THE
MAKING
OF
ECONOMICS

▼

Third Edition

E. RAY CANTERBERY
Florida State University

Wadsworth Publishing Company
Belmont, California
A Division of Wadsworth, Inc.

Economics Editor: *Stephanie Surfus*
Production Editor: *Andrea Cava*
Designer: *MaryEllen Podgorski*
Print Buyer: *Barbara Britton*
Editorial Assistant: *Cindy Haus*
Copy Editor: *John R. Ziemer*
Compositor: *Carlisle Graphics*
Cover Design: *Donna Davis*
Cover Art: © M. C. Escher Heirs
% Cordon Art—Baarn,
Holland. Photo: Vorpal Gallery

Printed in the United States of America   49
1 2 3 4 5 6 7 8 9 10—91 90 89 88 87

ISBN 0-534-06786-7

Library of Congress Cataloging-in-Publication Data
Canterbery, E. Ray.
  The making of economics.

  1. Economics—History. I. Title.
HB75.C25 1987   330′.09   86.13194
ISBN 0-534-06786-7

TO
KATIE,
JENNIE,
ANDREW,
AND
HEIDI

▼

CONTENTS

▼

PREFACE

▼

Change is the modern constant, and the study of economics offers no exception. As economic theory responds to modern economic problems and incorporates new methods of analysis, more readers feel the need for economics books that are transitional. The earlier editions of *The Making of Economics* were intended to bridge the gap between what economics has been and what it is becoming. This new edition is a continuing statement about the escalating desire for such a linkage as well as a sharpening vision of the destiny of economics.

The goals of this book are many. I want to convey accurately where economics has been, where it is now, and how it got to be this way. I want to discuss current developments in economics, and where economics might go from here. I want to catch the new sense of excitement by setting my sails in the winds of change. I try to accomplish my goals in the following ways:

1. By describing the development of economic organization from feudalism, to the market economy, to the complex mixed economy, to the present day.

2. By analyzing the ideas of those who formulated the basic principles upon which economics rests—Smith, Ricardo, Mill, Marshall, and Keynes—and those who have provided penetrating critiques of the mainstream economics of their day—Marx, Veblen, Galbraith, the monetarists, the new radicals (left *and* right), and the post-Keynesians.

3. By examining the social and intellectual influences that have shaped the thinking of the great economists. Perhaps the most incessant charge leveled against economics is that it lacks relevance. A major theme throughout this book is that economists of the recent past have tended to formulate economic laws as if they were

immutable laws of nature, with the implication that economic phenomena can be analyzed in the same way as physical phenomena. I question this assumption throughout the book and attempt to show that economics must deal with people as well as with inanimate objects. Since the first edition, the recognition of the social and political nature of economics has grown among economists.

4. By weaving economic ideas out of the fabric of economic history. Any subject, even a mathematical natural science, cannot avoid humanity and thereby avoid becoming humane when it is studied as history.

5. By examining the current economic crises and how economic theory is responding. My first three goals are relevant here. When chaos prevails, we often look back at the past to see where we are going.

In convergence upon these objectives, an accelerating trend toward optimistism and a sense of direction about the nature of new economic ideas characterize the recent editions. The dogmatic position formerly held by many economists that economic science had achieved its final and permanent state has softened, a mutation appropriately considered. The end of dogmatism could be timely. The world is beset by economic problems, and many of the problems we face—such as stagnation, unemployment, national budget crises, global debt crises—apparently have no solutions to which reasonable people can agree. It is important for all of us to try to understand how and why these crises have occurred. Because the present is rooted in the past, we gain a good deal of understanding from the study of the ideas of the great economists who have formulated the basic principles on which modern economics rests.

Our analysis is not concerned only with economic thinking, however. We also look at the social and economic conditions to which these economists responded and consider the relationship between *what* economists think and *why* they think it. Like men and women in every walk of life, most economists reflect the values of their society and want to be accepted by their fellow citizens as responsible members of society. Their thinking, therefore, is a reflection of their social world, and vice versa.

Our detailed study of economists will begin with Adam Smith (1723–1790) and continue to the present day. Smith thought and wrote as the Industrial Revolution was getting under way in England. Business and manufacturing firms were still quite small, with many competitors in the same field. Smith's economic theories conformed with this business atmosphere of intense competition, and thus he wrote, in a sense, what most of the eighteenth-century traders and merchants wanted to read. But there was more to Smith than met eighteenth-century eyes, otherwise his ideas would not have endured so long. He revolutionized economic thought, and much of what he had to say forms the basis of economic theory today.

Smith was profoundly affected by the English scientist and mathematician Isaac Newton (1642–1727), whose scientific work had caused great changes in the prevailing world view of most educated people. The universe pictured by Newton operated with the order and precision of a giant clock. Smith adapted Newtonian harmony to eighteenth-century commercial activity, finding, for example, an almost perfect equilibrium between supply and demand in a business world of perfect (or nearly perfect) competition.

Economics today still works with many of Adam Smith's assumptions, such as the world of perfect competition, even though the most powerful elements in the modern economy bear little resemblance to the world of Adam Smith. Natural science has undergone several revolutions since Newton's time; economics has not. Until the late 1970s, many economists, in the face of giant unmet crises, seemed to be content with mechanistic refinements of thoughts forged in another world. One of our purposes throughout this book will be to try to discover why this happened. We will also envision a future economics that might alleviate some of these crises.

History tells us that major steps forward in economic theory have resulted from attention to the realities of hunger, depression, inflation, war, social discontent, and other maladies. A return to a concern with such problems—and we shall examine many that plague modern-day society—may lead to a transformation of economics.

Economic crises are with us today because we have not yet resolved conflicts that have plagued humanity throughout 5,000 years of history. We are still quarreling over such fundamental issues as the degree of private ownership versus common ownership; individual freedom versus the common good; the virtue of private versus public monopolies; the advantages of rapid technological change versus the pastoral pleasures of an undisturbed natural world; and the gains of science versus its danger to human survival.

Any new vision must recognize the existence of conflict. We will see that the scientific system of Adam Smith has failed to resolve society's long-standing problems of scarcity, equitable power, equitable income distribution, work satisfaction, and poverty—not because of scientific imprecision but because of the assumptions underlying the system. Borrowing its assumptions from the Scientific Revolution that closed the Middle Ages, too much of modern economics supposes that people behave like inanimate particles. This obvious distortion of human values can continue to influence economics only if we continue to regard the science as an end in itself. To meet the crises of the postindustrial age, we must supplant naive eighteenth-century natural science with a concern for the survival of the human race.

▼   ▼   ▼   ▼

My reviewers and I are practical. We know that a question always arises about the potential audience for a particular book. The only prerequisite for *The Making of Economics* is an inquiring mind. The book can be read easily by a beginning reader in economics, as I do not presuppose any prior study of economics. I think that *The Making of Economics* will provide the beginning reader with meaningful insights, and I also think that the book will prove interesting and valuable to those who possess a sophisticated understanding of economic theory and history.

I wish to thank the many people who over the years have assisted in making this so. Among my many helpful readers were Ujagar S. Bawa, Bloomsburg State College; Thomas W. Bonsor, Eastern Washington State College; Don C. Bridenstine, San Diego State University; Les Carson, Augustana College; Gordon Galbraith, Portland Community College; James H. Horner, Cameron University; John W. Isbister, University of California at Santa Cruz; Thomas Iwand, University of Nebraska; Robert Keller, Colorado State University; Odin Knudsen, San Jose State University; Floyd B. McFarland, Oregon State University; James W. Nordyke, New Mexico State University; Don V. Plantz, Arizona State University; and Herbert D. Werner, University of Missouri. For the current edition I must add James Angressano, Hampden-Sydney College; Richard Ballman, Augustana College; James Horner and Robert Keller were called back into the game from the bench; Andrew Larkin, Saint Cloud State University; and Stewart Long, California State University.

I also have been fortunate in having inspirational friends and associates. John Q. Adams of the University of Maryland, John Boorman of the IMF, John Hotson of the University of Waterloo, H. Peter Gray of Rutgers University, Sam Skogstad of USAID, and Clifton Grubbs of the University of Texas (Austin) continue to serve as valuable and witty critics. For a few precious years at Florida State University, I had the instructive pleasure of engaging in some remarkable dialogue with the late Abba P. Lerner. I also thank Irvin Sobel, David Rasmussen, Edgar Fresen, William Laird, and Philip Sorenson for some enlightening discussions. I greatly appreciate the careful and critical reading of all portions of the manuscript that contained references to natural science by a leading physical scientist, Michael Kasha, then Director of the Institute of Molecular Biophysics at Florida State University.

John Kenneth Galbraith graciously read parts of the manuscript and, as always, was a source of kindly encouragement. The late Joan Robinson, Cambridge University, read the sections on the ideas of her friend John Maynard Keynes and provided essential insights and corrections. My dearly missed friend, the late Sidney Weintraub of the University of Pennsylvania, provided thoughtful and meticulous comments on the Keynesians and post-Keynesians. Still another friend, Mancur Olson of the University of Maryland, provided valued reactions to my interpretation of his *Rise and Decline of Nations*. Hyman Minsky of Washington University also devoted considerable thought to and several suggestions for my discussions of finance and investment. Finally, Gerhard Mensch of Case-Western Reserve University provided insightful comments on Chapters 15–17. I exonerate all of the readers from the responsibility for any errors.

Kathey Freeman and June Nolan were indispensable research assistants for the original edition. Kathey, now at the University of Denver, who read several drafts of the manuscript, was also a valuable critic. Brad Hobbs served a similar function on the third edition. Lyn Boone at Oberlin College and Susan Williams have provided valuable editing assistance. I wish to thank M. E. Sharp, Inc., and the *Journal of Post Keynesian Economics* for permission to use excerpts from my articles that appeared in the Spring 1973 and Fall 1984 issues.

Meanwhile, at Wadsworth, Stephanie Surfus has been my premier cheerleader, and Andrea Cava's production and editing skills have kept me sane. I hope—no, I *believe*—that, when you have closed the final page, you will agree that our goals have been met.

E. Ray Canterbery

1

VALUES
AND ECONOMIC
SYSTEMS

▼

Adam Smith (1723–1790), the first great professor of economics, lived and wrote toward the end of the Scientific Revolution and during the beginnings of the English Industrial Revolution. He was a teacher of moral philosophy (broadly speaking, what is today called *ethics*) and obviously not the first person ever to search for a coherent pattern in the apparent chaos of the natural and social world. He is famous because of his success in finding order and harmony in the turbulent business of buying and selling goods. He provided both a moral defense and a scientific blueprint for the market exchange system that is still a major component of the economic organization of the industrial market economies such as the United States, Japan, and the Federal Republic of Germany.

The plan of this chapter is first to define and discuss the general ways that economic activity can be organized and the specific forms that such organization has taken. Special emphasis will be given to feudalism, the dominant economic system of Europe during the Middle Ages. Next, we shall discuss how values and the authorities who express them have helped shape and defend various "idealized" economic systems, including Smith's favorite, the market exchange system that evolved out of feudalism.

Throughout this discussion we should keep in mind the distinction between a *natural* order and a *social* order. When we speak of law and justice, for example, we are usually referring to a human social order, such as the one we live in. But Adam Smith believed that the economic laws he talked about resided in nature and were discoverable by human reason. Social rules and laws also are important as a means of reconciling the private passions and interests of individuals to the interests of the whole group or nation. Smith's broader vision of society included social rules as well. Thus, while Smith lay bare the natural laws that

1

keep the market economy together, he warned that in the absence of certain social values each person would be hanged separately—by his neighbors.

ORGANIZING ECONOMIC ACTIVITY

The economic organization of a society is an important factor in its success or failure. A society must continue to produce goods and services or it will die. It must also find a way to distribute the benefits of production or production will cease. This second objective is closely allied with human values because production can be either coerced or voluntary, depending on what the society's members are conditioned to tolerate or demand.

Further, because the resources used in the production of goods and services are limited, any economic organization must answer three basic questions: (1) *what* goods and services will be produced, (2) *how* the available resources will be organized for production, and (3) *for whom* the goods and services will be produced. History shows us that these questions have been answered in a great variety of ways, but for our purposes all these ways can be summarized under four general headings: the customary (or traditional) economy, the command economy, the competitive market economy, and the cooperative economy.

The Customary Economy

In a *customary* economy, each economic function is prescribed by tradition. People do what they do because that is what they and their ancestors have always done. In ancient Egypt, for example, every man was required by the principles of the Egyptian religion to follow the occupation of his father. No one attempted to deal with an economic emergency, such as a crop failure, in a new way because there was already a traditional, known way of meeting such an emergency. In Western society until the fifteenth or sixteenth century, the allocation of tasks was very often hereditary, and a person's economic role was decided at birth. Among some ethnic groups even today, individuals will almost always choose their parents' occupation.

The Command Economy

In a *command* economy, those who produce goods and services are told what to do, like an army that takes orders from a commanding officer. The area of command may be only economic and may coexist with political democracy; people who enjoy abundant civil liberties may demand few economic freedoms. However, slave labor is also a kind of command economy. Again using ancient Egypt as an example, we find the pharaohs ordering some Egyptians to drag stones from quarries in the Arabian mountains down to the Nile; others to receive the stones that were transported down the river; and still others to use the stones in building roads, temples, and pyramids. All this took place while Egyptian agriculture continued to be organized along customary lines.

The Competitive Market Economy

In a *competitive market* economy, the system itself, not tradition or authority, decides what is produced and to whom the outputs are passed. Theoretically, all power is exerted by the market for goods and services. People select occupations according to their own initiative and skills. Families select from marketplaces whatever goods and services they want or need, and producers produce what consumers demand at competitive prices. Because there are opportunities for choice built into it, Adam Smith called the competitive market a "system of liberty."

The United States' economy is often pointed to as an example of a competitive market system, but Americans know that this definition is only approximate. There are few ingredients of a customary economy in the United States today, but a large part of the economy is "public," which means there is a considerable amount of centralized command from the federal government. Moreover, certain large sectors of the economy have only a few producers of a product and are involved in entanglements with giant labor unions in such a way that prices do not always materialize from an atmosphere of unfettered competition.

The Cooperative Economy

The *cooperative economy* is a compromise version of the competitive market economy. Specific quantities of products and prices are determined by a free market system; however, the distribution of incomes is regulated by a democratic government. In other words, the free market system is valued for its efficiency in production, but social judgment is preferred in deciding the distribution of incomes. The cooperative economy requires consensus politics and goal sharing as an integral part of an interaction between the producers in the private sector and government planning agents in the public sector. These efforts may be coordinated through study commissions and administrative boards that involve the joint participation of workers, management, financiers, and government representatives. Social goals would be based upon an extensive dialogue and debate among business leaders, government officials, and the news media. The cooperative economy would require widespread ideological flexibility and an understanding of the advantages of social cohesiveness.

The Scandinavian economies come closest to fitting the cooperative criteria, with the Swedish system being the closest prototype. Although more than 90 percent of Swedish industry is privately owned, the central government is given the authority to modify market forces in order to encourage conformity with social objectives. Sweden is often cited as an example of the "welfare state," in which the system relies on very high tax revenues (about 40 percent of the GNP), over half of which are redistributed in the form of welfare benefits. Moreover, the national income tax is highly progressive (the percentage of taxes being higher on higher incomes), from a rate of only 10 percent on very low incomes to 65 percent on high incomes. The social welfare services include tax-free yearly allowances for children, free education, national health insurance, and an old-age pension program. Most individuals belong to several of the widespread Swedish pressure groups that promote common interests and perform most of the coordinating function with the government.

CARICATURE SYSTEMS

I hope it is clear from the preceding section that the four general, abstract types of economic organization seldom exist in a pure form. There can be many variations of a customary, command, competitive market, or cooperative economy. And when we turn to the particular kinds of economic systems that exist in the modern world, we find that these systems, too, exist only in untidy mixtures. In describing socialism, communism, and capitalism, therefore, I call them *caricature* systems because I must exaggerate their characteristics in order to show what they would be like in a pure form.

Caricature socialism requires public or common ownership of all the means of production—land, labor, and capital, including machines, tools, and factories. In practice, however, socialism requires only that those branches of the economy *decisive* for its functioning be publicly owned.

Caricature communism could be achieved only in a society so affluent that goods and services were literally as free as air. Goods and services would be "free" (prices equal zero), under common ownership and control, and consumed by everyone according to individual desire. There would be no monies, prices, or wages. Even such massive affluence and abundance would require that wants be satisfied in such a way that a scarcity of any good would never occur, for a scarcity of a good would raise its price above zero. The Garden of Eden is an example of caricature communism, but even in that setting there was dissatisfaction and temptation.

Caricature capitalism is an economy based on private property and a two-way exchange system: one good for another or for equal value in money. Every person—worker, factory owner, consumer—is a free agent and does not have the power to influence prices, outputs, wages, or profits while engaging in two-way exchanges. Moreover, factory owners and workers never organize as groups in order to enhance their power over their economic destinies. This system depends on absolutely free competitive markets and requires the total dedication of each person to economic self-interest. That is, all people would yield to all temptations that would enhance their economic well-being. That includes a lot of activity that some people might call sin.

A *caricature cooperative* economy is one in which the income and wealth distribution is decided entirely by a democratic political process. It is based on the principle that a relatively equal income and property distribution is required in order to sustain political democracy. The allocation of resources through the production system is otherwise decided by free markets. Each person presumes that every other individual has similar preferences and derives similar satisfactions from each dollar of income and wealth. The absence of any ideological differences enable such a society to agree on higher rates of taxation on those receiving the highest incomes and a redistribution of income— either directly or through services—to lower-income families in the society.

FEUDALISM AND THE EVOLUTION OF ECONOMIC SOCIETY

We now turn from generalized types of economic organization and caricature systems to a discussion of feudalism, the major economic system of precapitalist Europe. We can better understand why Adam Smith was the embodiment of the new values of capitalism if we examine what preceded capitalism during the vast expanse of history known as the Middle Ages. The Middle Ages extended from the end of the Roman Empire in Western Europe (A.D. 476) to the beginning of the Renaissance (c. A.D. 1453), a period of about 1,000 years.

A great diversity characterizes the Middle Ages, a richness of variation that extends to space as well as to time. Life for the English peasant during the eleventh century, for example, was quite different from that of the city dweller in Venice or Florence. Moreover, there was sufficient progress during some centuries to warrant a distinction between the Dark Ages (from the end of the Greco-Roman civilizations through about the 900s) and the High Middle Ages of about 1000 to 1300. Even the Dark

Ages were not quite so dim as some historians have contended. And, although not within the scope of Western history, the Middle Ages were golden in Byzantium and the Arab world. Our generalizations here will apply to the dominant attitudes, conditions, and organizations of Western Europe, especially to much of England.

Real-world economic systems are usually in various stages of *becoming*. There are three general stages of precapitalist or premarket economic development: (1) primitive, (2) slave, and (3) feudal. In the primitive economy, all resources are held in common: everyone works the same land and shares in what is harvested. The commonality of "ownership," however, is virtually meaningless because the level of technology is so low that the resources cannot be developed or combined to produce goods in any substantial quantity.

When resources are sufficiently abundant that they become worth defending, slavery becomes a possibility. Slavery requires the ownership of humans as tools of production as well as the ownership of land. It is the ultimate example of a command economy. But slavery is viable only as long as the slaves can produce more than they consume.

Feudalism, the next stage, grew out of the slave economy of the Roman Empire. The relationship between master and slave changed to the extent that one human being was not supposed to own another outright, but there was bondage nevertheless. The lowest person on the feudal economic scale, the serf, was bound to the land and exchanged service for protection by his master, who, in turn, was given control over the land in exchange for service to *his* master, the king or duke. The ultimate control of both the serf and the land was in the hands of the king, who could transfer control from one master to another. There was, therefore, no market for either land or labor because such things were not sold, they were only transferred. The system depended to some extent on custom—serfs did not become kings—and to some extent on command. (The reader should remember that feudalism is not only an economic system but an extremely complex social and political system as well. It took different forms in different parts of Europe, and it was not a static system, even though its general outlines remained stable.)

The Influence of Antiquity

Historians are more or less forced to lump together huge spans of time and give them titles—such as the Ancient World or the Middle Ages—in order to give the past a coherent order; but obviously the transition from one period to another is not as simple a matter as some history books would have us believe. The Roman Empire, for example, did not die giving birth to the Middle Ages. A great deal of Roman civilization survived in one form or another, changing as medieval civilization began to develop. Some of Rome's economic legacies contributed to the growth of feudalism.

In almost every society, a minority depend on the labors of the majority to produce a surplus of goods to feed, clothe, and house the minority at a certain customary level. That is, the majority—even if they are slaves—must produce enough of the necessities of life to enable them to do their daily work and maintain their health, plus a little more. The distribution of the surplus goods—the "little more"—depends on the nature of the political and economic system and on the tastes of those in power. During antiquity, slaves were the main producers of such a surplus. The city of Athens in ancient Greece is celebrated as the birthplace of democracy, but even at its most "democratic," at least one-third of its population were slaves.

The Roman Empire was a centralized political bureaucracy that relied on slave labor both in the major cities and towns and also on the huge agricultural estates (villas). There were also large groups of free artisans and laborers. During the Dark Ages, those villas that had not been destroyed by barbarian raiders from the north and east became landed estates. The Roman cities—some in ruins—shrank to towns and villages. The slaves tended to remain slaves until a decline in population made labor scarce and expensive. They were then accorded some of the privileges enjoyed by other humans. The Church promised that those who chose to be baptized as Christians could not be sold into slavery, but this promise was not widely respected, in part because the Church itself owned slaves. In Milan in 775, a Frankish boy could still be bought for twelve *solidi;* the price of a horse was fifteen *solidi* the same year. A ninth-century bailiff of a Flemish estate belonging to the Abbey of St. Bertin tilled twenty-five hectares with about a dozen slaves. Slavery did not end with the Roman Empire. It continued in Western Europe, although on a greatly diminished scale.[1]

The Development of Feudalism

Thus far I have been stressing some of the major continuities between Greco-Roman civilization and the Middle Ages. But the "fall" of Rome is not just a figure of speech: major *dis*continuities occurred at the end of the fifth century, and people's lives began to change markedly in many ways. Feudalism emerged with these changes. The most important change was that citizens of the empire could no longer rely on Roman centralized control and legal authority for protection. Much of Greco-Roman knowledge was lost with the collapse of the political order.

By the end of the sixth century, Europe was profoundly uncivilized. To be "free," one had to be a warrior; one had to have weapons. War was a common form of economic activity. Pillaging (then a form of economics and politics) included the acquisition of cattle, ornaments, and men, women, and children, as well as weapons for the next assault. But successful aggressors were themselves obvious targets for plunder, and pillage was therefore a poor "solution" to the question of how goods and services could be produced and distributed. People had to be able to hold on to what they had; as a result, mutual self-protection societies began to evolve within the framework of the existing agricultural economy.

The owner of a large amount of land (I'll call such a person a *king*, although not all landowners were kings) could not personally control or supervise all he owned. Therefore, the king decentralized his landholdings and the revenues from them (often payments-in-kind) by "leasing" parts of his land to men less powerful than he, who were made noblemen by his own decree. These nobles, the tenants-in-chief, further delegated responsibility by in turn appointing subtenants, who actually did most of the work on the land. The right to farm the land obligated the subtenants (called *serfs*, or "free" peasants) to render military and other services to the noble in the name of the king.

In terms of the work they did, the serfs were like the slaves in the Roman economy, but a "contractual" set of obligations had been substituted for slavery. The sparseness of the population and the joint defense needs of the serfs and the nobles appear to have been the forces that made serfdom mutually irresistible to people in the early Middle Ages. We cannot be sure about population trends preceding and during the Dark Ages; but the general impression is that the population of the Roman Empire tended to decline from the second century onward. An apparently slow decline was speeded by a bubonic plague epidemic in the sixth century. The epidemic continued for over fifty years. The population of England in the sixth century was probably less than half a million. Labor in the early Middle Ages, therefore, was a scarce resource.

Thus, we can see that the feudal ties that bound the serf to the land had obvious advantages over slavery. The tenant-in-chief (or *lord*) did not have to worry that his slaves would be stolen, or, as long as he maintained his obligations to the king, that they would be taken from him. And the serf enjoyed at least some of the benefits of his own labor as well as a degree of protection from the pillaging barbarians.

A few more details will help clarify the kinds of mutual obligations that existed in feudal society. A man's status and his political rights and duties depended entirely on whether he held land "freely" (that is, voluntarily, in exchange for services) or whether he was "unfree"—tied to the land by custom and heredity.

Land was freely held in exchange for four general types of service: (1) knights' service; (2) specified services, such as money, produce, labor, and attendance at the lord's court (*socage*); (3) quartermastering certain military services, such as a given number of men in arms, transport, etc. (*serjeanty*); and (4) religious services (*frankalmoign*). A freeholding person could refuse service at any time and return his land to the lord and move on. A fifth type of tenure (*villeinage*) was unfree and created serfdom. The serf (or *villein*) was bound by custom and heredity to remain on the land. As custom would have it, the majority of the population were serfs.

The acts constituting the feudal contract were called *homage* and *investiture*. It was the custom for the tenant or vassal to kneel before the lord surrounded by his court, place his folded hands between those of the lord, and hence become his "man" (*homme*). The tenant or vassal took an oath of fealty of special obligation. The lord in turn reciprocated by investiture, handing to his vassal a banner, a staff, a clod of earth, a charter, or other symbol of the property or office given—the *fief*, as it was termed. Whether free or serf to the land, the peasant swore a form of fealty and was invested with the tenement he held of his lord. Even if the land changed lordships, the serf was tied by his unwritten contract to the land and fulfilled his obligations to the next lord. The manor often was passed to the next lord by inheritance.

Family connections had no effect upon the obligations of a man to his lord or king. On the other hand, the king and other lords had control over the families of their vassals. This meant that women and children had even fewer social rights than men. In England no woman could marry without the assent of her lord. In general the right to use land was inherited by the eldest son, whereas women could acquire a property share only by marriage. The unmarried daughters and the younger males were then sometimes left to beg at the gates of the manors. The intent of the feudal system was the survival of the fief, not necessarily of the family or its members.

The lord continued to have problems with invasions by foreigners throughout the early medieval period. The king depended heavily on mounted knights for defense, and the outfitting of *one* knight required an outlay equivalent to about twenty oxen or the farm equipment for about ten peasant landholders.[2] To take care of his military needs, the king exacted military duty and other services from his lords, who in turn reminded their knights of *their* military obligations. Military service was thus not voluntary but obligatory as part of the feudal contract.

The Manorial System

Economic activity in feudal society was generally organized around the life of a *manor,* a largely self-sufficient agricultural plantation controlled by a lord and tilled by peasants and serfs. Most of life's material essentials were provided in one place. These small, often isolated settlements were havens of civilization in an anarchic world.

Manorial organization had two basic aims: producing enough to keep the manor going, and providing authority and agricultural surplus for its lord. What was produced? Food, shelter, and clothing to keep the peasants and serfs in working order, the lord contented, and some surplus. How was it produced? In the custom of the manor. For whom was it produced? Beyond the workers' subsistence, virtually all products were distributed to the lord and king by custom. Although the manor strove for self-sufficiency, the uncertainties of agricultural production made necessary some exchange of products between manors, often on a "loan" basis.

The English manor is the kind most frequently described because it was the most durable. The agricultural peasant or serf would have about thirty acres to farm, consisting of relatively narrow strips of land scattered throughout the two or three open fields of the manor. Each year one field out of the two or three was left fallow and unenclosed for animal grazing. The cultivated areas were fenced. Mixed in among the peasants' land were the strips of land kept by the lord for his own use (his *demesne*). Each serf household owed *week-work* (one laborer) of about three days a week on the demesne farm. The serf had to supply his share of the needed oxen, heavy plows, and other implements.

Thus, in addition to providing for their own subsistence, the serfs supported the knights and provided surpluses for the lord and king. In return, the lords and the Church provided what little safety, peace, and justice there was. Today, feudalism seems an undesirable, even grotesque, economic system, especially for the serfs. There were some peasant uprisings in the Middle Ages, but by and large the serfs and peasants were merely living in the "manor" to which they were accustomed and did not envision a better arrangement. There was little they could have done to bring about change if they had so desired. Besides, they saw serfdom as an improvement over slavery. And they were right.

The Social Theory of Feudalism

In feudal society the serfs worked, the warriors fought, the clergy prayed, most of the lords managed (quite well!), and the king ruled. There were more conflicts between families and states than among these classes because social organization was hierarchical and relatively stable. A person born into serfdom gave little thought to the possibility of upward mobility into the noble class. Almost every kind of social bond was decided by either tradition or contract.

But whatever social form a society takes, some ruling idea is also needed to hold it together. At the time of the great Crusades of the twelfth century, chivalry flowered as a moral system fusing religion and the martial arts. Drawing inspiration from a pre-Christian past—the Trojans, Alexander the Great, and the ancient Romans—chivalry originally prized ancient pagan virtues, including pride, a sin in Christian theology. When Western Europe had to defend itself against Norsemen, Moslems, and other "pagans," the pacifist ideas of the Gospels were set aside, and the Church blessed the knight's arms and prayed for him.

Chivalry justified the knight's daily activities in a way that the much maligned merchant could only envy. As a "middleman," the merchant seemed to serve no productive purpose in an agricultural economy except to line his own pockets. The knight was equally suspect initially because his most effective tool was the death blow. Thus, the knight's sword had to be put to the service of widows, orphans, the oppressed, and the Church so that "God and Chivalry are in accord." Ultimately, however, neither chivalry nor business enterprise could be contained. Though chivalry thereafter governed the life of the nobility, it was—like all moral codes—more illusion than reality. That did not make it any less powerful as a social force, however. The Church provided the additional cement that was needed for holding medieval society together, however precariously.

The Church itself held a large number of manors and was accumulating wealth in the form of land, contributions from nobles, and tithes, a strict tenth of the *gross* produce of the peasants down to the potherbs in their gardens and two shillings in the pound from the personal earnings of the expanding class of shopkeepers and poor artisans. The Church's traditional opposition to worldly goods was directed toward the accumulation of wealth through trade rather than the accumulation of wealth per se.[3] Also, belief in original sin was so deeply embedded in medieval thought that reform or change was hardly worth considering: if human beings are *fundamentally* corrupted, there is no use in trying to change them or society.[4] Thus, in a way, religion was used to rationalize existing social and economic conditions.

The Church nonetheless—like the chivalrous knight—was supposed to be charitable. From its massive resources, gifts (*one-way* economic transfers) were given to the poor, but the required tithing was often a heavy burden on the lower classes. Indeed, the lay tithing plus other fees often created the poverty that the Church was called upon to relieve. The ability to "give" was itself an index of status, and the amount received could not be sufficient to alter the social station of the recipient. Because a substantial portion of landowners were clerics, the landowners' exhortation to be diligent to the lords and generous to the Church served virtually a double (they would have said noble) purpose.

Even prior to the twelfth century, the law and the power of authority were frequently interpreted as being God's punishment of humanity for its sins. The residue of this belief made the nastier work of the armored men on horseback (forcible suppression of heretics, the excommunicated, and enemies of the Holy See) easier, if less chivalrous than romantics would have us believe. Neither medieval thinkers nor tenants-in-chief tried to disguise the reality and advantages of a stratified society. Most important, a hierarchical social theory prevailed long after reality became something else.

The Rebirth of Markets

Commerce requires, among other things, a reasonably stable society in which to grow. For example, merchants must be able to travel safely so they can sell their goods in different towns. And society must be peaceful enough so there can *be* towns. By the mid-tenth century, conditions in Europe had sufficiently stabilized for a slow revival of commerce to begin. The terror of foreign marauders had declined. Warfare was still a way of life between local lords, but that, too, had declined somewhat. The security provided by feudal institutions contributed to population increases, and the number of manors grew. Indeed, by the thirteenth century, the best agricultural land had probably been occupied.[5]

Towns began to form in the densely populated areas. Crafts began to flourish, and crude manufactured goods such as armor and harnesses were traded for raw materials and food from the countryside. This increase in trade and the specialization of labor skills became the source of mutual reinforcement for commerce: for example, carpenters or blacksmiths could not be wholly self-sufficient and had to rely on trade and barter to acquire what they could not produce. Commerce that relies on barter (the exchange of one good for another), however, is cumbersome and inefficient, and in time the old Roman custom of using money in exchange for goods was revived.

But one of the most significant facts about the new towns is that many of them became independent of the feudal lords and had their own governments and their own defense. This was not an easy process; more than one town was looted by an angry lord because it refused to give in to his demands, but over the centuries the independence of towns became an established part of the European economy.

Europe has a great variety of resources and climates and different types of crops and livestock. Thus the potential for exchanging dissimilar commodities was always there once travel was made relatively safe. A substantial increase in international trade accompanied the Crusades, which began in the late eleventh century. In the twelfth century, the towns of northern Italy, central Germany, and Flanders became important commercial centers as trade and population continued to expand. By the thirteenth century, French champagne, Flemish wool, and the raw materials of German mines became part of a growing commerce that incited the development of banking and other new commercial institutions.

But we are getting a little bit ahead of ourselves. Let's go back to a medium-sized medieval town and try to reconstruct how it might develop from a bartering community into a marketplace, and the townspeople from artisans to merchants. One way such a change might begin is with the exchange of gifts. A large and busy gathering such as a religious festival would provide a good setting for potential exchange. Goods may have been brought originally for personal consumption during the festival, and barter among people who have brought new and different commodities would have been tempting. Eventually, such a religious festival might turn into a village fair, with the original religious motive almost forgotten.

Some one person—say a weaver who has managed to accumulate a small amount of cash—may decide to use his money to buy goods from people at the fair and later resell or barter them after the fair is over and they cannot be so easily acquired. Goods acquired one day may not be sold until many days later. The weaver may find that he has made a tidy profit, and he may decide to specialize in buying and reselling goods and let his wife do the weaving. He becomes a middleman. However, he dislikes the inconvenience and risk of carrying goods around the countryside (travel still isn't all that safe), so he picks out a spot in the town and opens a shop where he will sell his goods. Everything is going fine, and then his friend the carpenter opens a shop across the muddy street, selling exactly the same kind of goods. The medieval town has changed forever.

Thus, it is the independent merchant, operating at the frontiers of the customary or command economy, that can transform the nature of a community. This is the start of a *commercial* or *mercantile* economy that greatly diverges from the feudal organization. In particular, the rise of the independent merchant leads to a new value, the elixir of individualism, and potentially to a new economic system, the market economy.

VALUES, AUTHORITY, AND ADAM SMITH

Values

Which comes first, values and those leaders and authorities who reinforce them, or the events and circumstances that determine the values? Like the proverbial query about the chicken or the egg, this question can never be answered definitively. One thing about values is certain, however: they can become so deeply rooted in the life of a society that they are followed and believed in long after they are of any real use. Before we discuss the relationship between values and economic systems, we will have to define some terms.

A *value judgment* is a personal judgment made on the basis of an individual's own feelings about what are "right" thoughts and behavior. For example, a sixteenth-century bishop might believe that profit making is morally wrong and charity is morally right, whereas a shopkeeper of the same town might see no harm in profit making and no point in charity.

Ethical judgments are collective value judgments, principles of "right" action "binding" upon society's members or subgroups, that serve as guides for "acceptable" behavior. The bishop's judgment becomes an ethical judgment rather than a value judgment if a large segment of society shares his views.

We cannot fully understand the economic organization of a society unless we consider the values and ethics of its members. As we have seen, an economic system requires a set of rules to operate, but individuals must be personally motivated to follow the rules, or the system will collapse. Rules and personal values must intersect. An economic system is also based, to some extent, on faith, on a belief in its implicit values. Even a planned socialist economy is based on the belief, not the certainty, that it will achieve the political and social goals of the secular state. A set of beliefs, an *ideology*, can become an important source of authority.

The Bible as Authority

One of the functions of organized religion is to preserve and transmit a moral tradition that society can use as a guide to conduct. Religion helps people to know "what is right" and encourages them to do right, thereby helping to promote the harmony of society. In the Western world, the major religious moral tradition largely derives, in one way or another, from the Bible. For example, much of the early medieval ethic denouncing personal gain and embracing charity is found in the New Testament, which contains the history and teachings of Jesus Christ and his apostles. When the masses had no food, Jesus proved to be at the same time more efficiently productive and more equitable than caricature capitalism. "I have compassion on the multitude," he told his disciples, "because they have now been with me three days, and have nothing to eat . . ." (Mark 8:2). Seven loaves of bread and "a few small fishes" were used to feed four thousand people! Jesus also drove the moneylenders, who charged interest, out of the Temple.

However, the Bible has also been used in support of an exchange economy and the value of accumulation (personal gain). Parts of the Old Testament can be interpreted as a defense of private initiative, freedom in accumulating capital, and an *exchange economy* in which goods are given up not for charity but only in exchange for money or other goods and services. According to Genesis 47:15, "money failed" in Egypt and Canaan. All the Egyptians came to Joseph and said, "Give us bread: for why should we die in thy presence?" Joseph replied, "Give your cattle; and I will give you *bread* for your cattle, if money fail. And they brought their cattle to Joseph: and Joseph gave them bread *in exchange* for horses, and for the flocks, and for the cattle of the herds. . . ." The dominant Old Testament morality is not only an eye for an eye but also a cow for a cow, the two-way exchange that is a major feature of caricature capitalism.

It seems, then, that even an authority with the immense prestige of the Bible offers no absolutely clear justification for preferring one kind of economic system to another. Rather, it poses a choice in extreme terms: between charity and exchange or between altruism and selfishness. The terms of the choice are basic in the history of economic thought.

Adam Smith and the Ethic of Individual Rights

Throughout modern history, socialist, communist, and capitalist economies have been defended by appeals to different values and authorities. Western economic thought is dominated by defenses of caricature capitalism, which has been traditionally linked to the ethic of individual rights. As early as Adam Smith, the market exchange system was presumed to depend on the free expression of individual rights: the freedom to buy whatever one wishes, to hire whomever one wants, to work in whatever occupation one desires, to work for whatever employer one chooses, to decide freely to keep whatever share of one's earnings one wishes—that is, complete freedom to exchange and accumulate.

Smith believed that a world in which maximum individual liberty enabled the most single-mindedly ambitious person, acting according

to self-interest, to accumulate private property was in accord with natural instincts and therefore correct. This rampant individualism is for
a person's "own good" and leads to a collective harmony. If *everyone*
has the same rights and pursues them, the government's intervention
in the economy is not necessary. [Although Smith did not want public
authority meddling in private business, he did see a government role
in national defense, justice (especially in matters endangering private
property), and public works that were advantageous to society but could
not be profitably supplied by an individual or a small group.] He believed
that this kind of behavior found its best expression under the capitalist
system.

The capitalistic ethic leans toward the extreme of selfishness (fierce
individualism) rather than toward altruism. There is little room for collective decision making in an ethic that argues that every individual
should go his or her own way. As we have seen, the idea that capitalism
protects individual rights would have been rejected during the early
Middle Ages. "Individual rights" were predestined by the structure of
feudalism, governed by the pull of tradition and the push of authority.
Economics was based upon mutual needs and obligations.

Smith's view that capitalism and freedom are linked has proved to
be enduring, although it isn't the only ethic around. A leading modern
exponent of free markets is Milton Friedman, an economist identified
with the University of Chicago and once a columnist for *Newsweek*. In
Friedman's view, capitalism nurtures individual freedoms, the same liberties that Smith deemed essential for the development of free markets.
Thus, Friedman completes the circle between individual liberties and
capitalism by turning Smith's argument upon its head and closing the
system with a value judgment. Friedman contends that capitalism is
necessary for freedom but does not alone guarantee it. In his book
Capitalism and Freedom, Friedman writes: "The kind of economic organization that provides freedom directly, namely, competitive capitalism, also promotes political freedom because it separates economic
power from political power and in this way enables the one to offset
the other."[6]

There are, however, significant differences between Adam Smith
and contemporary defenders of caricature capitalism. Smith's work encompasses two major books. The first, *The Theory of Moral Sentiments*,
emphasizes the altruistic side of human nature; the second, *An Inquiry
into the Nature and Causes of the Wealth of Nations*, emphasizes self-
interest as leading to right actions. To Smith, *both* qualities lead to the
harmony of individual and national interests. He defines moral philosophy as the concern for human happiness and well-being, "the happiness and perfections of man . . . not only as an individual but as a

member of a family, of a state, and of a great society of mankind. . . ."[7] That is, the happy individual plays more than a purely economic role in Smith's vision of the orderly society.

Not all free marketeers have been as sociable. Friedman, for example, considers any intentional flagging in the race for maximum profits by business to be "subversive." According to Friedman, "Few trends could so thoroughly undermine the very foundations of our free society as the acceptance by corporate officials of a responsibility other than to make as much money for their stockholders as possible. This [social responsibility] is a fundamentally subversive doctrine."[8] But Smith observes that, no matter how selfish a person may be, "There are evidently some principles in his nature which interest him in the fortune of others and render their happiness necessary to him though he derives nothing from it except the pleasure of seeing it."[9]

Smith sees ultimate happiness coming from complete freedom to pursue self-interest, enlightened by an altruistic conscience. A person's empathy with others will deter undesirable social behavior. In *Moral Sentiments*, the pursuit of wealth is only one aspect of a person's desire for self-betterment; nevertheless, individual self-interest is desirable in the economic sphere because such selfishness results in societal harmony.

Individualism is certainly an appealing philosophy. It is almost irresistible if it can be shown to result in the collective good. It provides the best of everything. Smithian economic morality can accept the Old Testament virtues of exchange and accumulation without necessarily damaging the social goals expressed elsewhere in the Bible. Yet social life would surely be impossible unless self-interest were tempered by respect and compassion for others. Society is not always organized so that self-interest works to everyone's benefit. For example, the mentally and physically handicapped would suffer greatly in a purely competitive society, but they can live with dignity and make valuable economic contributions in a compassionate society.

Despite all this talk of the self-interest ethic and Smith's own qualifications in his *Sentiments*, economics slowly developed the claim of being value free. A *value-free* social science of economics claims to be unencumbered by the economist's personal judgment about what is right behavior or by collective societal judgments of what is proper action. Given even our brief historical survey, this notion appears odd. Adam Smith himself would not have agreed that social sciences are value free because he developed his own economic system from his perspective as a moral philosopher. Nonetheless, economists developed the notion that economics is value free in the same sense that natural science is. We shall have more to say about that later.

THE WORLD VIEW

We can see no universal principle that guarantees that a society will prefer the ethic of two-way exchange to an ethic of charity. Historically, real-world economic systems are mixed, containing elements of both extremes. And people can point to authorities in support of either ideal because most original sources of values are ambiguous enough to allow for a variety of interpretations.

Nevertheless, it is possible to generalize about societies and their values. One way of doing so is to try to discover what a particular society's world view is, what it believes to be truly important. A *world view* is a widely shared set of beliefs about the individual's relationship to the natural world, to his fellows, and to the Divine. Obviously not every single individual or group will assent to the dominant world view, and not all elements of the world view will be equally shared. But if a particular world view is generally shared by the majority, it provides a framework for the predominant moral values of the society and can be used to account for common patterns of behavior. In Western Europe, the world view was dominated by religion for many centuries. Today the place once occupied by religion has been taken over by science.

During the Middle Ages, the world view was dominated by the idea of the Cosmos, an all-encompassing harmony, a unified whole in which God's presence and spirit were embodied in all living things. Moreover, all parts of the Cosmos had their own immutable order. God had ranked his creatures from the most inferior ascending upward. Trees outranked herbs. Every herb, tree, bird, beast, and fish had a particular place and use given to them by God, their Creator.

Clearly, the medieval world view fit very neatly with feudalism, a highly structured economic system in which everyone had a specific place. Is the order of the Cosmos a mirror of feudalism, or was feudalism somehow patterned after the medieval conception of the Cosmos? The question probably is unanswerable. What is important for our understanding of the relationship between values and economic thought is that in this world view there is no conflict between "rational knowledge" and faith. The *Summa Theologica* of St. Thomas Aquinas (1225–1274) contains a complete and authoritative statement of medieval economic thought. Consistent with the world view outlined above, the proper life required that each class perform its obligations according to the laws of God and nature. St. Thomas deplored lending money for interest and trading for profit, but he expressed no preference for the equal distribution of private property. In fact, the main test for the propriety of any exchange of goods and services was whether or not the exchange threatened the class hierarchy. He thought a just price was a price that suitably supported the seller in his social rank.

St. Thomas's economic views are complexly intertwined with his religious faith. A science claiming to separate itself from religion was not born until the Renaissance. With this change came a new world view, which was to serve as a framework for Adam Smith's beliefs.

We have made plain the difficulty of trying to develop a value-free economics. A society's economic organization is in great part a matter of human choice, for contrary to notions of natural law, socialism or capitalism is not decided in Heaven and then handed down. Whether the mode of economic organization is mostly two-way exchanges or one-way transfers depends greatly upon the balance between the spirit of individualism and the sense of community, and the scale tips one way or another over historical time. The initial Smithian system takes into account both sides of the scale, but Western economic history has been dominated by the concept of individualism and hence is best defended by an economic theory built on the ethical base of self-interest.

2

THE NATURE
OF SCIENCE AND
THE ECONOMICS
PARADIGM

▼

We do not ordinarily think of the ideas of the Scientific Revolution and of Isaac Newton and Adam Smith as related, but they are. Newton had a powerful influence on all branches of science, including economics. His description of the motion of the heavenly bodies in space capped the Scientific Revolution and laid the basis for modern physics. In the eighteenth century, Adam Smith laid the basis for modern economics with his great synthesis, but he could not have done so without the work of Newton. The connection between physics, a natural science, and economics, a social science, outlived them both.

The values of a society have much to do with promoting or retarding science and scientific advance. The European Renaissance, beginning in the mid-fifteenth century, witnessed a shift from a reliance on institutionalized religion as a guide to daily activity toward increasing confidence in the independent human mind. This change in values was slow but immensely important: it encompassed the rise of modern science and scientific revolutions. During this period, however, there was never an absolute break between science and religion. Religious values continued to exert great influence, even within the revolutionary scientific world view that would evolve by the end of the seventeenth century.

Insofar as *natural* science during the Renaissance was allied with religion, it could never claim to be value free. And, because economics is an outgrowth of developments in scientific method and analysis that had their origin in the Renaissance, the question arises whether or not economics as a *social* science can be value free. We will see, for example, that the economics of Adam Smith (1723–1790) is a captive of the Scientific Revolution, a subperiod of the Renaissance that began with the work of Copernicus (1473–1543).

We will see that, just as natural science did not shun theological thought but actually made room for it, so the social sciences, such as economics, have been shaped by the world view—including the values, goals, and beliefs—into which they were born. Thus, if we are to portray accurately the growth of economic science, we must first delve a bit into the scientific method itself, whose initial momentum was generated within the study of the natural sciences. This broad perspective on the infancy of modern science will prepare us for a more insightful study of one of its subsequent expressions, economics.

SCIENCE AND THE SCIENTIFIC METHOD

A *true science* has established laws that can be proved by experiments in a laboratory. For example, Galileo's law of falling bodies (bodies of different weights fall at equal speeds) can be closely approximated time and again in laboratory experiments. [Galileo Galilei (1564–1642), the Italian astronomer and physicist, was a key participant in the Scientific Revolution that culminated with Newton.] The object of scientific inquiry can be either living (plants and animals) or nonliving (rocks and stars), but it must be something that can be studied in a careful, systematic way according to the *scientific method*.

The scientific method requires: (1) a statement of the scientific problem to be solved, (2) one or more suppositions (hypotheses of what the solution might be), (3) tests of the hypotheses to find out which one is correct, (4) a statement of the correct hypothesis, and (5) forecasts to predict outcomes. Economics is a science if economists use the scientific method to study and explain economic phenomena in a systematic way.

The scientific method is a rational process, based on logical principles. Logic, however, is not in itself sufficient basis for scientists' work. They also require *empirical* information—that is, information derived from observation and experiment. We saw that step (3) of the scientific method requires testing the hypotheses offered in step (2); it is at this point that empirical information becomes important.

Suppose that the following series of statements accurately reflects economists' views of how the goal of full employment is achieved:

1. All members of the labor force are employed when and only when business competition is all pervasive.

2. Business competition *is* all pervasive.

3. Therefore, all members of the labor force are employed.

The statements are logically consistent, but how can economists know that statement 3 is true? They could make an empirical test of it by finding out if everyone who is willing and able to work does in fact have a job. Or suppose economists wanted to test statement 1. If they wanted to be sure that business competition is responsible for full employment, they would have to measure the pervasiveness of competition.

Scientists who are occupied in testing hypotheses are performing ordinary, day-to-day scientific activity. Their work is scientific (or not) according to the standards of the scientific community to which they belong. We must make a distinction, however, between scientific activity and scientific advance. The process whereby science actually changes (advances) cannot be defined by day-to-day scientific activity.

As long as scientists find only what they expect to find, they are practicing science, but usually they are not making a scientific advance. Suppose that in the process of testing these statements the economists discover business monopoly (that is, *non*competition) existing side by side with full employment. This is an unexpected discovery. It contradicts the logical conclusion that business competition is necessary for full employment. There is evidently a basic weakness in the theory, and therefore the economists have failed, at least according to their internal standards. However, if they can prove a general association between monopoly and full employment, they may actually have advanced the science of economics. Revolutionary scientific advances, in other words, are almost always surprises to the majority of scientists who are tilling the vineyards of existing knowledge.

Two additional terms must be defined before we begin to consider scientific revolutions: the first is *normal science;* the second, *paradigm.*

Earlier I said that scientists belong to a scientific community. A scientific community is an invisible college that contains all those who practice or work at a particular scientific specialty; for example, medicine, chemistry, or biology. Practically all of the scientists in a given field have had similar educations, and they all work with the same technical literature. In addition, they share a belief in identical rules of exploration and common standards for correctness in their sciences, rather like players of a game who agree upon the same rules. This agreement on standards is a prerequisite for *normal science*, which is the kind of science practiced by nearly all working scientists at all levels of their profession. Normal science is based on the accomplishments of scientists in the past whose work has laid the ground rules for contemporary scientists. In contrast to normal science, the new scientific systems we will examine, such as the Copernican and the Newtonian, were forms of extraordinary science and, hence, revolutionary.

Closely related to the practice of normal science is what science historian Thomas Kuhn has called a *paradigm.* A paradigm is an outstanding example of scientific achievement that other scientists can use and follow in their own work. For example, Copernican astronomy is a paradigm. Its explanation of the movements of heavenly bodies was complete and convincing enough to attract numerous scientific followers, but at the same time it left problems for its followers to solve. A paradigm, then, is the body of knowledge that the members of a particular scientific community share; conversely, a scientific community consists of people who share a paradigm. As Kuhn puts it, "The study of paradigms . . . is what mainly prepares the student for membership in the particular scientific community with which he will later practice."[1]

In this book, the term *paradigm* will refer to the broadest, most general form in which a particular scientific idea can be expressed. The parts of the paradigm will be called *theories*, or *subparadigms;* they are the components of the more general model. This distinction will become clear when in Chapter 3 we discuss Adam Smith's famous economics paradigm, the market mechanism.

Smith's paradigm will also make clear that paradigms are not developed in isolation from the rest of society. Normal science is influenced by the values of the society in which it develops and by the state of knowledge in other fields of study. We shall see that this influence is not always one-way, however. Natural science has greatly influenced values in an industrial society, and economics has often been a conservative force, used to defend the status quo. The longevity of Smith's paradigm (his market mechanism idea was two hundred years old in 1976) is evidence for the latter statement.

With these definitions in mind, we can better understand the impacts of science on society and society on science. The nature of scientific revolution is most clearly seen in astronomy, where the medieval concept of the universe was ultimately overthrown. I shall use the Ptolemaic and Copernican scientific systems as examples of well-developed and easy to understand paradigms that illustrate the interaction between these scientific ideas and the changing values of Western society. Once unleashed, science had a tremendous impact on the world view.

EARLY CELESTIAL MECHANICS AND THE PTOLEMAIC SYSTEM

We must begin our discussion of scientific revolutions with two very simple statements: (1) there was a time when everyone believed that the sun revolved around the earth; and (2) today, everyone thinks that the earth revolves around the sun. The first belief found its most complete expression in the astronomy of Claudius Ptolemy (c. A.D. 140), the last of the great Greek astronomers. The second view is associated with

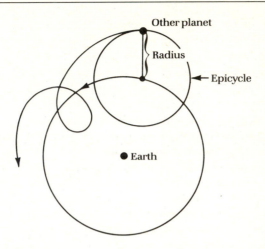

FIGURE 2.1 The Ptolemaic epicyclic system

Each planet moves in an epicycle whose center revolves around the earth. Because Mercury and Venus were always seen close to the sun, the centers of their epicycles are fixed in line with the sun and the earth.

Nicolaus Copernicus, a Polish astronomer (1473–1543), who was dissatisfied with Ptolemy's paradigm. The shift from Ptolemaic to Copernican astronomy is the first major event in the Scientific Revolution and one of the seminal changes in the history of Western thought.

Ptolemy's paradigm, a refinement of the astronomical theories of the Greek and Roman philosophers, is a complicated mathematical system that describes the movements of the heavenly bodies as they are seen from the earth. Ptolemy believed that the earth was a motionless body at the center of the universe. All of the heavenly bodies, including the sun, moved around the earth in a circular orbit, from east to west.

Even in the second century, however, it was obvious that the planets do not move around the earth in perfect, concentric circles. Sometimes the planets move relatively close to the earth; sometimes they appear to be moving backward. Ptolemy explained these apparently irregular movements by claiming that each of the planets, while moving in a larger circle around the earth, also moved at its own speed in a series of smaller loops. Each planet thus traced out its own peculiar orbit, called an epicycle, while circling the earth (see Figure 2.1). Whenever an irregularity "unexplained" by the paradigm appeared, a new epicycle was added, with the result that the system grew increasingly complex. (It is important to remember that, despite the unwieldy mathematical complexity of Ptolemy's paradigm, it was nevertheless a satisfactory explanation of what people actually saw when they looked at the heavens, and it could be used to predict most of the movements of the planets. To take the simplest possible example, it was clear to those who accepted the Ptolemaic paradigm that the sun and the planets moved around the earth because they could *see* them do so.)

According to Ptolemy, the earth was surrounded by a series of transparent globes, called celestial spheres. Each planet moved, it was thought, on its own epicycle in accordance with its own sphere. The sphere carrying the last known planet, Saturn, was believed to be the farthest from earth, the planets Uranus, Neptune, and Pluto not having yet been discovered. Beyond the sphere of Saturn was the sphere that made all the other spheres move—a sort of cosmic engine. At this point, astronomy joins hands with religion, and Ptolemy's mathematical paradigm gets involved with medieval philosophy.

Christian philosophers of the Middle Ages added a final refinement to the theory of celestial spheres. They placed God, the angels, and the saints beyond even the very last sphere, outside of time and motion, in "Heaven." According to this scheme, the earth was the motionless center of the universe, but also at the farthest point from God. The universe was viewed as a hierarchy, a series of steps with God at the top, humanity in the middle (on earth), and Hell below.

Much of the logic of Christianity and of economic organization during the early Middle Ages relied on this view of the universe. (Feudalism, for example, is hierarchical, with the landowner at the top and the peasant farmer at the bottom.) The stars were the lights of Heaven, and the earth beneath people's feet was Hell's roof. The hereafter was as important as the here. Human beings were not simply the select creatures at the center of the universe, they were God's *only* concern. But even though this Cosmos conformed well with the medieval urge toward hierarchy, the system created enormous difficulties for post-Ptolemaic astronomers.

The problem was that the Ptolemaic paradigm could not really explain the behavior of Mercury and Venus, the morning and evening "stars." Ptolemaic predictions of their positions did not match their actual movements. According to Kuhn, a scientific crisis begins when irregularities occur that cannot be explained by the conventional paradigm. The inability of the Ptolemaic paradigm to solve puzzles such as the relative position of certain planets was the breakdown that caused a scientific crisis in astronomy.

THE SCIENTIFIC REVOLUTION AND COPERNICUS

Although Copernicus was a truly revolutionary figure, we must not make the mistake of thinking that his work somehow changed people's ideas overnight. He developed what was to become the first step in a new paradigm, but he did not reject the old one. The feudal, hierarchical society of the Middle Ages was dependent on unquestioned religious faith, and Copernicus did not tamper with it. In fact, as late as the eighteenth century, most educated Europeans still thought in terms of hierarchy, discipline, order, divine providence, and stability. What Copernicus and other scholars did—sometimes unknowingly—was to drive a wedge between religion and rational knowledge, between faith and reason. This wedge was widened during the Renaissance by considerable skepticism about prevailing religious dogma, particularly among scholars. But the freedom to have one's own thoughts about the physical world was recognized by much of the Church leadership as a potential cause of chinks in its armor of authority. In great part because of such unresolved conflicts in authority, the Scientific Revolution emerged only slowly as a major force in Western Europe.

Any new version of the Ptolemaic-Christian paradigm of the heavens was certain to encounter stiff theological opposition. Reason and revelation were not separated easily or quickly. Yet, despite the Church's—and therefore society's—preference for remaining at the center of the universe, in the mid-sixteenth century Nicolaus Copernicus, the founder of modern astronomy, developed a new paradigm that moved the sun to the central position. He did so in a fit of mathematical frustration over the relative positions of Venus and Mercury. The movements of these two "stars" were more satisfactorily explained by a system in which the planets orbit the sun. Thus Copernicus's "new" paradigm involved only two changes in the old one: (1) the earth is no longer motionless but rotates on its own axis; and (2) at the same time, it orbits the sun. The positions of the sun and the earth were exchanged in the same scheme of crystalline spheres. Still, the shift to a sun-centered system was denounced by the Vatican as false and altogether opposed to Holy Scripture.

Copernicus's simplified paradigm gave astronomers better results in predicting planetary movements than the old paradigm, but the idea of a sun-centered universe was significant far beyond the realm of astronomy alone. More important, Copernicus became the center of an intellectual revolution. The new astronomy of Copernicus and, later, of Johannes Kepler (1571–1630) and Galileo Galilei (1564–1642) ultimately changed the world view of their contemporaries. For example, the telescope came into use early in the seventeenth century, and Galileo found mountains on the moon and spots on the sun, thus destroying the myth that the heavenly bodies were perfect. The belief that these bodies were arranged in a hierarchy also came under attack. With his telescope, Galileo could see the satellites orbiting Jupiter, which proved that all heavenly bodies did not circle either the earth or the sun.

As the vastness and complexity of the universe began to unfold, the human world seemed to change and grow small and insignificant. John Donne (1573–1631), an English poet and cleric, lamented his generation's loss of the old conception of order, proportion, and unity. Blaise Pascal (1623–1662), a French mathematician and religious mystic, drew a dramatic picture of humanity's lonely place in the new universe: "What is man in nature? A nothing in comparison with the infinite, an all in comparison with the nothing, a mean between nothing and everything."[2]

A modern psychologist might explain what was happening by saying that many people were suffering an identity crisis because of scientific discoveries. No longer, it seemed, was there one focal point of the universe, one world, created by God for human beings as the center of divine attention. Rather, it was uncomfortably clear that the universe was not necessarily made for the sole benefit of humanity. But no matter how insecure such knowledge might make people, scientific inquiry could not be stopped.

Copernicus's paradigm left many opportunities for development and refinement, and scientists continued to speculate about it. Two of Copernicus's most important followers, Kepler and Galileo, and their achievements must be briefly touched on. Kepler was a German mathematician who saw through the argument about crystalline spheres. He altered the Copernican paradigm by ridding it of the transparent spheres that Copernicus had taken over from Ptolemy. Kepler's planets moved through space in elliptical orbits rather than in circles. Galileo did not reject the concept of circular motion, but he was a source of great irritation to Church authorities for other reasons. His observations through his telescope, as we have seen, showed that the heavens could change, which contradicted Church doctrine. Other observations he made seemed to contradict the Bible. He defended his views with considerable energy, but eventually was forced, under the threat of torture by the Holy Inquisition, to deny his beliefs. (The Church feared that Galileo's ideas would aid the rising Protestants.) His scientific achievements were not lost, however, but were building blocks for a scientist who to this day overshadows Galileo himself: Isaac Newton (1642–1727). Whereas Kepler and Galileo had left many phenomena unexplained, Newton put all the pieces together in a system so well-designed that it did not dare fly apart.

NEWTONIAN MECHANICS AND NATURAL LAWS

In order to fully appreciate Newton's relation to Adam Smith and, especially, to more modern developments in economics, we need to consider the influence of one of Kepler's and Galileo's contemporaries. René Descartes (1596–1650), a French philosopher and mathematician, suggested that correct thinking proceeds on the basis that the human being possesses no senses. To Descartes, the founder of analytic geometry, mathematics was more reliable than sense perception. Things outside the mind could only be described through concepts created *inside* the mind; thus Descartes neatly split the world into two separate parts.

The basic notion derived from Descartes is the use of imaginary states. For example, by describing the body as "nothing else than a statue or machine of clay," Descartes was able to explain body functions logically, using only simple principles of mechanics, such as those used in making clocks, fountains, mills, and other machines. The imaginary state used by John Locke (1632–1704), the seventeenth-century natural-law philosopher who advocated limits to sovereign rule, was the "state of nature." The imaginary state used by Isaac Newton was the mechanical state of nature. Newton, however, placed constraints upon his imagination. He had an experimental bent and derived his system from actual observations (insofar as planets could then be observed) of the heavens. Nonetheless, it was Newton's imagery of the motion of the heavenly bodies in space that provided a philosophy for Adam Smith, and elements of mechanism were to remain in economics, devoid of the rich historical tapestry of Smith. Figure 2.2, a time scale for natural science and economics, enables us to envision the clustering of such thinkers (and events) in time.

About fifty years after the death of Galileo, Newton formulated the *law of universal gravitation*, which states that forces of attraction and repulsion among bodies in space keep them in motion and balance. Gravity, a force like the mainspring of a giant clock, causes the universe to run predictably forever, without breakdowns. Newton's new paradigm, based on the law of gravitation, stated that the planets move around the sun in Kepler's ellipses and in conformity to Galileo's law of falling bodies. The Newtonian system made concrete the idea that all phenomena, all experience, consists of the arrangement of atoms following mechanical, mathematically regular laws. Galileo and Kepler had understood the importance of the existence of such "natural" laws, but they had applied them only to special cases, such as falling bodies and the movements of planets. In his theory of gravitation, Newton found a cosmic law subject to precise mathematical proof and as applicable (he thought) to the smallest object as to the entire universe.

Newton's mechanics thus brought with it the *doctrine of scientific determinism*, the principle that all events are the inescapable results of preceding causes. For example, once a planet is found in the scheme of celestial mechanics, its position thereafter is completely and unambiguously disclosed for all time by the knowledge of its position at a *single* instant in time. Henceforth—until the work of Max Planck, a twentieth-century physicist—scientists conceived of nature as a giant mechanical contrivance whose behavior could be revealed by observation, experimentation, measurement, and calculation.

The notion of the Cosmos as mechanical, as a finely tuned, clocklike piece of machinery, would quickly become crucial for the world view of people in the early eighteenth century. It has two significant implications for religion. First, God is an artisan or craftsman who constructed an immensely complicated but reliable piece of machinery called "the universe." Second, after God created the universe and the rules by which it operated smoothly, he then more or less retired and left the machine to run on its own. In a world dominated by a mechanistic perspective, people found it more and more difficult to assess the value of anything, such as personality or morality, that could not be measured scientifically.

This does not mean, however, that the universe was amoral or valueless, for with Newtonian science a God emerged who was derivable from natural law and in harmony with the order of the universe he made. God, like his universe, was rational and dependable. This optimistic conception of *reliability*—intensified by the conviction that the Creator was kind and charitable—produced a profound sense of relief. For example, the American clergyman Cotton Mather (1663–1728) could argue: "Gravity leads us to God and brings us very near to Him." To understand the forces of gravity was to better comprehend God's wondrous ways.

By the beginning of the eighteenth century, Newton's great scientific synthesis had caused a revolution in the intellectual outlook of people. It was a source of inspiration for much of the liberal philosophy and theology of later centuries. Although one could no longer believe that the world had been constructed with humans at the center, one could at least be confident that the mechanics of the universe were perfect and that nothing could go wrong. And, what is most important for our purposes, the Newtonian world view is the view that has had the greatest impact, directly and indirectly, on modern economic science.

THE ECONOMICS FRAMEWORK

Because cause and effect were so certain and clear in physics and astronomy, many scholars assumed that history, human behavior, and economics would all be governed by natural laws. If laws are divinely

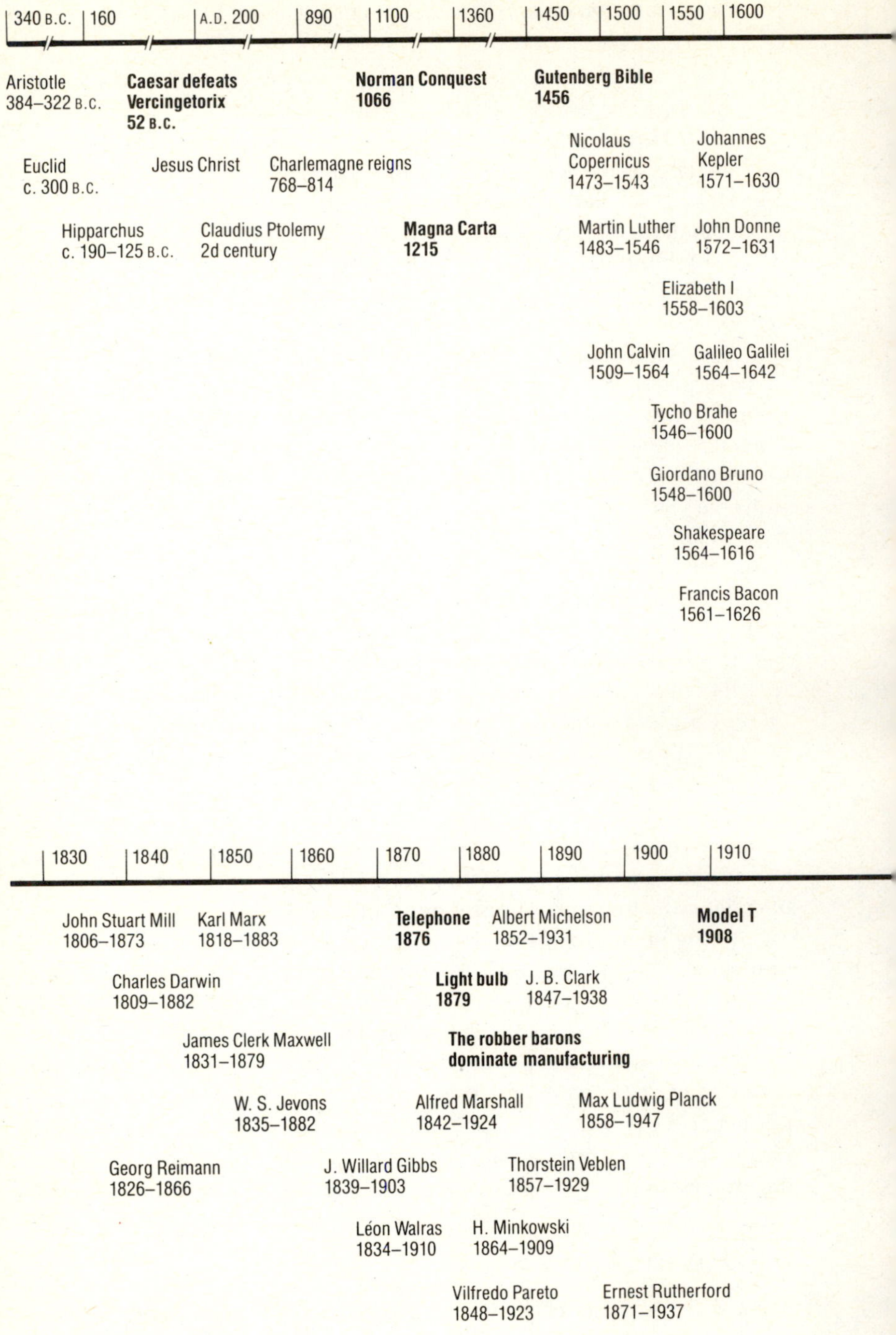

| 340 B.C. | 160 | A.D. 200 | 890 | 1100 | 1360 | 1450 | 1500 | 1550 | 1600 |

Aristotle
384–322 B.C.

Caesar defeats
Vercingetorix
52 B.C.

Norman Conquest
1066

Gutenberg Bible
1456

Euclid
c. 300 B.C.

Jesus Christ

Charlemagne reigns
768–814

Nicolaus
Copernicus
1473–1543

Johannes
Kepler
1571–1630

Hipparchus
c. 190–125 B.C.

Claudius Ptolemy
2d century

Magna Carta
1215

Martin Luther
1483–1546

John Donne
1572–1631

Elizabeth I
1558–1603

John Calvin
1509–1564

Galileo Galilei
1564–1642

Tycho Brahe
1546–1600

Giordano Bruno
1548–1600

Shakespeare
1564–1616

Francis Bacon
1561–1626

| 1830 | 1840 | 1850 | 1860 | 1870 | 1880 | 1890 | 1900 | 1910 |

John Stuart Mill
1806–1873

Karl Marx
1818–1883

Telephone
1876

Albert Michelson
1852–1931

Model T
1908

Charles Darwin
1809–1882

Light bulb
1879

J. B. Clark
1847–1938

James Clerk Maxwell
1831–1879

The robber barons
dominate manufacturing

W. S. Jevons
1835–1882

Alfred Marshall
1842–1924

Max Ludwig Planck
1858–1947

Georg Reimann
1826–1866

J. Willard Gibbs
1839–1903

Thorstein Veblen
1857–1929

Léon Walras
1834–1910

H. Minkowski
1864–1909

Vilfredo Pareto
1848–1923

Ernest Rutherford
1871–1937

FIGURE 2.2 A time scale for natural science and economics

| 1610 | 1630 | 1650 | 1670 | 1690 | 1710 | 1730 | 1750 | 1770 | 1790 | 1810 |

René Descartes
1596–1650

Cromwell, Lord
Protector of England
1653–1658

Adam Smith
1723–1790

**Spinning "Jenny"
1770**

**Battle of
Waterloo
1815**

**Telescope
1608**

Isaac Newton
1642–1727

**American Revolution
begins 1775**

Blaise Pascal
1623–1662

Jonathan Swift
1667–1745

James Watt
1736–1819

Christiaan Huygens
1629–1695

Alexander Pope
1688–1744

**French Revolution
begins 1789**

John Locke
1632–1704

David Hume
1711–1776

Jeremy Bentham
1748–1832

**Cotton gin
1793**

Pierre de Laplace
1749–1827

L. Carnot
1753–1823

David Ricardo
1772–1823

Thomas Malthus
1766–1834

J. B. Say
1767–1832

| 1920 | 1930 | 1940 | 1950 | 1960 | 1970 | 1980 |

J. M. Keynes
1883–1946

**Great Depression
begins 1929**

**IBM
1944**

**Laser developed
1960**

**Synthetic gene
1976**

Albert Einstein
1879–1955

E. H. Chamberlin
1899–1967

**The Pill
1952**

**Synthetic
DNA 1967**

A. C. Pigou
1877–1959

Werner Heisenberg
1901–

**Diesel locomotive
c. 1920**

Joan Robinson
1903–1983

**Man lands on
moon 1969**

Niels Bohr
1885–1962

Prince Louis
de Broglie
1892–1976

Erwin Schrodinger
1887–1961

Paul A. Samuelson
1915–

J. M. Clark
1884–1963

John Kenneth Galbraith
1908–

predetermined, scholars reasoned, then people should discover what these laws are so that they can cooperate with the "preestablished" natural order that controls them. In retrospect, this transfer from physics to other areas is puzzling because the natural laws were laws of motion governing the behavior of particles, not the behavior of people. Nevertheless, Newton's entire system—a machine running according to discoverable laws—became one of the unquestioned assumptions of European thinking. After Newton's time, any other world view would be measured and challenged by the one he had created.

This concept of order was the basis of the political philosophy of the French physiocrats who preceded the English classical economists. The physiocrats were named for *physiocracy,* the law of natural order. The ideas of these philosophers, taken from the natural sciences, were representative of those spreading through the literate classes in France and England by the middle of the eighteenth century. The physiocratic school was founded by François Quesnay (1694–1774), the court physician to Louis XV and Madame de Pompadour. The physiocrats' motto, *Laissez faire, laissez passer* (Let things be the way they will!), was to become the commercial battle cry of Adam Smith. And the slogan neatly summarizes the shared view of the physiocrats and Smith that the natural advantages of *free market competition* should not be spoiled by government interference.

The Scottish universities were highly active in spreading the ideas of Newton. Adam Smith was then one of the great Scots at Glasgow University. In an essay on the history of astronomy, he described Newton's system as "the greatest discovery that ever was made by man." Smith believed in a universe whose harmonious and beneficial organization is proof of the wisdom and goodness of its maker. He prophetically assumed that Newton's system would be the model for all scientific paradigms,· and he witnessed to his faith in Newton by successfully applying to social and economic phenomena the idea of the universe as a perfectly ordered mechanism operating according to natural laws. The harmony and balance that Smith saw as a natural and desirable consequence of commercial expansion and progress was the source of much of the social optimism of later centuries.

Once the economy had been set in motion by the hand of God, Smith believed, there was no need for any improvements. Attempts to repair it would only upset the mechanism and disturb its ability to function in an orderly way. In his founding of classical economics, Smith was no doubt driven by a desire to emulate the most widely respected scientific system of his time, and thus the impact of Newton on social science and society continues to this day.

CONCLUSIONS

We cannot ignore the influence of natural science upon the culture of which science is a part or upon the methods of social scientists. Science's impact has been extraordinary. People's sense of importance was greatest when the earth and they were at the center of the Cosmos. They were God's only concern. Insecurity accompanied uncertainty with the realization of the vastness of the unfolding, sun-centered universe. Although the Newtonian world view could not recapture for people their former sense of their own significance, Newton was able to reassure people of the orderliness and predictability of a universe governed by natural law. Moreover, God still was the unseen ruler: he merely worked in an indirect way as the universe's timekeeper and thermostat. On automatic pilot, the universe would function just fine, and, with growing optimism, society's leaders could be content in knowing that everything functioned best if left alone. Combine the appeal of natural laws with people's sense of impotence and we find, not surprisingly, that social scientists also decided to depend upon the preordained natural (or were they supernatural?) laws and avoid the policy ideas of mere people that would change the blissful, natural state.

Yet, no matter how persuasively it may masquerade as natural science, social science is related to human behavior. Moreover, codes of conduct that govern this behavior are as changeable as people's minds, and economics as a social science could not remain forever impervious to change. The great economists have been buffeted by changing values, historical events, differing perceptions of nature, and even by the structure of governments. An understanding of such historical flux can offer us considerable insight into the impact on society that value changes are having and will continue to have. Some economists are now saying that conventional economics is ripe for revolution, but any economic revolutionaries will have to go to the barricades against the genius of Isaac Newton as well as against Adam Smith and his followers.

3

ADAM SMITH
AND THE MARKET
ECONOMY

▼

*I am rich and I am proud of every penny I own. I have made
my money by my own effort, and free exchange and through
the voluntary consent of every man I dealt with—the voluntary
consent of those who employed me when I started, the
voluntary consent of those who work for me now, the
voluntary consent of those who buy my product. . . . Do I wish
to pay my workers more than their services are worth to me?
I do not. Do I wish to sell my product for less than my
customers are willing to pay me? I do not. Do I wish to sell it
at a loss or give it away? I do not. If this is evil, do whatever
you please about me, according to whatever standards
you hold.*[1]

AYN RAND, *ATLAS SHRUGGED*, 1957

The basic principles of caricature capitalism, distilled from Adam
Smith and other economic thinkers, can be summarized as follows: (1)
Capitalism is necessary for freedom (a belief that is still implicit in most
conventional economic thought). (2) Workers are (or should be) paid
according to their individual contributions to sales revenue. (3) Consumers are sovereign because they pay only for the legitimate production costs of goods. (This is an important element in Smith's view of
capitalism.) (4) The government has no role in business; a laissez-faire
policy is best. (5) If work is rewarded according to its effort and productivity, the economy will expand.

Perhaps these statements seem ordinary, familiar, and rather dull—
too far removed from the realities of the modern industrial democracies
(in which government accounts for a large share of GNP) to be meaningful. Yet, as we will see in Chapters 8 and 14, Ayn Rand's caricature
of capitalism was endorsed by Milton Friedman, the 1976 Nobel laureate

of economics science, and President Ronald Reagan. Ironically, the ideas were heralded as revolutionary because they were so old. There was a time, however, when these ideas and all they implied were revolutionary and new. Their 1776 spirit was captured by Adam Smith, who attempted to begin in social science what Isaac Newton had completed in natural science.

SMITH'S LIFE OF HARMONY

Adam Smith was born in Kirkcaldy, a quiet Scottish seaport where his father was controller of customs. Smith's life, like the economic world he imagined, was orderly and harmonious. Nothing very dramatic or very terrible ever seems to have happened to him. So far as we know, he had no burning passion for any woman, no romance. He suffered from a nervous affliction that made his head shake. And he was incredibly absentminded, capable of putting buttered bread instead of tea leaves into a teapot and then complaining about the quality of the tea. One day while showing Charles Townshend (1725–1767) the sights of Glasgow (population c. 25,000), Smith took him on a tour of the great tannery and absentmindedly walked directly into the tanning pit.

Smith was also highly gifted. He studied Greek and Latin literature at Oxford (which he hated). It was upon his return to Scotland and the University of Glasgow that he studied moral philosophy. In the eighteenth century, moral philosophy included natural theology, ethics, jurisprudence, and political economy. The science of economics as Smith conceived it was thus far more broadly based in his day than it is in ours. Smith's lectures on ethics, given when he was a professor of moral philosophy at Glasgow, became his first book, *The Theory of Moral Sentiments* (1759), which gained him almost instant recognition. His masterpiece, *An Inquiry into the Nature and Causes of the Wealth of Nations*, appeared in 1776. This remarkable book is the first and so far the only complete paradigm for economic science. It also became an important political force that helped to change English economic policy.

Smith was an advocate of freedom (closely linked to capitalism) and individualism, but history has not always been on the same side. In Chapter 1, we saw how the paternalism of feudalism was an impediment to individual liberties. In this chapter, a second impediment will appear—the economic system called mercantilism. Once we have looked more closely at feudalism and mercantilism, we will better understand Smith's rebellion and see why *The Wealth of Nations* was such a startling book. We will also examine the meaning of "natural liberty" and Smith's explanation of the societal harmony that results from self-interest.

THE SLOW EVOLUTION OF THE MARKET ECONOMY

When Smith wrote *The Wealth of Nations*, the market economy was a living reality. In order to absorb the significance of what Smith says, we must pick up our story of the rebirth and development of markets, begun in Chapter 1. Market development was in two stages: (1) the mercantile economy; and (2) the industrial economy, which we will discuss in Chapter 4. Although it is impossible to specify a particular moment in history when the transformation from feudalism to a market system was complete, we can identify the major forces that brought about the change.

Agricultural Surpluses and the Breakup of the Manor

The period from around 1000 to 1300 is called the High Middle Ages for a number of reasons, including a commercial revolution that occurred during those centuries. The rebirth of markets is an important element in this revolution, but other changes were taking place as well. For example, farmers began to use a more regular rotation system for the winter and spring sowing of crops. In the first year, a field would be planted with winter wheat or rye; in the second year, with grains and legumes; in the third year, it would lie fallow, plowed but unseeded. Crop rotation—the beginning of modern farming—helped to provide surpluses for seasons when the weather was unreliable.

Other innovations generated surpluses sufficient to feed both the peasant and the wandering merchant. By 1100 there were probably some 5,000 water mills in England, and water power became as important a source of energy as fire. The windmill, although less powerful than a water mill, was more adaptable for industrial use. The heavy plow, which had wheels inserted between the plowshare and the team, gave the plower a fulcrum so that heavier plowshares could be used on the moist, heavy soils of continental Europe. Nailed horseshoes and new harnesses made the faster horse a serious competitor with the ox in agriculture.

The marketing of surpluses had two effects. First, it released some labor from agriculture; and second, the manor became less self-sufficient and more reliant on purchasing. In time, the institution of the manor began to break up, although most of the feudal political controls it exercised did not. The change was very slow, evident only where the excitement of towns and trade was more attractive than the security offered by the manor. The building of castles and churches still sponged up much of the surplus food and labor. The nobleman was still ill at ease with carting and bartering, and he did his buying and selling through a middleman. In the rigid feudal hierarchy, there was still a vast gulf between the exalted religious and secular lords and the lowly farm laborers, who could not yet be replaced by machines.

Expanding Trade and Contracting Populations

As early as the First Crusade, beginning in 1095, adventuresome people broke loose from their feudal ties and became traveling merchants. And, virtually alone among Western cities, Venice remained a thriving commercial center. Venice developed a triangular trade in spices, silks, and ivories (Eastern luxuries) and timber, iron, and slaves (Western "necessities") between Western Europe, Muslim Africa, and the Levant. Moreover, Venetians, not blind to their own wares, became a famous source of glassware and salt, taken from the Venetian lagoons.

Extremely important to this medieval trade were the Jewish merchants. Their religion imposed no ban against moneylending, and thus they could make loans and increase the circulation of capital. They were also stateless, and therefore they could travel and sell their wares without the restrictions that feudal society often imposed, especially in wartime.

Although merchants attained commercial importance, their social standing remained very low. Even paupers enjoyed a higher social standing than merchants because of the continuing religious and, hence, social imputations against commerce and wealth. The poor could enter the kingdom of Heaven more easily than the rich, who had to buy passes through almsgiving. Rathier, the bishop of Verona, denounced merchants as gold-hungry. He was probably right. Only the brave and clever or the desperate and foolish carried on the commercial revolution of the Middle Ages.[2]

Towns expanded and trade and commerce flourished locally, regionally, and even internationally, but the "good times" of the Commercial Revolution did not roll forever smoothly. It unfolded in a broken series of leaps and bounds. Always lurking in the background of medieval life were the Four Horsemen of war, revolt, famine, and pestilence. War was endemic and often devastating. The "Hundred Years' War" between England and France (about 1387–1453), which seemed to have no beginning and no end, made a wasteland of much of France. The Wars of the Roses, an English civil war, kept the feudal armies of several barons busy for virtually the balance of the century. Crops and the weather were unpredictable, and famine was frequent.

England experienced widespread famine four times during the calamitous fourteenth century. This was good compared with France, where famine visited an unlucky thirteen times. Like modern-day famines, these were followed by epidemics spawned by unburied, rotting bodies. The most devastating outbreak was the Black Death (the bubonic and pneumonic plague) of 1348–1351, which had an especially disastrous effect in crowded urban areas. It is estimated that the population of Europe declined from 73 million in 1300 to 45 million in 1400. Both the famine and the plague appear to have been, at least to some extent, a consequence of rapid population growth, lack of sanitation, and inadequate medical knowledge.[3]

But the tide turned again. The plague subsided, and during the sixteenth century both the population and the volume of trade expanded, particularly in northern Europe. Italian city-states continued to dominate European commercial life, with Venice, Milan, Florence, and Genoa leading the pack. As population grew, the money wages of labor fell relative to the price of land. And this meant that the price of food rose compared with the prices of industrial goods. Agriculture relied upon large quantities of an increasingly expensive input—namely, land.

Weapons and the New Nation-States

Feudalism was characterized by relatively small political units. A tenth-century map of the area today known as France would show many separate counties and dukedoms, all owing feudal allegiance to the king in Paris, but the largest and most powerful of them were like independent states and could more or less do as they pleased. By the end of the Middle Ages, nation-states (integrated counties and kingdoms) in the modern sense had begun to emerge. A map of "France" in the early fourteenth century would still show many counties and dukedoms, but a far greater number were controlled directly by the king.

With the advent of new weapons technology, kings were able once again to extend protection over all their subjects without the knights as middlemen. Knights faced technological unemployment. As a result, the eligibility for entry into one of the orders of chivalry became more strictly controlled. Although tournaments often were used as a training ground for war, they increasingly were staged as Arthurian theatrical extravaganzas. The role of knighthood slowly gave way to the function-free privilege and limited occupational entry of the nobility.

In the Battle of Courtrai in 1302, the flower of French knighthood, heavily armored, was laid waste by foot soldiers, Flemish burgers armed with pikes. During the Hundred Years' War, the English longbow undid the French. And the successful breach of the walls of Constantinople in 1453 brought gunpowder to the attention of warriors and made the old-style walled city a questionable defense measure. By the end of the fifteenth century, civilization was blessed with both the handgun and the cannon.

Thus, nations and weapons grew up together. The nation-state took over from the feudal lord and his manor the functions of providing protection for the citizens—for a price, of course, because this new kind of "national" defense was not cheap either. The king needed revenue, and the citizens often were quite willing to pay for protection. In England and the Low Countries, for example, representative bodies began to set tax rates, and the king traded land and promises for additional revenue.

The Enclosure Movement

Another major factor changing the landscape, particularly in England, was the *enclosure movement*. (The pace of the enclosure movement was, of course, different in diverse places. It began in England in the twelfth century, moved rapidly during 1450–1640 and again in 1750–1860, and was virtually complete by the end of the nineteenth century. Yet the enclosures made little progress in the rest of Europe *until* the nineteenth century.) With the population increases of the sixteenth and seventeenth centuries, land increased in value for a number of reasons. There was an ever-growing market for food products, which made land valuable for agriculture. And there was an ever-growing market for wool; wool was a major industry in the late Middle Ages. A landowning noble didn't have to be very clever to figure out that it takes only one person to watch sheep in a pasture, whereas it might take as many as ten or twelve laborers to grow food on the same land. Thus much of the land that had once been open was fenced in (enclosed) so that the land-owners could profit from either farming or raising sheep.

The greatest loss to the smaller farmers was the common land upon which they had, by custom, fed their poultry, pastured their cow, and chopped wood for fuel. Many peasants were therefore compelled by dwindling economic prospects to sell their property and become day laborers in agriculture or go to the towns and work in the new factories. Discontent with these conditions was aptly expressed in a popular rhyme:

> *The law locks up the man or woman*
> *Who steals the goose from off the common;*
> *But leaves the greater villain loose*
> *Who steals the common from the goose!*

Thus, we have reached the point where people could sell their labor—to a woolen manufacturer, say, or a wealthy landowner. Labor was cheap. Land was also for sale by the Church, which needed more cash for bigger cathedrals, and by the king, who needed bigger armies to defeat his rivals. Land wasn't cheap at all; only the nobles or richest merchants could afford it. Gold and silver were flowing into Europe via Spanish and Portuguese explorations, and there was abundant coinage to make the market economies float. Not much more is needed for a market system. It was a slow revolution, but the traditional duties, values, and obligations of feudalism were gradually eroded by the use of money in an exchange economy. The old feudal order struggled in vain against this emerging cash economy. The pleasures of money and new economic and political organizations that emerged were worth certain sacrifices of privilege and security—at least for all those except the shrinking feudal aristocracy.

The Reformation and Other Ideas

The late medieval traveling merchant was the first recognizably modern "economic man," but, as we have seen, the commercial ethic was contrary to Church doctrine. As far as the Church was concerned, merchants were going to Hell. The morality of profit making continued to be suspect, despite intense efforts by merchants to give it a good name. But a gradual change in societal attitudes toward material accumulation from commerce was to come about, largely as a result of a series of events, beginning in the early sixteenth century, that have come to be known as the *Reformation*. This change is important, because private material accumulation is a prerequisite for capitalism.

The Reformation began as a religious movement within the Church, aimed at correcting (reforming) certain specific abuses of spiritual power, particularly the sale of indulgences.[4] (An indulgence was a partial remission of the punishment for a sin that had been confessed and repented.) In a sense, the Church itself engaged in economic-spiritual "capitalistic" exchange in order to gain capital: it sold indulgences to get some of the money it needed for operating expenses and new buildings, such as St. Peter's in Rome. The reformers—led by Martin Luther (1483–1546), a monk who became the leader of the movement in Germany—were outraged by what they considered a lapse from Christian ideals. Luther nailed his ninety-five theses to the door of All Saints' Church at Wittenberg with a rat-a-tat-tat in tune with the freer thought of the Renaissance. The Reformation ultimately culminated in a thorough modification of much of the Church's doctrine and the establishment of the Protestant Church.

The emerging merchant class was very active in this movement. Protestantism offered a haven to the worldly religious spirit of the merchants because it taught them that hard work and the accumulation of wealth were virtues. The stern and autocratic French theologian John Calvin (1509–1564) developed an interpretation of Christian beliefs that had particular appeal for the commercial classes. He riveted the attention of the faithful on some of the Old Testament values of accumulation and exchange. They could not, he argued, contradict Christ's teachings about the rich and the kingdom of Heaven (Matthew 19:24) because both books of the Bible were the word of God and the word of God was one. He taught that good Christians showed their faith by hard work and frugality. Because "Heaven helps those who help themselves," prosperity became an indication of piety. The temporal and the spiritual were happily married.

Protestantism offered the people of Western Europe, Scotland, and England a choice. They could look to the New Testament–oriented teachings of Martin Luther, or they could follow Calvinism, which had its severe and rigorous aspects but at least allowed one to accumulate money while suffering. The authority selected by the merchants was predominantly either Calvinistic or Judaic, both of which relied upon the Old Testament. [In England and Scotland, the followers of Calvin broke with the Lutherans in 1561. Calvin's principles are found in the creeds of the Presbyterian and reformed Protestant churches. John Knox (1505–1572) was Calvin's counterpart in Scotland.]

Thus, over some six centuries the forces that would guarantee the establishment of competitive market economies in much of Western Europe were grinding away at the economic roots of the manor and the political organization of feudalism. The most compelling forces were increasing agricultural productivity and surpluses, the resultant breakup of the manor, travel and exploration, the rise of the nation-states, the enclosure movement (especially in England), the buying and selling of land and labor (two important factors of production), the expanding use of money in commercial transactions and as revenue for governments, and an acceleration in the acceptance of the idea that wealth accumulation and economic progress were good.

MERCANTILISM, BIG GOVERNMENT, AND THE PHYSIOCRATS

We haven't quite yet reached the full market economy itself. We have one more step: an interruption called *mercantilism*, which was the prevailing European economic system in the years between the decline of feudalism during the early fifteenth century and the start of the Industrial Revolution (1780). Just as free competitive markets were about to unleash themselves, the rulers of various European nation-states decided in their self-interest to control the mercantile economy. These rulers still conceived of power in feudal terms, believing that national power came with a big treasury, swelled by tight controls on economic activity, especially international trade. Mercantilism (the term derives from the Italian word for merchant) was the first alliance in modern history between government and business. At first, the merchants were to be dominated by the government; later, they would do the dominating.

Mercantilism, like feudalism, worked in different ways in different countries, but the basic idea behind it was always the same: the government should manage the economy for the purpose of increasing national wealth and state power. Because power and wealth were equated with gold and silver, the government should (1) stimulate the output of domestic goods; (2) limit domestic consumption; (3) put tariffs on imports; and (4) try to create a favorable balance of trade—more exports than imports. The exports were paid for with gold and silver, which in turn could be used to build a strong army. The limits on consumption were aimed at the masses, not at the king and his court or the well-to-do landed gentry or merchants.

Gold and mercantilism tended to go hand in hand because precious metals were used as internationally acceptable money. Just at a time when trade was rapidly expanding in Europe, an acute shortage of gold and silver bullion developed. This monetary threat to trade was arrested by the influx of Spanish bullion, gold and silver mined by the Spanish in their American colonies. There was a price (or, we should say, prices) to be paid for the increased supply of gold: product prices tripled in Europe between 1500 and 1650. As the prices of simple manufactured goods rose much more rapidly than either labor's wages or land's rents, the rising merchant class benefited from these developments.

The accumulation of capital by the merchant class enabled it to extend the simple factory system during the sixteenth and seventeenth centuries. Such production did not constitute the modern type of factory, but it did increase the degree of specialization and productivity. Production, trade, and commerce thrived. Sensing the advantages of a new source of revenue, the monarchs in the new nation-states provided military protection for these commercial ventures.

However, not every nation had Spain's gold supply. In other countries, the monarch had to use monopoly powers to build up a favorable balance of trade for the nation. The nation-states were determined to never run short of gold again. The merchants of France and England experienced the happy—though not entirely unplanned—coincidence of building their nations while earning profits. In England particularly, the merchants and the landed aristocrats formed a smooth working alliance. Thus, the English merchants and the nobility developed a mutual protection association in which it was not uncommon for the merchants' daughters to marry into nobility.

As gold and silver were the coins of the mercantilist realms, most of the mercantilists were aware of a direct relation between the quantity of money and the level of prices under certain conditions. As one mercantilist quaintly expressed it: "Plenty of money in a Kingdom doth make the native commodities dearer." Thus, it would appear contradictory to encourage the influx of gold through a favorable trade balance. Would not this increase in the money supply raise prices and thus "make the native commodities dearer" or, as we might say today, cause galloping inflation? Higher domestic prices would then dampen exports, and there would go the mercantilist's prized trade surplus.

It may surprise you to learn that economists today still are divided over the answer to this question. Mercantilists did not like inflation much more than do today's pensioners. The mercantilists reasoned that increases in the amount of gold would "quicken trade"; that is, a swell in the money supply would result in higher levels of production (including the manufacture of guns and gunpowder), which would greatly offset any increase in the price level from the same source. Indeed, they saw an expansion of money and credit as essential to unimpeded trade growth. (Whether the money supply has its greatest impact on prices or on output is an issue we will return to in later chapters.)

The general notion that the level of economic activity is related to the supply of money is now known as the *quantity theory of money*. Its specific form has changed historically. The English philosopher John Locke (1632–1704) presented the most refined version of the theory in his day. He recognized that the money supply had to be increased along with production to keep business going so that merchants did not backslide into inefficient barter arrangements. Nonetheless, Locke believed that it is always difficult to decide the exact proportional relationship between the money supply and output because the amount of money required depends, as he put it, upon "the quickness of its circulation." Today's economist calls this quickness, or the rate at which money is turned over, the *velocity of money*.

The crudeness of the mercantilists' quantity theory of money certainly is understandable. They were practitioners not theoreticians, economic policymakers not philosophers. Adam Smith was not as forgiving. Even though many of the English mercantilistic restrictions had become outmoded by the mid-eighteenth century, much of Adam Smith's immediate fame was derived from his attack upon the mercantilists.

The pursuit of *national* gain dominated the mercantilist era. The new association between money and wealth (in feudal society, land was wealth), plus the new nationalism, led the nation-state to use economic policy as the main instrument for achieving its power goals. The mercantilists saw their nations in a struggle for supremacy and focused on conquest and the acquisition of colonies. National defense was the dominant organizing force of mercantilism, much as local defense had been for feudalism. From 1600 to 1667, the great powers of Europe were at peace during only one year.

Government regulations were widespread. For example, tariffs and other controls were placed on foreign trade to increase gold inflows. Gold, flowing into a nation as a result of the country's exporting more goods than it imported, had many uses. It could buy mercenaries to fill armies no longer conscripted from the manor, and it could buy the newfangled gunpowder and cannons. The government also regulated production, mostly in order to increase the production of exportable commodities.

The French mercantilist system developed by Jean Baptiste Colbert, minister of finance under Louis XIV from 1661 to 1683, brought virtually every aspect of economic production under government control. Trading companies owned by the Crown were established to trade with France's expanding colonial empire. Shippers and shipbuilders were subsidized by the state. Ports were improved and canals built. Colbert tried in many ways to improve French industry and commerce, including luxury industries such as glassmaking and lacemaking. Even the production methods and standards of quality of such industries were set by the state. He increased the tariffs on imported cloth and subsidized the immigration of Dutch and Flemish weavers and merchants into northern France. His intervention probably saved the French cloth industry from the competition of Dutch producers, yet the French economy did not flourish under Colbert's extreme mercantilist practices. (Louis XIV's policy of persecuting French Protestants also drove many members of the commercial classes from France.) An alternative policy was clearly needed.

Adam Smith was to argue that the mercantilists were mistaken about the nature and causes of the wealth of nations. His criticism, however, was preceded and, in a limited way, influenced by a group of French economic theorists called physiocrats, whom we met in Chapter 2. The physiocrats attacked the mercantilists where it hurt most, in their wealth. The physiocrats offered a different explanation of both the form and the source of a nation's wealth, claiming that land—a gift of nature—was the only *real wealth* because it enabled agriculture to produce a positive net product in excess of its production costs. Agriculture was the only truly productive enterprise. Yet the physiocrats saw a host of governmental restrictions, mercantilist subsidies, and privileges that protected industry and commerce. Unlike the agricultural industry, manufacturing produced only as much as it received and, therefore, generated no surpluses. Their beliefs led the physiocrats to advocate a policy of laissez-faire: The government should not interfere by husbanding unproductive commerce. Moreover, there should be no tariffs on the export of agricultural products.

The farmers received cash payments for their crops, and they had to pass these monies on as rent to those who had bought or retained the Church's and the king's land, the landed nobility. Manufacturers (an unproductive class) were also paid for the goods they produced. All people received payment for what they produced except the landowners, who collected rent but produced nothing. The physiocrats concluded that all the land should be taxed, no matter who owned it, a view that did not win much support from either the nobility or the clergy.

The physiocrats' attack on mercantilism was intended to eliminate the feudal landholders' tax exemption, the intolerable tax burden placed upon the farming peasants, and the protected status of manufacturers. Smith liked the laissez-faire side of the physiocrats' thought, but he rejected their attitude regarding the unproductiveness of manufacturing. His ideas would prove to be more durable than those of the physiocrats, partly because he had positive things to say about industry and, more important, because he said them on the eve of the Industrial Revolution in England.

Smith feared that commerce would be smothered by the blanket of mercantilist regulations. He noted firsthand in a celebrated tour of the Continent (1764–1767) that French peasants still wore wooden shoes or went barefoot in contrast to even the poor Scottish peasants. Smith did not believe that trade restrictions were beneficial or that gold was wealth. Gold was simply money, a wheel of circulation, whereas *product* was real wealth. Adam Smith saw an unimpeded expansion of markets as a liberating force, fresh air sweeping across all England and perhaps sweetening even France in its rush. Expanded commerce brought new products that would be purchased with the surpluses of the landed aristocracy. The expansion of markets would enable the economy to grow, and workers and merchants would be free at last, dependent upon neither lord nor bureaucracy. Smith believed that commerce was a civilizing influence and that mercantilism stood in its way.

ADAM SMITH AND THE TRIUMPH OF WESTERN ECONOMICS

The main ideas of Western economic thought originated, appropriately perhaps, in England, an island. The detached or isolated nature of English economics is epitomized by its insular birth. Adam Smith began a revolution in economic thinking with *The Wealth of Nations*, a new perception of economics required by a rapidly expanding commercial world in which the familiar tradition and command systems were becoming less and less important. The rise of the science of economics as a separate discipline thus paralleled the flowering of the market system, the accumulation of capital in private hands, and a dizzying upward spiral in the growth of the industrial factory system.

In the bustling world of the early Industrial Revolution, Smith was the right scholar for the right season—and, some would say, the right reason. Religion was failing to cover all the sins of the rapidly expanding merchant class, and the merchants needed a new economic philosophy. Smith's theories provided the justification for a growing economy in which money facilitates the efficient market exchange of goods and services. Although one can find in *The Wealth of Nations* some support for virtually any economic policy position, I shall focus on those basic ideas that dominated economic behavior through at least the nineteenth century.

Self-Interest, Division of Labor, Capital Accumulation, and Natural Law

Smith believed that the individual pursuit of *self-interest* in a two-way exchange economy would guarantee social harmony. In his economic behavior, an individual neither intends to promote the public interest nor does he know that he is promoting it. He intends only to provide for his own security. Smith wrote, "It is not from the benevolence of the butcher, the brewer, or the baker, that we expect our dinner, but from their regard to their own interest." He believed that self-interest and economic self-reliance were perfectly natural, grounded in "the desire of bettering our condition," which "comes with us from the womb, and never leaves us till we go into the grave." Economic self-interest is morally beneficial, too: "I have never known much good done," says Smith, "by those who affected to trade for the public good." But self-interest is not grasping and narrowly focused. It is enlightened by the "social passions" of generosity, humanity, kindness, mutual friendship, and esteem.

Growth in the production and sales of goods and services increased the wealth of nations. The starter key to the growth of wealth in a nation was the *division of labor:* the breaking down of a particular task into a number of separate tasks, each performed by a different person. Different specialist-occupations would develop, and the skill of each laborer would increase as the worker concentrated on doing only *one* thing well. In a famous example, Smith calculated that ten men dividing labor in a pin factory—one draws out the wire, another straightens it, a third cuts it, a fourth points it, a fifth grinds the top for receiving the head (which requires two or three distinct operations)—could make 48,000 pins a day or 4,800 each. One man doing all the steps could make perhaps 1, perhaps 20!

People are willing to engage in such labor because, by working in an occupation in which they are most productive, the workers can earn a sufficient amount of income to purchase commodities that they are inefficient in producing. For example, the individual who is an excellent baker does not necessarily have to be a good candlestick maker. For by being able to produce two loaves of bread for every candlestick produced by someone else, the baker can exchange approximately two loaves of bread for every candlestick. This, of course, was not done directly by barter but through a middle factor called money. The expansion of markets facilitates the specialization of labor because greater numbers of people consuming greater quantities give rise to the organization of more and more production in longer production runs in a factory system.

One way to enlarge the market is to pursue free trade in those goods in which nations enjoyed *absolute advantage*. Tea could be produced in England using less labor than would be needed for its production in the American colonies. Likewise, the colonies could produce tobacco with less labor than could England. England, Smith would say, had an absolute advantage in tea, the colonies in tobacco.

If the division of labor starts up the growth process, capital accumulation keeps it humming. According to Smith, the capital stock of the factory owner consists of fixed capital (machines, tools, plant) and circulating capital, a fund used for buying raw materials and for paying labor. The latter, a *wages fund*, grows as production and profits expand. Wages are paid to labor in advance of production and sales because of the time elapsing while production takes place. Savings by the manufacturer lead to capital amassment. The stock of wealth grows through such accumulation, and thus average payments to workers can increase as manufacturers use savings from expanding profits to hire more workers. The workers require as a minimum food, clothes, and lodging. Then as workers spend more on necessities, total demand increases, and even more is produced in the next period. And economic growth is *good*.

The concept of natural law is another important cornerstone of Smith's economics. By the mid-eighteenth century, most educated people believed that God did not control people and events personally but only indirectly, by means of laws at work in nature. Popular interpretations of the work of Isaac Newton, whose ideas were discussed in Chapter 2, helped to spread the idea that the universe was governed by natural laws. The Newtonian explanation that God created the universe as a self-propelled machine supports the virtues of individualism (self-interest) because, after all, what harm can one person do to the rest of society as long as the results of behavior will always be determined by some natural law? This view was bolstered in the political sphere by John Locke, who claimed that natural laws and natural rights existed prior to the formation of governments. Persons need be responsible only to themselves.

Besides justifying ungoverned individualism, this Newtonian world view also vindicated private property. Private thrift and prudence by individuals were now rewarded on earth, and sufficient accumulation would lead to the ownership of private property. And if one had accumulated a great quantity of private property, it must have been the machine's will. Once private property was accumulated, its protection was a *natural* right. Smith restated Locke's natural rights arguments in favor of private property and its protection. Government was to be feared because it alone could strip persons of their private property and hence also deprive individuals of their liberty. The sanctity of private property becomes a justification for a laissez-faire economic policy.

Smith transformed the virtues of natural law into the requisites of capitalism. Profits are "good" because they provide the incentive for capitalist savings. Capital accumulation is "good" because its technological consequences create a division of labor, which in turn facilitates mass production and the expansion of international trade. Without privately owned property, the master manufacturers could not assemble the means to build and equip factories and provide employment for themselves and a wages fund for others. [Smith used the terms *master*, *manufacturer*, and *master manufacturer* interchangeably. *Master* denoted both the craft skills of the manufacturer and the master-worker managerial relation. Smith wrote at a time when "manufacturers" were primarily identified with the half-entrepreneur, half-merchant of the domestic handicraft system. It was Karl Marx (1818–1883) who appropriately named the manufacturers *capitalists*.] All this was best for society and therefore should proceed naturally, without any governmental restrictions.

Smith's Theory of Value

One of the most difficult problems in economic theory is what determines the value of a product and the distribution of the income from its sales among all those who have a hand in producing it. Adam Smith did not give a complete answer to this question, and the last attempt at an explanation is nowhere in sight. Smith did, however, provide *his* explanation. As a first approximation, he relied on what has come to be known as the *labor theory of value*, the idea that the value of a product is equivalent to the labor required to produce it. In the "early and rude state of society" that precedes the accumulation of capital and the ownership of land, Smith said, commodities exchange in proportion to the quantities of labor required to produce them. In a nation of hunters, he suggested in a famous example, if it takes twice the labor to kill a beaver as to kill a deer, one beaver will exchange for two deer. In a nation of hunters, we can presume that money is not involved in such transactions. Hunters' incomes can be counted in terms of the numbers of beavers and deer that they kill. In this discussion, Smith focused upon supply forces and largely ignored demand.

Even in this primitive economy, specialization is important. Hunters who are also good runners will probably shoot more deer than beaver. Hunters who are good at sitting and waiting will be successful with beaver. Total "production" increases—more deer and more beaver—if hunters specialize in the type of pursuit at which they are best. And exchange or trade in animals will mean that all hunters ultimately gain more if they each stick to hunting only one kind of animal.

In this primitive hunting economy, we cannot make a distinction between the value of the commodity itself and the value of the amount of time required to produce it. The two values are essentially the same. In a more advanced economy, however, goods will be exchanged for money. Profits will be paid to those who own capital and rent to those who own land. In other words, there is a capitalist and a landlord with whom the value of a product (the income from its sale) must be shared. Either (1) the income going to the capitalist and landlord is an earned reward, or (2) workers are being deprived of an income share from the product that is rightfully theirs.

Which of these alternatives did Smith believe to be true? At points Smith sees labor time as the only real standard of value because the worker must always "lay down the same portion of his ease, liberty and his happiness." Yet, as Smith admits, the employer pays labor a wage that varies from the value labor places on itself. Suffice it to say that Smith did not make further use of a labor theory of value. Nowhere in *The Wealth of Nations* does he deny the right of the capital owner to receive profits or the landlord to receive rent. Indeed, he thinks that the presence of these income shares is "natural" in an economy that is growing and accumulating capital. The wages fund consists of *advances to workers* for which the fund's owner, the manufacturer, is entitled to a return. Smith argued that an average rate of wages, profits, and rents that is natural with respect to its time and place exists in every society. The interests of workers and landlords are harmonized by the progress embodied in capital accumulation.

The money price of a commodity is also a part of this natural economic balance. When a product sells for a price just sufficient to compensate the worker, the manufacturer, and the landlord at the prevailing, average rates of compensation, it is being sold at its *natural price,* or for exactly what it is "worth." In Smith's words, "The natural price, therefore, is, as it were, the central price to which the prices of all commodities are continually gravitating." Changes in supply and demand will cause the price of a commodity to rise and fall around the natural price, but these fluctuations are temporary because, according to Smith, the supply will always adjust to the demand. In the long run, then, the price of a commodity is determined solely by costs of production. The price of every commodity resolves itself into the sum of the "natural rates of wages, profit and rent." In the short run (a period when the manufacturer's productivity cannot be changed), prices are determined by the interplay of supply and demand under competitive conditions.

This whole process of price adjustment is part of the *market mechanism,* the natural laws at work in the world of commerce. Individual self-interest is the motivating force in this free market system. The built-in regulator that keeps the economy from flying apart is competition. For example, if a horseshoe manufacturer charges an exorbitant price for horseshoes, competitors will soon build blacksmith shops in town. Unless the blacksmith then lowers the price, he will be driven out of business by competition. Buyers, who are aware of all the outlets of horseshoes, will avoid the higher-priced establishment and buy their horses' shoes from alternative outlets. A large number of sellers, the consumers' knowledge of prices and outlets, and the mobility of economic resources limit the ability of any single supplier to influence prices. This emphasis on the forces of competition continues to dominate economic theory to the present day.

The laws of the market mechanism also determine the quantity of goods produced. An increased demand for baby buggies will increase their price at the current level of production, motivating manufacturers to make more of them, a depressing force on their rising price. However, resources used in the production of a commodity like bread already will have been shifted into the buggy industry. More buggies are precisely what society "wanted" in the first place. Smith emphasizes the maximization of liberty under such competition. The consumer has become king, shoving aside the feudal noble and the mercantilist planners.

The awe-inspiring laws of the market mechanism also regulate the income of the workers and manufacturers. When prices begin to rise in the baby buggy business, baby buggy profits will rise, too, until competition steps in and limits each manufacturer's profits. If a worker demands "too high" a wage, the manufacturer will simply hire another, "competing," worker. Or if wages rise in one occupation, such as furniture making, workers will move into that occupation for the higher income until a "natural" adjustment occurs: the increased supply of labor in furniture making limits the rate of wage (and income) increases. One embarrassing (and unexplained) exception is the rent of the landlords, which Smith calls a *monopoly price*.

Notice that the market is its own guardian in the sense that it is *completely self-regulating*. Whatever goes up—prices or wages—must either eventually come down or else go up a limited amount. Whatever goes down—well, you get the picture. Yet even with these ups and downs, a price will only temporarily vary away from the actual average cost of producing a good, that is, the natural price. The producers of commodities and services will be producing what individuals in society really want. Workers will be paid in accordance with what they can contribute to the production of those goods that the society desires. Everyone appears to be free, although actually everyone is controlled by the market itself because each person is too small a part of the system to influence its results significantly. An individual is "led by an invisible hand to promote an end which was no part of his intention." Adam Smith's economic system has been described as a world of *atomistic* competition in which no single, individual part of the market mechanism—worker or capitalist—is large enough to resist the pressures of competition.

Smith's views had a strong influence on the most enduring general policy conclusion in economic history: the marketplace would work properly only if *let alone*—the policy of laissez-faire. Although certainly not opposed to all governmental activity, Smith was strongly opposed to such intervention as regards the market mechanism. Only if the market were unfettered would the consumer continue to reign as king. For the same reason, Smith also opposed monopolization of the production of a commodity by one producer.

SMITH, REALITY, AND THE VISIONS TO COME

Smith's analysis of commercial capitalism was influential and widely acclaimed in the Western world. Later economists would develop Smith's theories and make them more precise, but none would match the richness of his explanation of life under a competitive market system. The popularity of *The Wealth of Nations* is primarily attributable to three specific forces.

(1) Smith's antifeudalist, antimercantilist, even antigovernment views struck a responsive chord in many of his readers. Expanding commerce had brought a measure of liberty and security to individuals. People whose forebears had lived in servile dependency upon royal masters and suffered continual warfare saw feudalism breaking down with the rise of a money exchange economy. They saw the pro-war policies of the mercantilists diminishing as expanded trade with neighboring states reduced political disagreement. Smith spoke of the beneficence of the Newtonian universe, of new liberties through natural law, and of the necessity for release from the arbitrariness of government, all of which found an eager, receptive audience in England, France, and elsewhere.

(2) With some important exceptions, eighteenth-century England approximated the model Adam Smith built. Business *was* quite competitive. The average factory *was* small. Prices often *did* rise and fall with demand. Price movements often *did* evoke changes in the volume of production. Wage changes *did* sometimes lead to shifts in occupation.

(3) The book is optimistic and democratic. It makes clear that the potential for sharing in the growing wealth of England is not limited to the wealthy landowners. Smith is concerned with *all* of society.

In fact, from the point of view of the ruling classes, Adam Smith was a radical. The rulers saw no advantage in a decentralized economic system in which the government's role was replaced by the "natural order." The French Revolution followed *The Wealth of Nations* by thirteen years, and many English people found in Smith's doctrines of freedom and his criticism of public policies a subversive spirit like that which lit the fires of the French revolt.

But Smith was not oblivious to weaknesses in his own system and faults in the world around him. He had doubts about natural liberty that were forgotten by his followers. For example, although the division of labor gives rise to the wealth of nations, it is also responsible for routinized operations that result in monotony and ignorance. Smith was one of the first to recognize that increased specialization may result in poorly motivated, alienated workers. He suggested that the monotonous life of the detail worker "corrupts the courage of his mind, and makes him regard with abhorrence the irregular, uncertain, and adventurous life of a soldier," so that he may increase the cost of national defense to fellow citizens because he may become "incapable of defending his country in war." The ease and security of the still mighty landowners also would leave them indolent and ignorant.

Smith found employers everywhere conspiring to keep wages below the level required to keep the worker "tolerably well fed, clothed and lodged." Smith also found merchants and manufacturers quick to attack high wages but slow to see the "pernicious effects of their own gains." He was concerned that capitalists might become so powerful that they would have an unfair advantage over workers. The business master, he argues, can always hold out much longer in a labor dispute:

> *A landlord, a farmer, a master manufacturer, or merchant, though they did not employ a single workman, could generally live a year or two upon the stock which they have already acquired. Many workmen could not subsist a week, few could subsist a month, and scarcely any a year without employment. In the long-run the workman may be as necessary to his master as his master is to him, but the necessity is not so immediate.*

By the time he had finished writing *The Wealth of Nations*, Smith had found sour notes in the purported harmony of Newton's natural order. He remarked in a famous passage that "people of the same trade seldom meet together, even for merriment and diversion, but the conversation ends in a conspiracy against the public, or in some contrivance to raise prices." Such giants as the East India Company, a mercantilistic monopoly chartered by the British Crown, went beyond the propriety of small private businesses, and Smith loathed it. "Artificial" prices above natural prices were an undesirable consequence of legal regulations, exclusive corporate privileges, statutes of apprenticeship, and monopolies. Yet, on balance, Smith believed that the civilizing effects of commerce were a blessing, well worth defending against the medieval and mercantilist forms of social organization.

CONCLUSIONS

The Wealth of Nations remains one of the great books of Western civilization. Like all great books, it is important at a number of different levels: (1) as a polemic that inspired the rejection of mercantilism in England; (2) as a work of philosophy that imposes order on social chaos; and (3) as a paradigm in scientific economics that can be used to study the market system. The themes of polemic, philosophy, and paradigm are intertwined; the reader cannot follow one strand without becoming involved with the other two.

In Smith's view, human welfare is at its highest when an unrestrained economy serves the needs and desires of the consumer. These requirements and wishes are met by the natural tendency of producers to manufacture and sell what the consumer really wants. The natural tendency to trade and exchange at costs and prices held low by competitive bidding leads to the increased efficiency garnered through specialization. Specialization results in investment in new machines, economic growth, and trade expansion. Capital accumulation keeps the national economy moving upward.

Smith eliminated the old painful moral dilemma between individual selfishness and social order. As long as competition reigned as the great equalizer and persons were otherwise civilized, there simply was no conflict between self-servers in the economy and maximum social welfare.

Smith provided the analytical framework and vision for economic science, and many economists today still accept them. They accept them even though natural law and Newtonian order have been known to give way to other principles as the basis for laissez-faire. They accept them even though competition—as we shall see in Chapters 5 and 6—sometimes has been seen as a Darwinian fight for survival rather than as an assertion of self-interest. They believe that there is a competitive market mechanism obeying certain laws of the market. The natural market system of balances follows a path of increasing national wealth. As long as the market mechanism is allowed to adjust freely to changing supplies and demands, capital accumulation will occur.

Does it all sound too good to be true? It was and it is.

4

THE INDUSTRIAL REVOLUTION AND THE OTHER CLASSICALS

▼

Our rulers will best promote the improvement of the nation by confining themselves strictly to their legitimate duties, by leaving capital to find its most lucrative course, commodities their fair price, industry and intelligence their natural reward, idleness and folly their natural punishment, by maintaining peace, by defending property, by diminishing the price of law and by observing strict economy in every department of the state. Let the Government do this, the people will assuredly do the rest.

THOMAS BABINGTON MACAULAY, "SOUTHEY'S COLLOQUIES ON SOCIETY," 1830

Adam Smith's economics paradigm became the basis for a school of economic thought. The *classical economists,* the first of whom was Adam Smith and the last, John Stuart Mill (1806–1873), dominated political economy for at least a century, especially in England. Although the classical writers differed sharply on details of economic theory, they agreed in their condemnation of governmental regulations in all but three areas: (1) national defense, (2) national criminal justice, and (3) public works and institutions that could not be profitably maintained by individuals or groups. Any regulations beyond those termed *rightful acts of government* were considered ruinous to commerce and industry.

The most prominent classical economists following Smith were Thomas Malthus, David Ricardo, James Mill, and his son John Stuart Mill. This chapter is concerned with their ideas. Broadly speaking, these men were nineteenth-century, middle-class liberals. They shared a belief in the liberal tradition of laissez-faire and private property protection so succinctly expressed by the essayist Macaulay in the epigraph to this chapter. Basically, *liberalism* was the belief that economic, political, and religious freedom were all elements of a program that would emancipate the middle class from domination by the government.

David Ricardo (with the help and encouragement of James Mill) developed the most influential refinement of Smith's paradigm in his three editions of *Principles of Political Economy and Taxation* (1817, 1819, 1821). James Mill himself provided a well-written summary of classical economics, *Elements of Political Economy* (1821); his son, the economist and social philosopher John Stuart Mill, followed with a widely used multiedition text, *Principles of Political Economy* (1848), which was still in use as a textbook in the United States as late as the 1920s. Except for Malthus, the classicals accepted Say's law of markets, which denied the possibility of a "general glut," or oversupply of goods, and had been developed in Say's *Traité d'économie politique* (1803) and by James Mill in 1808.

J. B. Say was a leading French advocate of laissez-faire whose radical (in the sense of fundamental, basic) views had incurred the imperial displeasure of Napoleon Bonaparte, who had difficulty keeping his hands off other countries, much less his own. *Say's law of markets* states that there is no need for government policy to bolster the total demands for goods because production under free market competition will always generate an equivalent amount of demand for the goods produced. A partial glut of goods might happen in the event of a particular commodity's being overproduced. However, this oversupply would automatically correct itself under conditions of competition. If one commodity is excess in supply and selling at a loss, another will be produced in insufficient quantity and selling at a sufficiently high price to attract the unemployed resources. As Say put it, "The creation of one product immediately opened a vent for other products." Total demand would always be sufficient.

Like Smith, Say believed that money was only a go-between for goods and not an asset valuable in itself. Hoarding of money therefore was irrational, and everyone, including producers, was not hesitant to spend money on something of value—namely, other goods. Ricardo stressed this aspect of savings by the capitalist. Savings would immediately be spent for investment goods and labor, which meant an income receipt by the resource suppliers. Again, total demand would always equal total supply. As a result of this belief in the impossibility of general gluts, where goods in excess supply go unpurchased, the classical economists advocated a hands-off policy for the government, even during economic depression.

We must also briefly mention here Karl Marx, sometimes viewed as a second branch of the classical tree. In the first volume of *Das Kapital: A Critique of Political Economy* (1867), Marx adopted some of the ideas of Smith and Ricardo—such as the labor theory of value and a mistrust of monopolies—but much of what he had to say conflicted with Smith's idea that social harmony would arise from the pursuit of self-interest and with Ricardo's and Malthus's defense of laissez-faire. In his own time, Marx was viewed by the traditional classical economists as the rotten branch of the family tree. Even today, Marx is considered a radical because he viewed capitalism as only one stage of development in an economy and thought that ownership of the means of production under a classless socialism was inevitable. It is therefore appropriate to treat Marx apart from the classical paradigm. This I do in Chapter 10.

It is important to remember that the classical school was not homogeneous. Malthus and J. S. Mill, for example, were, for different reasons, near the "radical" fringe of the new political economy. Malthus did not share Smith's optimism. He believed that unbridled population growth would rob people of the benefits of expanded capitalism. Mill challenged the classical school's faith in the universality and permanence of natural law. Most of all, Mill's humanitarianism, warmth, and empathy for the poor and the downtrodden were not shared by many of the other classical economists, especially not by Malthus. We keep Mill in the classical school because his "laws" of production are taken from the other classical economists. Unlike Marx, Mill accepted a continuing need for private property in the economy.

British classical economics emerged from the political struggles of the Industrial Revolution. Following the paths suggested by Smith and extended by Say, the classical economists lobbied for the freedom to own and move private capital. Their objective was political and revolutionary: they wanted the control of government taken forever from the hands of the landlords and placed in the hands of the merchants and manufacturers. The classical economists were sometimes significant actors in the political conflicts of their day, including the debates over free labor markets, the abolition of tariffs, welfare legislation, and free competition among manufacturers. Indeed, Ricardo and J. S. Mill were members of Parliament. Therefore, we need to describe the setting—the English Industrial Revolution and its political environment—in which these struggles took place so that we can understand the motivations and ideas of the actors.

THE INDUSTRIAL REVOLUTION

The Early Stirrings

By 1750, over a century of successful exploration, slave trading, merchandising, piracy, and war had made England one of the world's wealthiest, most powerful nations. Although much of its wealth had gone to the Crown and the nobility, a good deal of it was filtering down to a growing stratum of commercial middle-class people. This change in the distribution of income created an ever-growing market for food, utensils, beer, wine, clothes, etc. Rising consumer demands, in turn, confirmed the need for improvements in industrial procedures.

In a way, England was ready for the Industrial Revolution in the seventeenth century. The commerce and finance were there, and there was considerable industrial technology by the late sixteenth century. Yet the industrial explosion did not occur until the mid-eighteenth century. A look at the industrial situation in England in the first half of the seventeenth century will help us understand why.

Efficient, large-scale manufacturing is next to impossible using wooden machines; iron and steel are essential because of their durability. Iron was first cast with the heat of firewood and charcoal. Coal, a more efficient source of higher temperatures, was not widely mined until shortages of wood developed during the fifteenth century. Luckily for England, Wales turned out to be a prime source of coal. By 1527, coal was being mined in the lordship of Bromfield, where a mining lease for twenty-one years was granted to one Lancelot Lother.[1] In 1613, John Browne's armament factory in Brenchley was employing 200 people in the casting of guns, which made it a sizable factory. Around 1620, John Rochier, a Frenchman living in England, applied for a patent to produce steel by using hard coal and without using wood. By 1635, steel of sufficient quality to meet the needs of the cutlery industry was being produced in Sheffield and Rotherham. But despite all these signs of activity and growing industry, English iron and steel production was actually declining in the late seventeenth and early eighteenth centuries. To a great extent, the social attitudes of the landed gentry were responsible for the decline.

The landed gentry were prominent in both the coal and iron industries because they owned the land where the coal seams were discovered. They tended to be interested in quick profits, however, rather than in the investment of large capital amounts for long-term gains. The social pressure to live ostentatiously was too great for the latter course. Moreover, the highest purpose of the ambitious trader or small manufacturer continued to be the purchase of a landed estate. That is, wealth was still associated by tradition with land not with the profits of manufacturing. Much of the capital that flowed into England from sources such as commerce in slaves and tobacco also went into "conspicuous consumption." It took a special, new kind of attitude to accumulate capital for building industry.

The farmers who worked in the Lancashire cotton industry in its early stages had that new attitude. For example, the expansion of Matthew

Boulton's cotton mill was made possible by his father's lifetime savings in the hardware industry. The brewing industry was dominated by the Quakers, whose commercial instincts were quietly parsimonious rather than conspicuous. In good times and bad, the Quakers seemed good for what "aled" the Englishman.

Industry Explodes

If there were factories, some thriving industry, and markets before 1750, then what constituted the Industrial Revolution? It was the explosive nature of the change in industrial output, a sustained increase that was revolutionary when compared with what went before. After 1780, about every measure of production turned sharply upward. Between 1780 and 1850, the growth of the English national product per person averaged from 1.0 to 1.5 percent per year, a rate that doubled real (adjusted for price changes) output per person every fifty years.

More than half of the increase in the shipment of coal and the mining of copper that occurred in the eighteenth century took place between 1780 and 1800. More than three-fourths of the increase in broadcloths, four-fifths of that in printed cloth, and virtually all the exports of English cotton in the eighteenth century also occurred during the final twenty years of the century. Of 2,600 patents during the century, more than half were registered during this same period.

As early as 1709, a Quaker ironmaster, Abraham Darby, had used coal in the form of coke in his own blast furnaces in Coalbrookdale in Shropshire. Expansion in the iron industry was made possible by Darby's example and by James Watt's rotary-motion steam engine. The latter supplied a more efficient and reliable energy source for the blast required for coke smelting and improved steel making. Even so, no other entrepreneur followed Darby's example until mid-century. The number of blast furnaces quadrupled between 1760 and 1790 to over 80. By 1830, there were 372 and in 1852, 655. The production of pig iron was some 30,000 tons in 1770, one-quarter million tons by 1805, nearly three-quarter million tons by 1830, and 2 million tons by 1850.

The spectacular growth of the cotton textile industry is reflected by raw cotton imports used in cloth production. The average import from 1776 to 1780 was about 8 million pounds. In 1850, raw cotton imports were 620 million pounds. There were less than 2 million cotton spindles in 1780 and 21 million by 1850. Power looms were introduced in 1820; there were 50,000 looms by 1830 and 250,000 by 1850.[2]

It is perhaps impossible to overstate the impact that the Industrial Revolution had on England and, in time, the whole world. Many of the traditional modes of life were destroyed or changed beyond recognition.

For some, life became better; for others, it became much worse; but for everyone, life was transformed.

Can we now sort out the causes of this revolution? Economists are not in agreement on the relative importance of each cause, but without attaching a precise value to each factor, we can be generally correct on several major ones.

Increased agricultural productivity and population.   First, increased food supplies as a result of rising agricultural productivity led to population growth. More people meant more demand for new products. The enclosure movement, the breakup of the manorial system, and modifications in agricultural techniques hastened this process in England. In the seventeenth century, agriculture accounted for some 40 to 45 percent of everything produced in England, and hence its health was crucial. By 1730, the precarious balance between harvests and population had tipped in favor of feeding the people, although not all of them all the time. This increased agricultural productivity released cheap labor from food production. There eventually (perhaps by 1830) were interactions, too. Advances in steel making, for example, provided improved farm tools that also made agriculture more productive and efficient.

Capital accumulation.   Second, there was the capital accumulation that Adam Smith thought so important a contribution to economic growth. In England this capital accumulation was sustained by the institution of inheritance. Smith thought that more capital would mean more machines and therefore more productivity. As we have seen, the financial capital available in the seventeenth century had not been put to productive use. Thus, it was not only the accumulation of finance capital but the proper use of it that helped industry flourish.

Technological change.   Third, change in the form of new inventions for industrial use greatly accelerated during this period. The Industrial Revolution was related to the Scientific Revolution that we discussed in Chapter 2. The Royal Society of London for the Promotion of Natural Knowledge, of which Isaac Newton was an early president, was granted royal patronage in 1662, thus stimulating a general interest in science and enhancing its prestige. Though the majority of manufacturers in the late eighteenth century had little knowledge of science, a substantial minority, especially some of the most important, were members of scientific societies and therefore aware of scientific developments. It was an accepted fact that manufacturing was being improved by scientific progress.

The inventions came in convenient clusters. Before 1734 came the coke smelting of iron, the Newcomen steam engine, and John Kay's flying shuttle (for weaving). But, predictably, the greatest concentration came in the last third of the century, a time of even greater interest in scientific applications. Richard Arkwright, a barber who clipped hair near the weaving districts of Manchester, saw the need for a machine that would enable the spinners of the in-home (cottage) textile industry to keep up with the more technically advanced weavers. James Hargreaves met this need with his famous spinning jenny (patent, 1770), which increased the spinners' output eightfold. With two rich hosiers, Jedediah Strutt and Samuel Need, Arkwright also produced the water frame (1769), which enabled Arkwright's weavers to use cotton instead of linen thread in the vertical threads of cotton cloth. Until the water frame came into use, "cotton cloth" had not been made entirely of cotton, and Arkwright's cloth was of much finer quality. A decade later, Crompton's "mule," so-called because it combined the functions of the spinning Jenny and the water frame, pulled spinners' productivity up from eight- to tenfold. The English cotton industry was transformed.

The steam engine that Thomas Newcomen invented early in the eighteenth century was used to pump water out of the coal mines. This engine was more or less restricted to the mines, where the fuel was available and cheap. The engine was improved between 1776 and 1781 and reached its most powerful and efficient form in the hands of James Watt, who discovered how to lower the engine's fuel consumption and thus make it more widely useful. By 1800, there were perhaps 1,000 steam engines puffing away in England, with about 250 in the cotton industry.

We have already mentioned some early advancements in iron and steel making. A later development is puddling, the process of subjecting iron to heat and frequent stirring in the presence of oxidizing substances to convert it to steel, which was invented in 1784. Then, with improved steel, the first useful threshing machine was built for agriculture (1786), and the lathe was improved for industry (1794). Thus began a new era in which machines were used to produce other machines. Financial capital accumulation was merely important; the technology of the machines that were purchased with such investment funds was crucial.

All of this technological ingenuity was buttressed by the experimental bent of science. The Newcomen engine, for example, was based on principles demonstrated in scientific-technological experiments. Later developments of the steam engine emerged from the study of mechanics and hydrostatics. The *theoretical* descriptions of those engines were carefully studied by James Watt, who, along with Boulton, was a member of the Royal Society. And chemistry played a major role in the development of the bleaching and dyeing that was essential for colored cotton prints, even though important inventors in the cotton industry, such as Kay, Hargreaves, and Arkwright, had little or no scientific training.[3]

The commercial environment.   Adam Smith had argued that the rate of progress resulting from the accumulation of capital would depend on a favorable commercial environment, especially one that allowed competition and free trade. The seventeenth and eighteenth centuries had witnessed the increasingly rapid breakdown of mercantilist restrictions in England, in sharp contrast to the absolutism, the Colbertism, and the stagnation of the French economy during the same period. Patents protected the works of the English inventors, and, in general, property was made relatively secure by laws that favored its accumulation. These laws did not *cause* economic growth, but they helped to create an atmosphere that effectively rewarded business enterprise and allowed the Industrial Revolution to proceed.

It was an environment in which James Watt could come together with Matthew Boulton, already a wealthy manufacturer of simply made buttons and buckles, and form a company for manufacturing steam engines. The environment allowed Richard Arkwright and other industrialists of modest beginnings to retire as landed millionaires. Arkwright, once a lowly barber, was knighted as *Sir* Richard Arkwright.

Social change.   Finally, there was the necessity of social change that accepted innovations and profit making. Again, there is a contrast between England and France. In France, all religious dissenters to Catholicism were treated alike. In England, however, the normal educational and professional outlets for young men from prosperous business families who were dissenters were closed by a 1689 settlement. If the young man bought a landed estate, he had to join the Church of England and the Tory squirearchy as well. Thus the exit from mercantile pursuits into gentility was closed to the English dissenter, and this served the useful economic purpose of keeping the capital of well-to-do Presbyterians and Baptists in the family businesses.

THE SOCIAL SCENE: LIBERTY, FRATERNITY, AND INEQUALITY

The Industrial Revolution was a gradual process that took many years; indeed, it is still going on in developing nations. The age of Adam Smith saw two other revolutions that were briefer but no less important in their impact: the American Revolution of 1776 and the French Revolution of 1789. These political, economic, and social upheavals struck at the hearts of the European landed aristocracy and the old notions of the divine rights of monarchs. Many English people sympathized with the spirit of both revolutions.

The French Revolution destroyed all that remained of the super-structure of feudalism in France, but the original purposes of the rev-olution were sidetracked by the imperial ambitions of Napoleon. England, in an ultimately successful attempt to resist Napoleon's conquest of Europe, was involved in a series of wars with France from 1793 to 1815. These wars put a great strain on the type of English liberalism repre-sented by Smith and his followers. In 1794, the Habeas Corpus Act was suspended for five years, all secret associations were banned, all meet-ings attended by more than fifty persons had to be supervised, printing presses had to be registered with the government, and the export of English newspapers was prohibited. In perhaps the most dastardly blow of all, lecture rooms charging admission were legally classified as broth-els! In 1799 and 1800 the Anti-combination Laws prohibited any kind of combination of either employers or workers for the purpose of regulat-ing conditions of employment. If there was hope for the English liber-tarians amid this sea of oppressive legislation, it was the fact that the Anti-combination Laws were enforced against workers and embryonic labor unions but not against employers. The merchant class at least could breathe easily.

The Expanding Middle Class

When the smoke from the battlefields of the Napoleonic Wars cleared, it was apparent that, although the monarchies and the aristocracies still held political control, the *economic* power required for sustained po-litical dominance by any group was gradually passing into the hands of the expanding middle class. In the larger cities of England, France, and the Low Countries, the leaders of the old mercantilists' government-by-the-wealthy were reluctantly beginning to share their leadership in the business world with a small number of factory owners, the new "captains of industry." Moreover, there were some country lawyers, country doctors, freeholding farmers, and some schoolteachers who began to share some of the attitudes of the urban middle class.

To many of those in the middle class, the accumulation of money had not yet become an end in itself. For example, the sons of the old patrician families at the top of the middle class, whose fortunes had been made in colonial enterprises and earlier long-distance trade, tended to become bankers and merchants rather than manufacturers. They considered wealth to be only a *means* of gaining leisure in order to enjoy one's family and friends and, as suggested earlier, to secure landed property in order to gain status. The ideas of Adam Smith and other classical economists, which gave Calvinism a rational base, were to contribute to a change in this attitude.

As the old world of mercantilism disappeared, a new society was forming in England, France, and the Low Countries. A new type of "economic man" was emerging—hard-working, energetic, self-made. His virtues were self-denial, self-discipline, personal initiative, and personal risk for personal gain. He could not permit laxity in workers or see any value in welfare. One ambition dominated his life: to increase the output of his machines to their very limits. Thrift was his watchword, and every penny saved was for reinvestment in his business. High wages and government regulations were bad for business. He disallowed leisure and recreation for either himself or his workers. Factory management required long hours and diligent supervision, and he spent days over his machines and his ledgers, perhaps contentedly. He wasn't much fun.

It would be wrong, however, to put too much stress on general social change during this period. Factory chimneys crowded the horizon in cities like Manchester in England and Lille in France, but there were still hundreds of towns where economic life had not greatly changed since the time of the Italian poet Dante Alighieri (1265–1321). The overwhelming majority of the population of every European nation-state except Great Britain still lived from the land. The landowners still had substantial political power and were able to continue to enclose common lands and drive the farmers onto smaller tracts. (This process had left only one-fifth of English land unenclosed by 1810, about the time enclosures were gaining momentum in the rest of Europe.) The peasants and the small freeholders and renters were somewhat better off— freer to buy, sell, work for themselves, perhaps change their occupation. Yet life was still very hard for all the working classes, whether on the farm or in the factory.

The Working Class

Although Adam Smith had second thoughts about merchants and contempt for the landed aristocracy, the general thrust of his beliefs was that the elements of the economy would combine in a harmony of interests and a steady upward progression for society. Contrary to his expectations, however, as mechanization increased, clashes of economic interest also grew. The new factory system herded workers like cattle under a common roof, where they were closely supervised and required to work steadily. This involved a radical change in work style from the old in-home industries. The laborers also were often required to live in quarters that they did not own and under conditions over which they had no control.

What has come to be known as automation was also a source of conflict, even in the eighteenth century. New equipment often displaced laborers, sometimes resulting in open violence. In 1779 a mob of 8,000 workers attacked and burned an English mill. By 1811 protests against machinery were sweeping across England as workers sought revenge against the factory owners for widespread unemployment and low wages.

One of the worst abuses of the early factory system was the exploitation of women and children, who were considered valuable workers, especially in the spinning and printing factories. Indeed, the percentage of adult males in such factories was relatively small. Women and children had the fewest civil liberties and were physically least able to make effective protests against brutal or hazardous working conditions. They could be disciplined easily, forced, if necessary, to spend long hours at repetitive tasks, and they worked cheaply. Sometimes children as young as nine or ten years old were made to work twelve to eighteen hours a day under a supervisor who might beat them to keep them awake and at work.

The rate of population growth compounded the ugliness of early industrialism. In Great Britain between 1700 and 1750, the increase was only 8 percent; between 1750 and 1800, it was 60 percent (an enormous leap by the standards of the time); and an incredible 100 percent between 1800 and 1850. The industrial expansion was spurred on by the wars. As a result, the rapidly growing population was being pushed out of or pulled from the country, from the towns' cottage industries and into the cities' factories. Urban growth brought with it crowded conditions, slums, inadequate sewage, and all the other ills that remain common to many American cities today.

All of these social problems, and others, are common knowledge, yet there is little agreement among historians on the effects of industrialization on the English working class in the late 1700s and early 1800s. It is clear that, although industrialization was eventually to improve everyone's income level (not equally), the real wages (adjusted for price changes) of labor either declined or failed to increase noticeably during the Industrial Revolution. The rate at which surplus agricultural and cottage industry labor was moving into the factory towns and cities exceeded the growth in demand for it. After all, the new technology was labor-saving. The inventions of Arkwright and Hargreaves greatly reduced the labor requirements of cotton spinning, eliminating hand cotton spinning almost as fast as the machines could be built.

The English cotton industry is one of the crucial economic forces of this period, a good place to try to discover if the working class was better off during the Industrial Revolution. Statistics show that the change from cottage industry to the factory was in some respects an improvement and in other respects a worsening of living standards. Hand-loom operators had been employed in large-scale industry prior to the Industrial Revolution. As early as 1736, two brothers employed 600 looms and 3,000 persons in the Blackburn district. It was higher wages and *regular* employment that brought many of the workers out of the cottage industry and agriculture and into the Lancashire factories. It has been reported that male unskilled operatives in 1806–1846 could earn 15 to 18 sixpence and skilled operatives 33 to 42 sixpence a day, compared with some 13½ sixpence as agricultural workers in Lancashire.[4] The higher-paid Lancashire laborers could afford meat, whereas the agricultural peasants were living mostly on bread and water.

Those coming from the farm to the factory probably felt that industry demanded too much discipline in terms of steady working hours. Workers lost the freedom to schedule their own work. There were rare "model" employers, such as the utopian socialist Robert Owen (1771–1858), owner of the Lanark mills, but even his famous benevolence must be seen in context. He was praised in his own day because only 14 of the nearly 3,000 children that he employed over a twelve-year period died and not one became a criminal.[5] Owen's practices were of course exceptions. Elsewhere in England, thousands of male and female children from seven to fourteen years of age were compelled to work every day from six in the morning until six in the evening with only thirty minutes allowed for eating and recreation. These conditions were in great part a continuation of a tradition of harsh supervision in farms and workshops, which continued long after remedial legislation was enforced in the factories. And sometimes the children found the factory less intolerable than their home environment.

We are left, then, with the inescapable conclusion that the Industrial Revolution was no great boon to the workers, although urbanization and rapid population growth probably contributed more to adverse urban living conditions than did the factory system itself. At times when factory employment was high, workers' incomes obviously increased, but the expansion of industry did not in itself increase their share of the wealth of the nation. It was not until about the 1860s that the standard of living of the English working class significantly improved.

The Landed Aristocracy

During this period of rapid industrial growth, the landed nobility was reaping benefits from the rising price of food. And the rising, hard-working new industrialist class was expressing self-righteous indignation at the landowners who could profit while sitting on their land and at the factory workers who were demanding higher wages from a factory system that was built by the grace of self-sacrificing industrialists. Was this what Adam Smith meant by the all-encompassing harmony of interests? Not only did these conditions set the stage for some pessimism, but they also required some explanation. For this we turn to the "other classical economists."

THE PHILOSOPHICAL RADICALS IN GENERAL
AND JEREMY BENTHAM IN PARTICULAR

We can best appreciate the views of the other classical economists—Malthus, Ricardo, the Mills, and their followers—by examining some of the ideas that influenced their thinking. Indeed, most of post-Smithian economics is influenced one way or another by the philosophical radicals. These thinkers attempted to introduce a principle, analogous to Newton's in the natural sciences, on which a science of moral and social life could be founded. Beyond this, they hoped to provide the basis for a reform movement known as *Philosophical Radicalism*.

The movement is primarily associated with Jeremy Bentham (1748–1832) and James Mill (1773–1836). Bentham (like Smith) was influenced by the eighteenth-century Scottish historian and philosopher David Hume, who taught that all our ideas are derived from impressions, and therefore human behavior is ultimately the result of sense experience rather than reason. Bentham's social ethics assumed that pleasure was associated with moral goodness and pain with evil.

Bentham had taken his degree at Oxford. He left his entire estate to the University of London as its founder, after specifying that his remains be present once a year at meetings of its board. Stuffed and dressed, his skeleton is seated in a chair with his cane in gloved hand. To add to the macabre effect, the head on the body is wax, and Bentham's actual head (preserved) is between his feet. Since his death, Bentham has not missed a meeting!

Underlying Bentham's philosophy is the doctrine of *hedonism*: whatever is good is also necessarily pleasant. The sole aim of life should be to seek one's own greatest happiness. This doctrine, however, is not quite as individualistic as it might sound, because Bentham superimposed on it *utilitarianism*, the belief that an individual's conduct should be directed toward promoting the greatest happiness for the greatest number of persons. Legal, moral, and social sanctions act as constraints on acts of individualistic self-interest that might impede the greater good. Bentham thus departed from a strict laissez-faire position; he even advocated socializing the life insurance business.

Bentham applied these concepts to society as a whole, arriving at a kind of social arithmetic by adding up pleasures and subtracting pains from them. He argued that, because all individuals in society count equally, any action will result in identical experiences of pleasure and pain for each one. The total welfare of society is equal to the total welfare of all the individuals in it. Thus, if one person *gained* more welfare from a change in the government's policy on, say, rent control than a second person *lost*, the total welfare of society would increase. However, people do not necessarily associate their own interests with the general interest, and the kind of social behavior required for social harmony has to be learned. (He is rebutting Smith's claim in *The Wealth of Nations* that the natural—i.e., unlearned—pursuit of self-interest leads to social harmony.) Bentham saw education legislation contributing to the greatest happiness of the greatest number.

The book that was eventually to be called the first textbook in Philosophical Radicalism was published in 1793, *An Enquiry Concerning the Principles of Political Justice* by William Godwin (1756–1836), a political writer, novelist, and philosopher. (Godwin was at the stormy center of a distinguished intellectual circle. His wife, Mary Wollstonecraft, was an author and an early champion of the rights of women. His daughter, Mary Shelley, wrote *Frankenstein.* And his son-in-law was the famous poet and radical, Percy Bysshe Shelley.) Godwin proposed a simple form of society without government in which human perfection would ultimately be attained. He contended that the institutions of society that affect the distribution of wealth prevent the achievement of human perfection and ultimate happiness. Godwin called for an equal division of wealth that would provide for necessities and leave sufficient leisure time for the intellectual and moral improvements that would lead to such perfection on earth. The French philosopher Condorcet (1743–1794) had held similar views, although he relied more on science as a source of perfectibility.

These ideas have an obvious appeal, and many people seemed to want to believe them, but to others in Godwin's day they seemed naive and crudely optimistic.

THE DISMALNESS OF THOMAS MALTHUS

The fame of Thomas Malthus (1766–1834) rests on his theory of population growth, a theory that shows his total disagreement with Godwin and Condorcet. It was the excessive optimism characteristic of the eighteenth-century faith in the ascendancy of reason (a movement called the Enlightenment) that Malthus attacked rather than the more modest cheer of Adam Smith.

The origin of the name *Malthus* is as redoubtable as the famous Malthusian theory. Originally the name was Malthouse, as in the brewer's malt. No doubt because of the religious roots in the family tree, the name was modified, and in its new version Robert Thomas Malthus was enrolled at Cambridge in 1785. He is said to have been fond of cricket and skating at college, and he obtained prizes for Latin and English declamations. He became an ordained minister of the Church of England, but rarely acted in that capacity. After his fame as an economist was assured, Malthus became professor of history and political economy at Haileybury College, run by the East India Company in London.

Malthus believed that the tendency of the population to increase faster than the means of subsistence would be the principal obstacle to a future age of perfect equality and happiness. In the culmination of a dispute with his father (who sided with Godwin), young Malthus (then 32) in 1798 published anonymously "An Essay on the Principle of Population, as It Affects the Future Improvement of Society: With Remarks on the Speculations of Mr. Godwin, M. Condorcet, and Other Writers." The main theme of this work is that the general law of nature is the perpetual tendency of people to increase beyond their means of subsistence, a theme that pricked the balloon of belief in natural progress that rose from the Enlightenment.

Malthus the nonpracticing clergyman believed that the economic system was dictated by supreme order, but he could not agree with Adam Smith that all of the consequences of that order were necessarily beneficent; some of the problems appearing in nature could be downright unpleasant. Malthus saw room, however slight, for small motions by the "visible hand" of humanity. In this respect, he was influenced by Bentham's utilitarian ethics, the idea of "the greatest good for the greatest number," but he was not controlled by it. He tended to be much more conservative, even reactionary, than the other utilitarians.

Malthus did not share the utilitarian optimism about the progress of the human condition, and he defended the traditional English class structure (with the landed aristocracy at the top) that the utilitarians shunned. Thus, whether it was welfare legislation, tariffs to aid landowners, or the problem of preventing depressions, Malthus always came down hard on the side of preserving the existing class structure while relying upon the principle of utility for evaluating improvements. One could hardly argue that Malthus's personal values were kept out of his economic analysis.

Malthus illustrated his argument that people tend to increase beyond their means of subsistence with two numerical progressions. If there were no limit to the food supply, the population of the country would easily double every twenty-five years, at a geometric rate of increase. But the increase in food production under ideal conditions would be, as he put it, "evidently arithmetical." Thus we see the humans in the cities increasing in the ratio of 1, 2, 4, 8, 16, 32, 64, 128, 256, 512, and so on, and subsistence increasing as 1, 2, 3, 4, 5, 6, 7, 8, 9, 10, and so on. As Malthus put it, "In two centuries and a quarter, the population would be to the means of subsistence as 512 to 10: in three centuries as 4,096 to 13, and in two thousand years the difference would be almost incalculable."[6]

The tendency of the population to exceed food production was restrained by the "positive" checks to population—those events that raised the death rate. These are the natural laws of famine, misery, plague, and war. Poverty and regret are the natural punishments for the "lower classes." Relief for the "unworthy" poor, such as that provided by the English poor laws, only made matters worse, as more children would survive. Only the "class of proprietors" could be trusted with fecundity. The obvious, and gloomy, conclusion is that poverty is inevitable.

Malthus had some second thoughts as early as 1803, when he published a second edition of his essay. He saw that there might be morally acceptable "preventative" checks on population. Fewer marriages, postponed marriages, sexual continence, and strict adherence to sexual morality would reduce the size of families, although Malthus realized that these expectations were to some degree unrealistic. If effective, the preventive checks would reduce the birthrate. However, prostitution and birth control were ruled out on moral grounds. Malthus himself married late—thus practicing part of what he preached—but he eventually fathered three children. In his day, Malthus was Great Britain's foremost political economist. His dark presentiments about the future moved the historian Thomas Carlyle to call economics "the dismal science," an appellation that is still widely quoted and, some would say, apt.

Malthus's ideas about the moral inferiority of the poor were adopted in the Poor Law Amendment of 1834. All relief outside the prisonlike workhouses was abolished for able-bodied people. Relief applicants had to pawn all their possessions and enter the workhouse. Women and children usually were sent to work in the cotton mills, away from the temptations of the nuptial bed. The intent of the law was to make quiet starvation more dignified than public assistance. This system remained the basis of English poor-law policy until the eve of World War I. Vindicated by human law, Malthus died four months after the passage of the Poor Law Amendment.

Data can be produced both to substantiate and to refute the Malthusian population doctrine. The English data for 1250–1800 appear to fit the Malthusian specter. Declines in mortality and increases in productivity raised population growth; the swollen labor supply then lowered real wage rates and elevated the price of food relative to the rent on land. As wages fell, fertility declined and population growth slowed. However, the start of the Industrial Revolution broke this Malthusian cycle; rising living standards and rising fertility no longer went hand in hand because productivity was rising so rapidly.[7] Recent statistics on per-capita food consumption in Western Europe, North America, and Japan show the theory to be incorrect. However, certain areas of the world are similar to the agrarian world of Malthus's day and tend to support the theory. Humanity *is* threatened by its own replication in the poorest areas of Africa, Latin America, and India. Yet even in these areas, the recent development of new grain varieties, especially rice, wheat, and corn, may turn back the Malthusian tide. An increase in grain yields of up to threefold has been hailed as a Green Revolution that could end food shortages forever—or so it was hailed until the soaring price of chemical fertilizers dimmed the prospect. Malthus intrudes again: it is unlikely that even the Green Revolution can feed the world's population indefinitely at the present population growth rate in the poorest parts of the world.

It is clear, however, despite evidence in support of Malthus's views, that he overlooked some important variables. First, humans can reduce their fertility through modern birth-control methods. Second, advances in agricultural technology can result in increased yields in food production. It is true that the various neo-Malthusian theories predicting that the world's energy resources, which in part support agriculture, may someday become exhausted must not be ignored. But these theories may also underestimate the ability of humans to create new technologies to meet such threats. Godwin had argued that technological inventions were susceptible to perpetual improvement.

Malthus had an important influence on theories of evolution. Charles Darwin (1809–1882), the British naturalist, knew that it was possible to produce hardier varieties of plants and animals by selective breeding. He was searching for a theory of evolution that would account for *natural* selection. He had reached a dead end when, in 1838, he read Malthus's *Essay on Population*, apparently for amusement, as strange as that may seem. He was struck by what light the struggle for food and the geometric progression of population could shed on the evolution of plants and animals. Darwin borrowed those ideas Malthus had applied to humans and generalized them to cover the plant and animal kingdoms. As we shall see in Chapter 5, these Malthusian/Darwinian ideas became part of economic thought through a theory known as Social Darwinism, which shifted the idea of selection by nature to the competitive struggles of humans in their social and economic lives.

Before plumbing other depths of classical despair, we need to mention briefly another contribution of Malthus, his *theory of gluts*. Malthus strongly dissented from the position of Smith and Say with regard to the possibility of unsold goods. Malthus saw an unlimited human desire for goods (perhaps not as intense as that for sex). However, he suggested that, if the individual who wishes to buy has nothing to sell that others want, goods will remain unsold. A manufacturer will not hire a worker unless the laborer produces a value greater than that that he or she receives, a surplus equaling the employer's profit. Obviously, the worker is not in a position to buy back the surplus, so others must. Full employment is assured only if all output is bought.

Malthus worried about who would buy the surplus. He saw the capitalists as misers who were interested primarily in amassing fortunes, so they could not be counted upon. In this respect, the landlords constituted the preeminent class because, given the returns from nature, the landholders generated income in excess of their production costs. The genteel landlords also had a will to spend (for servants, if nothing else), and such spending was the best way to overcome economic stagnation. For this as well as other reasons, Malthus was soft on landlords, and his position was to lead to a confrontation with the formidable David Ricardo.

DAVID RICARDO, THE STOCKBROKER-ECONOMIST

The next important classical economist to be considered is David Ricardo (1772–1823), Malthus's close personal friend and intellectual adversary. Between them, they developed an economics that can be described as a tragedy in two acts. In Act I, Thomas Malthus pictured the dire consequences of overpopulation for humanity. In Act II, Ricardo showed that the lazy, leisure-loving landlords were the only beneficiaries of the economic system, while the industrialists, upon whom the nation looked as the source of national growth, become frustrated and powerless.

Ricardo was the third of seventeen children in a family of well-to-do Dutch Jews who had immigrated to England. In other words, his family was part of the population problem. Ricardo's formal schooling ended when he was fourteen and entered his father's stockbrokerage business. When he was twenty-one, he married a Quaker woman and joined the Unitarian Church, for which his father disowned him and banished him from the family business. He began his own brokerage firm with borrowed funds and was soon richer than his father. At the age of forty-three, Ricardo retired from business and devoted himself to economic studies. A few years later, he bought a seat in Parliament. By the time of his death from an ear infection at fifty-one, he had built an estate of about £725,000, a kingly sum in those days. The bulk of his estate was in land and mortgages, an irony that will soon become apparent.

Although Ricardo certainly would have included himself among those who saw the value of accumulating wealth, he was a person of firm convictions and high principles who often advocated policies that conflicted with his own interests. After amassing land, he advocated economic policies that were inimical to landowners. In Parliament, he represented a constituency in Ireland, where he had never lived, and he argued for reforms that would have deprived him of his seat. He was one of the richest men in England, yet he advocated a tax on wealth.

When, at age twenty-seven, Ricardo read *The Wealth of Nations*, he liked it so much that he acquired a taste for the study of political economy. His own first published work was a letter to a newspaper on currency problems. Ricardo became a national figure in economic analysis during the Bullion Controversy on the causes of the rise of prices during the Napoleonic War years. Ricardo argued that an overissue of bank notes had caused gold to have relatively more value than paper currency. He met James Mill, who in turn introduced him to Jeremy Bentham, and Bentham drew him into the small, tight circle of Philosophical Radicals. In 1811, Thomas Malthus introduced himself to Ricardo. Their subsequent friendship was close and long-lasting despite their heated disagreements on both theory and policy.

In order to understand Ricardo's contribution, we have to remind ourselves of the economic conditions in England and on the Continent in the early nineteenth century. Adam Smith had correctly seen that the establishment of a free, middle-class state required the freeing of business from mercantilist regulations, and to a great extent a regime of free industrial competition had emerged in England. The government of England and—after Napoleon's Waterloo (1815)—France denounced interference with the ʻorganization of production and with relations between masters and workers, including trade unions, which were prohibited. In other respects, however, mercantilism was by no means dead. In France, Jean Baptiste Say continued to proclaim Smith's gospel in a series of lucid attacks on mercantilism. In England, Ricardo stepped onto the stage to modify the ideas of Smith and Say to suit the developing economic conditions there.

The conditions that Ricardo confronted were the last vestiges of mercantilism in international trade regulation, the still powerful landed gentry, a rapidly growing population, and widespread urban poverty. Trade regulations he wanted to eliminate. Excessive profits from the land owned by the aristocracy he wanted to cut. Consistent with laissez-faire tradition, he did not want to interfere with the malignancy of poverty; he chose only to explain the disease. In his writings, he was able to explain the distribution of income shares among workers, capitalists, and landowners with more precision than Smith. And in this scramble for different slices of the economic pie, Ricardo saw the conflicts of interest.

The Debate over the Corn Laws

Ricardo's main theoretical arguments concerning the English economy were sparked by parliamentary debate in 1814–1815 over the proposed Corn Laws, which would prohibit the import of corn until the price on the domestic market increased a specific amount. The main debate was between the landowners and the industrialists. The landowners had expanded cultivated acreage as produce from the Continent was cut off by war. They believed that, when the wars in Europe ended, there would be a sudden flood of imported cereal grains (in general called corn in England), and they would be financially ruined. The landowners held control of Parliament, and the Corn Laws were passed against the wishes of the industrialists. The industrialists believed the Corn Laws to be special treatment for a favored few at the expense of their own capital accumulation, as higher food prices—which the Corn Laws would cause—meant they had to pay higher wages.

Malthus supported the landlords; Ricardo attacked them. A legislative issue became a contest in economic analysis. As the arguments evolved, it also became clear that the central issue involved a class conflict. How was the national income to be distributed among the various economic classes—the landlords, the business class, and the workers?

Lurking behind the debate was an idea that was later to be called *the law of diminishing returns*. This principle states that, the more one input of equal quality is increased in production while the quantities of all other inputs of *equal quality* remain unchanged, the smaller will be the resulting output increment. The added input has less and less of the other inputs to work with. In agriculture, this means that, the larger the population, with the amount of land fixed, the less food per person can be grown, even though *total* food production is higher. But both Malthus and Ricardo had another twist to this idea. They were concerned not only about the relative benefits to the various economic classes from tilling land of identical quality, but also about the effects of land use of varying quality.

Disagreement over "Rent"

The disagreement between Malthus and Ricardo rested on the issue of the landowners' profits, or "rent." Malthus observed that the most fertile land yields the greatest amount of produce for the least amount of labor and capital. As the population increases and the demand for grain swells, however, land of poorer and poorer quality must be brought under cultivation. The same number of workers and tools will yield fewer bushels of grain on the poor land, yet the price that the cultivator gets for the grain is the same whether it is grown on poor land or fertile land. The grain price may just cover the cost of production per bushel on the less fertile land and, as a result, create a surplus profit for the cultivators of higher quality. If, for example, landowners who have poor soil produce 500 bushels and their cost of labor and tools is £1,000, their grain is raised at a cost of £2 per bushel, which (let's assume) is the market price for grain. Then suppose that owners of more fertile land can produce 1,000 bushels for the same £1,000 cost. Their cost per bushel is only £1, and they are better off by £1 per bushel. Malthus called this surplus profit *rent*.

Ricardo's analysis of the landowners' position is similar but more precise. He defined rent as a compensation paid to the owners of the land for "the use of the original and indestructible powers of the soil." This rent is not the same as returns derived from improvements made on the land, which give rise to profits rather than rent. Malthus considered higher rents for landowners a good thing, but Ricardo did not.

Ricardo believed that labor was the ultimate source of the value of commodities (similar to Adam Smith's view of the hunters' economy, as we saw in Chapter 3). But, contended Ricardo, *some* capital is always required. Even in the hunters' society, neither the beaver nor the deer can be killed without a weapon. This capital, minor as it is, was made with labor from the past. Thus, even capital consists of past labor. Unlike Smith's theory, therefore, Ricardo's theory is a pure labor theory of value. For example, if it takes a total of 40 hours of labor to make a suit of clothes from sheeps' wool into cloth and into the sewn product, and 400 hours of labor to build a wagon from trees and iron ore into lumber and cast iron, then the wagon will cost ten times as much as the suit. Given the going rates of wages and profits, the cost of the production of a commodity reflects the amount of accumulated labor required to produce it. With few exceptions—such as rare paintings—the value of a commodity is decided by the costs of producing it. Therefore, Ricardo reasoned, the landowners' "rent" was not justified because it was created independently of the amount of labor necessary for the production of grain.

Even though the price of grain is the same everywhere, the labor and capital costs vary with the quality of the land. Landowners who have to work longer hours for their bushel of wheat (or work their laborers longer hours) sell it at the same price as farmers who own the richest delta land in the country. Unlike the role played by labor costs, rent does not determine the price of grain. Rather, the price of grain decides the amount of rent. For the landowners of poor land, the price represents only a return on their labor. The price also represents a return for the labor on the highly fertile land. But because laborers are required to work fewer hours per bushel of grain, the price also provides a gratuitous income that Ricardo called *economic rent*. Thus, the owners of the poor land receive only the wages for their labor; the owners of the fertile land also receive rent.

Unfortunately, as Ricardo ingeniously showed, the problem of rent reaches out to affect all of society. As population expands at a Malthusian rate, less productive land is brought into cultivation, there is a decline in per-capita food supply, and food prices go up. With higher food prices, the wage rate just sufficient to keep the worker alive must be higher than before. Ricardo called such a wage the *subsistence wage for the worker.* (Ricardo saw a tendency for wages to *remain* at a subsistence level, a principle often called the *iron law of wages.*) The higher wage has to be paid in industry as well as in agriculture. Like Adam Smith, Ricardo had the worker being paid from the capitalist's wages fund. Higher wages and therefore greater labor costs meant less profit for the industrialists, who, with lower profits, have fewer resources for savings to be accumulated for investment in new plants, equipment, and tools, or for hiring more workers.

If we look at the picture of society now emerging from Ricardo's analysis, it becomes clear why he argued that the interest of the landowner "is always opposed to the interests of every other class in the community." Business is declining because the industrialists do not have the profits for expansion. The workers are struggling along on a threadbare subsistence wage as food prices continue to rise. Meanwhile, the owners of fertile farmland are better off than ever. The landowners will not use their rent to invest in business because the businesses are not making any profits. The businesses are not making any profits because. . . .

Ricardo was opposed to the Corn Laws because he believed they would perpetuate the landowners' privileges and weaken the other social classes. He saw the industrialists as the source of productive social growth. Moreover, he saw the economy as self-adjusting in the absence of government barriers so that Say's law would preclude industrial crises.

Malthus disagreed. As usual, his dissent was a mixture of protecting the rich from the poor and economic analysis. Malthus saw progress with the landlords, believing that higher rents would enable them to make permanent improvements in the productivity of their land, while their spending on luxuries would prevent general gluts. More generally, Malthus was concerned with what a rapid expansion of manufacturing would bring with it: a concentration of population in the cities, where conditions, as all could see, were unhealthy. He thought employment in manufacturing was essentially unstable because consumers' tastes were likely to change at any time. This instability, he feared, would lead to worker unrest. Perhaps most important, Malthus believed that the evils of industrialization would undermine the cultural advantages of a society based on a genteel landed class. Malthus could not understand why Ricardo, a landowner himself, did not appreciate the virtues of people of his own kind.

Ricardo, like Smith, saw mostly good in the expansion of industry. He thought that unwise policies like the Corn Laws would lead the economy into a *stationary state*—a condition that Ricardo viewed with alarm. A sufficiently large decline in the industrialists' rate of profit and the consequent elimination of the capitalist motive for continued accumulation would mean the economic system would no longer expand. Population growth would cease, net investment would be zero, and per-capita income would stagnate. Free trade—the absence of tariffs—could delay the coming of the stationary state.

Again like Smith, he emphasized the importance and value of capital accumulation, of orderly growth and market equilibrium. He wanted business freed of restrictions that might reduce its ability to maximize profits so that saving and capital accumulation would continue. Ricardo was also an internationalist; he believed that national rivalries—tariffs, trade restrictions, and wars—would slow the development of capitalism.

Ricardo's Contributions

Ricardo's most lasting contributions to economics are (1) the nature of his own economic methods and (2) the importance he attached to income distribution. With Ricardo, economics loses touch with philosophy and becomes an independent discipline, detached from any principles except those generated by its own inner logic. Ricardo's theories are as basic, unadorned, and stark as Euclidian geometry. It is true that the idea of class conflict occurs, but there are really no people in Ricardo's thought, only idealizations. In Adam Smith's writing there are

diligent, flesh-and-blood workers busily specializing, and clever, calculating businessmen maximizing profits. Smith's disciple reduces Smith's
fully clothed, colorful economic portraits to naked, gray abstractions.

Still, we can never be sure when a pure abstraction might take on
real-world implications. For example, Ricardo tried to generalize his
simple corn model by finding an "invariable standard of value" in which
to express relative prices. The labor theory of value and a composite
commodity he called "gold" proved inadequate. In Chapter 15, we shall
see how Piero Sraffa solved the problem while clarifying some real-world
issues concerning income distribution.

There is, to be sure, an implicit human concern, even potential
tragedy, in Ricardo's view of income distribution. His main theoretical
concern was the division of the nation's income among the three main
social classes in the form of wages, profits, and rent. Wages would be
just sufficient to provide the crust of bread that would keep the worker
alive. (Sometimes the classical writers viewed subsistence, the minimum
conditions for life, in sociological terms so that the definition of what
was required to keep *both* body and a culturally defined soul together
could change historically.) Unless tariffs were discarded, rents would
increase as a share of the national income. And, if natural forces did
not keep the landlords in check, profits would drop below that level
required to keep the industrial economy expanding. But this was a
functional income distribution in the sense that not people but only
abstract factor inputs received wages, profits, and rents. The tragedy
was that the only beneficiaries of the system are the landowners, the
only economic actors who benefit from the natural properties of the
soil. And the landowners gained at everyone else's expense. Wages were
payment for work effort, and either profit or interest was the price of
capital, but rent was greater than just the price paid for the use of the
soil. Ricardo could not tolerate seeing the capitalist, the one responsible
for progress, in such a squeeze.

The two-act tragedy that I spoke of at the beginning of this section
was never played out. The Corn Laws proved to be ineffective and inefficient legislation, and they were repealed in 1846. To this day, Britain
does not have to depend on homegrown foodstuffs. Moreover, the population in Western Europe never exerted the pressures on land resources that Malthus and Ricardo had foreseen.

POVERTY AND OTHER FORMS OF COLD WATER

The policies advocated by the classical economists were ultimately to
benefit society by encouraging capital accumulation and economic
growth, but the gains were not equally distributed. As we have seen,

wage earners suffered especially heavy costs during the Industrial Revolution. Although Adam Smith was sympathetic to the working class, the effect of his main principles and those of Ricardo was to give businesspeople (especially industrialists) respectability in a society that had previously extended its greatest honors to the landowning nobility and the gentry. Industrialists achieved new status as promoters of the nation's wealth.

The sternest interpretation of the political economists defended child labor, sixteen-hour working days, unclean and unsafe working conditions, and five-minute lunch breaks by justifying them as an inevitable part of a free system. Poverty was represented as nature's own medicine, and if it was more widespread at one time than another, that was because society was in greater need of the medicine. Those who were well-off seemed content with these rationalizations of oppressive working conditions and inescapable poverty, which were perfectly consistent with a Calvinist work ethic.

It would be deceptive, however, to claim that the economic conditions of this period were met with universal enthusiasm. Although the general public may have agreed with Smith, Ricardo, and the merchants on the importance of liberty, the poverty and frequently horrendous working conditions failed to gain many champions other than the factory owners. The poets and novelists of the day were especially effective in questioning and exposing the values of commerce. At the time Ricardo was writing, the poet Percy Bysshe Shelley (1792–1822) attacked both business commerce and the Calvinist ethic in his "Queen Mab" (1813). Commerce, Shelley called "the venal interchange," and

> Commerce has set the mark of selfishness,
> The signet of its all-enslaving power,
> Upon a shining ore, and called it gold;
> Before whose image bow vulgar great,
> The vainly rich, the miserable proud,
> The mob of peasants, nobles, priests and kings,
> And with blind feelings reverence the power
> That grinds them to the dust of misery.[8]

Writers like Samuel Taylor Coleridge and Robert Southey shared these sympathies, though not with equal fervor. They sympathized with the working class against the merchants and the government that protected business interests at all costs. Indeed, these literary figures were part of the Romantic Age (c. 1760–1870), an era of literature and art that comprised an allergic reaction to the Enlightenment.

Dickens's Criticism of Industrial Society

Later in the century, the works of Charles Dickens (1812–1870), especially *David Copperfield* and *Hard Times*, offered memorable descriptions of life among the working classes and industrialists. Dickens himself was taken out of school when he was twelve years old and put to work with other boys his own age and younger, pasting labels on blacking bottles. His experiences in the blacking factory are bitterly recounted in the autobiographical *David Copperfield*. He touched on some of the social issues of industrialism in his journalism and in other novels as well, for example, *The Old Curiosity Shop* and *Bleak House*, but his most vivid picture of industrial society is in *Hard Times*, which tells about life in Coketown, Dickens's prototype of the industrial town. Dickens sets his story

> *in the innermost fortifications of that ugly citadel, where Nature was as strongly bricked out as killing airs and gases were bricked in; at the heart of the labyrinth of narrow courts upon courts, and close streets upon streets, which had come into existence piecemeal, every piece in a violent hurry for some one man's purpose, and the whole an unnatural family, shouldering, trampling, and pressing one another to death; in the last close nook of this great exhausted receiver, where the chimneys, for want of air to make a draught, were built in an immense variety of stunted and crooked shapes, as though every house put out a sign of the kind of people who might be expected to be born in it; . . .* [9]

Dickens contrasts the lives of three men in Coketown: Thomas Gradgrind, a retired merchant; Stephen Blackpool, a worker; and Josiah Bounderby, the factory owner. Gradgrind is a caricature—but not too broad—of the overprecise, calculating Benthamite, to whom everything is cut and dried:

> *A man of realities. A man of facts and calculations. A man who proceeds upon the principle that two and two are four, and nothing over, and who is not to be talked into allowing for anything over. . . . With a rule and a pair of scales, and the multiplication tables always in his pocket, sir, ready to weigh and measure any parcel of human nature, and tell you exactly what it comes to. It is a mere question of figures, a case of simple arithmetic.* [10]

Dickens's contempt for classical economics is shown by his naming two younger Gradgrind children Adam Smith and Malthus.

Blackpool is a power-loom weaver who looks older than his forty years because of his hard life. (In the plot of the novel, he is unjustly accused of a crime committed by one of Gradgrind's older sons.) To Dickens, the paternalism of feudalism has been replaced by the paternalism of the factory owner. The contrast between Blackpool's status and that of his employer, Mr. Bounderby, shows the harmonious private enterprise of Adam Smith in an unflattering light:

> Stephen came out of the hot mill into the damp wind and cold wet streets, haggard and worn. He turned from his own class and his own quarter, taking nothing but a little bread as he walked along, towards the hill on which his principal employer lived, in a red house with black outside shutters, green inside blinds, a black street door, up two white steps, BOUNDERBY (in letters very like himself) upon a brazen plate, and a round brazen door-handle underneath it, . . .[11]

Rather than a piece of bread for lunch, Mr. Bounderby was having a "chop and sherry." Taking some sherry but offering none to his employee, Bounderby says condescendingly,

> We have never had any difficulty with you, and you have never been one of the unreasonable ones. You don't expect to be set up in a coach and six, and to be fed on turtle soup and venison, with a gold spoon, as a good many of 'em do! . . . and therefore I know already that you have not come here to make a complaint.[12]

Mr. Bounderby knows what Stephen wants better than he does.

Dickens was neither an economist nor a philosopher, and some commentators on *Hard Times* have complained that he did not understand Bentham and utilitarianism. It could as well be argued that Shelley didn't understand commerce, and it would be equally beside the point. Their function as artists was to report and comment on what they saw, which was that, although industrialism was perhaps not evil in itself (Gradgrind and Bounderby are not "villains"), it led to abuses desperately in need of correction.

Some reforms did come out of these intellectual forces and from an outraged Parliament that was incited to hold hearings on factory and urban conditions. The Factory Act of 1833 was a great improvement over earlier legislation regulating working conditions. The factory hours of children between nine and thirteen were not to exceed forty-eight hours weekly, and up to age eighteen, sixty-nine. Most important, the act created the factory inspector. From the point of view of reform, one advantage of the factory system is that, because production is organized in one place, abuses of the system can easily be monitored and ultimately controlled. Contrary to the capitalists' interpretation of classical economics, government acts were getting into the laissez-faire.

JOHN STUART MILL: THE MOST HUMANE CLASSICAL

John Stuart Mill (1806–1873) was the last great economist of the classical school. His father, James, was also a well-known economist, author of *Elements of Political Economy*, who urged Ricardo to write, publish, and sit in Parliament. He popularized Bentham's ideas and helped found the Philosophical Radicals. He is most famous—or notorious—for the extraordinary education that he imposed on his son when John was a very small child. The senior Mill had nine children, and he wanted one to be properly educated to be a disciple of his and Bentham's ideas. John was that child. He began to learn Greek at the age of three. When he was eight, he began to study Latin. By the time he was twelve, he had mastered algebra and elementary geometry and was studying differential calculus. By that time also, he had written a history of Roman government. Apparently a late bloomer in economics, John Stuart Mill did not begin the study of political economy until the age of thirteen. Between his fifteenth and eighteenth years, Mill edited and published five volumes of Bentham's manuscripts. He was publishing original scholarly articles by the age of nineteen. When he was twenty, he had a well-earned nervous breakdown.

Much of J. S. Mill's subsequent life and career was marked by an attempt to overcome a childhood devoid of affection and tenderness. His father was harsh and sarcastic, his mother almost invisible. He had to replace the unreasonable demands that his father made on him with demands that he himself would want to meet. Bentham had ridiculed poetry, for example, as a childish game, but Mill overcame his intense, analytical training and became appreciative of poetry, particularly William Wordsworth's, which he considered an important factor in his recovery from his mental crisis. He learned to be moved by many of the romantic, revolutionary impulses of his age. Unlike Wordsworth and his friend Samuel Taylor Coleridge, another poet of the Romantic Age, Mill did not abandon his youthful radicalism as he grew older. It is an important element in his economics.

Mill's great summary of classical economics, *Principles of Political Economy*, appeared in 1848 and was the leading textbook in its field at least until the publication of Alfred Marshall's *Principles of Economics* in 1890. Its popularity is related in part to the improvements in the economic conditions of the worker, which appear to justify the book's optimistic tone. But the nature of the classical economic school was changing during Mill's lifetime, and he himself departed from some of the key concepts of the structure built by Smith and Ricardo.

Mill, like Smith and Ricardo, thought that the industrialist's rate of profit would continue to fall. He even agreed with Ricardo's explanation for a falling rate of profit. It was, he thought, inevitable with the increases in the cost of producing food in a growing population. He also agreed that there would be a stationary state for the economy. However, it was at this point that Mill began to part company with his famous predecessors. Smith and Ricardo saw the stationary state as undesirable, but Mill believed that such a state would be the *final result* of economic progress. And, unlike his predecessors, Mill emphasized the importance of a more equal distribution of wealth, a concept not unrelated to the stationary state.

Mill saw other motives for human behavior besides accumulation. He valued the indefinite accumulation of commodities but also wanted to direct human beings toward striving for higher goals. Mill saw that beside the "economic man" was walking a "noneconomic man," and he felt that political economy could not pretend that its conclusions were applicable to such a person. In England, he thought, it was not the *desire* for wealth that needed to be taught, but the *use* of wealth and the appreciation of the objects and desire which wealth *could not* purchase. As he put it, "Every real improvement in the character of the English, whether it consists in giving them higher aspirations, or only a juster estimate of the value of their present objects of desire, must necessarily moderate the ardour of their devotion in the pursuit of wealth."[13]

Once England had achieved a sufficiently high level of wealth, Mill saw no reason for a continued growth in production, as long as population growth were limited. (Mill did not want the laws of production repealed; he simply wanted the division of labor and capital accumulation to take the economy to a high plateau.) Admitting that a value judgment was involved, Mill wanted an economy in a stationary state of high production in which production ceased to grow. To Mill, the stationary state was a blissful, pastoral existence in which justice in the distribution of income ranked higher than the longing for more accumulation.

Mill's argument rests on a distinction between the laws of nature and what is merely customary—a distinction we dealt with in Chapter 2. In Mill's view, the economic laws of production follow nature's dicta. The laws of scarcity and diminishing returns derive from nature just as much as the laws of gravity and the expansion of gases. But although the factors of production must be combined according to scientific principles, the *distribution* of that production is an ethical issue, and the rules of distribution are customary. To Mill, the distribution of wealth obeys the laws and customs of society.

Even what a person has produced by his individual toil, unaided by anyone, he cannot keep, unless society allows him to. Where Ricardo saw the necessity of allowing natural price changes to keep the landlord from garnering all wealth, Mill could envision a law that would evict the landlord from his "own" land.

Whatever the economic conditions, then, if society did not like what it saw, it had only to alter those conditions. Society could—if it had the will—expropriate, redistribute, tax, subsidize, and generally raise havoc with the distribution of wealth initially decided by the economic machine.

However radical these ideas may sound, Mill was primarily a reformer within the system, a modest socialist. He favored free public education, regulation of child labor, government ownership of natural monopolies such as gas and water companies, public assistance for the poor, and, if labor wanted it, government enforcement of shorter working days. The *Communist Manifesto* of Karl Marx and Friedrich Engels was published the same year as Mill's *Principles*, but the relatively improving economic conditions in the 1860s and 1870s, bad as absolute worker poverty had been, kept the "radical" ideas of Marx underground, gave succor to the emerging optimism of mainstream English economics, and fed J. S. Mill's positive thinking. In Mill's many opportunities for the revision of the *Principles*, he remained a reformer.

Many economists have complained that John Stuart Mill was confused, but if that is so, the confusion is between what is called the heart and the mind. It has been the luck of economists since his day to watch society treading the path described by Mill, while they have been content to work with the more predictable laws of production. In any case, Mill's warmth, humanitarianism, and sympathy for the poor and disadvantaged took some of the chill off Ricardian economic science. As we shall see, however, later economists were to come in from the warm.

5

THE "AMERICAN DREAM"

▼

Nature, and Nature's Laws lay hid in Night.
God said, "Let Newton be!" and all was Light.

ALEXANDER POPE, "EPITAPH INTENDED FOR SIR ISAAC NEWTON," 1730

The "American Dream" has taken many different forms in the two centuries since the United States was formed. For some, the dream has meant the accumulation of wealth and the exercise of power. For others, it has meant simply the right to be independent and free. Whatever form the dream has taken, it has always been optimistic and based on a sense that America offered unlimited opportunity. The dream has gained much of its optimistic spirit from the eighteenth-century belief in a beneficent, finely tuned universe, an idea that, as we have seen, was given its most memorable scientific expression by Isaac Newton and its economic expression by Adam Smith.

HORATIO ALGER AND THE BENIGN UNIVERSE

In 1776, a remarkably gifted group of men saw enough political and economic strength in the American colonies to take enormous risks in order to put some of the liberal principles of the Enlightenment to work. They revolted against the English king at a time when Great Britain had a population of about 15,000,000 and the thirteen colonies only 3,500,000. A small, poorly paid, ill-supplied colonial army defeated the greatest power in the world (with, it is sometimes forgotten, some European help). This seemed to show that in the new world anything was possible. The frontiers were wide open, and the horizons seemed boundless.

English Puritans were among the earliest settlers of North America, and the growing country proved fertile ground for the Protestant ethic.

The main economic thrust of Calvinism and Puritanism was to condone and encourage the accumulation of wealth as both moral and prudent, a way of doing God's work. The Protestant ethic contributed to the rise of capitalism in Europe and America because it synthesized the goals of business and religion. Thrifty, industrious Protestants, making and saving money, were also assuring their own salvation.

By the mid-nineteenth century, the Industrial Revolution had spread from Europe to the United States. The marriage between the Protestant ethic and the American Dream produced, as we shall see, a number of interesting offspring. From about 1870 through 1910—a period in American history usually known as the Gilded Age—the American Dream assumed an almost entirely materialistic form. I shall discuss the effects the Industrial Revolution in the United States had on the economic scene and on economic science during this period in Chapter 6. In this chapter, I want to return to a further exploration of Newton's optimism and his analytics and also look at some other personalities who provide keys to understanding how the economics paradigm supported the American Dream.

We begin with an American clergyman who wrote fiction for boys— Horatio Alger, Jr. (1832–1899), whose name has become synonymous with a particular version of the American Dream. He updated the Old Testament stories of Noah, Abraham, Joseph, and David—good men who gain wealth through their virtues—in a popularized interpretation of the benign universe. The Horatio Alger stories inject into the Protestant ethic an element from Newtonian science, the idea of a universe that rewards. If the good beget riches, then it is fair to assume that the rich are good. Material success in the Alger stories results from a curious mixture of design and chance. The economic worth of labor is never mentioned, and inheritances come only to the "deserving," whose upward mobility is assured by their strong desire to improve themselves in terms of their marketable talents. In *Brave and Bold*, the hero Robert inherits close to $10,000. Now in easy circumstances, Robert decides to pursue his studies for two more years and increase his economic potential. He attends a famous school and makes rapid improvement. He then enters business life under the wing of a friend "and promises in time to become a prominent and wealthy merchant." Robert's good fortune has been the result of his good qualities and sheer luck.

The Alger stories are examples of American optimism at its shallowest. The most casual observation shows that material success does not come with any great frequency to the "good" or even to the wise. Yet the basic *value* behind the stories—nature knows best—runs very deep. Robert's "luck" must be the manifestation of some higher plan. During the nineteenth century, people were demanding scientific explanations for various social phenomena, including the uneven distribution of wealth. We shall see that ultimately they found these explanations in Newton, because Newton's scientific methods were adapted by three men for purposes having nothing to do with physical science: the biologist Charles Darwin, the philosopher Herbert Spencer, and the sociologist-economist William Graham Sumner.

Biological Darwinism was derived from Newton and Social Darwinism from biology. Darwin applied Newton's laws concerning the physical universe to the science of biology. (In Chapter 4 we saw that Malthus also influenced Darwin.) Herbert Spencer (1820–1903) combined the laws of thermodynamics (a branch of physics dealing with the mechanical actions or relations of heat) with Darwin's theory of evolution and developed a theory of human society, which he saw as an animal-like struggle. William Graham Sumner (1840–1910) popularized Spencer's Social Darwinism in the United States. Social Darwinism purported to explain why a few are rich and many are poor. And, like nature's laws hidden in the night, the ethics of Social Darwinism were concealed in the base of the neoclassical economics of Alfred Marshall, whose ideas will be discussed in Chapter 6.

Throughout this chapter, we will consider two important questions: (1) Do outstanding results from purely mechanical efficiency also give the best results in a *social* science dealing with humans? (2) If the conditions of society become increasingly better and more orderly, as the Social Darwinists suggest they will, can we therefore conclude that the best social policy is to have no human rules or policies at all? The first of these two questions will arise again in Chapter 9.

Conciseness and elegance of exposition combined in a conceptual scheme of great generality is the ideal scientific paradigm. The Newtonian system in the physical sciences became such a paradigm (classical mechanics) and the one that all scientific disciplines have aspired to emulate. Certain inquiries yearning to be scientific have also tried to imitate all or part of the paradigm. The nineteenth-century social scientists, like the biologists, wanted to be, or wanted at least to appear, *scientific*. Social Darwinism, for example, retained the idea of natural harmony and equilibrium that characterized Newton's world, despite the fact that it is difficult to be either concise or elegant when defining and discussing relations as varied and changeable as those among humans. Nonetheless, not content with Smith's metaphor of harmony and balance (see Chapter 2), economists went on to transfer the equilibria of Newtonian mechanics to economics, giving the *impression* that a

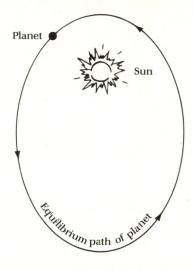

Planet

Sun

Equilibrium path of planet

FIGURE 5.1 Kepler and Newton's ellipse

balance among contending economic forces was good, just as equilibrium in the natural order was desirable in itself.

THE ANALYTICS OF EQUILIBRIUM AND OPTIMIZATION

In both the physical sciences and economics, *equilibrium* is a state of
balance between opposing forces or actions. Equilibrium is either static
or dynamic, depending upon whether the object in a state of balance
is stationary or in motion. In physics, an object in dynamic equilibrium
is moving along a path over time that is predictable. Suppose we want
to find the force required to keep a planet moving in its elliptical course.
We turn to Newton's formula, which related the elliptical courses of the
planets to the sun's "attractive powers."[1] This force—based upon a mysterious X-factor Newton called *gravity*—is sufficient to keep the planet
in a predictable path and thus in dynamic equilibrium, as illustrated in
Figure 5.1. In this way, the planets and comets move in free space and
preserve their motions.

    The planet is in dynamic equilibrium because it would take an
enormous force to propel it out of its known path.[2] If we consider the
speed of the planet in its orbit, then time change becomes a unit of

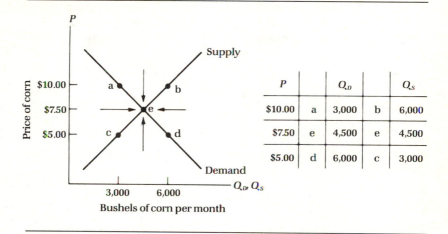

FIGURE 5.2 Equilibrium price

measure especially applicable to the study of mechanics. But even in physics, time turns out to be arbitrary.

Equilibrium in Economics

The classic example of static equilibrium in economics is Alfred Marshall's explanation of *equilibrium price* maintained by the forces of supply and demand, as illustrated in Figure 5.2. The figure shows letters (*a, b, c, d*) representing different quantities of corn supplied and demanded at different prices. Farmers will supply a greater number of bushels of corn per month the higher the price paid to them. (*Why* will be explained in detail later.) Consumers will demand a greater number of bushels of corn per month if the price is lowered. This is the normal *law of demand,* in which the quantity of corn demanded increases as the price of corn declines. The equilibrium price is reached when the forces of supply and demand are in balance at *e*. Once established, this price will persist and the market elements will be in a state of rest.

A more detailed explanation of the figure will make the concept clearer. Suppose the price (*P*) of corn were $10 a bushel; the quantity demanded (Q_D) is *a*, and the quantity supplied (Q_S) is *b*. At this price, the quantity of corn that farmers are willing to supply (6,000 bushels) exceeds the quantity that consumers are willing to buy (3,000 bushels). This excess supply of corn, the distance *ab* or 3,000 bushels, leads to a

falling market price. The falling price, in turn, causes the quantity demanded to rise and the quantity supplied to fall. Now suppose that the
price of corn were $5 a bushel, with the quantity farmers are willing to
supply given as c and the quantity buyers are willing to purchase given
as d. At this lower price, the bushels consumers are willing to buy (6,000)
is in excess of what producers are willing to supply (3,000), which results
in a shortage. The shortage exerts an upward pressure on the existing
$5 a bushel price, which in turn affects the quantities supplied and
demanded. All of these forces reach a balance when the price per bushel
reaches $7.50—the equilibrium price, where demand and supply be-
come equal.

Optimization and Efficiency

Another important concept from the physical sciences that has
been used in economics is *optimization*, the achievement of the best or
most favorable conditions in a given situation. Once economists identified the stability that accompanies economic equilibrium as an optimum condition, they had difficulty disassociating "optimum" from
"favorable." Physicists no longer attach that value to stability. The second
law of thermodynamics provides an example of mechanical optimization. The first law says that the total amount of energy in the universe
remains constant; the second law states that the availability of that
energy for a specific job depends on how closely the energy can be
confined to the job at hand, which leads us to the steam engine.

The steam engine was the first harnessed energy source sufficiently
efficient to move trains, such as those that began to crisscross the western United States during the second half of the nineteenth century. Coal
is burned in the steam engine to produce heat, heat boils water and
converts it to steam, the steam pushes the piston, and eventually the
wheels turn and the train moves. The optimal steam engine would be
one in which all the available heat is converted to work. This can be
shown very simply: heat going into the steam engine from the burning
coal = (heat expelled from the engine) + (work done by the steam engine), where (heat expelled from the engine) = zero degrees. In thermodynamics, this equation represents the "best" possible result, a
genuine optimum when the only criterion is *mechanical efficiency*. Such
an efficiently optimal steam engine is just one of many possible examples of equilibrium optima in physics.

An example of an equilibrium optimum in economics is the balance
between output and price for a product manufactured by a firm under
conditions that permit maximum profits. (Profits begin when a firm's

revenues exceed the costs required to generate nonzero profits; maximum profits are simply the greatest point of difference.) This is a Smithian type of equilibrium that supposedly benefits the consumer because the firm's price for a product will just equal the cost of producing another product unit. This equilibrium is sometimes used to show that capitalism is the most "efficient engine" of enterprise, and, in order that economists could emulate the physical sciences, it has been expressed in Newtonian calculus.

Yet there are obvious pitfalls in pressing the similarity between economics and the physical sciences. For one thing, an optimum according to the criterion of mechanical efficiency is not necessarily relevant to a social situation involving humans rather than physical particles. The best steam engine is one that converts *all* energy into a form usable for work, but such a conversion would not be good for society because an economy without *potential* energy for work ceases all production. Moreover, social and economic optima involve choices and decisions and judgments, which are excluded from mechanical optima. The very fact that people, collectively, can decide under what form of economic organization they want to live has a significant effect on economic optima.

THE SOCIAL DARWINISTS

In the preceding sections, we have seen that it is possible to move directly, if not always wisely, from the analytics of motion and thermodynamics to that of economics, but such a transfer of concepts is often more roundabout. For example, Darwin was inspired by Newton's physical laws and, in part, by Malthus's treatise on population. Darwin developed the theory of natural selection: changes favorable to survival in a given species tend to be preserved in nature, and unfavorable changes tend to die out. The eventual result is the evolution of a new species. Herbert Spencer took Darwin's ideas (which he misunderstood) and the concept of entropy (explained below) from the physical sciences and merged them into a "scientific sociology" that came to be known as Social Darwinism.

Spencer and the Scientific Basis of Social Harmony

To understand Spencer and Social Darwinism, we need to examine the concept of *entropy,* which is derived from the second law of thermodynamics. Energy cannot be lost, but it can become unavailable for work because of a qualitative change that it undergoes: the heat from coal (for instance) turns water to steam, and the steam is dispersed into the atmosphere. The energy has become dissipated or randomized instead of permanently confined in a usable way. The Humpty-Dumpty of energy-organized-for-work cannot be put back together again. Entropy is a measure of the amount of degradated, unavailable energy in a system. As a generalization, there is a tendency in physical processes toward disorder.

Spencer applied the entropy concept to biology, retaining the idea of an irreversible transformation but otherwise turning entropy on its head by saying that the evolutionary process tends toward *increasing order*—it is neg-entropic. The biological-social process, according to Spencer, is an evolution from primitive life forms that were in a chaotic state because they were in transition—becoming something else—to *homo sapiens*, which is the final, highest, and most orderly life form. In effect, Spencer isolated humanity from the environment, as if people were alone on the planet, and the physical world were designed solely to serve their purposes.[3]

One implication of Spencer's theory is that, because humanity's conditions are getting better and better and society is becoming more orderly through natural law, the best social policy is to have no human rules or policies at all. Why interfere with natural progress? Likewise, Spencer's belief in natural order and progress led him to ignore the possibility of social conflict. The process of evolution would end in an "equilibrium" of peace and happiness. Spencer's scientific sociology does not conflict with Smithian notions of harmony or with classical laissez-faire doctrines. Again, to aid the poor, either by private or public aid, interfered irreparably with the progress of the race. The Darwinian law that the fittest, most adaptable members of a species survive can be construed to mean that the existing order of things is "best" since it is arrived at by a natural, selective process; the same claim can be—and was—made for the social status quo. Thus, while Horatio Alger's heroes could achieve in fiction the American Dream of rising to the top, the doctrines of the Social Darwinists helped to preserve a social process that made sure such successes were in fact infrequent. Social programs equalizing the odds for success and allowing some of the "unfit" to move up would have been repugnant to the Social Darwinists.

Spencer also resolved the genuine religious crisis that had been caused by Darwinism for many Christians. To put the matter very simply, if Darwin was right, then the Bible was wrong; if human beings had evolved from lower forms of life, then the account of the creation of man and (inferior) woman in the first chapter of Genesis was not true. Spencer settled the issue with his *doctrine of the unknown*. Whatever science might learn, the true sphere of religion—the worship of the Unknowable, Descartes's world beyond experience—is by its nature unassailable. There will always be *something* that we do not know. Noah Porter, a Congregational clergyman and head of Yale University, had surrendered to the evolutionary forces by 1877, when in an address he found "no inconsistency between the findings of this museum on the one corner [which contained evidences to prove evolution] and the teachings of the college chapel on the other."[4]

Religion was therefore able to accommodate science to some extent, although many people were repelled by the idea that humans descended from apes. (The controversy over whether or not Genesis should be taught along with evolutionary theories as a kind of separate but equal doctrine of the origins of life was revived by the "Moral Majority" during the early 1980s.)

The Social Darwinism of William Graham Sumner

The most vigorous and influential Social Darwinist in America was the sociologist William Graham Sumner, who made a striking adaptation of Darwin's theories to conservative thought.

Sumner brought together "three great traditions of western capitalist culture: the Protestant ethic, the doctrines of classical economics, and Darwinian natural selection."[5] He ingeniously put Newton, God, and the science of biology all on the side of classical economics and the emerging neoclassical economics, bridging the gap between the economic ethic set in motion during the High Middle Ages and the scientific thought of the nineteenth century. His sociology equated the hardworking, thrifty person of the Protestant ethic with the "fittest" in the struggle for survival. It also reinforced the Ricardian principles of inevitability and laissez-faire with a hard-bitten determinism that seemed both Calvinistic *and* scientific. Monetary success in the capitalistic society was the fulfillment of the classical idea of an automatically benevolent, free competitive order.

Other interpreters of Darwin shrank from a direct analogy between animal struggle and human competition, but Sumner did not. He saw economic competition as an admirable reflection of animal existence. In the struggle, people went from natural selection to social selection of fitter persons and from "organic forms with superior adaptability to citizens with a greater store of economic virtues."[6] This selection process depended on the workings of unrestricted competition, which Sumner compared to a natural law, as inevitable and necessary as gravity. When liberty prevails, those people of courage, enterprise, good training, intelligence, and perseverance will come out on top. Sumner's literary output peaked at about the same time as the monopolistic power of a handful of American financial tycoons, around 1900.

Ideas similar to Sumner's were promoted by some of those who had proved themselves fit in the struggle. Here is John D. Rockefeller, business tycoon and founder of Standard Oil, explaining competition to the Sunday school class he was teaching:

> The growth of a large business is merely a survival of the fittest. . . .
> The American Beauty rose can be produced in the splendor and
> fragrance which bring cheer to its beholder only by sacrificing the
> early buds which grow up around it. This is not an evil tendency in
> business. It is merely the working-out of a law of nature and a law
> of God.[7]

John D. was not promising anyone else a rose garden.

Despite his faith in liberty and freedom, which was doubtless sincere, Sumner's writing has a distinctly antidemocratic tone. For example, he was worried that the distribution of income in a competitive process might be supplanted or complemented by partial distribution of income by vote, a fear that supported arguments against the graduated income tax. Taxing the rich at higher rates than the poor would be burdening the superior with the support of the inferior. Sumner admitted that a person with capital has a great advantage over the person who has none, but, he suggests, this does not imply that one person has an advantage *against* another. Capital is accumulated through self-denial, and hence its possession proves that the advantage has been secured by the superiority of the person who accumulated it. The capitalist is by definition virtuous, while the ordinary noncapitalist may well be a nonfrugal sinner.

Like a latter-day Calvin, Sumner provided an evangelistic science to those budding neoclassical economists who shared his beliefs. At the same time, Sumner and Spencer provided scientific support for the guardians of a process that kept the rich rich and the powerful powerful. This defense of caricature capitalism came at a providential time, because free enterprise was facing the challenges of such diverse political groups as the Greenbackers, Grangers, trade unionists, Populists, and Socialists. Farmers supported both the Greenbackers, who favored an eight-hour workday, an income tax, and votes for women; and the Grangers, who opposed the unjustifiably high freight charges of the railroads.

Social Darwinism as Faith

I said earlier that, when confronted by the issues that Darwin raised, religion was to some extent able to accommodate science. But in time certain religious leaders began to behave as though religion could not survive without the support of science. Indeed, the apex of the Social Darwinists' influence may be a watershed in the development of modern American theology. Where science did not replace religion as the authority, religion co-opted science, appropriating scientific principles and concepts to rationalize existing economic conditions. In the United States, nearly all the leading nineteenth-century teachers and writers on Smithian-Ricardian economics were either members of the clergy or religious sympathizers. The unifying theme among these American economists was the idea that God had established natural laws in the physical and human universe that had equal certitude, the most important natural law being the right to private property and its accumulation. None, therefore, saw any conflict between science and religion.

The tradition began with the Reverend John McVicker at Columbia University and, by the end of the century, was to include Henry Vethake at the University of Pennsylvania; the Reverend Samuel P. Newman at Bowdoin College; the Reverend Joseph Holdich at Methodist Wesleyan University; the Reverend John Bascom at Congregational Williams College; George Opdyke, a businessman; the Reverend Francis Wayland of Brown University; Marcius Willson, a secondary school teacher; Henry Carey of the wealthy commercial class of Philadelphia; and many others.

McVicker believed that any attack on wealth and power was also an attack on religion, moral discipline, the institution of marriage, and the sacredness of property. He judged the virtuous poor as happy as the rich. Not only did Bascom put economics on the same footing as physics, but he also viewed production as "more provocative of virtue than virtue itself." And, because the love of profits is the "best" of human impulses, the first purpose of government is the protection of private property. Property, argued Wayland, is an exclusive right founded on the "will of God." He thought poor laws vicious because they destroyed the natural stimulus of self-help. Science is a systematic arrangement of God's laws, including the law that "no man can grow high without industry and frugality." Carey felt satisfaction that his writings had done much to "justify the ways of God to man."[8]

The example of these men shows that not only did religion and science begin to walk hand in hand, but that, with the general public's acceptance of Newton and then Darwin, science became a new faith, an American scientific religion. The steel industrialist Andrew Carnegie became one of its disciples. He describes in his autobiography his troubled mental state concerning what he believed was the collapse of Christian theology, a tension that he relieved by reading Darwin and Spencer:

*I remember that light came as in a flood and all was clear. Not
only had I got rid of theology and the supernatural, but I had found
the truth of evolution. "All is well since all grows better," became
my motto, my true source of comfort. . . . Nor is there any
conceivable end to his [the human being's] march to perfection.
His face is turned to the light; he stands in the sun and looks
upward.*[9]

When materialism and economic growth began to become dominant values, the Protestant ethic came to the defense of the new ac-
quisitive spirit. But when Darwinism seemed to trample on the truth of
the Biblical origins of humans, social science gained in power relative to
religion. What stronger source of authority could people seek than a social science with its feet firmly on the ground and propped up by biology and physics? The doctrines of Spencer and Sumner may seem cold-
blooded today, but they have never entirely died. They have survived even
the progressive legislation of Franklin Roosevelt's New Deal administration in the 1930s. Americans attempting to live the life of the Darwinian
prototype struck down one piece of legislation after another that was
aimed at making income distribution more equal. When the general
manager of the Atlas works of Pittsburgh was asked what might be done
to raise the wages of workers from seventy-five cents a day, he could re-
ply scientifically: "I don't think anything can be done. . . . The law of the
'survival of the fittest' governs that." Wealth was distributed according to
the laws of nature, and people must not try to fool Mother Nature.

The God of this new science was a deity made very much in the
image of the American industrialist, although this mirroring of dominant interests is not as antireligious or as uncommon as it may seem.
A portrait of Christ will always tell us more about the culture of the
artist who painted it than it will about the nature of God. And we have
already seen Western religion taking on the coloration of competitive
capitalism during the Protestant Reformation and, later, monopolistic
capitalism under Social Darwinism.

To the extent that this new science fails, it falters as a faith, and we
might have to return to the worship of Spencer's Unknowable. The fate
of economic science was by this time in the stars of Newton. Can a
science about people and their institutions derived from a science of
particles in motion and the lower animals in a closed habitat also succeed as a *faith?*

The startling answer unfolds in the next and later chapters. As we
shall see in Chapter 14, a new Social Darwinism—though a minority
view—had a tremendous impact upon public policy during President
Reagan's first term.

6

ALFRED
MARSHALL AND THE
U.S.A. PURITANS

▼

*U.S.A. is a group of holding companies, some aggregations of
trade unions, a set of laws bound in calf, a radio network, a
chain of moving picture theaters, a column of stock quotations
rubbed out and written in by a Western Union boy on a
blackboard, a public library full of old newspapers and
dogeared history books with protests scrawled on the margins
in pencil. U.S.A. is the world's greatest river valley fringed with
mountains and hills. U.S.A. is a set of big mouthed officials
with too many bank accounts. U.S.A. is a lot of men buried in
their uniforms in Arlington Cemetery.*

JOHN DOS PASSOS, *U.S.A.*, 1930

We saw in Chapter 4 that the picture of industrial society in Charles
Dickens's *Hard Times* is in some respects more accurate than any economic analysis. Similarly, John Dos Passos's novel *U.S.A.* is a far richer
description of economic conditions between the Civil War and the Great
Depression than the typical American economist's treatment of the period. The range of *U.S.A.* is very nearly as wide as its title suggests.
Among the many subjects that Dos Passos dramatizes is that social
recognition in the United States, and the power that went with it, could
be bought. In their drive for money and power, such men as John D.
Rockefeller, Cornelius Vanderbilt, J. P. Morgan, Jim Fisk, Jay Gould, and
others who controlled giant financial enterprises, nearly gained a stran-
glehold on the American economy between 1880 and 1930. Conventional economic theory did not address the issues their power raised.
It occupied itself with thrift rather than fraud, with conventional rather
than conspicuous consumption, and with perfect competition rather
than monopoly. The excesses of the millionaires of the 1890s to 1920s
were ignored while economists busied themselves with refinements of
a theory that found competition and income distribution to be perfect.

The high priest of economic science during this period was Alfred Marshall (1842–1924), an Englishman whose name is virtually synonymous with *neoclassical economics*, a resurrection and reinterpretation of the doctrines of Adam Smith. In this chapter, we shall examine Marshall's work and discuss the ways in which he and his followers modified the classical economics paradigm. We should ask if economic science would have benefited society if it had been in closer touch with reality between 1870 and 1930. The question is important because if Alfred Marshall and the other neoclassicals retain center stage as Smith's understudy for as many years as Adam Smith had been the principal actor, then economists will still be relying on the neoclassical subparadigms in 2001.

ECONOMIC MAN AND PERFECT COMPETITION: SOME PARADIGM REFINEMENTS

Adam Smith's paradigm, with the later addenda of David Ricardo, remained intact for about a century. Then during the 1870s the *marginalist school* of economics developed, and marginalism, more or less within the old paradigm, dominated Western economic thought until at least the mid-1930s. Marginalism is still the dominant mode of analysis in microeconomics. (*Microeconomics* is the study of the determinants of relative prices of commodities, the relative employment of the various factors of production, and the resultant market distribution of income by pricing of the factors of production.) The marginalist school developed more or less independently in several countries. Its major representatives were Karl Menger in Austria, Hermann H. Gossen in Germany, Léon Walras in Switzerland, W. Stanley Jevons and Alfred Marshall in England, and the "Austrian School" of Friedrich von Wieser and Eugen Böhm-Bawerk (following in the footsteps of Menger).

Among these men, Léon Walras (1834–1910) is especially remembered for his application of mathematics to economics. In the mid-1870s, he published a complex mathematical general equilibrium theory, which, instead of using only two commodities and deciding at what equilibrium rate they would exchange, embraces all commodity and factor markets simultaneously. Also, in a lead followed by most of the neoclassicals, Walras defined *capital* as machines, instruments, tools, office buildings, factories, and warehouses. This classification, narrower than Smith's, made capital one of the *several* productive inputs on the same footing as labor and land. Walras's inspiration was Newtonian mechanics, still the most universally admired scientific paradigm.[1] He

was determined to demonstrate that the harmony of the spheres operated in his idealized free enterprise system as well as in the heavens.
Walras's view is like Newton's in that his economic universe is much
like a machine, with prices moving up and down, functioning like levers
and pulleys. Although he was held in relatively low esteem among economists in his own day, Walras is now regarded as perhaps the greatest
of the pure theorists, a change that reflects the continuing fascination
with pure mechanical systems. (He also had a now-forgotten side: he
was active in formulating policies aimed at improving human welfare.)

As we shall see, Walras's general equilibrium notion differs from
Marshall's view of markets. Walras's system is very much in the tradition
of Quesney (Chapter 2) and J. B. Say (Chapter 4) in the sense that full
employment is guaranteed by automatic market adjustments. Walras
discusses not only stability in one market but also multimarket stability.
Suppose that all markets except the wheat market and one nonwheat
market are in equilibrium. (In order to be strictly correct in Walrasian
economics, *at least one other* market must be in disequilibrium if any
particular market is in disequilibrium; that is, an excess demand in one
market must have an excess supply counterpart in another market or
markets.) At the present price of wheat, the amount of wheat demanded
is greater than the amount supplied. When the Walrasian criterion is
applied to the wheat market, the price of wheat must be raised to eliminate the excess in demand.

Because all markets are interdependent, however, this price increase must upset equilibria in other markets because such equilibria
were defined with reference to the initial price of wheat, which turned
out to be the "wrong" price. Thus, further adjustments in all other
markets must be made, and then again in the wheat market, and so
forth. In this way, the whole system moves inexorably toward multimarket equilibria.

The question naturally arises as to how enough could be known by
all market participants about all quantities and all prices so that simultaneous equilibria could be achieved. Walras's solution to this problem is his theory of *groping*. Walras assumes that buyers and sellers
announce the amounts they wish to trade at prices "cried at random."
For example, buyers reduce their price offers when there is an excess
supply and increase them when there is an excess demand. They continue to cry out their uncommitted intentions to purchase until they
hit upon a price that just clears the particular market (the equilibrium
price). Both buyers and sellers in this way discover the true equilibrium
price before they ever undertake to exchange any goods. As economists
have always liked the idea of specialization, they began to refer to a

Walrasian auctioneer, who would cry out the prices, relieving the individual participants of this responsibility.

The Walrasian system may seem extremely abstract, because it is. The influence of Descartes's rationalism seems to have pushed Walras into a narrow analogy of Newton's system.[2] In a modern economy, individuals do not cry out prices or wage rates, and auctioneers are engaged only on special occasions. Moreover, according to Walras's strict logic, economic theory leaves no room for economic policy. If Walras was correct about multimarket equilibria, the world has no need for economists.

In order to understand fully the principles of all the marginalists, we must return to the utilitarian moralist Jeremy Bentham, whom we met first in Chapter 4. Bentham's concept of human nature was consistent with the philosophy of self-interest and had influenced Malthus, the Mills, and Ricardo. In the first chapter of *Introduction to the Principles of Morals and Legislation* (1780), Bentham argued that "it is in vain to talk of the interest of the community, without understanding what is the interest of the individual. A thing is said to promote the interest, or to be *for* the interest, of an individual, when it tends to add to the sum total of his pleasures: or, what comes to the same thing, to diminish the sum total of his pain." Bentham's hedonism (the doctrine that whatever is good is also necessarily pleasant) provides the foundation for the marginalists' calculus of pain and pleasure, a theory purporting to prove that perfect economic competition maximizes pleasure while minimizing pain.

In this context, the point of change in pleasure or pain is called the *margin*, a concept Marshall and his school used to explain economic behavior. *Marginal pleasure* would be an extremely small increase in pleasure per some arbitrary unit of time and could be expressed in Newton's calculus. The marginalists saw people as rational balancers (at the margin) of pleasure and pain in a world of perfect competition. This balancing act, described with elegant mathematics, was called equilibrium, of course. Thus, Bentham's hedonism, utilitarianism, and rationalism became building blocks for the construction of a scientific abstraction that came to be called the economic man.[3]

We have already seen that during the Industrial Revolution the idea of the *economic man* (or person; the sex is not at issue) had practical uses; for the marginalist, its purpose was in its abstract quality. The marginalists imagined a world in which people act in response to conscious and consistent motives, inclinations, or desires. Nothing is capricious or experimental; everything is deliberate. For example, someone would never impulsively buy a new fishing pole. People know what the consequences of their actions will be, and they act accordingly.[4] The purpose of human action is to benefit the person who acts. Every person is the final and absolute judge of his or her own welfare. The consumers and producers are hedonistic, lightning-fast computers of pleasures and pains. They have no past and no impact on the future.

Moreover, there is perfect mobility in all economic adjustments and no cost involved in any movements or changes. There is no cost in traveling from Chicago to San Francisco, whether it be to buy a new dress or to accept a new job. Finally, there must be perfect, continuous, costless intercommunication among all individual members of the society. This assumption requires that all the elements entering into economic calculations—effort, commodities, etc.—be continuously variable and divisible without limit. This fractional divisibility permeates marginalist thought and its calculus.

Abstract economic man requires a society of *perfect competition*, an idealized laissez-faire world, in which to exist. Perfect competition is based on the following assumptions: (1) the number of buyers and sellers is so great that no single one can influence the market price of either the material used in production or the final commodity. (2) For theoretical purposes, all products of the same generic name are substitutable for each other. A dress is a dress; the individual preferences of the person who buys one are irrelevant. (3) There is complete freedom of entry into production in the market being analyzed. There are no restrictions resulting from the high cost and risk of setting up business, nor is there any barrier due to such things as license regulations.[5] (4) Every consumer and every producer has perfect knowledge at all times. The woman looking for a new dress knows that all prices on dresses available in the economy are ultimately identical, and the dress manufacturer knows all the alternative profit returns for producing products other than dresses. (5) Distance to all markets is zero miles; the woman buying a dress may do so in Chicago, where she lives, or in San Francisco. Except for (2), these assumptions are implicit in Adam Smith's market mechanism, discussed in Chapter 3. In this paradigm, a *monopolist* is any economic man who is the only seller of a product.

THE MARGINALISTS' BRIDGE

Like the classical economists, the early marginalists believed that economic laws were natural laws that should not be tampered with. They also shared with the classical economists a strong faith in individualism, believing competition to be the great regulator that would convert the brute selfishness of individuals into a collective virtue. But the fundamental agreements between the two schools should not obscure the differences. The classical economists were primarily concerned with

TABLE 6.1 Diminishing Marginal Utility

Hierarchy of want	I	II	III	IV	V
Want	To avoid starvation	To be clothed	To be housed	To be transported	To enjoy luxury
Commodity or service to satisfy want	Food	Clothes	House	Horse	Ale
1-unit increase	5	4	3	2	1
Another-unit increase	4	3	2	1	0
Another-unit increase	3	2	1	0	
Another-unit increase	2	1	0		
Another-unit increase	1	0			
Another-unit increase	0				

the production side of the private enterprise system over the long run. Much of *The Wealth of Nations* is about producers' dividing up their labor in order to increase production. Thus, while David Ricardo emphasized cost of production (supply) as the main determinant of the value of commodities, the early marginalists (William Jevons, Karl Menger, and Léon Walras) focused on demand. Marshall suggested that the values of commodities (prices) are decided where demand *and* supply meet in equilibrium.

The early marginalists focus on the point of change between variables at which decisions by consumers and/or producers are made. They extend the marginal principle to all of economics. Their conception of the value of products is in the tradition of Bentham: a product is an object or service that can give pleasure or prevent pain. Hence, their idea of value is based on psychological satisfaction. This subjective valuation and the concept of marginalism is illustrated in Table 6.1, which is patterned after an example used by the Austrian Menger in 1870.

The table illustrates what is known as the law of *diminishing marginal utility*. The table shows five human wants that can be satisfied by the purchase of commodities or services. First, a person will rank his or her wants in descending order of their importance (I, II, III, etc.). Then, we can see that different levels of satisfaction will accrue from consuming more and more units of the object that satisfies a particular want (to avoid starvation, to be clothed, etc.). Menger used Arabic numbers (5, 4, 3, 2, 1, 0) to indicate the amount of *extra satisfaction* associated with each unit increase (marginal increase) in the quantity of the good. Declining numerical values represent the diminishing want-satisfying power to an individual of additional units of the same commodity or service.

We can see from the table that each unit increase in the consumption of food gives less additional satisfaction than the immediately preceding unit. Satisfaction in avoiding starvation tends to diminish as consumption increases. For example, the sixth unit increase in food yields no extra satisfaction.

Marginal utility lies somewhere behind Marshall's concept of demand, but he wants to reduce the unscientific subjectivity of utility. He attempts to do so by using money as a measuring device, much as kilowatt hours meter electricity usage of any type. The other marginalists would say that, if a suit is three times as useful to you as a pair of trousers, then you will pay ninety dollars for the suit and thirty dollars for the trousers. Marshall shifts this around, saying that, *because* you are willing to pay three times as much for the suit as for the slacks, the suit is three times as useful to you. Marshall's explanation is preferred by economists today because prices are quantifiable in terms of money, and psychic satisfaction is very difficult to measure.

MARGINALISM AND THE THEORY OF DISTRIBUTION

A second element of marginalism that is closely related to classical economics is income distribution. John Bates Clark (1847–1938), America's foremost marginalist economist, is the outstanding theorist in this area. About 1880, Clark also developed some of the ideas of marginal consumer satisfaction and its influence on demand independently of the work of the English marginalists. Clark conceived a marginal productivity theory of income distribution, adding intricate detail to the workings of the perfectly competitive labor market of classical economics. This theory can be best summarized in Clark's own words from the opening paragraph of his *Distribution of Wealth*: "It is the purpose of this work to show that the distribution of the income of society is controlled by a natural law, and that this law, if it worked without friction, would give to every agent of production the amount of wealth which that agent creates."

Clark's theory is partly derived from the classical *law of diminishing returns*: if the amounts of a producer's capital, land, and managerial skills remain constant while labor is added, then the output of each additional worker will eventually decline because the worker has fewer and fewer units of the other inputs to work with. Clark said that capital (now meaning only factories, machines, etc.) had a similar kind of diminishing marginal product characteristic. He also claimed that, however wages may be adjusted by bargains freely made between individuals, the rates of pay resulting from such transactions tend to equal that part of the product of industry traceable to the labor itself. [Because wages are paid in money in a fully monetized economy, the extra products of labor in physical output units (marginal physical product) must be multiplied by the price of the product in order to obtain the *value* of labor's contribution (marginal value of product, under perfect competition) and hence the "appropriate" wage rate.] The same statement holds for capital. The rights of both labor and capitalists to private property are absolute and should be protected by the state. Laissez-faire policies are best because, insofar as private property rights go unobstructed, such rights assign to all people what they have specifically produced. In the private enterprise system, the division of the total income from production into wages, interest, and profits is completely equitable because every person is paid exactly what he or she is worth.

It would be unethical for the government to interfere with the "natural laws" of income distribution because, according to Clark's theory, the distribution and accumulation of income and property are a reflection, over time, of the worth of the individual. At the same time, however, Clark, like Adam Smith, feared monopolies. He was not blind to the industrial concentration that was going on in the United States, and he saw that such concentration might jeopardize perfect competition.

THE NEOCLASSICAL NICETIES OF VICTORIAN ENGLAND

In the nearly one hundred years between the publication of *The Wealth of Nations* and the emergence of the marginalists, it would seem that economic thought was dominated by a group of like-thinking scholars who found little basic disagreement among themselves and little wrong with society. We know that this is not strictly true—Malthus and J. S. Mill were in conflict with Smith and Ricardo on certain issues, for example—but it appears to be true because the simplified classical-neoclassical paradigm is so well-suited to the ethics of Western society, and this version prevailed throughout this period.

Paradigms sometimes outlive their greatest usefulness because the inherently conservative task of normal science practitioners is to refine the existing paradigm. I propose to call the most zealous of the para-digm refiners *apostles. An apostle is a student of an economics paradigm who both advocates the paradigm as a matter of faith and refines its scientific appearance and form.* In a scientific sense, the apostle exhibits paradoxical fidelity. Most economists have been apostles of Adam Smith, but some, such as Alfred Marshall, are sufficiently masterful and original to claim their own followers. Marshall is thus both an apostle of Smith and a leader in his own right. (After you have read Chapter 9 on positive economics, you will realize that an apostle is a positivist disciple. The positive economist is defined in that chapter.)

The marginalists smoothed the path for the neoclassical revision of the standard economics paradigm, a revision that was substantially different from classical economics in certain details. Yet, because the underlying classical superstructure so well revealed by John Bates Clark was still intact, the neoclassical "revolution" had all the excitement of a Sunday school picnic.

The major source of postclassical changes in the economics para-digm (excluding changes in mathematical or statistical technique) was Cambridge University in England. The association there of Alfred Mar-shall, Arthur Pigou, Joan Robinson, Piero Sraffa, and John Maynard Keynes accounts for Cambridge's unique stature in the world of aca-demic economics during the first half of the twentieth century. At the head of this distinguished teacher-student lineage stands Alfred Mar-shall. He is best described as neoclassical rather than marginalist be-cause his purpose was to preserve the legacy of the classical economists while refurbishing their thought with some ideas of his own. He differed somewhat from the classical economists in allowing room for modest departures from laissez-faire in the direction of cautious reform. He shifted the focus of economics toward individuals and small, "repre-sentative" business firms.

Once again, Marshall was an example of the right professor of eco-nomics for the right season of economic history. Victorian England was at full sail in front of the steady breeze of late nineteenth-century ex-hilaration and progress. With improvement in the wind came optimism about the course of industrial society and some basis for it. Average real wages began to rise after 1850, and increasingly fewer ordinary laborers were begging, stealing, sending their children off to work in the mills, or simply starving to death. Because of technological changes, the work-week began to decline.

Why did the English system perform, for the most part, so well during the second half of the nineteenth century? The British success was based upon its near monopoly position in world industrial pro-duction until well past mid-century, its consequent development as the premier trading nation of the world, and its related role as international banker to the Western world. International trade was required for British prosperity for two reasons: (1) Britain's giant industrial machine produced goods and services well in excess of the purchasing means of the average British worker. (For much of the century, the British worker had sufficient income only to buy necessities.) (2) Because of the small size of Britain and its limited natural resources, it relied upon less developed countries, such as India, for imports of food and raw materials.

The less developed countries and Britain had a complementary relationship. Great Britain's relationship with the industrializing advanced nations (such as the United States, France, and Germany) was potentially a competitive one as they became more like the English. In the meantime, however, England and the chief European nations united on a gold standard between 1863 and 1874, which simplified the operations of financing world trade. Importantly for Britain, world trade financing centered on London because of Britain's large reserves of gold and its expertise in international finance.

As we shall see, even when Britain appeared to be at the peak of its powers, events began moving against it. Even then, the sun's movement with respect to the British Empire was short of proverbial. Nonetheless, the Victorian climate of economic expansion gave rise to a group of clarifiers who examined the workings of the system in considerable detail but who expressed no fundamental doubts about its basic worth nor made unsettling forecasts about its future. Among the foremost of these men were W. Stanley Jevons, John Bates Clark, and, of course, Marshall.

Marshall's Background

Marshall was a mixture of mathematician, physicist, economist, and moralizer. He came from a strict Evangelical Protestant background, and his father had intended that the younger Marshall be ordained in the Evangelical ministry. (Something of the atmosphere of Marshall's youth is suggested by the title of a tract that his father wrote in opposition to the feminist movement: *Man's Rights and Women's Duties.*) At Cambridge, however, Marshall switched his studies from theology to mathematics and physics and eventually to economics. He rebelled not against orthodox theology but rather against the further study of the classics then required for the ministry.

Alfred Marshall arrived in economics at about the same time that English intellectuals began to feel the influence of the theories of Charles Darwin and Herbert Spencer. The ideas of Darwin that had the widest dissemination—usually through interpreters such as Thomas Huxley—concerned the physical and biological struggle for existence, natural selection as a result of individual differences, the survival of the fittest (Spencer's phrase, not Darwin's), and the evolution of the species. Marshall is a disciple of Darwinian evolutionary progress, Christian morality, and the utilitarian ethics of Bentham. To Marshall, evolutionary progress meant that the entire society materially improved, not just the hardy few, as the Social Darwinists had claimed. His general philosophical bent can be illustrated by a passage in which he describes his feeling about economics when he first began to study the subject: "Its fascinating inquiries into the possibilities of the higher and more rapid development of human faculties brought me into touch with the question: how far do the conditions of life of the British (and other) working classes generally suffice for fullness of life?"[6] As an economist who was trained both in the ministry and in physical science, Marshall shared Adam Smith's vision of earthly material advance. As a moralizer, he tended toward cautious optimism. In the first half of the eighteenth century, Alexander Pope had epitomized a certain kind of Newtonian optimism by his claim that "Whatever is, is right." According to the economist Joan Robinson, the moralizing of Marshall " . . . always came out that whatever is, is *very nearly* best."[7]

Two other significant intellectual influences on Marshall were the renowned physicist James Clerk Maxwell and the mathematician W. K. Clifford. When Marshall's serious study of economics began, J. S. Mill's and David Ricardo's versions of the Smithian system were still unchallenged. Marshall, a trained mathematician and personal friend of Clifford's, focused on the theoretical rigor of Ricardo and began to involve himself with diagrams and algebra. Marshall is the founder of the modern diagrammatical methods of economics. His general technique was to work out a problem first in mathematics, draw the diagrammatics, and then eliminate the mathematics from the presentation by relegating it to footnotes. (In a curious reversal, today's advanced textbooks in microeconomics consist mostly of Marshall's footnotes rather than the basic substance of human economic life.)

Marshall's Contributions

Marshall agreed with other conservative economists that economic laws are natural laws, although not necessarily good ones, and that it is *usually* best to allow the laws to work themselves out unrestrained. Marshall's idea that price is determined at the equilibrium point of supply and demand was extended to create an entire Newtonian system in which all the elements of the economic universe are kept in place by mutual counterpoise and interaction. Marshall's more precise working out of the concept of equilibrium assured the permanence of the intricate watchworks of neoclassical economics.

Yet it is fair to say that Marshall's followers departed less from the mechanics of natural law than he did. Marshall's great textbook, *Principles of Economics*, is an impressive sociology of nineteenth-century English capitalism, permeated with a broad historical sense of the evolution of economic institutions, for all of its analytic apparatus. His apostles, unfortunately, chose to develop only Marshall's analytics and not his idea of historical evolution.[8] An overly simplified Marshallism that disregarded history pervaded the college teaching of economics until, according to one economist, "Many of the more lively intellects got thoroughly sick of it."[9]

Marshall's most important contribution to economics was to combine the production theory of the classical writers with the demand theory of the marginalists into the famous "Marshallian cross." Imagine a graph with the price of a commodity on one coordinate and the quantity demanded or supplied on the other. (An example is Figure 5.2 in Chapter 5.) The graph depicts the quantity supplied as rising with price increases and the quantity demanded falling. The idea that the quantity demanded declines as price rises is derived from the marginalist concept of diminishing marginal utility as a result of increased consumption. The point at which demand and supply cross, like the blades of a pair of scissors, is the equilibrium price of a commodity. Marshall's theory is, of course, far more complicated than this brief explanation even begins to suggest. The point to remember is that Marshall's detailed working out of the mechanism of supply and demand together to determine an equilibrium commodity price was *conceptually* revolutionary.

Although Henry C. F. Jenkin (1833–1885), a professor of engineering who turned to economics in 1868, had alluded to the concept of elasticity in an 1870 publication on supply and demand, Marshall extended the idea until it was his own. As he put it, "The *elasticity* or *responsiveness* of demand in a market is great or small according as the amount demanded increases much or little for a given rise in price."[10] Very simply, economics teachers define price elasticity of demand for beginning students as the percentage change in quantity demanded divided by the percentage change in price. The flexibility of the elasticity idea enabled Marshall to extend it to supply and to factor markets as well as to income classes.

It is important to note one difference between the general approach of Marshall and that of Walras. Marshall introduced the idea of *partial equilibrium,* in which prices and quantities in markets other than the one under consideration were held constant or assumed to be small in their effects. A simple example will clarify the difference. Suppose Marshall were constructing the demand curve for English wool. He would define the demand for wool as related to the price of wool with the prices of other commodities, money income, and consumer tastes held constant. On the other hand, Walras would define the demand for English wool in relation to the prices of all commodities, including the price of wool. (Money income and tastes still would be presumed constant.) Walrasian general equilibrium is exactly like the solution of any system of simultaneous equations. In order to simplify matters, Marshall was willing to examine the functioning of one market at a time as if it were in isolation from the balance of the economy. Perhaps this explains why Marshallian economics still occupies elementary economic textbooks as well as advanced texts, whereas Walrasian economics appears in advanced texts and in esoteric economics journals.

For a number of reasons, the changes that Marshall brought about in economics were not in his own time described as revolutionary. For one thing, there is no sharp break between his values and those of the classical economists. Both defended capitalism for about the same reasons. Second, Marshall's ideas were known by and discussed with his students, colleagues, and others who met and talked with him long before he committed them to print. By the time he was only thirty-five, Marshall had privately worked out the foundations of his entire system. According to Marshall's onetime student and biographer John Maynard Keynes, Marshall kept "his wisdom at home until he could produce it fully clothed . . . ," partly because he feared being wrong.[11] And third, Marshall's style and presentation are modest and understated. The *Principles* introduces many concepts for the first time without any suggestion that they are novel or remarkable. The style is simple, unadorned, and unemphatic. The book seems to be an ingenuous attempt to disclaim any credit for discovering the economic truths it is so earnestly in pursuit of. Passages assigning error to earlier economists are few. *Principles* reads as if it had all been said before, and in saying it the earlier economists had made virtually no mistakes.

Nevertheless, despite what seems an innate predisposition to accept the status quo, Marshall had a greater flexibility toward laissez-faire economics than many of his classical predecessors. His compassion for human well-being was genuine. The student who today associates Marshall's name with the Euclidean diagrammatics of microeconomics is probably unaware of what Marshall wrote in the preface to his *Principles:* "The study of the causes of poverty is the study of the causes of degradation of a large part of mankind." In his *Industry and Trade,* Marshall admits that "associated action" by capitalists and other businesspeople may restrict output to the national disadvantage, but he left it to his favorite pupil and successor to the Cambridge chair in political economy, Professor Arthur C. Pigou, to work out some of the details of the negative fallout from private industry. Yet the inadequacy of perfect competition is only faintly perceptible in the writings of either Marshall or Pigou.

Marshall's influence was and is enormous. An economist of the day said (in 1887) that half the economics chairs in the United Kingdom were occupied by Marshall's former students.[12] The marginalist/neoclassical school still dominates the study of economics in Western countries, along with a modified Keynesian school, while both share the international field with Marxism. The marginalist subparadigm rules, even though by the 1880s its underlying assumptions about pure competition were too unrealistic to warrant its use for policy guidance. Marginalism preserved the ideological foundations of classical economic theory after the conditions that had produced that ideology had greatly changed.

We have seen that the classical school directly served merchants and gave them respectability in a new commercial-industrial world. Marginalism also favored business and anyone else who defended society's status quo. Marginalism is the economics of conservatism, favoring all those whose interests commit them to the preservation of things as they are—employers, landowners, the wealthy in general. Though the maximization of self-interests and profits eventually leads to material benefits for the whole society, there are social problems attendant on the concentration of wealth. As we shall see in the next section, some of these emerged when marginalist/neoclassical economics was at the peak of its power.

THE ROBBER BARONS: COMPETITION AFTER THROATS HAVE BEEN CUT

The Civil War (1861–1865) marks a period of great change in the American economy. During the half century after the war, per-capita gross national product grew at an average annual rate of about 2 percent. In the 1860s, pig-iron production in the United States more than doubled, and then doubled again in the 1870s and in the 1880s. By the 1880s, the average annual value of manufacturing exceeded that of agriculture for the first time. What had happened in England during the first half of the nineteenth century was happening again in America during the second half. It has been called the Second Industrial Revolution.

The Second Industrial Revolution

Science and its application, technology, had a great impact on both of these revolutions. The Second Industrial Revolution was marked by technological advances in railway engines, chemistry, electrical science, and a new power source, the internal combustion engine. The marriage of American inventiveness and organized science had implications for industrial competition. Some of the new technology—in the steel industry, for example—required businesses to enlarge their scope of operations, including plant facilities, machinery, and equipment. Industrialists found that greater efficiency could be achieved with a larger scale of production, which economists later called economies of scale. Such plants and the fixed capital outlays they required might seem small in today's trillion-dollar economy, but some of the outlay was huge relative to the virgin consumer market.

The new forms of steam, electrical power, and internal combustion made machines more powerful and automatic. The development of transcontinental railways, huge steel-producing plants, machine tools, precision manufacturing that made it possible to interchange parts among different plants making the same items, automatic machine operation through the industrial use of electricity, and (perhaps most important of all) moving assembly lines all began to transform American industry into something quite different from Adam Smith's world of small shops and factories.

The industries of mass production, most of European origin, fed upon each other. Sir Henry Bessemer first produced steel in large quantities at low unit cost by injecting air into holes in the bottom of a large vessel containing molten iron. This direct conversion of pig iron into steel caused the cost of production to fall "to about one-seventh its former level."[13] The uneven quality of Bessemer steel was overcome by William Siemens's open-hearth process in the 1860s. Both of these men were practical professional inventors, masters of applied science rather than scientists. Because of the switch from rails made of wood covered with iron strips to rails of solid iron during the 1850s and 1860s, there was a substantial increase in the total demand for iron. Later, more durable steel rails replaced iron rails (between 1873 and 1877). In turn, British ships and American railways made of steel and engines powered by steam created larger markets for an increasing number of basic commodities in the last quarter of the nineteenth century. Mass markets began to match mass production.

Not only were methods of production transformed, but the nature of business organization changed as well. Some business leaders became advocates of laissez-faire economic policies without any reservation whatever. For example, Amasa Leland Stanford, president of the Central Pacific Railroad from 1863 until his death in 1893, wrote in his 1878 annual report to stockholders: "There is no foundation in good reason for the attempts by the General Government and by the State to especially control your affairs. It is a question of might, and it is to your interest to have it determined where the power resides." Stanford believed business should hold the upper hand over government. Despite the visible signs of a concentrated economy, in which particular goods are produced by only a few firms, the neoclassical economists went right on assuming perfect competition, ignoring the fundamental changes in the nature of commerce. (At the time of Stanford's statement, incidentally, he was making profits from the construction company that received government funds to build his railroad.)

The Rise of the Robber Barons

The amount of capital needed to finance large-scale industry made it necessary for business to look to private banks and the stock and bond markets for money. Gradually, a separation appeared between the financial control of business and industrial enterprises and the means by which production took place. Joint stock companies—so maligned by Adam Smith himself—enabled persons to own a company through common stock ownership without being involved in production or management. With few government regulations on business behavior, the separation of ownership and production opened the door to irresponsible financial manipulation. At the same time, competition became too intense for its own survival, although it remained entrenched in business ideology. For large business enterprises, competition became obsolete because it was too risky. Investments in plants and equipment were too high for success to be trusted to the workings of the market mechanism, where competition was a kind of genteel balancing act. For example, Andrew Carnegie was the owner of some amazingly efficient steel mills and so enthusiastically competitive that he would undersell other mill owners even if doing so required forgoing immediate profits. John Pierpont Morgan, a banker, issued bonds for Carnegie's efficient steel company and for hundreds of other steel companies, bringing them under a single control. With the formation of the United States Steel Corporation, the production of one-half of the steel used in the United States now hung on the decisions of one man, a banker. U.S. Steel epitomized the combination of large-scale, low-cost production, separation of ownership, and just plain greed. Its techniques of business competition were so cutthroat that by 1901 it appeared that U.S. Steel might become a monopoly.

Robert Heilbroner gives a dizzying example of the kind of big-money hanky-panky that enabled Henry Rogers and William Rockefeller to buy the Anaconda Copper Company in 1881 without spending a single dollar of their own money:

> *1. Rogers and Rockefeller gave a check for $39 millions to Marcus Daly for the Anaconda properties, on the condition that he would deposit it in the National City Bank and leave it untouched for a specified period. 2. They then set up a paper organization known as the Amalgamated Copper Company, with their own clerks as dummy directors, and caused Amalgamated to buy Anaconda—not for cash, but for $75 millions in Amalgamated stock which was conveniently printed for the purpose. 3. From the National City Bank, Rogers and Rockefeller now borrowed $39 millions to cover the check they had given to Marcus Daly, and as collateral for this loan they used the $75 millions in Amalgamated stock. 4. They now sold the Amalgamated stock on the Market (first having routed it through their brokers) for $75 millions. 5. With the proceeds, they retired the $39-million loan from the National City Bank, and pocketed $36 millions as their own profit on the deal.*[14]

During the Middle Ages, a *robber baron* was a feudal lord who preyed on and stole from people passing through his domain. The term was revived in the last quarter of the nineteenth century to describe those relatively few businessmen who controlled American industry. Besides Carnegie and Morgan, they included Jim Fisk, Peter A. B. Widener, Jay Gould, Charles Tyson Yerkes, James R. Keene, James J. Hill, John D. Rockefeller, H. H. Rodgers, George F. Baker, William Rockefeller, William C. Whitney, and George F. Baer. All these men became twenty-five years of age between about 1860 and 1870, which means that their adult attitudes and behavior emerged during the years immediately before and after the Civil War. These men mastered at least one problem posed by the war: mass production and the attendant necessity for large-scale production. They also had something else in common that made them representative of their financial generation: At least seven of those listed above were churchgoers, and six were actively interested in church affairs. J. P. Morgan was probably the most prominent layman in the Protestant Episcopal church. Half of the seventy-five multimillionaires in the New York of the 1900s were communicants of Morgan's church.[15] The Rockefeller brothers were prominent Baptists. Many of the Robber Barons believed that God was their ally both in this life and thereafter. John D. Rockefeller said, "God gave me my money," and Baer attacked labor during the coal strike of 1902 by saying, "The rights and interests of laboring man will be protected and cared for—not by the labor agitators, but by the Christian men to whom God in his infinite wisdom has given the control of the property interests of this country."[16]

It would be a mistake to think that these men were hypocrites. Religion, like economics, often takes on the coloration of the community in which it is practiced. We saw in Chapter 3 that Calvinism and Puritanism accommodated the accumulation of material goods and a devout spiritual life with relatively little difficulty. The accommodation suited the American business ethic very well. Morgan and E. H. Harriman, irresponsibly battling for control of a railway, brought on a financial panic, yet they worshipped. Rockefeller ruthlessly drove competitors out of business, but he sang hymns with the Sunday school children at the Euclid Avenue Baptist Church. Some of the Robber Barons had huge slush funds for buying votes in Washington and in state capitals. They reorganized railroads in ways that sometimes ruined stockholders. They fleeced the public on the exchanges by making exorbitant profits in stock-watering operations. Still, they all fully expected to be marked present when the roll was called up yonder. The Old Testament religious ethic of an eye for an eye and a tooth for a tooth was one to which Morgan, Gould, and Fisk could easily relate. Even from the pulpit, Henry Ward Beecher, among others, preached variations of the theme that richness is goodness. Samuel J. Tilden, a lawyer for the railroad interests and wealthy in his own right, gave secular expression to his belief at a testimonial dinner for Junius Morgan (J. P.'s father) in 1877:

> You are, doubtless in some degree, clinging to the illusion that you are working for yourselves, but it is my pleasure to claim that you are working for the public. [Applause.] While you are scheming for your own selfish ends, there is an overruling and wise Providence directing that the most of all you do should inure to the benefit of the people. Men of colossal fortunes are in effect, if not in fact, trustees for the public.[17]

During the time when the Robber Barons were coming of age, economics and natural religion were virtually inseparable. Both the natural and the social sciences were supportive of the ethics of the reformed Protestant churches. The Reverend John McVickar of Columbia University stated: "That science and religion eventually teach the same lesson, is a necessary consequence of the unity of truth, but it is seldom that this union is so early and satisfactorily displayed as in the researches of Political Economy."[18] The universe was governed by natural laws set in motion by God, and the commercial competition that economists saw as a metaphor of Newtonian mechanics was also assumed to be ordained by the deity. Natural law could be invoked in defense of monopoly almost as easily as in defense of competition. Later, Henry P.

Davison, one of Morgan's partners, could tell a Senate committee investigating monopoly, "If in practice it were wrong it could not live. . . . Things correct themselves."[19] Henry Ward Beecher, then the most renowned of American divines, expressed his wish to meet Herbert Spencer in Heaven and preached natural selection to the rich at the Plymouth Church in Brooklyn during the 1860s and 1870s. Beecher comforted the rich parishioners on the rectitude of their wealth even as he comforted (some of) their wives in bed.

A belief in natural law led the Social Darwinists and most neoclassical economists to a conclusion that suited the business community very well: laissez-faire is desirable. The Social Darwinists' laws are derived from their understanding of nature and support the idea that the people cannot and should not change society through collective action. Business leaders, including the Robber Barons, also concluded that survival of the fittest was a law of nature and human regulations were unnecessary. They came to see their competitive struggles as essentially no different from the struggles for survival that take place in nature.

Alfred Marshall and the neoclassicals did not offer an alternative theology. Indeed, businesspeople would have received the same spiritual advice from economists as they did from Morgan's church. Yet the state of competition after about 1870 resulted in predatory practices that were destructive of social harmony. While orthodox economics continued to enshrine Darwinian competition, giant trusts were staking out monopoly claims throughout American industry.

Undetected by the neoclassicals, economic conditions in Great Britain also had greatly changed by 1870. In mid-century, Britain had produced perhaps two-thirds of the world's coal, perhaps half of its iron, five-sevenths of its small supply of steel, and about half of the cotton cloth produced on a commercial scale. Britain's chief rival, even then, was its ex-colony, the United States. Nonetheless, as the United States, France, and the German confederation continued to industrialize, Britain's relative advantage began to shrink. Beginning with the last decade of the nineteenth century, Britain was one of a group of great industrialized powers but not the leader. Moreover, the industrialized world experienced a long depression that blemished the Victorian boom (1873–1896).

This is not to say that British industry was failing completely; rather, other nations' economies were succeeding all too well. Moreover, the international business climate was creating storms on the British seas just at a time when Britain's resources were strained to their limits and existing British technology was fully exploited. [20] Britain faced new competition from two directions. First, the less developed nations now had alternative outlets for their raw materials and food—namely, other industrialized countries. Second, the United States, France, and Germany were competing with Britain for worldwide industrial sales. Britain's colonial empire was an informal one as long as it did not have to vie with other industrialized nations for the attention of the less developed countries. This changed drastically. From the 1880s, imperialism—the political division of the world into *formal* colonies of the great powers combined with the *deliberate* establishment of economic dependencies—became popular among all the industrialized nations. When its power had been mostly economic, the British Empire had a benign appearance. However, the political form of colonialism shifted Britain toward strident imperialism.

There were also other less noticed changes. Even though real wages had increased during the Victorian era, they had not advanced uniformly. As much as 40 percent of the working class lived in what was then called poverty; about two-thirds would, at some time or other in their lives, become paupers. Not more than 15 percent of the working class lived in what was then regarded as comfort.

It is no wonder that by the early 1870s British trade unionism (like giant enterprises before it) became a fly in the soup of perfect competition. The trade unions initially included only skilled and better-paid craft workers and therefore were not large. In the closing years of the century, however, unskilled workers began forming large organizations of their own. The turn of the century, in fact, marks the origins of the British Labour Party.

There was a crisis in economic theory because the doctrine of perfect competition fit reality less and less well at home and abroad. The eyes of the economic world were again to turn toward Cambridge.

CRISES AND SCIENTIFIC REVOLUTIONS

What is a "crisis" in theory all about? We must remember that a scientific group will vigorously oppose any fundamental changes in its paradigm. The basic paradigm of a science, such as Adam Smith's economics paradigm, is frequently regarded as sacrosanct by those who work with it. Because they believe it adequately explains most observations and experimental outcomes, they see no reason to change it. According to historian of science Thomas Kuhn,

> *Further development ... ordinarily calls for the construction of elaborate equipment, the development of an esoteric vocabulary and skills, and a refinement of concepts that increasingly lessens their resemblance to their usual common-sense prototypes. That professionalization leads, on the one hand, to an immense restriction of the scientist's vision and to a considerable resistance to paradigm change. The science has become increasingly rigid.*[21]

What Kuhn calls *professionalization* is another term for normal science, the day-to-day activities by which scientists accumulate information and develop the precision of their theories. Such activity is non-revolutionary and has the effect of making the ruling scientific dogma more defensible and less easy to challenge. Alfred Marshall's apostles, for example, refined classical economics into a logical-mathematical-geometrical juggernaut that economic realities could not stop.

Although normal science does not contain within itself the seeds for change, change will emerge slowly because of external pressure. The development of new theories is usually preceded by a period of scientific insecurity caused by the failure of normal science to find solutions to new problems: a crisis, in short. The crises that cause fundamental changes in social science result from problems emerging in *society*. Societal conflict, in turn, is the antecedent for conflict within academic social science (although modest paradigm changes can begin because of in-house scientific failures). Social scientists may discover that they cannot solve or even adequately describe either strictly academic or societal problems using the dominant paradigm. Certainly the classical economic theory of perfect competition and the social harmony that was supposed to result from it failed to explain the Robber Barons and the monopolistic practices of certain industrialists in the United States from the 1880s through the 1920s. A social crisis was at hand.

MRS. ROBINSON, MR. CHAMBERLIN, AND NOT-SO-PERFECT COMPETITION

By the turn of the century, giant combinations had appeared in virtually every major American industry. The American Sugar Refining Company controlled about 95 percent of the business. The Pullman Palace Car Company controlled 85 percent of its industry. James Buchanan Duke's American Tobacco Company controlled about 80 percent of the nation's tobacco production. On top of these combinations came the merger movement of 1897–1904, which we will discuss in Chapter 13. More than 1,000 railroad systems had been consolidated into 6. About 100 public utility companies controlled some 1,300 plants. The administrations of Harrison, Theodore Roosevelt, and Taft made a number of significant and determined efforts to control giant business. In particular, Roosevelt exhibited much blood and thunder but was a little stick against the strong undercurrent of probusiness sentiment in the Congress and the courts. Reform was often slow and ineffective. In a 1911 ruling concerning John D. Rockefeller's Standard Oil, the Supreme Court set forth its famous "rule of reason," which stated in effect that not the size and power of businesses but only the illegal or unfair use of them should be regulated. This ruling has more or less dominated the government's attitude toward business ever since.

Although surrounded by examples of *im*perfect competition, economists did not develop a theory to account for it until the 1920s. Piero Sraffa, a Cambridge economics teacher and a former student of Marshall's, suggested that economists analyze the business firm as a monopolist rather than as a perfect competitor. Sraffa argued that the unit cost of production of a commodity may decline as the output of the firm increases. For example, when the production of bicycles increases, the amount of overhead cost to keep lights burning in the factory remains constant. But if one divides the number of bicycles into the total cost of electric lighting, the unit cost of illumination falls. With this new light on the subject, Sraffa concluded that demand rather than competition may be the factor that limits the increased size of a firm. Business firms, however, can manipulate demand to some extent by making functionally identical products appear to be different. Bicycles can be built in different sizes, painted different colors, and given different names. The real world is not the monotonous one of perfect competition in which every commodity of a particular type looks like every other. Manufacturing and marketing devices can influence consumer preferences and infringe somewhat on the consumer's sovereignty. This kind of competition, which we see all around us every day, is imperfect because it does not depend on simple laws of supply and demand.

A widely acclaimed reexamination of paradigmatic perfect competition came from another Cambridge economist, Joan Robinson, who published her *Economics of Imperfect Competition* in 1933. Robinson was affiliated with Cambridge as both a student and a teacher. Following the lead offered by Sraffa's work on decreasing costs, she began her work on imperfect competition and dragged fellow economists kicking and screaming into the new conceptual world of monopolies. Meanwhile, at Harvard University in Cambridge, Massachusetts, the economist Edward H. Chamberlin (1899–1967) had submitted a doctoral thesis on the same subject. His work was also published in 1933. We do not have space here to go into great detail concerning the theories of Robinson and Chamberlin, except to note that, like Sraffa, they both focused on the firm rather than the industry. A large joint-stock firm, not subject to the ravages of Smithian competition, could engage in nonprice competition by attracting buyers through special features and services rather than the normal method of competition, which is to reduce prices. An automobile producer, for example, might build an automobile that riders would have to step down into and call it *Hudson*. The producer could then advertise such an automobile as being unique in this respect and, assuming that buyers actually prefer to take such a step, the firm could attract new consumers with its new design without reducing its price.

Chamberlin and Robinson did disagree. He saw the advantages of imperfect competition, whereas she saw its wastes and argued for government intervention to put a stop to it. The world of monopolies is still ignored by some economists, and the imperfect competition that lies between the pure monopolist and the pure competitor remains a virtual no-man's-land of ambiguities for most of us.

CONCLUSIONS

In the skillful hands of the neoclassical economists, the political economy of Adam Smith became just plain *economics*. Certainly economics now looked more like a science. The rigorous defining of the economic man and the assumptions behind perfect competition added greatly to the precision of economics. Whereas Adam Smith and the other classicals had focused on longer-run capital accumulation and economic growth, Alfred Marshall demonstrated how demand in both the short and the long run helped to decide the value of commodities. The "Marshallian cross" was made possible by the hedonistic-utilitarian-rationalistic legacy of the classical-neoclassical bridgebuilders. Marshall's translation of these ideas into plane geometry provided an incredibly useful tool for problem solving. The supply-demand concept continues to occupy much of the normal science time logged by academic economists.

There was, however, something rather disturbing about all this scientific activity. Even at the time that Alfred Marshall was enjoying his stature as the high priest of economics, the counterpart in reality for his economic model could not be found in England. The Robber Barons were making a shambles of the idea of harmony from individualistic self-interest, and large-scale production leading to industrial concentration made neoclassical economics less and less relevant to the United States. Joan Robinson and Edward Chamberlin countered with theories of imperfect competition, but the uncertainties in their theories were no match for the balanced forces achievable in theory by the Newtonian-like clockwork of perfect competition. Its absence in reality bothered few economists at the time. Part of the failure of imperfect competition to become a full paradigm is a result of the considerable distraction caused by the Great Depression. For the neoclassicals, the worst was yet to come.

7

J. M. KEYNES: THE END OF FRUGALITY

▼

*The decay spreads over the State, and the sweet smell is a
great sorrow on the land. Men who can graft the trees and
make the seed fertile and big can find no way to let the hungry
people eat their produce. Men who have created new fruits in
the world cannot create a system whereby their fruits may be
eaten. And the failure hangs over the State like a great sorrow.*

JOHN STEINBECK, *THE GRAPES OF WRATH,* 1939

John Steinbeck's novel *The Grapes of Wrath* is an intensely dramatic story of the suffering and privation experienced by poor farmers
during the Great Depression of the 1930s. In contrast to Steinbeck's work
and other American literature of this period, we find some of the most
prominent economists assuring us that everything is all right and the
economy will correct itself. Arthur Pigou, the great summarizer of the
neoclassical theory of employment, blandly explains that "with perfectly free competition . . . there will always be at work a strong tendency
for wage rates to be so related to demand that everyone is employed."[1]
Yet in 1933 almost 25 percent of the civilian labor force in the United
States was unemployed. Pigou's own England was in its second decade
of debilitating depression.

The Great Depression was the source of the second major crisis
faced by economic science. The Depression sidetracked the theory of
imperfect competition, relegating it to a mere advance in the technique
of economic analysis and not a revolutionary idea or ideology. The
differentiation of goods was of little concern to those who were unemployed or on welfare; they were more interested in whether or not
there would be anything to eat tomorrow. Joan Robinson's theories and
the Depression were the introductory elements to the only widely
acknowledged revolution in economic thought since Adam Smith: the

120

Keynesian Revolution instigated by yet another student of Marshall's at Cambridge, John Maynard Keynes.

As we have seen, the marginalist/neoclassical school concentrated on the development of *microeconomic* theory, which deals with individual industries and firms and the relative prices of specific commodities. During periods of economic depression or crisis, governments often called on economists to give advice on economic policies affecting the entire population. Economists were thus required to combine the various strands of microeconomic theory to explain *general* economic conditions. The study of the behavior of the entire national income, price level, and employment is called *macroeconomics*; it focuses on the "added-up" outcomes from the whole system rather than on components of it. Our first task in this chapter will be to explore neoclassical macroeconomic theory. We shall see that its laissez-faire policy implications were irrelevant during the Depression. Keynes helped to change the idea that government should stay out of the economy. Second, we will examine the genesis and general nature of Keynesian economics. It appeared at first that Keynes had provided an entirely new economics paradigm, but he did not. Instead, he created an enormously influential subparadigm still embedded in Smithian economics, one that dominated national macroeconomic policy from the end of World War II until about 1965, when the subparadigm met a counterrevolution from modern Smithian apostles.

NEOCLASSICAL MACROECONOMICS, GLUTS, AND UNEMPLOYMENT

Say's Law of Markets, Again

In their analysis of national income and employment, the neoclassicals were, for the most part, content to update the theories of the French economist and popularizer of Adam Smith, J. B. Say (Chapter 4), who had argued that price adjustments would prevent a supply of goods in excess of demand. Manufacturers, who need labor, raw materials, and new machines to produce a stream of finished goods (supply), make income payments out of sales revenue to labor and to the owners of materials and machines. In turn, this income is respent to purchase the finished goods. The circle is closed. The economy continually refurbishes itself, and there is little or no lag between the receipt of money and its expenditure. Perfect competition precludes uncertainty about the future and eliminates any need to stuff wages into mattresses or to keep profits in the company safe. The fact that income is immediately respent—one way or another—makes either chronic shortages or gluts impossible.

This theory does not mean that no one ever saves any money. It means that the amount of money saved is always equal to the funds demanded by business firms for investment purposes, and therefore the money is never idle. The interest rate that savers receive for postponing consumption is equal to the rate that investors pay for use of the money. The interest rate is a self-regulating mechanism that maintains a "correct" equilibrium and guarantees that savings will always just equal investments.

How is full employment guaranteed—except for temporary lapses that can be explained away? Once again, perfect competition comes to the rescue. First, a high wage rate will attract more workers. Second, a lower wage rate will make producers willing to hire more workers. In neoclassical economics, the wage is expressed in money of constant purchasing power, a *real* wage rate. Adjustments in supply and demand will presumably equalize the workers' need for more income and the producers' need for more revenue. The "right" wage will be the equilibrium wage rate, arrived at when the quantity of labor demanded is precisely equal to the quantity of labor supplied. This rate will prevail in a perfectly competitive labor market. If it should happen that the number of workers offering their services is greater than the number demanded, then—according to the theory—some of these workers must be unwilling to work at a wage that equals their market worth. If the wage rate is temporarily above the equilibrium rate and workers are unemployed, they can fully employ themselves simply by going to a potential employer and offering their services at a lower rate. Workers unwilling to accept these conditions of equilibrium are *voluntarily* unemploying themselves. Full employment is theoretically always attainable. If you are out of work and one of your children has just fainted from hunger, don't worry. Just wait until the natural market forces return the wage rate to equilibrium.

The Quantity Theory of Money, Again

Although Alfred Marshall initially embraced Say's law without much qualification, his view of money loosened the law a bit. In Marshall's view, individuals demand cash primarily in order to engage in commercial transactions. The demand for cash holdings or *cash balances*, however, derives from liquidity needs. That is, people prefer to hold some cash balances to bridge the time gap between the receipt of money income and its expenditure. If this preference is such that the stock of money turns over at, say, an average rate of four times a year, a money supply equal to one-fourth of the money value of national production will be held in cash balances at any time. Thus, the demand for cash (which Marshall denoted as k) equals the reciprocal of the rate that money is turned over, or its velocity of circulation. Let V be velocity, and k equals $1/V$: in our example, $k = 0.25$.

Nevertheless, Marshall viewed people with "excess" cash balances as somewhat irrational. Money was not viewed as an asset to be held solely for its own sake. Thus, Marshall's k becomes a fixed value because the turnover rate of money (V) would be constant. If, on the average, income is spent three months after its receipt, $V = 4$ is a stable four times a year. Individual commodity prices are not related to the money supply or to the overall price level because holdings of financial assets (such as cash or checking accounts) are never substituted for holdings of goods and services. There are no cash balances beyond those required for day-to-day household needs and business trade so that money received from the sale of products is always used (ultimately) to purchase *other* commodities. After all this is said (and done), the requirements of Say's law are more or less met in Marshall, as in most of the classical economists. That is, cash is held only temporarily in order to buy either consumer or producer goods, so that a particular output calls forth an equal value in expenditures. A slippage in Say's enforcement occurs only if V varies.

It would be a mistake, however, to conclude that all the neoclassical economists were unified in their faith in the quantity theory of money and the exactitude of Say's law. An important exception was John Gustav Knut Wicksell (1851–1926), a Swedish economist who theorized about the business cycle. Later I shall discuss Wicksell as one of Keynes's precursors.

Meanwhile, back in Cambridge, the theory of automatic employment adjustment was restated during the 1930s by Arthur Pigou, Marshall's favorite student. Throughout the Depression, Pigou maintained that, whatever the state of demand for commodities in the economy, wage changes will always create a tendency toward full employment. In explaining temporary unemployment, he suggested "that such unemployment as exists at any time is due wholly to the fact that changes in demand conditions are continually taking place and that frictional resistances prevent the appropriate wage adjustment from being made instantaneously."[2]

THE GREAT DEPRESSION

Although the Great Depression provided overwhelming evidence to the contrary, the myth about full employment still persisted among economists who subscribed to neoclassical theory. For example, Lionel Robbins, a professor of economics at the University of London, wrote in

1934 that "... in general it is true to say that a greater flexibility of wage rates would considerably reduce unemployment. ... If it had not been for the prevalence of the view that wage rates must at all costs be maintained in order to maintain the purchasing power of the consumer," he added, "the violence of the present depression and the magnitude of the unemployment which has accompanied it would have been considerably less."[3] Robbins believed that the free market had become choked by business monopoly, the growth of trade unions, and an increase in governmental regulations. The return to full employment only awaited the removal of these restrictions and the unleashing of free market forces.

The statistical appendix to Robbins's *The Great Depression* contradicts its policy recommendations. Robbins believed that a decline in wages was a necessary precondition to a decline in prices that would culminate in a stampede of consumers rushing to buy merchandise at bargain prices. Yet his measure of the cost of living in the United States shows it dropping nearly 25 percent between the end of 1929 and the end of 1933, while his index of industrial production is dropping by almost the same share during the same time span. The stampede for consumer goods seems to have been sidetracked. His index of composite wages in the United States shows them dropping by about one-fifth from the end of 1929 through the end of 1933, while his data show the number of workers unemployed increasing from nearly zero to over 13 million in 1933—one-quarter of the U.S. labor force.[4] When his advice was requested from a British committee investigating economic recovery measures, the eminent Arthur Pigou offered the same policy remedies as Robbins: get the roadblocks out of the way of the market mechanism, and national income will rise and full employment return.

The Great Depression lasted for over ten years in the United States, from 1929 until the mobilization for World War II in the waning months of 1940. In the United States, the last great economic crisis of the Depression lasted from the spring of 1937 to the summer of 1938. During that year, industrial output dropped by about one-third and unemployment rose by about one-fifth, leaving about 6.5 million people unemployed in 1937 and about 10 million in 1938. After six years of crisis, the unemployment rate was higher in 1938 than it had been in 1931 (see Table 7.1), probably as a result of a sharp reduction in the federal budgetary deficit plus a sharp contraction in the money supply. The money supply can be greatly influenced by the actions of the central bank, the public-bank lender of last resort to private banks. The central bank also directly and indirectly affects rates of interest. Still the discount rate, the interest rate the central bank charges for loans to private banks, dropped to an extremely low 1 percent in 1938. And yet—contrary to the neoclassical view—business was apparently not optimistic about returns on invest-

TABLE 7.1 Great Depression Unemployment Rates
(percent of civilian labor force)

1929	3.2%	}	Peacetime prosperity
1930	7.0		
1931	15.9		
1933	24.9		
1935	20.1	}	The Great Depression
1937	14.3		
1938	19.3		
1939	17.2		
1940	14.6		
1941	9.9	}	World War II begins
1942	4.7		

ments in machines, people, and plants. For example, machines more than ten years old made up about 44 percent of the total in use in industry in 1925; by 1940 this share had increased to about 70 percent.

When English neoclassical economists were asked, "How can unemployment be eliminated?" they quickly responded with their standard answer: "Remove the impediments to wage and price flexibility, and full employment is automatic." The idea that full employment could be generated through governmental means generally was not considered a solution to an economic puzzle. Phenomena that will not fit the normal science view are often not seen at all. The behavior of normal scientists does not include the invention of new theories, and such scientists are often intolerant of those invented by others. Indeed, one criterion for choosing problems during normal science phases is that they fit known theories. Thus, even though real-world observations of conditions during the Depression directly conflicted with the neoclassical paradigm, they simply remained invisible to most economists.

J. M. KEYNES: THE NEOCLASSICAL HERETIC

Because the classical economics paradigm continued to serve as the unsteady prop for economic science, the science was changing more slowly than the values and institutions of capitalism. One important economist who recognized this fact was John Maynard Keynes (1883–1946). In 1919, his *Economic Consequences of the Peace* cast doubt on the supposed national economic virtues of frugality and accumulation. He suggested that World War I had "disclosed the possibility of consumption to all and the vanity of abstinence to many."[5] [Throughout this chapter, *consumption* refers to expenditures by households on durable consumer goods (refrigerators, automobiles, etc.); nondurable consumer goods (milk, bread, shirts, beer, etc.); and services (of mechanics, hairdressers, doctors, lawyers, etc.).] Keynes recognized that a basic change in social values had taken place. Great disparities in wealth, once thought essential to the goal of capital accumulation, were no longer acceptable to most people in capitalist society.[6] Keynes's doubt that adequate expenditure would stabilize the economy put Say's law in danger of being violated.

Keynes's background is eminently English and gentry, including his education at Eton and King's College, Cambridge, where he heard Alfred Marshall lecture on economics. Keynes's father, John Neville Keynes, was himself the leading logician-philosopher among the neoclassicals, and everything in the younger Keynes's training prepared him to be a normal science practitioner of economics. But his genius eventually made him a scientific maverick. We would have had to go back to Karl Marx, who died the year Keynes was born, to find an economist of comparable influence.

Keynes was far more than an economist. He was an incredibly active, many-sided man who also played such diverse roles as principal representative of the Treasury at the Paris Peace Conference, deputy for the chancellor of the Exchequer, a director of the Bank of England, trustee of the National Gallery, chairman of the Council for the Encouragement of Music and the Arts, bursar of King's College, Cambridge, editor of the *Economic Journal*, chairman of the *Nation* and later the *New Statesman* magazines, and chairman of the National Mutual Life Assurance Society. He also ran an investment company, organized the Camargo Ballet (his wife, Lydia Lopokova, was a renowned star of the Russian Imperial Ballet), and built (profitably) the Arts Theatre at Cambridge. While doing all this, he played an important role in the development of the economics faculty at Cambridge.

Keynes's lifestyle diverged greatly from the severe spartan airs of Alfred Marshall. A bibliophile and supporter of the arts, Keynes seemed most at home in the lively company of artists and writers. He was a central figure of the literary circle known as Bloomsbury, which included writers Leonard Woolf, Virginia Woolf, Clive Bell, E. M. Forster, and Lytton Strachey. (Strachey and Keynes had a short-lived love affair.) The opinions of this charmed group of twenty or thirty determined the artistic standards of England. Though Keynes could be extremely rude and devastating in arguments with "fools," he was almost always outwardly cheerful—as effervescent as the champagne that he consumed with thinly veiled delight.

Until Keynes, those who criticized neoclassical macroeconomics were considered unable to use the tools of their trade competently. Keynes expressed a lack of confidence in laissez-faire governmental policies, denying, in an essay called "The End of Laissez Faire," the metaphysics of natural liberty and the close relationship of private and social interest with enlightened self-interest. Yet even when a paradigm is failing, it is not replaced unless an alternative can solve puzzles more effectively. The economists continued to be complacent about the internal consistency of the neoclassical paradigm and the full employment that unfettered capitalism would generate. Keynes and the great numbers of unemployed during the Depression were not nearly so content.

For one thing, there was the shift in values noted earlier; during the twenties and thirties, attitudes toward wealth and work were changing. The early capitalism of the Industrial Revolution stressed labor *and* thrift. There had been a dedication to work and a rejection of consumption for its own sake, including leisure, which was equated with idleness. As early as the turn of the nineteenth century, however, people began to look at work as a secular activity leading to the enjoyment of the money it brought. The commitment to work and thrift were watered down by devotion to consumer pleasures. By the 1920s—the time of *The Great Gatsby* and the charleston—more Americans saw work as a path to luxury and leisure than as a thorny path to heaven.

THE KEYNESIAN REVOLUTION: THE MOMENTARY OVERTHROW OF A PARADIGM

The Precursors

As I noted above, the neoclassicals were not unified, and Knut Wicksell, in particular, appeared out of step with the monetary orthodoxy in most respects. As he had no academic appointment until 1896, Wicksell depended upon a small income from journalism and popular lecturing on birth control, prostitution, and universal suffrage. This unusual dual career led to a brief prison term in 1909 for his ironical remarks about church doctrine. So, too, his mapping of an up-and-down course for capitalistic economies seemed ironical to the English neoclassicals.

Wicksell's is a tale of two interest rates. There is a *natural* rate of interest in the economy. The natural is the *real* rate in the sense that it is not based upon the money supply. It is that rate of interest at which the demand for loan funds by business firms and the supply of savings exactly agree. The natural rate is the rate that equals the expected rate of profit on capital equipment. Therefore, the natural rate of interest is just right to bring into balance real saving and investment without changing prices.

Although the natural interest rate cannot be objectively observed, banks can interfere with the market rate of interest on loans because of bankers' abilities to create credit. A market interest rate above the natural rate would produce a cumulative downswing of the economy. The demand for investment funds by business is slashed because of the high cost of borrowing compared with expected returns on capital equipment. Prices and incomes fall. This economic decline is cumulative, because the deficiency of a demand associated with slumping incomes offsets any potential stimulus resulting from falling prices.

If we view Wicksell's idea from a slightly different perspective, we can see why he is said to have anticipated Keynes. With the natural rate of interest above the market rate, the savings planned out of income must be less than the investment planned by business. The savers are responding to what banks will pay them for forgoing consumption; the producers' optimistic plans are based upon what they presume to be the profitability of their capital. Such an excess in investment plans creates an economic expansion. On the other hand, a natural rate of interest below the market rate implies that investment plans are smaller than savings plans. In that instance, a cumulative contraction could be initiated. In either case, the price level and national money income have to adjust once more in order to generate the equality between savings and investment.

Monetary policy implications in Wicksell's view are strong. If only the monetary authorities will act to preclude any gap between the natural rate of interest and the market rate, the business cycle can be eliminated and a stable price level achieved. The significance of Wicksell's thought is in a monetary theory of the cumulative process of business expansion and contraction in which (unlike the quantity theory of money) the money supply affects the general price level *indirectly*, through the interest rate. (As is so often the case, this was a rediscovery. The indirect mechanism was first stated by Henry Thornton in 1802, during the classical period; this version appeared to be acceptable to David Ricardo at the time.) A major difficulty in Wicksell's analysis comes from his presumption that the economy is fully employed when the upturn initiated by the differential of the natural rate and the market rate begins. Thus, he viewed depressions and inflations essentially as monetary phenomena. Wicksell left for Keynes the problem of dealing with unemployment.

Others nibbled away at the edges of conventional theory. In the mid-1920s, D. H. Robertson, a student, then a friend and colleague of

Keynes at Cambridge, attacked the classical theory that assumed that all savings generated in the economy would be immediately invested. In a simple model, savings is a residual—the difference between a household's income after taxes and its total consumption. Robertson showed that the savings of a community did not necessarily lead to a new investment of the same quantity, an investment pessimism that was eventually to be a piece of the mosaic of Keynes's general theory.

In 1930 Keynes published his *Treatise on Money*, which was intended to be his definitive statement on economic theory. He was not satisfied, however, and within a few months began rethinking the fundamentals of his book and developing ideas for a new one. The *Treatise* had been criticized by a group of younger economists at Cambridge, and their objections aided Keynes in the further development of his own thoughts. Two important figures in this group are the late Joan Robinson (mentioned in Chapter 6) and Sir Richard K. Kahn, one of Keynes's pupils. (Others include James Meade, Austin Robinson, and the late Piero Sraffa.)

In an article called "The Theory of Money and the Analyses of Output" (1933), Joan Robinson succinctly explains how *actual* savings and investment can be equal at all points of time and yet not equal in terms of *schedules* of *desired* savings and investment. Actual savings and investment are those statistically measured quantities that were not spent by consumers (savings) and were spent by manufacturers and business for new plants, equipment, tools, and inventory changes (investment). This behavior actually happened. But a savings schedule shows the various amounts households will *plan* or desire to save at various possible income levels. Similar reasoning applies to an investment schedule. In this article, Robinson also explains how *unplanned* investment might occur in such a way as to maintain the actual measured savings-investment equality.

Keynes had outlined a primitive version of an idea later called the *multiplier* in a 1929 pamphlet advocating the use of public works. Kahn refined the idea of an *employment multiplier* in a subsequent *Economic Journal* article (June 1931). He showed that government expenditure on public works will be distributed to workers in the form of wages, a large part of which will be spent on consumer goods and services. The store merchants will then spend a large fraction of their receipts from the consumers, and so on and on and on. If the government hires 200,000 workers to rake leaves and, as a result, employment in consumer-goods industries (secondary employment) is increased by 400,000, total employment is increased by 600,000 and the employment multiplier is 3.

Keynes's Policy Suggestions

Keynes's new ideas steadily developed from 1931 to 1934. In the early months of the Depression, Keynes said that the fundamental cause of the slump was a lack of new plants and equipment as a result of the "poor outlook" for capital investment. Increased profits would stimulate investment, but they must not be achieved by cutting costs, which would be deflationary. Profits can be restored *either* by inducing the public to spend a larger share of their incomes *or* by inducing business to convert a larger portion of its revenue into investment, but not by both. Keynes was still relying in part on classical and neoclassical theories, because he believed that an increase in consumption would come out of a reduction in the savings otherwise available for business investment. He did not yet envision the possibility of both total consumption spending *and* total investment spending increasing simultaneously.

Keynes told his British radio audience in 1931 that *increased spending* was necessary to counteract the Depression. His intuition proved to be more powerful than the classical-neoclassical economic theory. Keynes attacked thrift, a classical and neoclassical virtue, because he saw the fallacy of expecting large savings to be offset by investment when there were virtually no investment opportunities in sight.[7] He urged families to spend more and the government to increase its public works expenditures. Arthur Pigou's suggested policy alternative of wage reductions would, he felt, only make matters worse.

In 1931, Keynes also served on the Macmillan Committee, which was to investigate and make recommendations about economic conditions in Britain. In an argument that was similar to his later theory of the multiplier, Keynes and other dissenting members of the committee argued that, because there was already a high level of unemployment in the private sector of the economy, public spending by the government would not divert resources away from private investment. The commonsense version of such a multiplier effect pictures the net national product as a series of repetitive, continuous flows of expenditures and income. The dollars spent by the government are received as income by say, Rowntree, who in turn spends it so that Rowntree's consumption becomes part of the income received by say, Shrewsbury. Although Keynes admitted that public-works programs might in the short run have an adverse effect on business confidence, he thought that, on balance, increased central government spending would be helpful and desirable. These minority recommendations contrast sharply with the conservative, orthodox, and generally neoclassical arguments in the main body of the Macmillan report. Keynes was beginning to suggest that, if free markets did not produce working people and humming

TABLE 7.2 The Multiplier Process

	Change, income		Change, consumption		Change, savings	Initial change, investment
Assumed increase, investment						$5.00
First round	$5.00	=	$3.75	+	$1.25	
Second round	3.75		2.81		0.94	
Third round	2.81		2.11		0.70	
Fourth round	2.11		1.58		0.53	
Fifth round	1.58		1.19		0.39	
All other rounds	4.75		3.56		1.19	
Totals	$20.00		$15.00		$5.00	$5.00

factories, then it would be necessary for the government to intervene to restore higher levels of economic activity.[8]

A Breakthrough: The Multiplier

We saw earlier that Keynes's colleague Richard Kahn had polished the idea of the employment multiplier, which Keynes adapted to his own purposes. Many economists had thought and written about the multiplicative effects of government spending coming from successive rounds of consumer spending, but none had been able to articulate an acceptable new theory.[9] Keynes borrowed Kahn's mathematics and used it as the key link in his arguments for government intervention. He used the term *investment multiplier*: if government or industry invests an initial $1 billion and consumption rises by $1 billion as a result, the investment multiplier is 2. The multiplier shows that three aggregates— consumption spending, savings, and investment spending—are all re- lated to the level of national income. At the risk of some oversimplifi- cation, the multiplier relation can be shown in a schematized example (see Table 7.2). The example assumes that every consumer plans to spend three-quarters of every dollar of after-tax income and intends to save one-quarter of every dollar. In addition, business investment rises by $5 billion as a result of improved profit expectations. Table 7.2 shows what happens.

In this process, the $5 billion is multiplied by four because only one-fourth of all income increments go unspent. After all rounds are played, the change in savings caused by the change in investment will be equal to the original investment increment. Higher investment spending, either private or public, multiplies itself in terms of national income changes, and out of higher wage disbursements workers are able to save more. Therefore, higher levels of savings finance even higher levels of investment.

According to neoclassical economics, savings and therefore consumption depend mostly on the rate of interest, but in the Keynesian multiplier, consumption depends on income. Keynes described a stable psychological propensity in the community, a *propensity to consume*, in which consumption increases and decreases with income, though not as fast. Irrespective of the speed, consumers reliably spend more when their income rises and less when it falls. If income is an important variable in a consumption relation, it must also be important in a savings relation, because saving is simply "not consuming." To justify any particular level of employment, there must be an amount of business investment to absorb the difference between total output (at that level of employment) in excess of consumption. That is, the economy's savings and investment must jibe with the desired employment (and output) level.

As the months of depression rolled on, Keynes watched businesses refuse to invest even though interest rates were very low, and he concluded that investment must also depend in part on forces in addition to the interest rate. In other words, the standard neoclassical explanation of the relation between interest and investment simply did not fit the facts. A theory of how the level of income is decided was needed to replace the theory of how the rate of interest is determined. Once this fundamental idea was understood, a revolution occurred in economic theory. Surviving fragments of early drafts of Keynes's great work, *The General Theory of Employment, Interest, and Money*, published in 1936, show that as early as 1932 he was using the multiplier concept in his theoretical system. Yet during these writing and advising years, Keynes was considered by most other economists to be only a thorn in the otherwise flawless rose garden of neoclassical economics—a barren thorn that had produced nothing new.

The Multiplier, Aborted Plans, and National Income

The main argument of Keynes's *General Theory* is that the changes in wages and interest rates assumed inevitable in the neoclassical tradition either (1) will not occur or, if they do occur, (2) will not bring about full employment. Although workers are willing to work at lower *real* (price-adjusted) wages when the decrease is brought about by a rise in prices, workers resist cuts in their *money* wages. The workers simply "feel" richer with higher money wages and are not as sensitive to the condition in which such wages buy fewer goods, a state Keynes called *money illusion*. On the other hand, a decline in money wages alone would not increase employment. Even though a reduction in wage costs would enable producers to raise output levels and reduce prices, the money wage decline reduces the income that is the well-spring of consumer demands. The bolster to total demand in the economy must come from some other source. In any case, massive wage cuts were an impractical policy notion.

Interest is not the price that is paid to people to save (forgo consumption), higher savings do not necessarily mean lower interest rates, and therefore it might not be possible to push interest rates below a certain level. Rather, higher *intended* savings mean lower *desired* consumption, and the resultant decline in demand for goods and services will result in lower production levels, less income from which to save, and therefore lower savings than originally intended. These lower than expected savings will match a level of investment depressed by lower consumption. This equality can be achieved at levels of total demand (and spending) insufficient to employ the entire labor force.

Total possible *output* (supply) of goods and services in the economy depends mostly, according to Keynes, on the size of the labor force. The greater the number of persons employed, the higher the possible output. (The existing state of technology, the money wage rate, and the in-place numbers of equipped plants are "givens." As we will see in Chapter 8, the precise role of the wage rate is different in different chapters of Keynes's *General Theory*.) Total *demand* equals the sum spent in consumption, in business investments, and by the government. When total planned demand exceeds total output, then output rises to meet the demand and national income tends to rise too. Conversely, if total planned demand is less than total potential output, then output and hence income tend to fall. [By definition, the dollar value of output equals the value of total income. Income receipts equal the payments (including profits) made to the owners of the factors—land, labor, and capital—used to produce the output.] Although gaps between intentions and reality can occur, Keynes agreed with the neoclassical economists that tendencies were toward a *national income* equilibrium. But the neoclassical tradition said that this equilibrium is always at a level of output sufficient to maintain full employment.

Keynes wasn't buying the latter argument. He attacked this Newtonian type of equilibrium by contending that the simultaneous occurrence of such natural equilibria in all markets—labor, money, and commodities—at exactly full employment was improbable. Furthermore, the failure of the equilibrium process could have dire social consequences. By way of illustration, let's look at Table 7.3.

When total demand equaled potential output (in the "before" column at $490 billion), the neoclassical economists cried "equilibrium"

TABLE 7.3 Employment, Output, and Demand

Possible levels of employment (in millions)	Potential output (in billions $)	Total demand (in billions $)		Tendency of employment, output, and income	
		Before*	After*	Before*	After*
85	$530	$520	$525	↓	↓
80 { Labor force	510	505	510	↓	Full employment
75	490	490	495	Equilibrium	↑
70	470	475	480	↑	↑
65	450	460	465	↑	↑
60	430	445	450	↑	↑

*"Before" is the demand schedule prior to a government policy change; "after" is after a change in government spending.

and "Victory!" This level was considered equilibrium because, at any other level of output, demand would be "too low" or "too high." But Keynes focused on the idea of *disequilibrium in terms of full employment*. To the neoclassical cry of "Victory!" he replied, "Equilibrium in *all* markets, my tea biscuit. A national income equilibrium does not necessarily occur at a level of output that fully employs the labor force." Private business investment, dependent as it is on uncertain expectations, cannot be counted on to guarantee full employment. At this point government spending comes in.

In Table 7.3, a constant level of government spending and the given private spending schedules will give an equilibrium income level no higher than $490 billion and employ no more than 75 million workers, leaving 5 million out of a total labor force of 80 million unemployed. [Keynes actually followed classical tradition so that total output increased (with employment), but at a decreasing rate because of diminishing returns. This complication is not necessary to establish the national income equilibrium, and, for simplicity, constant returns are displayed in Table 7.3.] Assume further that the investment multiplier equals 4. Keynes would have argued that somehow we need to generate $20 billion in additional output and income in order to raise output to the $510 billion necessary to employ everyone. With an investment (and other spending) multiplier of 4, we need only generate an extra increment of $5 billion in spending. Only the government, contended Keynes, can be expected to take a hand in stabilization policy and increase its net spending (i.e., minus taxes) by $5 billion. (A spending increase not accompanied by an equal tax increase causes a government deficit.)

The "after" total demand column shows the new, post-government-spending-increase schedule. At the *new* $510 billion national income equilibrium level, the entire labor force of 80 million is employed. However, Keynes did not think that even this "equilibrium" was stable. He emphasized that such things as fluctuations in profit expectations could destroy it. For the most part, Keynes saw the real world oscillating unsteadily between equilibria.

Money and Uncertainty

At this juncture, you might have the impression that Keynes was not interested in the economic role of money and therefore was uninterested in monetary policy. Such a conclusion would be a mistake. Even in Marshall's more refined presentation of the quantity theory of money, money is viewed as influencing only the overall level of prices while individual prices and output remain unscathed. As we have seen, in the quantity theory of money, cash balances are used or demanded for one purpose, to complete business transactions.

In contrast, Keynes thought that holding cash balances for their own sake is perfectly rational. For one thing, people cannot predict the future reliably, and the holding of cash balances is a safeguard against unforeseen contingencies. Moreover, under certain economic conditions cash, though non–interest earning, is a relatively more attractive asset than bonds. In short, Keynes viewed money itself as an asset worth holding or demanding. As he put it, to hold cash "lulls our disquietude." Given this preference for cash, higher savings levels may not push interest rates low enough to stimulate the economy.

The rate of interest required for our parting with cash in exchange for earning assets measures the "degree of our disquietude." Rather than as a neoclassical reward for puritanical abstinence, the interest rate was viewed by Keynes as a reward for illiquidity. That is, the interest rate was seen as a payment for individuals' giving up some of their cash assets. Keynes called the sensitivity in the amount of cash holdings desired or demanded in response to the rate of interest the *liquidity preference.* This responsiveness to interest rates was dependent upon a variety of opinions about what was uncertain. This emphasis upon the individual's desire to hold money as an asset constituted a sharp break from the theory of Marshall.

The essential difference between Keynes and the neoclassicals with respect to money is linked intrinsically to the market for bonds. In an organized market, the price of bonds varies with supply and demand. However, the dollar amount of interest paid for holding a bond is fixed.

For example, take a bond, any bond, that sells for $100 and for which the holder receives $10 in interest income per year. The annual interest rate on such a bond is $10/$100 or 10 percent. If the supply of bonds greatly diminishes and therefore the price of the bond in question rises to $200, the interest rate is now $10/$200, or 5 percent. Of course, if interest rates are continuously high, there is the advantage of earning a lot of interest for the sacrifice of giving up some cash holdings.

Although the bondholder buys the bond because the interest return is greater than the zero percent cash yields, the bond price can fall. If the bond was bought at a relatively high price (low interest rate), a subsequent small drop in its price will cause a loss in the value of the bondholder's capital sufficient to wipe out the small amount of interest income earned from illiquidity. Suddenly cash is a relatively more attractive asset than a bond.

In Keynes's mind, this point is where the trouble really begins. If bond prices are so high that individuals do not *expect* them to go any higher, the preference for liquidity or hoarding cash and keeping it idle may be almost unlimited. If virtually everyone holds onto cash—almost irrespective of what is happening to the overall level of individuals' savings—a limit to the decline in the interest rate has been set. The economy is in what Keynes's friend and colleague D. H. Robertson was to christen a *liquidity trap*. Even though the interest rate may seem exceedingly low, it may not be low enough to incite business firms to borrow money and invest in new plants and equipment. Indeed, if business prospects are sufficiently dismal, a *negative* interest rate may be required to stimulate investment.

Thus far, our discussion has related solely to the *demand* for cash or money to be held. We have not said anything about where the *supply* of cash or money originates. Keynes envisioned money coming into existence along with debts, which are contracts for deferred payment. Stated slightly differently, money comes into being because there is a lag between the production of commodities and the receipt of cash. The time gap is filled by the banking system, which finances goods in the process of being produced. Such money is created "inside" the private enterprise system. This is Adam Smith's idea of circulating capital, except that it is channeled through the modern banking system.

In the modern economy, most money is held in the form of checking deposits, a liquid asset for the individual and a liability for the private bank. The modern banking system functions on the basis of fractional reserves so that a large share of any deposits it holds can be loaned out to business firms. Loans by one bank become new checking deposits for a second bank, which in turn can loan out a large share of these deposits, and so on throughout the banks in the system. In this way, the money supply is multiplied with a mathematical regularity similar to Keynes's multiplier. The money supply grows as long as more loans are being made to businesses for expansion, the financing of inventories, or the financing of production processes.

If it so chooses, the government may also create debt through its deficit spending. Governmental expenditures greater than tax revenue can be financed by selling bonds to the central bank. This exchange increases the money supply. Such money is created "outside" the system. The supply of money therefore depends chiefly on the actions of private commercial banks and the monetary authority in response to the demands of individuals, businesses, and government.

Uncertainty and Money

The combination of the supply of money and the demand for money sets the level of interest rates. Unlike the crude version of the quantity theory of money, money supply changes can influence income and the price level only *indirectly*, through the money rate of interest. Then, if expected business sales revenues are sufficiently high and interest rates sufficiently low, firms will borrow from private banks and engage in active investment activity. If the filament supplier to General Electric sees its sales prospects brightening, it may borrow to buy more modern production equipment to meet its client's needs. Again, however, the interest rate may not fall low enough because of the liquidity desires of the public, or else the great uncertainty regarding investment prospects may be too great to entice business to invest at *any* rate of interest.

Recall Alfred Marshall's favoritism toward both the quantity theory of money and Say's law, and you can see the severe damage done to Marshall's theory by Keynes's view of money. First, the turnover rate of money (V) is no longer a constant. If the demand for money is sensitive to interest rate changes (bond price movements) or to mood shifts regarding economic prospects, V might as well stand for volatility. The rate of turnover of money will vary with the swings in desire for cash (liquidity) on the part of the public. Money balances no longer will stay precisely equal to those funds required for day-to-day household needs and business trade. No longer will the money received from the sales of products be exactly equal to purchases of other commodities. The broken link in Say's chain of events is the desire by individuals and business firms to hold money balances when they think that bond prices can go no higher.

Keynes certainly did not mean to imply that money does not matter. Rather, he attempted to show how money is an active ingredient in producing the levels of income, output, and employment in the economy.

Nonetheless, this message was lost to some of Keynes's interpreters because of the overwhelming need to move the economy out of the Great Depression, whose conditions coupled a liquidity trap with the gloomy business expectations depicted by Keynes. In such a double trap—where interest rates cannot be pushed any lower and business investors are wary—monetary policy is of no avail. The central bank cannot increase the money supply if private bankers are unwilling to make loans. Private bankers will not make loans if they have no takers. The interest rate will not fall to zero because individuals do not expect to see bond prices go any higher (interest rates any lower).

During such a monstrous slump, the only recourse is for the government to spend more than its tax receipts and sell its debt (bonds) to the central bank. The consequent government outlay raises aggregate demand, which leads to a renewed flow of output and increases employment and income, which further has a multiplier effect. The focus of an important group of Keynes's interpreters, the fiscal Keynesians, upon deficit financing is better understood in the dimness of what seemed to be the twilight of capitalism.

THE KEYNESIAN REVOLUTION: WHY?

Thus, whereas the English neoclassical economists assumed that full employment was automatic, Keynes advocated government action to guarantee it. During periods of unemployment, private spending usually would have to be supplemented by public expenditure, a recommendation that flew in the face of the virtue of frugality—or so it seemed. In the *General Theory*, Keynes argued that there are three underlying assumptions of neoclassical economics that would all topple if any one of them fell: (1) supply creates its own demand (Say's law); (2) the real wage is equal to a dollar amount that will cover the discomfort of the extra labor; and (3) there is no such thing as involuntary unemployment in the strict sense.

What was really a reformation of economics was called a revolution because Keynes's approach in many of his works was literary, unlike Marshall's, and because Keynes had earned impeccable credentials as a yeoman neoclassical economist. And of course the severity of the economic conditions that Keynes described was important too. Other economists could not extinguish the fires lit by economic realities when the flames were being fanned at Cambridge, England, itself. The way that this revolution—or reformation—started provides insight into the forces that can assure the success of scientific revolutions.

In attacking Say's law, Keynes was in effect also attacking his former teacher Alfred Marshall, the man who had begged Keynes to shift from mathematics and philosophy into economics, because Marshall was once a staunch defender of the general validity of the law. In finding examples of Marshall's defense of Say, Keynes had to turn to Marshall's early work because, as he grew older, Marshall became more skeptical about the French economist's "law." Keynes admitted that "it would not be easy to quote comparable passages from Marshall's later work," but the clear implication was that it could still be done.

This is the same Keynes who had taught straight Marshallian doctrine with the fifth book of Marshall's *Principles* as the center. Joseph Schumpeter has pictured Keynes, the young teacher, "of spare frame, ascetic countenance, flashing eyes, intent and tremendously serious, vibrating with what seemed ... suppressed impatience, a formidable controversialist whom nobody could overlook, everybody respected, and some liked."[10]

We can imagine the same person, although much older, assailing the neoclassical theory of unemployment, which was tantamount to attacking another of his teachers, Arthur Pigou, who invited the student Keynes to breakfast once a week. Keynes's rationale for attacking the substance of Pigou's *Theory of Unemployment* is that it was the only available detailed account of the classical theory—which is a compliment of sorts, although Keynes's critique is no less devastating for that.

As a result of Keynes's assault on Marshall, Pigou's review of the *General Theory* was harsh and intemperate. Yet Marshall had been generous to the writers who preceded him, and Keynes could have been charitable to Marshall (and Pigou). Why wasn't he? Joan Robinson offers an explanation for Keynes's motives:

> [He] went out of his way to pick out the interpretation of Marshall most adverse to his own views, to pulverize it, mock it and dance upon the mangled remains, just because he thought it a matter of great importance—of real, urgent, political importance—that people should know that he was saying something fresh. If he had been polite and smooth, if he had used proper scholarly caution and academic reserve, his book would have slipped down unnoticed and millions of families rotting in unemployment would be so much the further from relief. He wanted the book to stick in the gizzards of the orthodox, so that they would be forced either to spew it out or chew it properly.[11]

Robinson's view is supported by a passage in Keynes's correspondence with Roy Harrod, another disciple, in which Keynes says he wanted to be "sufficiently strong in [his] criticism to force the classicals to make rejoinders."[12]

Academic history is filled with the stifling of intellectual inquiry because of emotional attachments and loyalties to old teachers and old ideas. Marshall in particular had discouraged dissenting comments from his pupils. Pigou had rushed to attack Keynes because of his loyalty to Marshall, but thirteen years later he had calmed down sufficiently to reread Keynes's book. In what Joan Robinson describes as "a moving and noble scene," the now-retired Pigou returned to Cambridge after Keynes's death to give two lectures to the undergraduates in order to say that he actually agreed with most of the *General Theory* and had given Keynes an unfair review.

Despite all of this infighting and counterattacking, the *General Theory* was not nearly as revolutionary as it appeared. Keynes was blessed with extraordinary luck that he parlayed to his advantage. His academic reputation was superb in that strict scientific sense that had become associated with all Cambridge economists because of Marshall's influence. And the *General Theory* was greatly strengthened by the help of the bright young economists who surrounded Keynes. Some of its pieces were worked out by others, and over time its vitality increasingly depended on amendments related to degrees of imperfect competition. Moreover, Keynes guaranteed a large audience for the book by his vigorous attack on Marshall, Pigou, and the British Treasury's view of economic policy. And, of course, the conditions during the Depression provided an instant display for Keynes's dire conclusions. By now it was clear that the tremendous technical competence of the neoclassical economists at Cambridge had kept the classical tradition alive long after the paradigm had the power to solve a crucial economic problem.

CONCLUSIONS

There is no agreement today among economists about what constitutes the revolutionary elements in Keynes's work. According to a Noble Prize–winning scholar, "The revolution was solely the development of a theory of effective demand: i.e., a theory of the determination of the level of output as a whole."[13] Keynes himself wrote the famous socialist playwright George Bernard Shaw in 1935, "You have to know that I believe myself to be writing a book on economic *theory* [italics added] which will largely revolutionize—not, I suppose at once, but in the course of the next ten years—the way the world thinks about economic problems." There is more truth in the latter argument than in the former. Lord Keynes was never renowned for his modesty. Economist Robert L.

Heilbroner emphasizes the *policy* consequences of the revolution: "There was no automatic safety mechanism after all! . . . A depression . . . might not cure itself at all; the economy could lie prostrate indefinitely, like a ship becalmed."[14]

As we try to sort out these varying interpretations, certain elements begin to dominate. First, the emphasis of classical and neoclassical economics was on prices in specific markets, including interest rates, rather than on the determination of total income and employment. The classicals stressed long-run prices as decided by production costs, whereas the neoclassicals emphasized short-run prices clipped out by the blades of supply and demand. Classical production or supply is decided by the resources of the economy rather than by total demand. As both schools relied on free market outcomes via Say's law, before the *General Theory* there was a macroeconomics theory but no macroeconomic policy.

As we shall see in the next chapter, Keynes's interpreters were divided from the outset, strongly disagreeing on what Keynes really meant. The initially dominant Keynesian view was favored by the conditions of the time. Therefore, the revolutionary antidepression policy carried the day. However, Keynes's failure to replace Marshall's price theory at the *micro*economics level (Keynes thought it unimportant to his main arguments) opened the door to an interpretation that led to a theoretical counterrevolution. Theory is the battleground upon which economists decide the vanquished.

Yet the structure of neoclassical economics had made the nightmare of any long-term inadequacy of total demand an impossibility. Keynes showed that the Depression was a result of just such an inadequacy of total demand by consumers, investors, and the government—which *was* a revolutionary notion. (As we will see in Chapter 15, Michal Kalecki, a Polish Marxist, had derived pretty much the same analytical system as Keynes from Marx's premises. However, Kalecki makes more explicit the roles of imperfect competition and income distribution.)

There is no doubt that Keynes had an enormous impact on antidepression policy in England, and his ideas had a great effect on post–World War II stabilization policies throughout Europe. In terms of human welfare, Keynes's greatest contribution was to suggest persuasively that national governments had an obligation to their constituencies to guarantee sufficient levels of total demand in order to fully employ the nations' labor forces. In Great Britain, this new ethic meant the end of frugality *and* laissez-faire in governmental economic policy. The consequence has been a very low level of British unemployment during most of the post–World War II years. In the United States, this new ethic led to the Employment Act of 1946, which committed the federal government to follow policies that would provide employment opportunities for those able, willing, and seeking work. Keynesian economic policies were vigorously pursued by the Truman Administration, and a modified Keynesian policy paradigm was perhaps most successfully followed by the Kennedy and Johnson Administrations prior to the escalation of the Vietnam War in 1965.[15]

As Kuhn has suggested, even modest changes in paradigms generate such loud objections from the specialists that, when change does occur, it is guaranteed a reception as a "revolution." However, *The General Theory* was written not in order to solve puzzles about hypothetical conditions but out of an urgent concern that governments would fail to end the massive unemployment and deprivation of the 1930s. We have lost or forgotten much of Keynes's message on social injustice—namely, the growth of wealth is not dependent on the abstinence of the rich—and therefore one of the chief justifications for great inequality is removed. Most of the postwar economists focused on the "equilibrium" tendencies that Keynes used for the purposes of argument, thus obscuring his stress on the uncertainty of the future and the fluctuations in national income and employment. If we rush unthinkingly into the arms of equilibria every chance we get, we are simply substituting a mechanical analogy for history. At equilibrium nothing can be done—because we are already there.

We shall visit the various postwar Keynesian models in the next chapter. Then in Chapter 9, we will see Keynes subjected to unimaginable paradigmatic technicalities. Finally, we will witness a counter-counter-revolution (held at the barricades until Chapter 15) led by a surviving force of Keynes's original coterie. Will they restore the humanistic meaning of the Keynesian Revolution? This is the most exciting story because the last chapter has not been written.

8

THE BASTARD
KEYNESIANS
AND THE
MONETARISTS

▼

*"When I use a word," Humpty Dumpty said, in rather a
scornful tone, "it means just what I choose it to mean—
neither more nor less."
"The question is," said Alice, "whether you can make
words mean so many different things."
"The question is," said Humpty Dumpty, "which is to be
master—that's all."*

LEWIS CARROLL, *THROUGH THE LOOKING GLASS*, 1872

Keynes's classic tract left considerable room for interpretation. As John Kenneth Galbraith has suggested, Keynes's work had long been held suspect by his colleagues because of the clarity of his writing. "In *The General Theory* he redeemed his academic reputation. It is a work of profound obscurity, badly written and prematurely published."[1] If forgiveness for Keynes's style is warranted, it is in the knowledge that he was entering territory as yet largely uncharted by economists.

Keynes's vagueness and volatile historical circumstance gave birth to at least three schools of "Keynesians." They are the fiscal Keynesians, the neoclassical Keynesians, and the Keynes's Keynesians, who became the post-Keynesians. The fiscalists and the neoclassicals are the bastard Keynesians—in the judgment of post-Keynesians, that is.[2] The post-Keynesians want to retain Keynes's original stress on uncertainty as well as his social intent. In the rubble of Keynes's own obscurities in the *General Theory*, we can find harbingers of all the Keynesians who would follow.

The first goal of this chapter will be to describe the various interpretations of Keynes by the fiscal Keynesians, the neoclassical Keynesians, and the Keynes's Keynesians, as well as their implications. Second, the monetarists, who fomented a counterrevolution against Keynes *and* the Keynesians, will be examined. The developments by the bastard Keynesians and Milton Friedman, the monetarists' leader, culminated in an "era of positive economics," in which the precision of the economists was compared favorably with that of physicists. Positive economics will be discussed in detail in the next chapter.

THE FISCAL KEYNESIANS

The original fiscal Keynesians were centered at Harvard University. Keynes's most important American recruit in the later 1930s was Alvin H. Hansen, a professor first at the University of Minnesota and later at Harvard, who initially was a critic of the *General Theory*. Hansen was a prestigious figure in American academia, and the economic establishment could ignore neither his tardy endorsement of Keynes nor the views of his students, among whom was Paul Anthony Samuelson. When Samuelson's textbook, *Economics: An Introductory Analysis*, was first published in 1948, it aroused a storm of dissent because it devoted so many pages to Keynesian theory. Ultimately, however, the text was to instruct millions around the world in fiscal and then neoclassical Keynesianism. Most important, Samuelson's text made Keynes an accepted part of American economic thought.[3]

Paul Anthony Samuelson: Enfant Terrible Emeritus

Paul Samuelson went on to become the 1970 Nobel Memorial Laureate of Economic Science and reigns today as one of the most esteemed liberal economists in the United States. Samuelson was born in 1915 in Gary, Indiana, where his father was a druggist. Gary was then a company town created by U.S. Steel. Samuelson claims that he learned at an early age the concept of the Keynesian multiplier, for as the steel mills flourished, his father's drugstore business also grew. When his family moved from Gary to Chicago, Samuelson attended public schools and later the University of Chicago. Even at that time, the economics department of the University of Chicago was the center of laissez-faire philosophy.

When Samuelson won a Social Science Research Council fellowship, he selected Harvard University for his graduate studies. Still remembered at Harvard as a prodigy and an *enfant terrible*, Samuelson frequently became impatient with his professors and corrected them in their own classrooms. As a graduate student, he wrote a paper for Alvin Hansen that was published in 1939 and brought Samuelson worldwide fame.[4] In that article, he demonstrated mathematically that the capitalistic economic system was inherently prone to a business cycle

though it was not wildly unstable; the ups and downs of business activity tended to dampen themselves. Samuelson was educated not only
by the economist Hansen but also by the great mathematical statistician
and physicist E. B. Wilson, whom Samuelson revered.

In 1940, Samuelson, a mere instructor in the economics department
at Harvard, crossed the Charles River to a full professorship at the Massachusetts Institute of Technology, where he has been a popular teacher
ever since. At the end of World War II, Samuelson began teaching the
course in basic economic principles out of which his textbook evolved.
The centerpiece of Samuelson's *Economics* was Keynesian economic
principles, and it was the first textbook to present such material to
beginning students. Samuelson's book popularized the idea, despite its
then radical nature, that unemployment could be ended by governmental spending or tax cuts, the intentional creation of governmental
deficits. This influential work has dominated postwar teaching in economics much as Marshall's text prevailed during the early twentieth
century. Unlike Marshall's book, however, Samuelson's text has undergone drastic revisions from time to time. An economics adviser to President John F. Kennedy during the early 1960s, Samuelson continued for
many years thereafter to voice his opinion on the national economy
through regular contributions to *Newsweek*. Samuelson's column was
considered sufficiently radical during the Nixon Administration to win
him a place on Nixon's enemy list.

The Keynesian Cross

Samuelson's 1948 version of Keynes's thought became associated
with the "Keynesian cross," the seminal concept for postwar fiscal policy. Post-Keynesians appear to believe that it was really a double cross.
The *cross* refers to the intersection of Keynes's aggregate demand function and a 45° line, a relation first expounded in Samuelson's *Economics*.
Samuelson viewed the Keynesian cross as having a significance as great
as the Marshallian cross for demand and supply curves because it provided a guide for fiscal policy.

In Chapter 7 we referred to potential output or supply and total
demand in dollars that are not specified as either real or money dollars.
At that juncture and for those purposes it did not make any difference.
The Keynesian cross (Figure 8.1) is drawn with the assumptions that
production technology and the size of the labor force are givens, and
thus unchanging. The values are expressed in money terms. On the
vertical axis is the total dollar value of expenditures for consumption
and investment goods. On the horizontal axis is the dollar value of
national income or product.

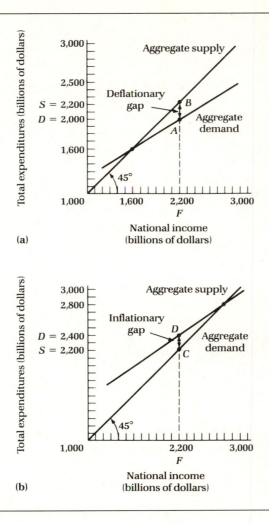

FIGURE 8.1 The Keynesian cross: deflation (a) and inflation (b)

There are two posts to every cross. The aggregate demand post is the total amount of expenditures for consumer and investment goods that will occur at particular levels of national income. For example, a national income level of $2,000 billion will result in a much larger level of spending for goods and services than will an income level of $1,500 billion. As Keynes surmised, total demand rises with national income, but not in a one-to-one or proportional fashion.

Now let us look at the aggregate or total supply post. In the Keynesian cross, which has earned the alternate title of the "45° model," as national income rises, the dollar value of goods and services potentially supplied rises by the same amount. That is, every time incomes received rise by one dollar, the total goods and services that could be made available also rise by a dollar.

Suppose that an economy were operating in such a way that, to employ every worker who wanted a job, the national income level would need to be at $2,200 billion (Figure 8.1(a)). At a constant technology and with the positions and shapes of the curves depicted, the national income cannot reach that high. In national income "equilibrium," the level of expenditures in the economy must be just equal to the dollar value of goods and services supplied. This condition is met at an income level of $1,600 billion. With the national income at $2,200 billion, the dollar value of goods and services supplied (S) would be $200 billion in excess of the total that would be demanded (D) at that national income level. Samuelson referred to this particular condition, the distance AB, as a *deflationary gap*.

True to Keynes's philosophy, the deflationary gap could be eliminated and full employment achieved if government expenditures were sufficient to fill the gap; that is, at a level of $200 billion. This condition would raise total demand to $2,200 billion (point B). The multiplier (of 3) would increase national income from $1,600 to $2,200 billion. Then the equilibrium level of national income *and* full employment would be simultaneously achieved at $2,200 billion.

It is easy to see why this particular diagram became popular after the nation had experienced the Great Depression. The Keynesian cross best depicts the state of affairs existing at that time. However, when national income advances as a result of fiscal policy stimulation, part of the increase could come from rising prices and another part from the increased physical quantity of goods and services. The diagram does not make a distinction between the two sources of increases in income and expenditures. Nevertheless, this limitation did not prevent Samuelson and the fiscal Keynesians from using the same diagram to explain inflationary conditions.

Suppose that the conditions of the economy are those of Figure 8.1(b). Then the level of national income required for full employment ($2,200 billion) is to the left of national income equilibrium, which is now at $2,800 billion. Samuelson referred to the distance CD as an *inflationary gap*. If this does represent the state of affairs, the dollar value of national income must be inflated in national income equilibrium. This is the case because, with no additional workers available to be employed, the goods and services on hand must be rationed by the raising of prices. The total dollar demand of $2,400 billion at $2,200 billion national income is $200 billion *greater* than the total dollar value of supply.

There is a problem with this explanation of inflation. In this simplified construct of Keynes's theory, the only cause of inflation is too much demand relative to supply—too much air pumped into the industrial balloon. This kind of inflation is the variety we have called *demand pull*. It follows that inflation can be cured by shifting the anti-depression policy of Keynes into reverse. If total demand can be lowered (to $2,200 billion in this example) the price level will be deflated to its previous level. The prescribed policies then would be to let some of the air out of the balloon with cutbacks in government spending, increases in tax rates, and upward movements in the interest rate, all of which would diminish spending on investment goods. In the parlance of our times, a "tight federal budget" and "tight money" deflate the economy.

It is important to note a hidden element. The presumption is that the entire distance between the national income exhibiting stable prices ($2,200 billion) and the actual national income ($2,800 billion) is composed entirely of price inflation. Otherwise, the fall in national income from restrictive monetary and fiscal policies would reduce production and diminish the employment associated with that production. The balloon would not descend gently.

THE NEOCLASSICAL KEYNESIANS

The Hicks-Hansen Synthesis

The *General Theory* was barely in the hands of the public when Professor John R. Hicks, an English economist, reinterpreted Keynes's theory in neoclassical terms. The impact of Hicks's message was delayed by the success (or illusion of success) of the American Keynesians in carrying the Keynesian cross to President Franklin Roosevelt during the Great Depression as well as to the millions of students reading Samuelsonian economics.[5] Economic science accorded its highest accolade, the Nobel Prize, to Hicks in 1972.

The neoclassicals generally saw the irreducible whole of an economy in *real* terms, and Hicks followed this time-honored tradition. In the Hicksian version, the values in Figure 8.1 would be adjusted by a price index. Obviously, this alteration causes even more difficulty. It is very difficult to describe the causes of price inflation when no prices are present!

Keynes had left the door to neoclassical reconstruction open by only a crack, but Hicks—at that time only semiconverted from neoclassical apostleship—saw the slender shaft of light. In response to Keynes's criticism of the neoclassical theorists for their imperfect description of how interest rates are established, Hicks retorted that Keynes's theory of the interest rate was itself flawed. In his description of how interest rates are determined by the demand for and supply of money, Keynes neglected to mention that interest rates are also in part influenced by the levels of savings and investment. Keynes had stressed that we need to know the income level in order to know the demand for money, crucial in determining interest rates. However, the national income level also affects the savings and investment levels and, in turn, the interest rate. The "savings" used for investment at higher income levels in part come from bank loans at a rate of interest itself influenced by the demand for such loanable funds. When attempting to put income, investment, and the demand for money all together in explaining interest rates, Keynes was remarkably unclear. Nonetheless, Hicks missed Keynes's main point—namely, that expectations *outweighed* the interest rate in the investment decision and in individuals' preferences for liquidity.

The classical writers had emphasized the duality of the supply of savings (including loanable funds out of income) and the demand for loanable funds in establishing interest rates. Hicks suggested that *all* of these elements are more or less equally important. What was required, therefore, was a merger of the classical and the Keynesian schemes. From the classicals, Hicks adopted the notion that although savings were higher at higher interest rates, savings also differ at various levels of income; from Keynes he borrowed the notion that the desired amount of money will vary also at different levels of national income. These factors, combined with the Keynesian notion of investment plus a given money supply, offer the key to the determination of the interest rate.

It is not necessary to describe all the details of the intricate curves and intersection points that Hicks's theories displayed. Suffice it to say that he demonstrated the possibility of simultaneous equilibrium both in the money market between the demand and supply of money and in the investment and savings equality. Equilibrium was once again possible in all markets! At least, the neoclassicals were quick to seize upon that interpretation.

The American Keynesians might have been spared Hicks's reinterpretation. However, Alvin Hansen, the leading American Keynesian at the time, prominently displayed Hicks's curves in a new book in 1953.[6] Even Hansen's acceptance of the Hicksian interpretation might have been forgotten without the aid of his former student Paul Samuelson. Apparently, universal equilibrium was irresistible to someone trained in mathematics, with an interest in physics, and with an eye for Newtonian metaphor. Samuelson incorporated the Hicksian system into his famous textbook, now in multicolored displays, and in the 1961 edition Samuelson was jubilantly referring to the rapprochement as the "grand neoclassical synthesis!"

Increasingly, the difference between Keynes and the original neo-classicals was described merely as a debate about the exact shape of "various curves." True, there may be extreme regions (extremely low) of income in which interest rates would no longer fall. True, there may be ranges in which interest rate movements will not do much in the way of stimulating investment spending. However, judicious use of fiscal policy will guarantee that the economy would operate well within the range in which general equilibrium in all markets is possible. As to the product markets, Keynes's system had left them in whatever state of competition the reader preferred, and the neoclassicals naturally chose *perfect* competition.

The neoclassicals smelled blood. Keynes's central argument was that no mechanism could achieve simultaneous equilibrium among the product, labor, and money markets—a general equilibrium. On the one hand, Keynes had argued that workers might resist downward wage movements because they are subject to a "money illusion." In a practical sense, powerful trade unions could do just as well as the money illusion in accounting for wage rate rigidity.

But there had to be more to Keynes than this. Even Pigou, the neo-classical, had asserted that unemployment could be attributed to wage rigidities (and thus price stickiness). Rather, Keynes saw cuts in money wages as leading to declines in aggregate demand, which would offset the stimulus to production from a lower wage bill. Unemployment would either increase or, at best, remain the same. Therefore, wage slashes could not be expected to reduce unemployment even if that option were avail-able. Keynes made clear that the possibility of money wage cuts is itself an illusion; in the real world, workers are unwilling to attempt to in-crease employment by lobbying for cuts in their own money wages.

What began as an attempt by Hicks to elucidate Keynes mounted into counterrevolution. An idea from Arthur Pigou, Keynes's old tutor, and Don Patinkin, an economist at the University of Chicago, suggested the same alternative mechanism for restoring equilibrium. Keynes had sealed his own fate with his concession that competitive product mar-kets would not alter his conclusions. When effective demand falls in response to declining incomes (at the lower wage rates), product prices under competitive conditions decline. People hold liquid assets such as cash, which have no corresponding liabilities held by other parties. In Patinkin's view, these holdings of wealth influence the level of con-sumption much in the same way that income influences consumption.[7] When prices fall, the real value of cash is enhanced. Consumption expenditures advance, the demand for labor to produce these commodities moves up, and *voila!* full employment returns. This phenomenon is termed a *real balance effect*.

For the neoclassical faithful, the main impact of Patinkin was to show that general equilibrium is possible—not probable—with flexible prices. They did not wait to consider all of his thoughtful qualifications. (Patinkin has made clear in subsequent writings that he wants to be remembered for his stress upon the difficulties, not the ease, of reaching universal equilibrium.) Like cub reporters with a hot-breaking story, they ran to their telephones and communicated the message to apostles everywhere.

One problem with Patinkin's (and, earlier, Pigou's) view is that the two-thirds of U.S. income generated solely from individuals' own labor is not sufficient to put the working class into a highly liquid or cash position. If the workers are unemployed or receiving very low wages, it may take a colossal price decline before they feel *really* wealthy again. A second, perhaps crucial, factor is the time lag required for all of these adjustments to take place. Patinkin himself thought that the length of time that might be necessary for the adjustment makes laissez-faire an impractical solution. While the unemployment rate hovers around 20 percent, workers will not quietly wait eighteen months for prices to decline 50 percent, consumption to rise 10 percent, and employment to increase after another six months' lag.

To many individuals, the specter of masses of workers streaming into department stores during an economic depression because their cash balances were suddenly "excessive" was black comedy. But it was the possibility that equilibria everywhere could be attained if all the curves were drawn "just right" that accelerated the heartbeat of the neoclassical apostles. The elegance of the argument, not its practicality, carried the day for economic science.

Thirty-seven years after Sir John Hicks had unwittingly set the stage from which a counterrevolution would be launched against Keynes, he recanted.[8] He now admits to a deeper meaning in Keynes's view of money, investment, and uncertainty. But most economists paid scant attention to his reversal. They were too busy at the blackboard drawing the curves they had relied upon for almost four decades.

KEYNES'S KEYNESIANS

The Wages of Inflation

Another model is set forth in Keynes's economic analysis; its neglect by the fiscalists was probably related to the Great Depression. The neoclassical Keynesians also ignored it, due to the influence of Hicks and, later, Patinkin. One part of this model is contained in chapter 21 of the *General Theory*, "The Theory of Prices." The second part of the alternative model dominates chapter 22, "Notes on the Trade Cycle," but indeed is spread throughout the book. In this regard, Keynes put forth a theory of business fluctuations based upon the importance of uncertainty. In chapter 21, Keynes described conditions in which prices could begin to rise prior to full employment, as depicted by what is now called the *Phillips curve*, which is discussed in detail in Chapter 13. Keynes postulated that, for any particular industry, the price level is dependent upon the payments to those who produce goods and services, which therefore enter into the cost of production. If the technique of production is given and the requisite equipment in place, the general price level depends largely upon the wage rate. Prior to the achievement of full employment, increases in total effective demand are divided in their effect between swelling output and pumping up prices.

The foregoing implies that the total supply line is not the simple 45° guide of the fiscal Keynesians. Because wage rates are the major component of the unit cost of production, an increase in the wage rate would entice producers to reduce their output levels. In turn, if they raise prices to reflect the increased cost of production, the price level also will go up. It is possible for production (and therefore employment) to retrench even while prices are rising. Such an outcome was viewed as an anomaly within either the fiscalist or the neoclassicalist vision of Keynes.

Who is going to worry about emphasizing a new theory of inflation during and immediately after the worst depression in modern history? Nonetheless, it is this more complete total demand and total supply picture from Keynes that was seized upon by the self-proclaimed legitimate heirs of Keynes, the post-Keynesians. Their story will be detailed in Chapter 15.

The Case of the Missing Auctioneer

Before we leave the subject of Keynes and his many models, we need to mention a second attempt to resuscitate his theory. Two economists—Robert Clower and the unpronounceable Axel Leijonhufvud—attempted to provide an explanation for the disequilibrium described by Keynes. Their central contention is that the *general* equilibrium described by the neoclassical counterrevolutionaries requires instantaneous price and output adjustments in the economy. This complete clearing of markets, however, requires a "Walrasian auctioneer," a reference to the theory of Léon Walras, who had everyone "groping" for the correct prices. With an auctioneer calling out prices of everything, including prices of labor (wage rates), every actor in the economy would have sufficient information to make precise adjustments, so all market prices would be true equilibrium ones.

In the real world, however, there is no auctioneer. The prices, including the wage rates, that prevail are imperfectly established because individuals do not have complete information. That is, people act on the basis of prices that are "wrong" in the sense that they are not equilibrium prices. According to Leijonhufvud, the responses of individuals are restricted to those their incomes will allow. Thus, markets adjust to any disturbances by production changes and income reactions, and only belatedly by price variations. Keynes's true world is one of imperfect information, and real-world persons will not wait for all these price adjustments to occur. This fact diminishes the practicality of the general equilibrium that the neoclassicals furtively embraced.

The Clower-Leijonhufvud view of Keynes's economics, therefore, is concerned with incomplete information, sluggish price adjustments, production rather than price adjustments, and incomplete trading at prices that are not equilibrium prices because the Walrasian auctioneer is nowhere present. Again, markets are not self-adjusting.

Keynes himself took an even more drastic view of uncertainty than did Clower-Leijonhufvud. For example, Keynes compared the stock market to a "game of Snap, of Old Maid, of musical chairs." In his restatement of the *General Theory* a year after its publication, he emphasized almost to the exclusion of anything else the uncertainty of knowledge and foresight as *the* cause of chronic unemployment of resources.[9] Not only would Keynes then abandon equilibrium in favor of disequilibrium, but he would also question the efficacy of policies based entirely on *dis*equilibrium models. Full employment equilibrium then could only be approximated through governmental intervention. This may well have been one of Keynes's central messages.

Keynes and the Problem of Economic Growth

One of the problems with the *General Theory* was sensed at the outset by some of Keynes's associates at Cambridge. They perceived that much of Keynes's theory is essentially static, or timeless, so that much of the economy can be seen only as a sequence of snapshots rather than as a continuous moving picture. Keynes's theory thus is more applicable to short-run or business cycle behavior than to long-run economic growth behavior. The snapshot shows us the way we are today but little about what our economic conditions might be over several years. Though Keynes himself alluded to economic processes over time and acknowledged the uncertainty with which producers viewed the future (and thus the unpredictability in forecasting their investment in plant and equipment), the American interpreters of Keynes developed a simplified theory that obscured the role of expectations in the economy.

The dynamic version of Keynes, which specifically views his theory over a period of time, originated with Sir Roy Harrod and, on the American side, Evsey Domar, in the 1930s and 1940s. Though not on the grand scale of Malthus, Ricardo, or Marx, the theories were substantial in their content and impact.

Harrod and Domar dramatized a major element that had been glossed over by Keynes. With respect to the investment multiplier, Keynes neglected to mention that continuous investment augments the capacity of firms to produce goods because it adds to the number of machines and plants. In order, therefore, to warrant this extra capacity, it is not enough to experience a one-time increase in investment of a fixed amount. Investment, a reservoir for "supply" in the Harrod-Domar view as well as a source of demand in Keynes's view, must grow at a sufficient rate to generate enough (multiplied) income to buy (given the propensity to consume) enough goods to warrant the available equipment and plant; otherwise, plants and equipment will not be fully utilized. IBM must not only build and equip a new plant, it (or a firm in another industry) must build a second plant lest the demand for office equipment be inadequate to justify the first plant.

As harmless as the Harrod-Domar thesis might sound, it raised a perplexing question about the future of capitalism. The dual role of investment, generating both demand and industrial capacity, implies that an unplanned capitalism is inherently unstable. There is little reason to presume that some natural law will equalize the rate of growth in income (multiplier) with the rate of growth in capacity (a second multiplier) from a given growth of investment. If expanding investment gives rise to a growth rate of demand less than that of capacity, the resultant unwarranted or excess capacity will cause a recession. Even if demand and capacity expand at the same rate, this rate may not be sufficient to employ the entire labor force at its growth rate. Keynes's greatest dread, unemployment, might follow. Conversely, if demand grows faster than capacity and the labor force, inflation is the likely result.

We have seen that a dynamic yet stable economy depended upon an unlikely triple coincidence of economic factors. As a result of the growth rate of investment, demand and the industrial capacity to satisfy it must expand at the same pace. Following upon the heels of the Great Depression, the Harrod-Domar view seemed to throw some light upon the darker side of capitalism, its tendency toward bust and boom. Thus, the Harrod-Domar view is in the tradition of Keynes's disequilibrium economics.

Those who would construct growth theories that depict an economy in which steady and stable growth is possible reject Harrod and Domar's premises. This "dynamic duo" had assumed that, given the state of technology, the ratio of labor to capital is fixed in the production of any particular commodity. If such a relationship is fixed, changes in wage rates or the return to capital would not alter the labor and capital mix.

Two American economists in the mid-1950s were associated with the evocation of a new neoclassical ball game suggesting the opposite. The key new player was Robert Solow, Samuelson's younger colleague at MIT.[10] Solow on first and Samuelson at shortstop abandoned the presumption that production takes place at fixed proportions of capital and labor. In the neoclassical growth form, the interest rate is responsive to changes in the levels of savings. Variations in the interest rate then will lead to adjustments in the capital-to-labor mix. All these adjustments are sufficiently fine that the economy never really diverges from its stable path. Thus, the threat to capitalistic stability is eliminated.

The development of neoclassical growth theory soothed the nerves of Harrod-Domar readers by showing how changes in labor's wage and capital's price would keep the capitalist economy on a path of steady growth. The economy could be compared to a long-distance jogger who never changes pace and yet runs forever. Neoclassical growth theory still dominated macrodynamics in the late 1970s: the theory, like the economy, had the endurance of the long-distance runner. In Chapter 15, however, we will see post-Keynesian growth theory gaining rapidly at the decade's turn.

THE MONETARISTS

The neoclassical counterrevolution set the stage for the ascendancy of the monetarists, whose roots lay in an exclusively American group in the late 1950s. They derive their ideas from the monetary theory of the classical economists, and they believe that a sophisticated version of the quantity theory of money best explains the macroeconomy. As we have seen, this is tantamount to an endorsement of a refined Say's law of markets, especially the interpretation of that law as proof of the self-correcting nature of the market system. Once the money supply is growing at a correct rate, the monetarists rely on Marshallian or Walrasian price theories to explain the substructure of the economy. (The term *monetarist* apparently was coined by economist Karl Brunner in 1968. However, monetarism's close connection with the quantity theory of money gives its most influential branch a long history.)

The Equation of Exchange, Once More

The story of the monetarists really begins with the equation of exchange, an idea that has had at least nine lives. The modern expression of the equation of exchange was formulated by Irving Fisher in the 1920s. Fisher studied mathematics under the eminent J. Willard Gibbs and then taught mathematics at Yale University for three years before switching to the economics department in 1896. Fisher was drawn toward economics by the magnetism of William Graham Sumner. He and Fisher agreed that civilization could be rescued only if the trends of physiological decadence and excessive reproduction of inferior persons could be reversed. Fisher's stand in favor of Prohibition, therefore, was not casual moralizing; he contended, along with Henry Ford, that workers would be more productive if they did not drink alcohol. As far as I know, no one has recorded the views of the capitalist beer producers on this issue. Fisher, who not only taught but also practiced economics, amassed a fortune from the invention of a visible card index system that was marketed in 1910. His company merged to form Remington Rand, Inc., in 1926.

Fisher's *equation of exchange* can be written as

$$\text{(Money Supply)} \cdot \text{(Velocity)} =$$
$$\text{(Average Price)} \cdot \text{(Number of Transactions)}$$

This formula is clearly recognizable as *Say's identity*. (The term *identity* is used instead of *law*, because this equation is true *by definition*, whereas Say's law is an explanation of market adjustments in the individual markets that enabled Fisher to infer usefulness to this equation. See Chapter 4 for a more extended discussion of Say's law.) If the money supply is multiplied by its rate of turnover, the result is the dollar value of expenditures. The average price of commodities multiplied by the number of commodities purchased yields the total dollar value of production. Hence, it follows that total expenditures equal the value of total national product. But this is true *by definition*.

Fisher molded the equation into a theory; he maintained that there is a direct causal relationship between the quantity of money and the general price level. All other elements held the same, the general price level will vary proportionately with the quantity of money: the price level rises when the money supply goes up. Some of the mercantilists would have agreed. The main contribution of Fisher to their formulation is the inclusion of bank deposits or checking accounts as a part of the money supply.

We have to rearrange the terms in the equation of exchange in order to obtain the *quantity theory of money*:

$$\text{(Average Price Level)} = \text{(Velocity / Number of Transactions)} \cdot \text{(Money Supply)}$$

If the rate of turnover of money (V) is a constant, and the quantity of goods and services produced (Q) is also unchanging, the price level will vary with the money stock by a constant (V/Q). Thus, concluded Fisher, we have an exact formula whereby a dollar increase or decrease in the supply of money could raise or lower prices by some constant fraction of a dollar. The turnover of money (V) is unlikely to remain constant, he quickly added.

During the Great Depression, which Fisher survived, a boost in the money supply would, in Fisher's view, have turned the economy around. The latter achievement would depend, however, on a direct connection between the money supply and the quantity of goods and services produced. This factor demands that the number of transactions or total output not be constant and also that the money velocity remain constant.

Fisher's ideas were forged prior to Keynes's *General Theory,* and no thought was given to the possibility that increases in the money supply might not have this salutary effect because the pessimism about future economic conditions combined with low interest rates would motivate both individuals and producers to hoard their money. Therefore, Fisher was undeterred in forming an association to promote the regulation of the money supply and thus stabilize economic activity. This reformist impulse did not prevent Fisher from losing $8–10 million in the stock market crash that closed the 1920s.

The Modern Quantity Theory of Money

Milton Friedman: The darling of the neolibertarians.   The newest interest in the quantity theory of money came with the publication of Milton Friedman's *Studies in the Quantity Theory of Money* in 1956. Friedman, described earlier as a contemporary exponent of Smithian laissez-faire, also is the modern monetarists' guru. The two roles are not unrelated. Friedman emerged by the late 1950s as the leader of the Chicago school of economics.

Friedman's fame is such that he became the thinly disguised hero of a novel, *Murder at the Margin,* authored by two economist-admirers.[11] The novel tells of a short, balding, articulate, brilliant professor of economics (an apt description of Friedman) who solves a murder through the use of Chicago-style economics. As the fictional Professor Spearman puts it: "I am interested only in economic laws, laws that cannot be broken." Though the murder violated human-made law, the murderer slipped up because the economic law remained intact.

Be that as it may, Friedman has been more than simply an unabashed supporter of free markets and the business community. He has
insisted that the free market is the basic assumption behind what he
calls "positive economic analysis," so his faith in the virtues of free
market processes meshes with his description of what constitutes scientific economics. Perceived by the small but influential neolibertarian
movement as a man who favors limited government, Friedman is one
of the leading proponents of that group.

Like Galbraith, Friedman is a political activist. Like Samuelson, he
once wrote a column for *Newsweek*. However, he and Samuelson do not
serve the same political party. Friedman emerged as Senator Barry Gold-
water's major economic adviser in 1964, supporting the presidential
hopeful on such fundamental issues as the volunteer army, law and
order, restricted governmental spending, the unlimited virtues of capitalism, individualism, and antibusing. Friedman returned to politics on
the coattails of Richard Nixon in 1968; thereafter, he advised Ronald
Reagan.

Born in Brooklyn in 1912, Milton Friedman was the son of poor
Jewish immigrants. His father dealt in wholesale dry goods, and his
mother worked as a seamstress in a New York sweatshop under the
type of working conditions in England decried by Lenin. When the
family moved the short distance across the Hudson River to Rahway,
New Jersey, Friedman's mother ran a retail dry-goods store while his
father commuted to his wholesale business. When Milton was fifteen,
his father died, leaving very little money for the education of his son.
Though raised in a religious environment, the boy had lost all interest
in spiritual matters by the age of thirteen.[12]

Despite the jokes correlating Friedman's New Jersey background
with his conclusion that everyone is motivated by pure self-interest, the
sharp contrast between the 100 percent dominance of self-interest and
zero percent altruism is not a mere cocktail-time stereotype. Friedman
thinks highly of neolibertarian philosopher and novelist Ayn Rand, even
though he finds the doctrinaire faith of some of her disciples intolerable.
(Alan Greenspan, the former chairman of the President's Council of
Economic Advisers under President Ford, was one of Rand's "moderate"
disciples.) One foil deserves another, and Ayn Rand has written that
"Capitalism and altruism are incompatible; they are philosophical op-
posites; they cannot co-exist in the same man or in the same society."[13]

Friedman's faith in "value-free" science began early in his academic
training. Perhaps his greatest aptitude was for mathematics and statistics. When he graduated with a double major in mathematics and economics from Rutgers University in 1932, Friedman received offers of
graduate scholarships from Brown University (in mathematics) and the

University of Chicago (in economics). He went to Chicago, but lack of funds forced him to leave after his initial academic year. A job as a waiter was not sufficient to supplement his tuition scholarship.

Friedman moved to Columbia University, which offered him a much larger fellowship. He completed work on his doctorate in 1941, but the acceptance of his dissertation was delayed until 1946 because his evaluators disliked his attack on physicians, whose organization restricts entry into medicine and therefore tampers with the laws of supply and demand. This episode represented for Friedman a personal encounter of the most disturbing kind with not one but two groups of enemies of the free market system.

The linkage of money and the GNP.   Friedman's fame as an economist stems from his development of monetarism. The monetarist doctrine states: (1) changes in the money supply by the central bank and the government constitute the only predictable element that influences the total level of expenditures and industrial activity in the economy. (2) Government intervention of *any* kind—regulation of business, taxation, spending, subsidies—interferes with the proper functioning of the substructure, the free markets. (3) With (1) and (2) operating, the only policy required to guarantee long-run full employment and full-time price stability is to direct the central bank to expand the money supply 4 to 5 percent annually, a rate about equal to the noninflationary growth potential of the economy.

Friedman's version of the monetarist doctrine apparently was originally inspired by the belief that Keynesian economics would cause such a growth in the size of the government that private enterprise capitalism would be destroyed. However, the monetarists' reaction is against the fiscal Keynesian position, a "bastardized" interpretation of Keynes that opens the door to attack by those who fear inflation. In its latter stages, the monetarists' faith has been bolstered by a host of empirical findings showing the money supply and the money value of gross national product to be highly correlated. One-way causation is inferred from this correlation: the monetarists presume that money supply changes move the money value of the GNP, whereas Keynes's *General Theory* pictured the two aggregates interacting. If an arrow indicates the direction of causation, for the monetarists, M→GNP; whereas for Keynes, M⇄GNP. By the late 1950s, monetarism became part of the "counterrevolution" against the Keynesians as Friedman made a wholesale endorsement of a sophisticated version of the old quantity theory of money.

In order to understand Friedman's version, it is instructive to modify slightly Irving Fisher's equation of exchange by putting the equation in terms of income:

$$\text{(Money Supply)} \cdot \text{(Velocity)} = \text{(Price Index)} \cdot \text{(Real National Income)}$$

This equation brings us closer to Alfred Marshall's approach, also called the Cambridge cash-balance approach. To Marshall, money served as an abode—though a temporary one—for purchasing power between the time of purchase and the time of sale. As before (except retaining national income), we have

$$\text{Money Supply} = \text{(1/Velocity)} \cdot \text{(Price Index)} \cdot \text{(Real National Income)}$$

The reciprocal of velocity $(1/V)$ can be seen as the fraction of the *money* value of national income [(PRICE INDEX) · (*REAL* NATIONAL INCOME)] that the public wishes to hold as cash balances. It is analogous to Marshall's k in Chapter 7. In order to derive the quantity theory of money, rearrange the terms so that

$$\text{Price Index} = \text{(Velocity)} \cdot \text{(Money Supply / Real National Income)}$$

As indicated earlier, the rate of turnover of money (V) depends upon the stability of its demand. As long as the demand for money to hold is relatively stable, only changes in the money supply can cause price changes. We must quickly add that this is so only if the money supply has no effect upon real national income. In Friedman's exposition, the demand for money, and therefore V, can vary. However, the *variation* is constant (another definition of money demand "stability"), and thus price changes still can be accurately predicted from money supply movements.[14] The "predictive" equation is derived from the percentage changes in the above price relation:

$$\begin{aligned}
\text{Inflation} = &\ \text{(\% Change, Velocity)} \\
&+ \text{(\% Change, Money Supply)} \\
&- \text{(\% Change, Real National Income)}
\end{aligned}$$

With real output growing at its full capacity rate and with a stable growth in velocity, price inflation is directly related only to the growth rate of the money supply.

Keynes had suggested that the effect of money on real income in the private economy is indirect, through interest rate movements and investment. The monetarists envision any output effect as direct but very temporary. These transitory output perturbations flow from adjustments in the composition of household assets, including goods and services. Thus the sophisticated theory focuses upon the demand for money within a balance sheet or "portfolio" setting. This formulation is somewhat Keynes-like (not Keynesian) in the sense that money is viewed as wealth, that is, as an asset.

These demand formulations relate only to final wealth holders, to whom money is one of several forms in which wealth ends up being held. It does not apply to business enterprises, which view money more as working capital or as an inventory. In the monetarists' view, the demand for money to hold is related to incomes (measured in various ways), expected returns from various wealth forms (stocks, bonds, goods and services, etc.), and the *expected* price level.

You will recall that the strict monetarist's arrow between the money supply and GNP marks a one-way street. Such changes in the money supply must come from "outside" the economic system. If business borrowing and the private banking system alone were to add to the money supply, producers' activities would be changing the money supply rather than the other way around, the money supply increments enlarging producers' sales revenue. Instead, for "outside" money supply increases, Friedman relies upon an imaginary helicopter dropping greenbacks from the sky upon palms-up citizens. This corresponds to a government printing and delivery system. Economists call this an *exogenous* change in the money supply; critics might call it a "helicopout."

After money has fallen on our heads, the new money *supply* level is higher than the cash balances *desired* by the public. Therefore, the public must rearrange their portfolios to maximize their returns; the "unwanted" cash is allocated among more goods, more stocks and bonds, and more savings certificates. The demand for goods and services rises, and prices go up as well. If it is expected that prices will continue to rise (an expectation probably reinforced by the public's belief in the quantity theory of money), the demand for goods and services rises even faster. Thus, you can see how the aerial drop of the money supply causes the money value of GNP also to give flight.

The bulge in demand for real output is a temporary bubble because individuals base fundamental spending plans upon their "permanent income," the income they expect to receive over their entire lifetimes. The long run—in real terms—is for the most part set. For the price level, it is a different matter.

It is rather easy to envision this extreme version of monetarism, however improbable the vehicular delivery system. When money is created solely by the interaction of producers and private bankers, however, the picture loses its focus. The story must run roughly as follows. When private money is used for private purposes, it is always used in "just the right" quantities for "legitimate" purposes. Thus, the privately generated money supply will be just sufficient for production needs and will grow at the same rate as output, and there is no price inflation problem. However, contrary to Friedman's theory, the money supply and GNP would be hopelessly intermixed in terms of the direction of cause and effect.

The price inflation aspects of money supply bursts are emphasized by the monetarists because they see the long-term or natural unemployment rate in the economy as unalterable. This view of a *natural* employment rate again is reminiscent of Adam Smith. The monetarists' stress on the price level leaves the results from Friedman's quantity theory of money about the same as from the crude earlier versions. In the longer view, the monetarists see the classical solution in the real value of production and national income come under the money supply spell. During such a period, the price level is a joint outcome of the monetary forces deciding the money value of GNP and the "real" forces determining real GNP. It is like the classical "veil of money." When the veil is lifted, the real values of goods, wages, and interest rates are the same as they would have been if money had not existed!

What about the short run, that time in which most persons live in a real sense? Unemployment, even for a few weeks, or severe price inflation of a few months can cloud our lives. As we observed above, the delicate portfolio-balancing act of the ultimate wealth holders would cause changes in output at less than full employment (as goods are bought) as well as alterations in prices as the wealth holders bid up prices. The monetarists' theory, which claims to predict the money value of GNP ($P \cdot Q$), unfortunately cannot distinguish between changes in that total attributable to P or Q. It does not separate output from price effects.

If monetarism is an attack on Keynesians, it must also be an assault upon fiscalists, or those who advocate the use of government taxes and spending to stabilize the economy. Such is indeed the case. The quantity theory of money and the monetarists' deep-seated fear of inflation can be tied directly to the fiscal mechanism. It is here that a knowledge of aerobatics is crucial.

The helicopter money drop will not succeed unless the government, the fiscal authority, prints the greenbacks. New money is created by the government by budget deficits, wherein tax revenue falls short of governmental expenditures. Without this element, the helicopter has no cargo. As long as the amount of money created "inside" the private economy by private commercial banks is sufficient to keep the economy growing at its "natural" growth rate, the economy stays on a steady course. It is those damnable helicopters carrying government-created money that cause rising prices. Blame the helicopter, chastise the government, ground the central bank (Federal Reserve), but in the monetarists' vision labor unions and business enterprises are blameless for inflation.

CONCLUSIONS

If Keynes were alive today, it is doubtful that he would be a Keynesian. Certainly he would reject the Keynesians if he still believed in his social vision, which began to take form in the 1920s and which was vindicated (in his mind) during the Great Depression. Keynes's early interpreters made good use of his antidepression nostrums. Nonetheless, the fiscal Keynesians' version of what Keynes meant was not enduring. It did not work well when turned against inflation, and it displayed fatal weaknesses in its premises that the state of competition in product markets was irrelevant and that general equilibrium was as certain as certainty.

The grand neoclassical synthesis says it all. The arrangement was always there; it only needed a fine-tuned economy and somebody to write the lyrics. The United States provided the one, and Sir John Hicks supplied the other. (Hicks was later to recant.) Though the result was a small measure for the neoclassicals, it was turned into a major score for the classical monetarists. The new cadence was in step with Say's law.

Prices were doing all the adjusting required for equilibria everywhere. The business cycle was self-adjusting, and economic growth was steady. Surprisingly, the born-again neoclassicals were not finished with Keynes. They were to redesign all the levers and pulleys of supply and demand in such a precise and positive way that economists would question equilibrium only at the risk of being defrocked. When inflation was too great to be explained by the merely rational economic man, the superrational economic man was invented. Keynes's theories were taken out of historical time because the past, present, and future are indistinguishable in equilibrium. Keynes had the neoclassicals right where they wanted him!

9

THE ERA
OF POSITIVE
ECONOMIC
SCIENCE

▼

*The position we have to combat seems to rest on the
inference, characteristically drawn by the "best minds" of our
race, that since natural objects are not like men [something
we needed the Scientific Revolution to discover], men must be
like natural objects.*[1]

FRANK KNIGHT, *"FREE SOCIETY: ITS BASIC NATURE AND PROBLEM,"*
1948

The main purpose of this chapter is to describe and evaluate the struggle of economists to establish their discipline as a science on an equal footing with the natural sciences. During this period—roughly from the early 1950s through at least the mid-1970s—the lust for "scientific purity" in economics has sometimes known no bounds, including those of common sense. In this struggle, refinements of economic thought were made by attempting to separate "economics-with-value-judgments" from so-called objective economics so that Newtonian scientific simplicity and balance might be achieved. The battle for scientific status has been won, but economics achieved its coveted scientific consensus only by embracing value judgments from another age. Moreover, the economic policy failures of the 1970s and early 1980s greatly tarnished the scientific facade of economics.

In their drive to establish an unassailable paradigm, economists have sometimes mislaid the real world. In order to imitate the characteristics of Newtonian physics, they narrowed the scope of economics and lost or set aside many of the broader humanistic concerns of Smith, Ricardo, Mill, and Keynes. In the meantime, as we shall see in Chapter 16, the United States and perhaps other economies have moved into supra-surplus economies that mock the traditional assumption of scarcity so that new economic systems are in the making. In mathematics and the natural sciences, dramatic advances have brought staggering increases in knowledge; yet in a special sense economic theory hung back during the era of positive economics, despite the unceasing evolution of economic institutions.

The characteristics of positive economics are associated with Paul Samuelson and Milton Friedman, who blaze among the stars of the economics firmament. The plan of this chapter is to define positive economics, to elucidate the roles of Samuelson and Friedman in these developments, and to evaluate positive economics in the light of scientific developments in physics as well as social reality. Let us turn our attention first to the meaning of *positive economics*.

THE CHARACTER OF POSITIVE ECONOMICS

The age of Keynes seemed the ideal time for the refinement of existing theories. The mathematization of economics was incomplete. Economic data mushroomed, and the computer was invented to process it. During the Kennedy Administration, the economic policy of the fiscal Keynesians seemed to have its expected results. It was an era of euphoria, in which Keynesian fiscal and monetary policy replaced Say's law. Keynes himself said, "If our central controls succeed in establishing an aggregate volume of output corresponding to full employment as nearly as is practicable, the classical theory comes into its own again from this point onwards."[2] Economic science had come full circle to orthodoxy once again.

Harmony was again the order of the day. A sense of system, of security, and of control was abroad, and confidence ran high that vast economic difficulties would indeed be manageable. The sense of potential mastery over such problems was nurtured by the widespread feeling that if a problem is quantifiable—if it can be expressed in mathematical language and symbols—then it is ultimately solvable, just as any properly articulated mathematical formula is reducible to one indisputable solution. With the advent of the computer and sophisticated techniques of data collection and utilization, economic science came to rely more and more heavily on the tools of mathematics. Economic theory building today is more intricate, elaborate, precise, and consistent than ever before, and much of this improvement has come to it from the sphere of mathematics, the handmaiden of the natural sciences.

There can be little doubt that the union of mathematics and economics is here to stay. To some extent, however, the influence of mathematics has transformed the discipline of economics, teaching it to mimic its positive nature. A *positive* fact is one that can be known to be true apart from all value judgments, cultural biases, or erosions of time.

A positive truth does not change; $2 + 2 = 4$, and no opinion, world view, fashion, or necessity can alter that equation. (The requirements of finding such an unalterable "truth" are themselves illustrated by our equation. The algebra defines terms in such a way that $2 + 2 = 4$ *by definition*. Hence, the truth is a truism.) Positive facts are not necessarily mathematical facts, but mathematics certainly embodies the pinnacle of positive science—no subjectivity can encroach, no compromise need be forged, a truth once demonstrated can be expected to remain immutable and perfect.

Such positive knowledge is an enviable thing, and no science can be faulted for desiring that degree of certitude. Positive science is an ordered science; order facilitates understanding, and understanding yields solutions. Yet pitfalls await the discipline that, imitating mathematics, single-mindedly sets its sights on positive truth. Not only must that science reject as irrelevant all cultural, ethical, and nonuniversal aspects of a given problem, it must also risk claiming as positive certain truths that are in fact tinged with some era's beliefs, colored or shaped by some culture's values and presuppositions. It also risks confusing the truth with mere arguments in a circle, such as 4 must equal $2 + 2$ because $2 + 2$ equals 4.

If economics was to become like natural science, then, something had to be done about the kind of lapses in scientific attitude that even such great thinkers as Smith and Marshall were guilty of because of their compassion. Too visible for the sake of unimpeded natural law, the hearts of Smith and Marshall sometimes appeared upon their sleeves. Economists, uncomfortable with such preoccupations, moved to eliminate the "political" in political economy and to make their discipline truly "positive." Values and ethics had to be kept strictly apart from economic analysis; in particular, the subspecialty called "welfare economics" was believed to be compromised and burdened by personal values and moral concerns.

POSITIVE ECONOMICS AND VALUES

Positivism was first identified with the French philosopher Auguste Comte (1798–1857). Comte saw the human mind developing in three stages—theological, metaphysical, and positive; the third stage could explain social life through laws of social behavior akin to the laws of natural science. The aim of such science also is closely connected with the tradition of scientific investigation that originated with Francis Bacon and Descartes and reached its highest form with Newton. Within this tradition, the goal of science is to discover the "connections," to use Newton's term, among phenomena and express them as general laws of nature. Science was not to ask the *why* of things but was merely to organize and systematize knowledge of *how* phenomena occur, in order to predict and control nature.[3]

What does the term *positive science* mean to economists? John Neville Keynes—John Maynard's father—made a series of helpful distinctions in his work, *The Scope and Method of Political Economy*. First, he characterized *positive science* as a body of systematized knowledge about what *is*. Then he described a *normative science* as a body of systematized knowledge about what *ought to be*. And last, he described an *art* as a system of rules for the attainment of a given end. "Ought-to-be's" necessarily reflect the values and therefore the personal judgments of an individual even when those values are influenced by that person's culture. Collective ought-to-be's are culturally determined *ethical* judgments that serve as guides for social and personal behavior. The biblical injunction against murder is one example of an ethic.

In addition to the influence of society upon an economist's personal values, the norms of the scientific group to which the economist belongs constrain and help mold the individual's activity. As Thomas Kuhn has reminded us, the scientific community has agreed on the desirability of certain analytical treatments and scientific instruments. The choice of methods used, such as the calculus, is related to what "type" of science is preferred. The criteria for accepting or rejecting theories, professional objectives, theoretical assumptions, and the like, are all based upon the values of economists themselves. Therefore, normative judgments that include the observer's personal values, cultural ethics, and policy views appear in economics. Speaking of normative— that is, nonpositive—economics, one economist has said that "judgments in normative economics are concerned with what is best for society, what ought to be, from the observer's point of view." Cultural influences on the methods of positive economics are inescapable. Indeed, "it is precisely differing cultural influences acting upon methodological differences which caused the theoretical systems of classicals, neoclassicals and Keynes to differ."[4]

Is it possible to draw a clear-cut line between positive and normative economics? When we try to do so, we find that the problem of definition becomes formidable. On the one hand, we find scientists whose personal beliefs are identical to those prescribed by society's ethics and whose assumptions—like those of Ptolemy, who kept the earth and human beings at the center of the universe—are strongly biased in favor of the status quo, even though the issue of conscious bias may never occur to them or anyone else. Yet Ptolemy was a genius and an immensely important figure in the history of science. Ptolemy's assumptions were not viewed as being derived from his personal values; was he therefore a positive scientist because his premises were rooted in society's acceptance of hierarchical organization? On the other hand, we find scientists who, although they have no quarrel with society as such, find themselves in deep conflict because their own science contradicts prevailing values. The Italian philosopher Giordano Bruno (1548?–1600), for example, was burnt at the stake for defending the astronomical theories of Copernicus, who placed the sun at the center of the universe. It seems hardly fair to describe Bruno's position as normative and therefore unscientific.

The crux of the issue is that, if positive economics proscribes certain areas of inquiry, it may be erecting a barrier for economists as scientists that economists as citizens may feel impelled to leap over. To put it another way, if a positive economist's *assumptions* about reality conflict with reality, the result may be the advocacy of policies that are desirable to few people, including the economist. In this light, we can understand how it is that Paul Samuelson sometimes advocates policies that are unrelated to the economics of his *Foundations.* One way or another, positive economics has relied upon the stereotype of the economic man and of the conditions of perfect competition that do not accurately portray human or economic reality.

This conflict between theory and reality can be illustrated by a passage from Lewis Carroll's masterful fantasy *Through the Looking-Glass* (1872). The child Alice and the quarrelsome twins Tweedledum and Tweedledee are walking in the woods and find the Red King asleep under a tree. Imagine the king as an economist dreaming a positive economic theory and Alice as a variable about to be discarded either to simplify the mathematics of the theory or to eliminate a value judgment. Alice, who is an extremely sensible child, remarks that no one can guess what the king is dreaming about.

> "Why, about you!" Tweedledee exclaimed, clapping his hands triumphantly. "And if he left off dreaming about you, where do you suppose you'd be?"
>
> "Where I am now, of course," said Alice.
>
> "Not you!" Tweedledee retorted contemptuously. "You'd be nowhere. Why, you're only a sort of thing in his dream!"
>
> "If that there King was to wake," added Tweedledum, "you'd go out—bang!—just like a candle!"
>
> "I shouldn't!" Alice exclaimed indignantly. "Besides, if I'm only a sort of thing in his dream, what are you, I should like to know?"[5]

Alice's responses are those of a normative person. Tweedledum and Tweedledee, for our purposes, can be interpreted as dedicated apostles of positive economics. They continue to goad Alice, and she finally cries, "I *am* real." "You won't make yourself a bit realler by crying," Tweedledee remarked; "there's nothing to cry about." Be that as it may, a person's feelings—and the person too—cannot be ignored in the making of economics. Thus, the distinction between what is and what should be is not as clear as one might suppose or hope. When economists say, "There are 6 million workers unemployed," that is a positive statement. But when an economist personally asserts, "In the United States the number unemployed should never exceed 4 million," that is a normative statement. The neoclassical economists spun a dream theory of employment, but when they awoke, they found real Alices crying about the poverty and unemployment all around them. Their perspective as scientific economists presumably prevented them from making useful corrective policy recommendations, but Keynes in England and many economists in the United States argued for expansionist governmental policies by going outside the paradigm *as citizens*.

With this introduction to positive science, we are ready to turn to the views of Paul Samuelson and Milton Friedman.

TWO POSITIVE ECONOMISTS

As we have seen, advocates of positive economics claim to be concerned only with what is, not with what ought to be, although Paul Samuelson and Milton Friedman disagree on what that claim entails. Samuelson prefers to construct syllogistic theories (see Chapter 2) in which nothing in the conclusion has not already appeared in the premise. For example, Samuelson's famous theory of revealed preference, which says (in mathematical form) that a higher price for one commodity than for a second reveals the true relative preference of the individual who purchases the higher-priced product, is a restatement of the marginalist's utility theory. Jevons (see Chapter 6) suggests that consumers will prefer the product that gives them the greater satisfaction. Samuelson states that, other things held constant, the consumer is willing to pay a higher price for products that are more gratifying.

Friedman, on the other hand, sees a theory as a framework for prediction. His test is not whether a theory is "right" or "wrong" but whether it "works." If a theory suggests that the gross national product, or GNP (the total money value of goods and services produced by the economy during a given period), grows when the money supply expands, and events appear to confirm this theory, then that fact is sufficient to show that the theory works. Friedman does not ask if the assumptions of the theory are correct.[6]

Samuelson's methods make him a narrow Aristotelian; Friedman is a narrow empiricist (see Chapter 2)—although my judgment about their narrowness would undoubtedly cause them to think me less than broadminded. At any rate, let us pursue their methods in greater detail. We may discover that their assumptions that they are positive scientists are themselves illusory.

Samuelson's Foundations

Among economists, Samuelson's stature is derived from his *Foundations of Economic Analysis* (1947), a book that is largely responsible for making mathematical economics part of the mainstream of economics scholarship. The *Foundations* is not a work of remarkable originality. Primarily, it amplifies what Léon Walras had begun in the 1870s: the working out of the mathematical mechanics of neoclassical economics. Samuelson brings the mathematics up to date and in line with advancements in thermodynamics, which, as we saw in Chapter 5, are largely derived from Newtonian physics. The *Foundations* expresses the economic essentials of Smith, Walras, and Marshall in pristine, resolute, unassailable mathematical form. Indeed, the domination of the era of positive economics by Smith's refined paradigm and Newtonian laws of motion was mostly a result of the magnetic attraction of *Foundations* to modern economists.

Methodologically, Marshall and Samuelson are linked across the years by the influence of the physicist James Clerk Maxwell, a contemporary of Marshall and an important influence on him. (Early in their university careers, both Marshall and Samuelson entertained the idea of becoming physicists.) In the speech he gave after receiving the Nobel Prize in economics in 1970, Samuelson said that he discovered one of his important ideas on consumer demand theory while reading Maxwell's "charming" *Introduction to Thermodynamics*. In the same address, one that contains more references to physics than to economics, Samuelson laid another economic discovery at the feet of his physics teacher at Harvard, Edwin Bidwell Wilson, one of J. Willard Gibbs's few students. Using an insight apparently provided by Wilson's lectures on thermodynamics, Samuelson was able to assert that raising any input's prices while holding all remaining input prices constant will reduce the amount demanded of that input. (Even the most simple propositions often require intricate mathematics to establish *formal* proofs.)

Though it is doubtful Samuelson intended it, his choice of mathematics and style eventually led to the replacement of Marshallian economics with a "choice-theoretic economics." Samuelson demonstrated that each and every part of microeconomics could be reduced to a simple maximization problem. An equation would be written that told what was to maximized—profits, wages, or prices—or minimized, depending upon whether the maximizing agent was a buyer or a seller. The choices required to maximize (minimize) were always subject to constraints. Indeed, choice was viewed as the singular economic act of selecting among *restricted* alternatives. The choices of the family shopper are restricted by the household budget. The choices of the business decision maker are restricted by competition from other firms, the cost of productive resources, and technology. However, since all the restrictions are "givens," they quickly became unimportant in economic theory. In other words, maximization was always possible (mathematically), given the constraints required to solve the optimization problem.

Perfect competition emerged from choice-theoretics as the "ideal." We have Samuelson's word for it from his preface: "At least from the time of the physiocrats and Adam Smith, there has never been absent from the main body of economic literature the feeling that in some sense perfect competition represented an optimal situation." Even Milton Friedman has called Smith's idea no more than "the maximization-of-returns hypothesis." Once out of the bag, choice-theoretic economics was difficult to control; it dominated the articles published during the 1970s in the "leading" U.S. economics journal, *The American Economic Review.* At Chicago the maximization scheme was extended to the most personal decisions, those involving marriage, extramarital affairs, homosexuality, divorce, and choice of religion. The gain from marriage by men or women was shown to depend upon their income, human capital (lifetime income), and relative wage rate differences. The number of extramarital affairs was found to depend upon optimal allocation of leisure hours between spouse and paramour. The individual's religious commitment was also "explained" by the household's optimal allocation of time. Homosexuality was simply another optimal choice: presumably the author had overlooked the advantages of autoerotism over both homosexuality and heterosexuality since self-stimulation requires fewer inputs and less time.[7]

Milton Friedman and Economic Prediction

We must now take a closer look at Milton Friedman's conception of positive economics, which, he says, "is, or can be, an 'objective' science, in precisely the same sense as any of the physical sciences." Friedman suggests that the main task of positive economics is to provide a system of generalizations that can be used to make "correct" predictions

about the consequences of any change in circumstances. Positive economics must be judged "by the precision, scope, and conformity with
experience of the predictions it yields."[8]

According to Friedman, policy recommendations are dependent
on predictions about their consequences. For example, if an economist
recommends a slower money supply growth rate to slow inflation, that
is equivalent to a prediction that business investments or consumer
spending, or both, will respond by also slowing down. Ideally, such a
prediction accurately forecasts the future implications of such a policy.
Friedman also argues that a "correct" governmental economic policy
should be derived from positive economics because that approach yields
conclusions that are, and *deserve to be*, widely accepted. At this early
stage in his description of positive economics, Friedman is making a
value judgment by suggesting that the conclusions of positive economics *ought* to be widely accepted. Yet such an acceptance is justifiable
only by tautology: "what is" is what economists describe, and "what is"
is what economists should study. We can better understand this view
of positive economics if we look at a couple of examples of prediction
and what they assume.

In the Newtonian world, the average person identifies cause and
effect according to the proximity of events. Suppose that you are playing
golf on a cloudy day that threatens rain and your partner has just sunk
a long putt on the eighteenth hole. She shakes her putter in the air in
exultation at having sunk the putt, a bolt of lightning strikes the eighteenth green, and she falls to the ground. Like a good Newtonian, you
assume that the bolt of lightning caused your golfing partner to fall. She
may have stumbled or had a heart attack, of course, but whatever actually happened, you don't assume that she *caused* the bolt of lightning
to strike. There is no confusion about cause and effect, although in this
particular instance there may be error.

In economics, Friedman and his fellow monetarists see a close association between changes in the nation's money supply and changes
in the gross national product. In Friedman's words:

> There is perhaps no empirical relation in economics that has been
> observed to recur so uniformly under so wide a variety of
> circumstances as the relation between substantial changes . . . in
> the stock of money and in prices; the one is invariably linked with
> the other and in the same direction [emphasis added]; this
> uniformity is, I suspect, of the same order as many of the
> uniformities that form the basis of the physical sciences.[9]

But the elements of the money supply and the GNP do not have
the cause-and-effect simplicity of the lightning bolt and the golfer. As

suggested in Chapter 8, the two economic variables move together in such a way that one can never be quite certain whether the money supply causes the GNP to change or whether the GNP causes money supply to change. Friedman argues that for the purposes of scientific prediction we do not need to know which is cause and which is effect. Unlike Samuelson, Friedman sees no need to formulate assumptions that are "realistic" in the sense that they explain real-world phenomena; what is important is that the assumptions provide accurate predictions. The golfer causing the lightning would be no problem for Friedman. The money supply ↔ GNP prediction leads to a policy conclusion: there ought to be a legislative rule prescribing the annual rate of growth of the money supply, thereby removing it from the uncertain, unskilled human hands of central bankers. Of course, the policy suggestion *now* presumes one-way causation, money supply → GNP. (Friedman's test of intelligence for monetary authorities is their acceptance of his ideas.)[10]

Friedman contends that he arrives at his policy position by observing that policymakers are wrong at least half the time. But unless Friedman is practicing some as yet unknown science of absolute certainty, how can we be sure that his criteria for testing the abilities of policymakers are correct? If humans are basically irrational or incompetent or both, then by what guides can we evaluate Friedman's ideas? The only guide can be natural law, handed down by the court of Mother Nature.

Many economists disagree with each other on fundamentals because some are monetarists (and also laissez-faire advocates in the Smithian tradition) and others are not, but surely this difference would be nonexistent if economics were a science in the same sense that physics is. (Disagreements among physicists occur, but usually over the interpretation and acceptability of evidence rather than procedure.) The issue I am raising has nothing to do with scholarly integrity on one side of the fence or the other. I am simply pointing out that the influence of cultural ethics and personal values is to a considerable degree deterministic and outside a person's ability to control, even as a scientist.

We have been unable to pinpoint positive economics, perhaps because it has several definitions. It certainly means something different to Friedman than it does to Samuelson.[11] Samuelson's *Foundations* and his neoclassical synthesis in *Economics* point toward laissez-faire, a value usually in conflict with the recommendations voiced frequently in columns he once wrote for *Newsweek*. Friedman's technical writings and policy advisories do not exhibit this inconsistency. Nevertheless, I suggest as a working definition that positive economics is an ideal that takes society's ethics for granted, avoids personal value judgments except when they coincide with society's, and minimizes its reliance on statements that it regards as empirically unverifiable. This definition leaves many unanswered questions. For example, is positive economics an ethically desirable system? Does it subvert its own ethically neutral aims in its guise as the scientific incarnation of the status quo? How do we—or can we—explain the fact that scientific paradigms in part determine society's values? Had Copernicus, Bruno, Kepler, and Galileo been strictly positive scientists and avowed the ethics of their societies, Albert Einstein (1879–1955) might have had to work out his theories on the assumption that the earth is the center of the universe.

TWENTIETH-CENTURY PHYSICS:
A RETURN TO COPERNICAN UNCERTAINTY

Certainty may pervade the metaphors that the social sciences borrow from the natural sciences, but no such certainty exists today in the natural sciences themselves. Nineteenth-century physics was confident about absolutes. But modern physics has become increasingly conditional and has even brought value judgments back into the natural sciences.[12] If economics wants to be a metaphor of modern physics, it must at least try to catch up with a paper published by Albert Einstein in 1905.

Crisis and the Theories of Relativity

The crisis of belief in Newtonian science came about when scientists began to examine Newton's concept of the infinite emptiness of space, the "lumniferous ether," a void occupied only by light through which the earth and all the other planets move. The Newtonian paradigm implied that the speed of objects through this ether was limitless, but scientists working in the late nineteenth century failed to verify the existence of the ether because they could not detect *any* apparent motion of the earth through space.[13]

Albert Einstein, at the age of twenty-six, resolved the crisis by accepting the observations about the motion of the earth and then pressing on to the conclusion that the velocity of light is the highest velocity possible anywhere in the universe and is a constant. A number of important consequences followed, all of them generally lumped together as the "theory of relativity," although "theories," plural, would be more correct. These theories called into question basic notions about the nature of time and space. Einstein's views upset widely held notions about the nature of time and space that depended on traditional mechanistic explanations.

Relativity is a difficult concept to grasp, but that should be no deterrent to students of economics. If the speed of moving bodies cannot be measured with respect to the medium through which they travel, then there is no absolute fixed point from which to describe the nature of motion. Space is meaningless without bodies, and their positions and motions can be described only with reference to one another, that is, relatively. Because time duration is measured by the distance traveled by light at a constant speed between one body and another, time itself can no longer be regarded as an absolute, as Newton had presumed.[14]

Everyday observations of rhythmical events, such as sunrise or sunset or the ticking of a clock, lead most people to the commonsense—but wrong—idea that everyone experiences the same interval between the same two events. Einstein corrected this error by defining time and distance as mutually dependent. The simultaneity of events depends on the viewer's frame of reference because the measure of time varies with the location of the person doing the measuring. The notion of cause and effect no longer has its ordinary meaning. Einsteinian simultaneity requires a sameness of time that depends on a sameness of place.

Einstein is further suggesting that there is no *scientific* basis on which it is possible to select one temporal-spatial reference point over another.[15] This theory does not challenge the fundamental lawfulness of physical phenomena. (Einstein defended the principle of causation and order to his dying day, contending that "God does not play dice with the universe.") But it does radically shift the position of the scientific observer to a far less absolutist position.

Quantum Uncertainty

The German physicist Max Planck (1858–1947), who reportedly chose to study physics rather than economics because the former was less difficult, launched what was to become the new quantum physics in 1900. He suggested that energy forms such as light can be exchanged only in discrete packages, or *quanta*. The *quantum theory* appeared to discredit the commonly held belief that light traveled in waves and further undermined the imposing structure of Newtonian mechanics.

What is the major change in physical theory that occurs when the new quantum theories are combined with relativity? If a particle can be spread out as a wave, then it cannot be said to be a particle at any specific place with certainty. The doubt thus created was epitomized by the German physicist Werner Heisenberg's uncertainty principle, which showed that the absolute certainty of knowing both the position and the speed of a particle is impossible. Heisenberg (1901–1976) demonstrated that the more accurately the position of a particle is measured, the less precision can be obtained in the determination of its speed. The interdependence between the measure and what is measured is illustrated by the case of the nurse who asked a patient how well he was doing. The patient replied, "Quite well," and died from the effort required to respond.

The implication is that, if nature is only probable and not "definite," then can nature be causal? Can we always be sure that a cause precedes its effect? If particles are spread out over a wavelength and traveling at high speeds, the application of Einstein's relativity theory tells us that an effect from a particular frame of reference may precede its cause. The principle of determinism—in the sense that phenomena are governed by the predictable causality of a natural order—has been seriously challenged.

With randomness as the essential component of nature, prediction in physics is now more limited than it was.[16] Objectivity in measurement is a problem for everyone, including the physicist. Scientific definitions have now acquired an even more elusive nature. Even mathematical "truths" have come to be viewed as metaphysical, that is, beyond the comprehension of the ordinary senses. By the "time" we locate a particle's position, its speed has changed.

Physical scientists now recognize that science is an element in the interplay between nature and human beings, not merely a neutral description of nature. Science can describe nature only in terms of the questions that scientists pose. Even in physics, the scientific world view has ceased to be entirely positive. Paradoxically, people have acquired a newly defined importance in this state of uncertainty, a significance in the Cosmos they have not enjoyed since the Middle Ages. When it is recognized that designating an appropriate reference point for scientific observation is in a certain sense artificial (i.e., the designation is "constructed" and does not arise from nature), then the human being is once again at the center of things.

These new ideas have had a wide cultural impact. Historians, among others, began to question the idea of historical "laws" and became skeptical that history was a science. The famous American historian Charles A. Beard (1874–1948), in a 1933 address to the American Historical Association, called for a rejection of the analogies with the science of Newton and Darwin that had held historical assumptions in bondage.

Throughout this intellectual turmoil—for that is precisely what it has been—many economists have remained placidly content with the world view prescribed by nineteenth-century physics. As we will see in

Chapters 10–12, however, some "nonorthodox" economists never accepted the idea of a positive economics in the first place.

To the extent that positive economics sees the world from one particular viewing platform—that of Smithian self-interest and Darwinian survival—economic science can be misleading. Nonetheless, economists are presently divided between extending the Darwinian base to all aspects of life or building an economics upon different behavioral premises. Modern science looks at nature from the point of view of a person, not of a god. If people are once again the focal point, could science be expected to serve more humane goals? Would economics become less positive and pursue more normative concerns for the future of humans? Or would economic theory continue to see people as if they were particles at a time when physicists no longer see particles exclusively as particles?

THE ECONOMISTS' CRITIQUE OF POSITIVE ECONOMICS

Far from the Apostles' Crowd

Orthodox economics had become immune to criticism from Marxists and other radicals because the positive economists had been inoculated with mathematics and simulated Newtonian mechanics. They had soared out of effective critical reach. However, by the early 1970s, attacks came from within. Among the occupants of the economics Trojan horse were the presidents of the leading economic associations around the world.

Exclusive reliance on mathematical model building, oversimplification of reality, overspecialization, and misleading econometric tests drew the criticism of at least seven such distinguished academics, including Kenneth Boulding and John Kenneth Galbraith. The 1974 president of the Eastern Economic Association, Barbara R. Bergmann, criticized the "static equilibrium models based on simplistic assumptions about behavior."[17] Similarly, E. H. Phelps Brown, the 1971 president of the (English) Royal Economic Society, bemoaned the ease with which equations had been set up on oversimplified assumptions about human behavior.[18]

In 1967, one of the most distinguished practitioners of econometrics, Wassily Leontief, another mathematical economist and 1973 Nobel Prize winner, concluded that, in emphasizing abstraction for its own sake, economics had taken a wrong turn. The 1968 president of the Econometric Society, F. H. Hahn, has expressed similar misgivings. When it comes time to interpret the conclusions of the mathematical model, said Leontief, the assumptions on which the model has been based are too easily forgotten. "But," he argues, "it is precisely the empirical validity of these *assumptions* on which the usefulness of the entire exercise depends."[19] In questioning the validity of assumptions, of course, Leontief clashes with Friedman's positive science ideal.

James H. Blackman, the 1970 president of the Southern Economic Association and currently the National Science Foundation's section head for economics and geography,[20] has expressed his anxiety about the effect of economics on society. He sees economists building irrelevant models, which can all too often achieve questionable lives of their own if their formal mathematical properties are sufficiently attractive.[21] Instead, he feels, scientific research should address itself to significant social issues whose solution will benefit the "public good."

As we have seen, economics has been infused with cultural and value-laden presuppositions from the beginning. We have discovered deep and lasting historical-ideological bonds among business leaders, natural scientists, the Church, and orthodox economics. This is hardly surprising. Early on, I commented on the fact that every economic system requires rules, an ideology to justify such standards, and a conscience that motivates the individual to follow them. Our precontemporary economic writers, including Adam Smith, Alfred Marshall, and John Maynard Keynes, recognized the role of morals in society. Usually economists wrote separate treatises on these issues, a practice discontinued in the present age. While emphasizing self-interest in purely economic dealings, Adam Smith recognized that *social life* is impossible unless the hard pursuit of selfish material gain is softened by respect and compassion for others.

The late Joan Robinson even cautioned that "to eliminate value judgments from the subject matter of social science is to eliminate the subject itself, for since it concerns human behavior it must be concerned with the value judgments that people make."[22] The neoclassical apostles did not eliminate the moral problem by invoking unenlightened self-interest as an economic virtue; they merely gave this value the respectability of "scientific" endorsement. Moreover, by conceiving of all individuals as automatons, they projected a mythical societal harmony that had thus far been realized only for the physical universe by Newton's model.

Robinson further suggested that the function of social science is different from that of the natural sciences; Robinson saw the task of social science as an attempt "to raise self-consciousness to the second degree, to find out the causes, the mode of functioning and the consequences of the adoption of ideologies, so as to submit them to rational criticism."[23] She saw the economists' doctrine of laissez-faire as an ideology that served only special interests. Values also change. Indeed, it is hardly conceivable that an economics paradigm derived from the institutions, values, and ideology of one century or culture could be applicable across all space and time.

The energies of the positive economists were directed at purging economics of real time and, thus, history. To the extent that they succeeded, they also failed. An economics theory free-floating in a timeless void cannot witness very many real-world social events. As we approach the twenty-first century, the Western industrialized nations and Japan appear to be entering a new era in which positive economics may have even less to contribute to the resolutions of concrete and urgent economic quandaries. We will have more to say about this in Chapter 16.

ECONOMIC IDEALIZATIONS: PERFECT COMPETITION AND ECONOMIC MAN

To understand why economists often appear unmoved by the shifting values of their culture, we should look at another device that contemporary economic theory has borrowed from the physical sciences—the use of idealizations. An *idealization* is an imaginary (or ideal) state that assumes, for purposes of observation, what is physically impossible given our present knowledge of nature. For example, physicists can hypothesize frictionless surfaces and perfect vacuums, but these are conditions that are inferred from observation and do not occur in nature. In physics, the argument that these idealizations are explanations of things that exist would be absurd. Idealizations may be useful abstractions, but they cannot explain the real world.[24]

In positive economics, there was often a confusion between an idealization and reality. However, the stereotypes or idealizations of "perfect competition" and "economic man," the underlying behavioral assumptions of positive economics, are not real forms of human behavior. Let us look more closely at these economic idealizations.

Perfect competition is supposed to protect individualism and maximize choices through diversity. However, private enterprise expands its market and economizes production by designing products that, to some degree, appeal to everyone. The high-budget blockbuster movie, such as *Raiders of the Lost Ark* and *Out of Africa*, is an example: these movies seem to appeal to everyone to some degree, but products made with *everyone* in mind are not designed for *anyone* in particular. The "surprise" successes of lower-budget off-beat movies, such as the first *Rocky* and *The River*, attest that in the postindustrial society the thirst for entertainment cannot be quenched by a common brew. Meaningful choice requires a diversity of products, and to the extent that business enterprise fails to provide that diversity, advertising must create apparent differences. But differentiation of products in turn limits competition. The competition that expands markets, differentiates products, and lowers prices below the average costs of competitors is a major cause of monopoly. Indeed, the whole concept of free choice under perfect competition does not even fit with the idea of the bloodless economic man, who, in effect, is *not* free to choose but merely satisfies materialistic urges in a pursuit of self-serving hedonism.

The idea that the economic man is always consciously and consistently motivated by pure materialistic self-interest assumes that the producer and consumer take nothing else into consideration while engaging in economic activity. The chemical manufacturer, then, would see no damage in dumping wastes into the Mississippi River. On the contrary, however, no one is free from social needs and obligations. There are few, if any, individuals whose relations with others involve *only* the exchange of goods. All of us live within a broader social environment than that described by the economic man prototype. There may be some people whose sole aim in life, like the economic man's, is material accumulation. In reality, such people are few in number.

As Marc J. Roberts of Harvard suggests, "Current economic theory is built upon a classic, simplified view of man and his psychology. Economic man, if anything, is even more simplified than Platonic man."[25] In order to render the participants perfectly predictable in its imitation of Newtonian science, economics has adopted a naive eighteenth-century view of human behavior. Such a view completely discounts aesthetic life, intellectual life, and a multiplicity of other human goals.

Nonetheless, the reigning idea of positive price theory and choice-theoretic economics is that the economic man under perfect competition enjoys an optimal situation. According to Friedman, "Existing relative price theory, . . . which reached almost its present form in Marshall's *Principles of Economics*, seems . . . both extremely fruitful and deserving of much confidence for the kind of economic system that characterizes Western nations."[26] If the truth be known, Marshallian economics has since collapsed into its choice-theoretic caricature. Thus, the economic man lives on even though he is an ideal type of primitive morality that confuses naivete with objectivity.

Just as Newton based his system on the assumption that time and space are absolute, so economists posited a system with economic man at its center and positive economics as its fixed orbit. But positive economics has not worked out as the economists had hoped. It is fraught with the malady of circular reasoning. And economics is full of value judgments. There has been a confusion between imaginary economic models and economic reality. Furthermore, in theory there is sometimes a jumble between ideal paradigm types and extreme paradigm types. A focus on beginnings and endings that often ignores the process in between may be permissible in the physical sciences, but it is inadmissible in the social sciences.

We have seen the astronomical viewing platform shift from the earth (Ptolemy) to the sun (Copernicus and Newton) to either (Einstein). These different points of view were possible even though the major relations of the physical universe remained the same! And the universe remained intact while Einstein switched the point of view from flatland to curvedland. The main distinction in point of view between Newton's and Einstein's theories of gravitation lies in the *conventions* each accepts about the geometry of space and time. The two points of view have almost identical consequences for ordinary earth time. The Einsteinian convention (curved space) gives a more accurate and consistent view of the nature of the universe, especially its size, but even it is an idealization—although a highly complex one—and increasingly phenomena are being observed that seem to violate its conventions. Caricature capitalism is also an idealization, relying on abstractions and conventions, such as looking at economic activity through the eyes of economic man. Does this point of view give us an accurate and consistent view of the economic universe? Positive economics is a scientific ideal derived from the natural sciences in which the personal values of economists are minimized while the ethics of society are accepted as given, but positive economics captured and froze the Newtonian world view. We must have doubts that an economics paradigm inspired by Newtonian physics, conceived during the Industrial Revolution, hardened into mechanics during the period of the Robber Barons, and polished to a high glitter by the positive economists is crucial any longer in describing reality.

WHERE PHYSICS AND ECONOMICS PART

From Idealization to Ideology

The use of idealizations in the social sciences results in some special problems that do not come up in the physical sciences. Physical scientists can depend on the fact that the physical universe remains fairly stable, that Euclidean geometry and Newtonian physics, given the right circumstances, are still useful. Neither social behavior nor human idealizations can alter the speed of light. But social scientists are faced with changeability. The people of a society can alter their economic goals, even switch to a new form of economic organization, as in the changes that have brought us from feudalism through capitalism. Moreover, choice-theoretic price theory can lead to the official belief that perfect competition exists, or even to the belief that it *should* exist. The idealization thus becomes ideology.[27]

Policymakers especially tend to confuse economic idealizations with reality. National pricing policy, for example, usually assumes perfect competition. Much of the reluctance to use any form of "incomes" policy by U.S. administrations has resulted from the idea of many firms competing vigorously, an ideal approached only in the past (if at all) and now residing in the imaginations of the managers of firms that restrain competition behind the paradigm's back. Obviously, economists cannot help formulate rational policies to stabilize price levels with a paradigm that assumes perfect competition, especially when policymakers fail to distinguish the assumption from the reality.

If we can believe physicists, the concept of Euclidean or flatland space in most solar-system problems is still the most convenient to work with. Whether or not Euclidean geometry actually describes "what is" is not important to the solution of a given problem. But in Friedman's positive economics, we encounter an altogether different situation. By definition, positive science claims to describe "what is." However, the idea that we can use the most convenient assumptions in economics contradicts the claim that economic science describes "what is." If the resulting theoretical conclusions only serve to restate whatever assumptions Samuelson selects, we necessarily know no more than we knew when the assumptions were formulated. And, in this case, necessity is the mother of convention.

When economists build idealizations and say that those idealizations describe "what is" in the economy, the implication is that either the nation must do the impossible by living up to the idealizations, or else it must remain as the economists believe it to be. There is a strong societal predilection for subscribing to policies that do not alter existing conditions. There are pitfalls to treating the status-quo economy as if it were perfectly competitive. It is naturally presumed that all social problems have already been solved by the "magic" of the market. On the other hand, when policies drawn from the economic model do vary from society's shifting ethics, economists may insist that positive science must prevail, and positive science itself becomes an ethical system. If society fails to conform to the model, there is something wrong with society.

The Implications of Newtonian Equilibrium
for Economics

As we have seen, mathematics has been essential to the development of natural science. Newton had to invent calculus in order to formulate his theories.[28] In its attempt to gain stature as a science, economics, too, adopted mathematics. While applying the calculus, economists often assume that the processes generating these values are continuous and smooth so that equilibrium is inescapable. Because they often assume that social change matches the continuity of conventional, mechanical clock time, they expect people and their economic activity to march in step with such time.

This notion of continuous and smooth social change—like the movement of planets through a frictionless space—best fits neoclassical economics. But despite these assumptions, social change does not have the continuity characteristic of clock time. Even the value judgments of society can be free of the time dimension. As we have seen in earlier chapters, the economic value judgments of Adam Smith's earliest eighteenth-century apostles are identical to those of Ayn Rand's twentieth-century novels. People are capable of believing in any values at any time. Yet the neoclassical economist insists that social change occurs along a straight line with a smooth regularity, matching the ticks of a mechanical clock. Neoclassicists discount the impact of influential individuals, inventions, and technological change because such persons and events are unique and therefore veer off the time line. They concern themselves with patterns of change and development independent of such forces. In reality, however, it is just such forces, not time itself, that can account for social change. When new seed varieties introduced in Asia in the 1960s resulted in a doubling or tripling of the rice crop, the time interval for the decade was no different from that of any other decade. The length of the second, minute, and year remained invariable. It was technology, not time, that made the difference. But the calculus has not generally captured that kind of reality.[29]

Though Alfred Marshall used mathematics in his footnotes, he could never have intended that much of his original thought would be lost among the symbols of today's textbooks. Few students today will learn, for example, that Marshall had much to say about the process of technological change. In fact, Marshall characterized capitalism as progressive and dynamic. He postulated stationary states of equilibrium only to examine static forces in isolation, "holding constant" for a moment the role of dynamic change. The same Marshall who popularized the technique of *ceteris paribus* also said that "as it is, the economic conditions of the country are [not stationary but] constantly changing." He also warned that "all suggestions as to economic rest . . . are merely provisional, used only to illustrate particular steps in the argument, and to be thrown aside when that is done."[30] And in the first pages of the preface to *Principles of Economics*, he expressed a progressive view of Darwinian social evolution when he said that "the main concern of economists is thus with human beings who are impelled for good and evil, to change and progress." Regrettably, as a result of mathematical oversimplification into choice-theoretics by his apostles, Marshall's neoclassical paradigm is now only a shadow of its original substance.

A similar fate awaited the economics of John Maynard Keynes. Although Keynes was a gifted mathematician, he had misgivings about the use of mathematics in economics, fearing that it might distract economists from the complexities of the real world. It was with good reason that Keynes felt such reservations; the calculus of equilibrium stripped Keynes's short-run economic theory of its original psychological and historical meanings. Bare of Keynes's qualifications concerning uncertainty, instability of employment and income, and disequilibrium, it appears that this vulgarized Keynes has nothing new to say. As Joan Robinson says, "For a world that is in equilibrium there is no difference between the future and the past, there is no history and there is no need for Keynes."[31]

Criticism of mathematical economics, however, must be kept in perspective. Mathematical economic models are extremely useful in developing analytical techniques that may help formulate theories to explain the behavior of society and its economic structure. However, the economist who is able to generate broad, creative generalizations about economic ills and social problems that cannot be easily expressed in precise notation should not be condemned as an imperfect Cassandra, whereas the mathematical model builder receives accolades for being precise yet incorrect. If nothing else, the more eclectic economist can remind the model builders of the true implications of their hypothetical structures. It is as much the economist's job to identify possible social problems and raise survival questions as it is to build analytical tools for precisely evaluating solutions to hypothetical questions.

As the Newtonian clock ticks on with the precision afforded by its calculus, economic time bombs are exploding at irregular intervals in our society. They will be ignored by a paradigm preoccupied with the caricature of economic man, the idealization of perfect competition, and the hidden value judgments of positive science. Whether the idealization of perfect competition is confused with reality or with an extreme that becomes a goal in itself, the result is generally the same. The status quo is either defended with an unrealistic rhetoric or else preserved with do-nothing policies. An insistence upon pristine simplicity in economic theory will hide from our view life-enhancing and even life-saving variables. The resulting restriction of economic science to games and puzzle solving will fail to provide guidance for solving the real crises of contemporary and future economic life.

10

PARADIGM
LOST:
KARL MARX

▼

*'What the hell are you getting so upset about? I thought you
didn't believe in God."
"I don't," she sobbed. . . . "But the God I don't believe in is
a good God, a just God, a merciful God. He's not the mean and
stupid God you make Him out to be."*

JOSEPH HELLER, *CATCH-22*, 1955

Every science has its radical fringe, made up of those who are
discontented with the methods or conclusions of normal science and
want to change them. In the natural sciences, intensified activity on the
fringe has resulted in what philosopher Karl Popper calls "extraordinary
research," such as Einstein's in 1905, and revolution, such as the theory
of relativity. As we saw in Chapter 9, the crisis that led to the overthrow
of absolute time and space and the establishment of the relativity principle was the failure to prove the existence of the ether. The proliferation
of competing theories, the willingness to try anything, the overt expression of discontent, the debate over fundamentals—all these are symp-
toms of a transition from normal to extraordinary research.[1]

Economics has experienced at least four crises since Adam Smith
(the Robber Barons, the Great Depression, the inflation-unemployment
trade-off, and simultaneous inflation and unemployment) but only one
revolution: the Keynesian *policy* revolution discussed in Chapters 7 and
8 succeeded in replacing some of the members of the orthodoxy, the
"ins" with the "outs." We have seen that John Stuart Mill refined Ricardo's economic theory and also contributed some original ideas on economic reform. Mill helped to gain recognition for the trade union
movement in England and bring about tax reforms, but he had almost
no impact on the classical paradigm itself. Similarly, Mill's contemporary
Karl Marx (1818–1883) constructed an alternative but more complete

paradigm based on classical foundations. Marx was to become an enormously influential thinker, but Marxian economics has been repulsed
in England and the United States, in part by neoclassical economists
who claim Marx's theories are alien to scientific discourse.

In this and the following two chapters, I want to explain, in turn,
the ideas of Marx, the American institutionalists, and the new radicals
of the Left, in an attempt to understand why all "radical" assaults on
the neoclassical stronghold from left of center have thus far failed and
to evaluate the chances for the emergence of a new paradigm.

Economic thought is *radical* (1) when it opposes the prevailing orthodoxy of economics, and (2) when its basic theoretical concepts are
not approved of by more than a majority of academic economists. (This
definition may not satisfy the new radicals discussed in Chapters 12
and 14 because it is insufficiently political—my radicals can disagree
with economists' methods without advocating a whole new society.)
According to this definition, at least four famous contemporary economists are radical: the late Joan Robinson of Cambridge, John Kenneth
Galbraith of Harvard (emeritus), Wassily Leontief, and Kenneth Boulding
of the University of Colorado. Robinson's ideas have been discussed in
earlier chapters, and we will discuss Leontief (again), Galbraith, and
Boulding later. For now, we must turn to the most renowned radical of
all, Karl Marx.[2]

NOTES ON MARX

Marx was born in Trier, in the German Rhineland of the Prussian kingdom, where his father was a lawyer. Marx belonged to what he would
have called the *bourgeoisie*, that is, the capitalistic middle class as opposed to factory workers or laborers, who have no capital. Marx's family
were Jews who converted to Christianity when Marx was a small child.
He grew up in a more or less liberal, intellectual atmosphere and intended to have an academic career, but political events made that impossible. He turned to journalism and became increasingly outspoken
in his denunciation of political oppression in Europe, for which he was
eventually exiled to England.

Marx's name is always associated with Friedrich Engels (1820–1895),
a fellow German who was his lifelong associate and collaborator. Books
have been written on the question of how much or how little Engels
contributed to the doctrines of "Marxism," but that need not concern
us. It is generally agreed that Engels is the better writer while Marx is
the more profound thinker, a meticulous, somewhat ponderous scholar
with little gift for rhetoric. Their backgrounds and personalities contrast
as well. Engels was an upper-middle-class capitalist, rather handsome

and athletic—the figure of one who liked to fence and to ride with the hounds—with a taste for wine and working-class women. Marx was gruff and slovenly, and his domestic life was a scene of almost continuous squalor, disorder, and poverty. Engels supported the Marx household from 1848 on.

Yet the two shared one thing: a detestation of the status quo and a fierce conviction that it must change. Engels's father sent Friedrich to Manchester, England, to work in the family textile business. Engels was already a convert to socialist theory, and what he saw in Manchester confirmed his beliefs. He wrote what is still perhaps the strongest indictment of industrial slums ever written: *The Condition of the Working Class in England in 1844*, a staggering description of hopeless filth, despair, and brutality. Marx read Engels's work and admired it, and their collaboration began, most famously and notoriously with the *Communist Manifesto* of 1848.

Because of this work, Marx is better known as an advocate of revolution than as a classical economist. In 1848, after all, it took a great deal of courage to say, "Let the ruling classes tremble at a Communist revolution. The proletarians have nothing to lose but their chains. They have a world to win." Prussia still believed in the divine right of kings, had no parliament, no freedom of speech, no right of assembly, no liberty of the press, and no trial by jury. Such despotism dominated most of the seats of power in Europe.

The *Manifesto* was part of the European revolutionary fervor of 1848. The work has had a long history, but its first and most immediate impact was on Marx's own fortunes: he was exiled from Belgium, where he was then living. On the next day, a long-awaited revolution broke out in Paris. The new French government invited Marx to come to Paris. Other cities—Naples, Milan, Rome, Venice, Berlin, Vienna, Budapest—revolted. Europe was, for the moment, ablaze. But by June 1848, the Paris revolt had nearly spent itself as the National Guard gained the upper hand. The cold water of the old order was thrown on the revolutionary fires throughout Europe, and they were put out. In July 1849, Marx was expelled from the Rhineland by the Prussian government. He then went to London, where he lived until his death in 1883.

THE INFLUENCE OF HEGEL

Before we consider Marx's place in the history of economic thought, we must first examine the beliefs of a philosopher who influenced Marx enormously: Georg Wilhelm Friedrich Hegel (1770–1831). Hegel's philosophy is extremely complex and at times almost absurdly difficult to understand, but its relevance to Marxism is at least fairly clear.

Hegel saw the course of history as the gradual realization by human beings of their own nature, which is identical with Mind, Spirit, or God, terms that Hegel used interchangeably. Spirit is a self-generated creative energy whose ultimate goal is to become fully conscious of itself in its role as Spirit. Contrary to Descartes and the rationalists, matter and Mind are not ultimately separable, and all things, all earthly events, are the result of the growth of the Spirit toward the ideal. We can follow the course of this growth to some extent by using a method of reasoning Hegel called the *dialectic*: One fact (thesis) works against another fact (antithesis) to produce a wholly new fact (synthesis). For example, feudalism (thesis) encountered a new force, the market economy (antithesis), and the result of this encounter was an entirely new system, capitalism (synthesis). Properly understood, history is a dialectical progression of the self-realization of the Spirit, the goal of which is perfect freedom.

However, humanity's progress toward self-realization is not smooth. The Spirit can become alienated from itself, which is for both Hegel and Marx one of the worst conditions of mankind. Alienation occurs when the Spirit confronts a world that appears real (i.e., aligned with the Spirit) but is in fact of human origin. People are alienated when they become hostile toward a former attachment to an object, a behavior, or an idea for reasons that do not emanate from a higher spiritual source but from human imperfection. Alienation is resolved when the Spirit recognizes the object of the hostility for what it is—human error—and unites itself once again with itself. (An obvious difficulty with Hegel is that he thinks on a level of abstraction that is beyond most people's grasp.) We noted in earlier chapters that the God accepted by Newton, Darwin, and the neoclassical economists was easily reconciled with the world of capitalism. But for Hegel, because humanity itself is Spirit or God in the process of self-realization, contentment with capitalism is illusory, and alienation is the eventual result. For Hegel, humanity is the manifestation in history of the self-alienated God.

In a sense, Marx turned Hegel inside out. Instead of seeing Man (used here to mean all people) as self-alienated God, Marx saw organized religion ("God") as a reflection of self-alienated Man. The human species creates God in its own image through organized religion. Thus, Man projects an idealized image of himself as "God" and worships this imaginary spirit. Marx believes that, as soon as Man discovers the error of artificial image worship, he becomes estranged from himself, and his own ungodly earthly creation becomes hateful to him.

Man overcomes alienation by taking God back into himself and recognizing that human individuals are the proper objects of love, care, and worship. As Robert C. Tucker explains Marx's view, "Religion is a phenomenon of human self-estrangement."[3] Whereas Hegel saw history as a series of detours on the road to the self-realization of God in Man, Marx, although he also had a progressive idea of history, saw God as yet another roadblock.

The basis of Marx's world view is broadly humanistic, affirming the worth and dignity of Man and Man's capacity for self-realization through reason. There is little evidence that Marx himself had any great affection for the masses of people that his system is supposed to free. He was dedicated to Man's thinking powers, and his own reasoning told him (as did Hegel's) that the forces of history and self-realization were inescapable.

Marx is an evolutionary determinist: he believed that the course of history is predetermined not by "God" but by the evolutions of entire social systems from lower (slavish) to higher (democratic and socialistic) forms. The Social Darwinists described the struggle of *individuals* in accordance with certain natural laws. Marx focused on a *class* struggle, in which one group overthrows another and thereby decides which economic system is to prevail. The landlords win under feudalism, the merchants under mercantilism, the capitalists under capitalism, and everybody under communism or socialism (these last two terms are used by Marx and Engels more or less interchangeably). Institutions such as organized religion slow the progress from lower to higher social orders, and the historical process could be speeded up by destroying them. Marx believed he was putting Man and his "true" rationality back at the center of the universe. As we have seen, however, those who subscribed to the Newtonian world view had a different idea about what rational people ought to think: man had to be satisfied to subordinate himself to natural laws.

MARXIAN ECONOMIC ALIENATION

Marx saw in the relationship of human beings to their government a process of alienation similar to the one he perceived in religion. Just as humans extend the idealized attributes of the species to a supreme deity, so they project social power into a separate sphere, the state. And the state dominates them. Political alienation, however, is an institutional reality, and its resolution requires an actual social revolution—that is, a collective act in which the citizens repossess the social power that they gave to the state.[4]

The state is intertwined with and at times indistinguishable from the economic life of society, which is yet another sphere of human self-alienation. Here we can clearly see the influence of Hegel: the Spirit, or God, did not create a materialistic world; the production of material goods was an entirely human undertaking, and hence, alienating. Marx believed that the workers and the owners of the means of production would be prevented from developing their full human potential because of their slavish devotion to producing more and more goods for the marketplace. Eventually the "animal spirits" that drove people to the accumulation of profit would be exposed as simply a lower stage in human intellectual development.

Because of the intensity of alienation, of obscured self-realization, that the capitalist stage of economic development caused, Marx saw some advantages to feudalism compared to capitalism as a form of economic organization: its social relations were paternalistic and personal, and work was not solely a means for making and accumulating money. Under pure feudalism, labor was used only to produce consumer goods that were more or less consumed at the site of production rather than sold in exchange for money. To Marx, when the middle-income group, or bourgeoisie, got the upper hand, it

> put an end to all feudal patriarchal, idyllic relations. It has
> pitilessly torn asunder the motley feudal ties that bound man to
> his "natural superiors," and has left remaining no other access
> between man and man than naked self-interest, than callous "cash
> payment." It has drowned the most heavenly ecstasies of religious
> fervor, of chivalrous enthusiasm, of philistine sentimentalism, in
> the icy water of egotistical calculation. It has resolved personal
> worth into exchange value. . . .[5]

Because of its influence on Marx, Hegel's world view could be called the grandfather of positive economics. Like Hegel's, Marx's system is a dynamic one, concerned with human development throughout history, and his premises are positive in the scientific sense discussed in Chapter 9. His detailed description of capitalism remains a definitive contemporary statement of what that economic system was like in the nineteenth century, and he assumed that his predictions were accurate about what capitalism would become. Capitalism was an extension of Man's self-interest that he would grow to dislike, a stage of history's progress that was alien to Man and not the culmination of civilization. When Man's final "scientific" state is achieved, it will be what it *should* be, and, moreover, objectively determined. That is, Man's self-realization that *what is* (capitalism) is unendurable *should* and *will* alter the historical process. The process of the self-development of the human species will, according to Marx, culminate in communism.

Thus, because they are concerned both with what is and what should be, Marx's arguments provide a valuable description of the interconnection between positive and normative economics.[6] When

Man arrives at a true perception of reality, he will at the same time experience the economic system that is best for him. (This view is contrary to neoclassical economics, in which the market system is first, last, and always.) Marx's conclusions are value related, but they emerge from a positive science. Whether there are holes in Marx's scientific method or omitted variables is another question. The system *is* scientific.

THE MARXIAN ECONOMICS PARADIGM

Let us look at some of the details of Marx's economics paradigm and how it differs from the models provided by Adam Smith and David Ricardo. Whereas Smith was euphoric about emerging capitalism as a permanent state for society and Ricardo feared that this industrial utopia would not be realized because of the political strength of the landowners, Marx saw capitalism as only a necessary evil. It was only one stage in the development of economic organization and would be superseded by a higher state where private property would not exist.

He agreed with Smith and Ricardo, however, and with most other classical economists, that the value of a commodity was decided in some way by the amount of labor time necessary for its production, but he leaned more heavily than the others on a labor theory of value. Though different labor has different abilities, Marx saw skilled labor as a multiple of unskilled labor. A *given* quantity of skilled labor was considered equal to a *greater* quantity of unskilled labor so that, for example, one skilled worker might equal two unskilled workers. In addition, there is a difference between the labor value of a commodity and its exchange value. The *labor value* of any commodity is equal to the amount of average labor time required for its production. The capital owner who must pay a price for labor treats labor power as just another commodity. The factory owner pays a subsistence wage just sufficient to keep the worker alive, at work, and able to reproduce the commodity. This wage rate, therefore, is the equivalent of one day's labor power as a commodity. (Marx defines subsistence wage in various ways, sometimes culturally.) But the factory owner also uses machinery to produce goods, and therefore current labor will produce a certain amount of commodity value above its own value. In other words, the *exchange value* of the commodity produced is greater than its labor value. Marx called the difference between the two *surplus value,* which is the source of the owner's profits. In today's economic terms, this surplus would be the *sum* of rent, interest, and profit.

Absolute and Relative Surplus Value

Most of the other classical economists had argued that the capitalist had accumulated the financial capital to buy the plant and its machinery through hard work and thrift. Marx discounts the implied high ethical nature of the factory owner and suggests that labor value itself produced the machinery and the plant for further production. He makes a distinction between *absolute* surplus value and *relative* surplus value. The former is the excess of new value created in a day over the value of the labor power bought by the manufacturer. It can be increased only by lengthening the working day. The latter arises out of improvements in technology that reduce the labor time required to produce a product. This applied technology mechanizes the production process and leads to a higher degree of specialization for the worker.

In fact, relative surplus value is the motive force behind the accumulation of capital. It is something for the manufacturer to admire and claim. The more capital and the higher the state of technology in the plant, the greater the output from a labor force of a given size and, presumably, the greater the profits. The greed for riches and the desperate pursuit of exchange value is boundless. A market system in conjunction with the relative surplus value that exchange makes possible provides the motivation for the acquisition of more and more capital. Marx believed that the original, postfeudal justification for private property came from this desire to accumulate capital and increase profits through market exchange.

He also rejected the notion that capital as property was ever accumulated through the frugality of the few. In a rather colorful passage, Marx noted:

> *This primitive accumulation plays in Political Economy about the same part as original sin in theology. Adam bit the apple, and thereupon sin fell on the human race. Its origin is supposed to be explained when it is told as an anecdote of the past. In times long gone by there were two sorts of people; one, the diligent, intelligent, and above all, frugal elite; the other, lazy rascals, spending their substance, and more, in riotous living. . . . Thus as it came to pass the former sort accumulated wealth, and the latter sort had nothing to sell except their own skins. And from this original sin dates the poverty of the great majority that, despite all its labour, has up to now nothing to sell but itself, and the wealth of a few that increases constantly although they have long ceased to work. Such insipid childishness is every day preached to us in the defense of property.*[7]

Monopoly Capital

Adam Smith believed that the division of labor would increase productivity and that competition would prevent monopoly. Marx, on the other hand, believed that changing technology as well as increasing competition would create larger and larger firms owned by fewer and fewer entrepreneurs. A higher state of technology will require a larger plant and more capital for production. Competition means that the strong dominate both the weak and the less strong, which ultimately leads to monopolistic practices. Monopoly capital means that enormous wealth will concentrate in the hands of a few, who can price commodities without much regard for the consumer. Thus, laborers as consumers fail to gain the benefits that Smith alleged they would. (I should note that the seeds of concentration—the thirst for profit, higher levels of technology, larger plants—in Marxian capitalism are no different from those rediscovered by Piero Sraffa in the 1920s. See Chapter 6.)

Worker Alienation

In his famous *doctrine of increasing misery*, Marx argues that the conditions of labor will worsen relative to the improved conditions of the factory owners. When the relative lot of the workers becomes intolerable, they will rise up against the factory owners in a social and economic revolution. Behind this doctrine is one of Marx's most influential ideas: the theory of estranged labor, which shows how capitalism alienates and dehumanizes workers. The theory rests on what Marx believed to be two incontrovertible facts about industry. First, laborers did not control the nature of the product, it controlled them and dictated their labor. Second, factory workers did not work for themselves but for their employer. Any benefits accrued to the workers would have to be consumed in their leisure hours; there was no direct satisfaction from work. These conditions are the cause of general worker alienation—worker is estranged from worker and all workers are estranged from the employer.

Alienation develops in the market exchange system for a number of reasons. For example, the very *type* of labor required by capitalism is dehumanizing. Marx and Smith both believed that a finer and finer division of labor would increase productivity, and also that, as Smith put it, "the man whose whole life is spent in performing a few simple operations . . . generally becomes as stupid and ignorant as it is possible for a human creature to become." Marx concluded that, insofar as the division of labor leads to specialization, it is evil, not only because of the monotony of the work but because specialization divorces workers from their fellow workers and from the end product of their efforts.

Even if the accumulation of capital results in wage increases for the workers, the increases will not be in proportion to the advances in profits for the capitalist. Absolute levels of income may be enough to stave off hunger, but as relative income differentials continue to widen, social discontent will begin to stir. Work does not enhance the satisfaction of a need, it is merely a means of satisfying needs external to it. In Marx's words:

> What, then, constitutes the alienation of labour? First, the fact that labour is external to the worker, i.e., it does not belong to its essential being; that in his work, he does not affirm himself but denies himself, does not develop freely his physical and mental energy but mortifies his body and ruins his mind. The worker therefore only feels himself outside his work, and in his work feels outside himself. He is at home when he is not working, and when he is working he is not at home.[8]

The worker was no longer the craftsman creating; he had become the servant of a new industrial process. Even the word *master*, which had meant the master of a craft, came to mean a person who was the master of other people.

We can now trace the course of the polarization between workers and employers. With the increased concentration of industry and augmented monopolistic power, more and more of the wealth of the nation sifted through the hands of workers and piled up at the feet of the factory owners. What Adam Smith merely detested—monopoly—Marx saw as inevitable. Added to this potential for conflict is the workers' attitude toward work itself. As the workers begin to see their labor as drudgery, they lose the recreation or delight that might come from a change of activity. We must remember that during the Industrial Revolution an enormous change in labor took place from direct hand production—like that still done today in certain arts and crafts—to a production system requiring routine operations with the help of tools and machinery. (One reason that unions were unattractive to workers in the early days of the trade union movement in England is that many workers felt that membership in a union meant acquiescence in a hated factory system.)

The Business Cycle

Marx developed the first sophisticated model of the business cycle, the ups and downs of industrial output and employment levels, sometimes crudely called boom and bust. Prosperity is followed by a depression, which is followed by prosperity, and so on. Marx believed that the successive depressions would become increasingly severe, so much so that the workers would finally revolt. His argument is technical, and we can do no more than summarize it here.

The Industrial Revolution began with a surplus of agricultural and cottage-industry workers seeking employment in factories. The surplus of workers enabled factory owners to keep the wage rate at a subsistence level (Ricardo's iron law of wages), but as industry expanded, the demand for labor grew until full employment ensued. At these higher levels of labor demand and employment, the owners of capital had to pay higher and higher wages to get enough workers for their factories. Labor-saving machinery, however, turned out to be an alternative: with it, the same number of workers could produce more, or fewer workers could produce the same amount. The problem of high wages could be temporarily solved by replacing workers with machines—what is known today as technological unemployment. Marx thought the number unemployed this way sufficient to be termed an "industrial reserve army."

So far, so good—for the capitalist. But, beyond a certain point in this process, factory owners began to defeat their own purposes. The new labor-saving machinery increased the factory's productivity, but the extra goods began to flood the markets just at the time the workers' incomes were being restricted by that very same machinery. Lower income meant lowered consumer demand. As sales revenue fell, the producers stopped making plans to add to a capital stock that was by now producing in excess of what could be sold. (Even today economists look to the capital-goods industry for a portent of what is going to happen in the business cycle.) A decline in the demand for durable goods and machinery has been a relatively accurate forecaster of economic downturns in the capitalistic system. The decline eventually causes unemployment, lower total wages, and falling national income. Up to this stage, Marx had anticipated Keynes's theory of insufficient total demand.

Contrary to Keynes, Marx believed that recovery from these cyclical slumps was automatic. However—and contrary to the neoclassicals— the assurance of economic recoveries did not guarantee the survival of capitalism. Moreover, the causes of recovery were different from those espoused by the neoclassicals. The surviving large business firms bought the failing small firms and restored profits, but the cycle became increasingly fragile. Each time the business cycle turned downward, it plunged deeper. The Great Depression of the 1930s and the great downturn of 1981–1982 would have surprised Marx less than the fact that there were no revolutions following them.

In fact, many people made premature predictions about the death of capitalism during the thirties, and the American Communist Party gained a number of adherents in those years. But the mixed enterprise system of the United States bears only a family resemblance to the kind of capitalism that Marx was attacking. For one thing, the American economy is bolstered by enormous spending in the name of national defense against Soviet bloc and other communist nations. For another, the government often intervenes on behalf of both the capitalists and the workers. Marx correctly saw the government as the enforcer of property rights and the protector of the entrepreneurs' economic power. For example, minimal capital gains taxation and low or avoidable inheritance taxes are measures that protect private property. He believed that governments would even go to war to expand the size of markets for products and provide roads, railroads, and canals in the interests of profitable commerce.

The United States has not been a fertile ground for Marxism. Avowed Marxists have been denied academic positions in most American universities. As late as 1978, a distinguished political scientist was denied an appointment as chairman of an academic department in a major state university because of his Marxism. The most prominent of present-day American Marxist economists is Paul M. Sweezy. Through the Monthly Review Press, Sweezy has provided a publishing outlet for Marxist economists, including himself.

The main function of the "older" American Marxists has been to update Marx's ideas about monopoly capitalism. They have described in detail the behavior of modern corporations. Sweezy (along with the late Paul Baran) depicts monopoly capitalism as a system made up of giant corporations. They see these corporations as profit maximizers and capital accumulators managed by company executives whose fortunes are tied to the corporations' success or failure. In contrast to competitive capitalism, the big corporation is a "price maker." In order to avoid price instability, price competition is minimized and the system is characterized by nonprice forms of competition. Prices initially are often set by the largest and most powerful firm in the industry, such as U.S. Steel or General Motors, and the others follow the leader. A modified form of this behavior is not precluded; for example, in the cigarette industry, big companies take turns initiating price changes.

With a ban on price competition, the sellers of a given product or of close substitutes have an interest in seeing that the prices established maximize the profits of the industrial group as a whole. Even though they may fight about relative shares of profits in the industry, none wishes to fight over the division of a smaller pie. Sweezy and Baran see this as decisive in determination of the price policies and strategies of the typical large corporation.

In Sweezy and Baran's view, price making by the giants does not spell the end of all competition. Competition takes new forms and even new intensity. The lower-cost and higher-profit company can afford the advertising, research, development of new product varieties, extra services, and so on that enable it to fight the battle for market shares. Such a firm has a strong incentive to seek continuously to cut costs faster than its rivals. Consequently, monopoly capital will become even larger.[9]

Baran and Sweezy point to Thorstein Veblen as one of the first economists to recognize and analyze many aspects of monopoly capitalism, particularly its emphasis on advertising and salesmanship. (The ideas of Veblen will be explored in the next chapter.) Although Veblen could hardly be described as a Marxist devotee, we will find (see Chapter 12) that some of the new radicals of the Left took up Marx's mantle during the 1960s and 1970s. It appears that Baran and Sweezy are describing modern corporate reality in an advanced stage of development that Marx could not possibly have imagined in its detail. One therefore cannot help but wonder why American Marxists are considered so radical.

Marx anticipated, in some detail, the evolution of capitalism, but he underestimated the resiliency of the combination of government, the military, and industry. The system that Marx wanted overthrown is now only vestigial, and the potential for revolution has consequently diminished. If whatever the American economy is today is to be replaced by a Marxist one, it is not pure capitalism that will be overthrown: you cannot overthrow what does not exist.

11

THE
ICONOCLASTS:
VEBLEN AND
GALBRAITH

▼

. . . these expert men, technologists, engineers, or whatever
name may best suit them, make up the indispensable
General Staff of the industrial system; and without their
immediate and unremitting guidance and correction the
industrial system will not work.

THORSTEIN VEBLEN, *THE ENGINEERS AND THE PRICE SYSTEM*, 1921

This, not the management, is the guiding intelligence—the
brain—of the enterprise. There is no name for all who
participate in group decision-making or the organization
which they form. I propose to call this organization the
Technostructure.

JOHN KENNETH GALBRAITH, *THE NEW INDUSTRIAL STATE*, 1967

The original meaning of the word *iconoclast* was a person who destroyed sacred images out of objection to their veneration. Today the word is used in a general way to refer to anyone who attacks the fundamental beliefs of a society, an institution, an academic discipline, or all three. In economics, Thorstein Veblen and John Kenneth Galbraith qualify as notable contemporary iconoclasts because of their vigorous denunciations of many of the tenets of neoclassical theory. Veblen (1857– 1929), a brilliant eccentric, dissected the neoclassical paradigm in response to the excesses of the Robber Barons (see Chapter 6) and also founded the only uniquely American branch of economic thought, the *evolutionist* or *institutionalist* school. Galbraith (1908–   ), the best-known contemporary evolutionist, has continued the attack on the neoclassicals. Where they see weakness, he senses power. Where the neoclassicals advise against intervention with natural market forces, Galbraith contends that economic forces left to themselves tend to work out in favor of the powerful.

VEBLEN AND THE EVOLUTIONISTS

Five figures dominate the evolutionist/institutionalist school: Veblen, who provided the framework for the general approach of these thinkers; Wesley C. Mitchell, who conducted statistical studies and stimulated empirical research in the United States; John R. Commons, who urged the government to legislate economic reforms and greatly influenced the reform-oriented research of the University of Wisconsin's economics department; Clarence Ayres, who, until his death in 1972, was perhaps the only well-known evolutionist/institutionalist teaching such economics at mid-twentieth century; and Galbraith, probably best known as the author of *The Affluent Society* (1958, 1969), *The New Industrial State* (1967), and *Economics and the Public Purpose* (1973). Today, the evolutionist group calls itself the Association for Evolutionary Economics; it began in 1967 to publish its own journal, the *Journal of Economic Issues.*

What makes the evolutionists iconoclastic? As we have seen in earlier chapters, general social crises usually precede and give rise to discontent with the reigning social science paradigm. At the turn of the century, Veblen was incensed by the uneven distribution of wealth and income and the overemphasis on making money. (Veblen began his advanced studies at Yale in 1882, the year that Herbert Spencer began a grand tour of the United States that culminated in a "last supper" at Delmonico's, then the famed watering hole of the New York rich.) Other economists read Marshall's *Principles*, enjoyed and apologized for the status quo, and saw little or no need for reform. Veblen, however, described a nation controlled by a few millionaires, Robber Barons who had accumulated vast wealth largely through financial manipulation, the kind of keen operations illustrated in Chapter 6.

Personally, Veblen was a strange man, seemingly out of step with others of his era. He had furtive eyes, a blunt nose, an unkempt mustache, and a short, scraggly beard. He was aloof and dressed simply, usually in tweeds. He appeared to have only two indulgences—smoking an expensive brand of Turkish cigarettes and finding lost balls on golf courses. In his golf walks, he had the air of being in a world apart from everyone else. In many ways, he was.

Veblen was also out of step with the conventional economic thought of his day. For example, J. B. Clark's *The Distribution of Wealth: A Theory of Wages, Interests, and Profits,* published in 1899, argued that the returns from capital were determined by the marginal physical product of capital and the perfectly competitive prices of finished products. Veblen's approach to capitalism is quite different and makes him an important sociologist as well as economist. He contends that those who accumulate wealth do so for reasons that go beyond the simple satisfaction of physical wants: the rich accumulate and consume wealth in a way that displays that wealth because the display is indicative of power, honor, and prestige in a materialistic culture.

Veblen's first and most popular book, *The Theory of the Leisure Class* (1899), introduced a number of terms that slowly became a part of conventional economic language, such as *leisure class; pecuniary emulation* (popularly known as "keeping up with the Joneses"); and, most famous of all, *conspicuous consumption,* the phrase he coined for the display of wealth described in the preceding paragraph. Around the turn of the century Commodore Vanderbilt, a skillful entrepreneur who also robbed the public with abandon, spent $3 million to build a house, the Breakers, that provided his suitably corseted wife with something more than minimal shelter. Vanderbilt was able to buy Vanderbilt University for only a half million, a sum that puts his conspicuous household consumption into perspective.

Veblen's book also originates the evolutionist argument about economic institutions, using a Darwinian biological metaphor in a novel way. The Darwinians had said that, in the evolutionary development of biological organisms, natural selection allows the fittest to survive. According to Veblen, institutions also evolve, except that there is always a *cultural lag* between the ideas of today and existing institutions that are based on the ideas of yesterday. "Institutions," says Veblen, "are products of the past process, are adapted to past circumstances, and are therefore never in full accord with the requirements of the present."[1] Veblen argues a kind of upside-down Social Darwinism, saying that evolution is an inertia-producing force because "these institutions which have so been handed down, these habits of thought, points of view, mental attitudes and aptitudes, or what not, are ... themselves a conservative factor."[2] As it turns out, the surviving institutions are the *least fit* for the present.

This Veblenesque world is the antithesis of the simplistic society envisioned by positive economics. Because the wealth of the leisure class shelters it from changing economic forces, it tends to accept the dictum that whatever is, is right. In fact, maintains Veblen, whatever *is* institutionally is very likely to be wrong because it will not have evolved at the same pace as the fundamental social conditions that institutions ought to reflect. Institutions cannot change quickly enough to accommodate social conditions.

Veblen did not develop a new paradigm that could be used as an alternative to neoclassicism, but he is nevertheless important because he did so much to broaden the scope of economics, bringing into play such "nonpure" economic forces as social institutions and psychological attitudes toward wealth. Veblen has made many economists stop and think about their bloodless, skeletal models of economic behavior. He is also a brilliantly witty writer; even if *The Theory of the Leisure Class* were bad economics—which it is not—it would still be a work of unique genius, perhaps a masterpiece, one of the few works of economic theory that can be read for pleasure and relevance today.

THE EVOLUTIONIST ECONOMIC THEORY

The basic ideas of the evolutionist/institutionalist school can be briefly summarized. (For brevity's sake, I am going to call this school *evolutionist* from now on, although its "institutional" aspect will not be ignored.) Evolutionists are holistic; that is, they study the economy and the society of which it is a part as an entire, organized pattern of group behavior. They believe that the collective economic action of a society is greater than the sum of its parts. They are concerned with a culture of customs, social habits, modes of thinking, and ways of living. Such patterns of thought and behavior can be broadly characterized as institutions; they need not be physical but can include shared beliefs or images, such as the Horatio Alger myth, the Puritan ethic, the idea of laissez-faire, and general attitudes toward trade unionism, socialism, or the welfare state. None of these ideas is determined by "natural" economic laws.

Where other economists may still be concerned with the notion of individualism, the evolutionists contend that *group* social behavior is the more significant factor in economic analysis. This contention leads evolutionists to wonder why economies mutate, and what the implications are for economic policy as attitudes about, for example, the income distribution change. Evolutionists reject the positive economists' acceptance of "what is" and ask, "*How* did the economy get to be what it is and *where* is it leading us?" Their defiance of conventional economics is largely rooted in their emphasis on change, which they see to be more basic to economic life than Newtonian equilibria.

The evolutionists also have a different view of competition than Adam Smith bequeathed to his followers. Smith saw competition as an essentially beneficial impulse because it kept business in check, but

Veblen saw it as predatory and despicable. Veblen's economic man is more psychologically complicated than Smith's and lives in a world where the fact of competition causes serious clashes of interests among social classes. This notion of the inevitability of class conflict suggests that Veblen has Marxist affinities, but they are superficial. People form groups to protect their mutual self-interests, and because there are different interests, there are inevitable conflicts, but the basic *values* of the different groups are never in question. The trade unionists don't want to overthrow the bankers, for example, because they are too busy emulating the conspicuous consumption of the wealthier group. Even the field of sexual infidelity, once thought to be the poaching ground for only the wealthy male, eventually was invaded by the masses. The workers don't want to eliminate the managers; they want to join them. Competition is in the service of a holistic value—the love of money. If there were an equitable distribution of wealth and income, this pernicious and pointless competition would not exist.

The evolutionists have many basic differences with neoclassical economics. The neoclassical school depends on stable equilibria in its analysis, whereas the evolutionists reject them. The neoclassical theorists see a person as an individual economic unit; the evolutionists see people as members of special interest groups. Neoclassicals tend to favor a "hands off the economy" policy for the government; evolutionists favor liberal, democratic reforms designed to bring about a more equitable distribution of wealth and income. A strong case can be built that the controversies raging today between two schools of economic thought—conventional and radical—emerge indeed from clashing value systems.

Even though the evolutionists gained adherents, in Veblen's day the neoclassicals ultimately held onto majority opinion among economists and society at large. The failure of the evolutionists to retain a consensus may provide a gauge for the possible success of radical economics of the Left today. Veblen's rejection of the analytical tools of economics and its general mode of thought was probably too complete, and he offered no acceptable substitute. The evolutionary arguments that addressed themselves to a whole society seemed to many economists too broad, while the neoclassical tools grew increasingly sharp with use. Veblen and the evolutionists did not provide an economic model that would be widely understood and appeal to economists struggling to assume the cloak of science. Veblen also had to struggle against a tendency in the seminaries of higher learning that he ascribed to all institutions—the dislike of innovation.

A paradigm must consist of parts reducible to a few basic principles before it can be easily passed on in books and classrooms. One economist has said, ". . . the essence of an orthodoxy of any kind is to reduce the subtle and sophisticated thoughts of great men to a set of simple principles and straightforward slogans that more mediocre brains can think they understand well enough to live by . . ."[3] The evolutionists, despite their individual brilliance, could not produce a reducible orthodoxy. They were not so much outthought as they were outbred by those who could understand the simple mechanics of Newtonian neoclassicism. For extraordinary science to become normal (i.e., orthodox), it must be sufficiently dilutable to be swallowed by more than a handful of potential apostles.

Nevertheless, the evolutionists continue to influence economic thought. Veblen, for example, helped to direct attention away from the perfect competition model as a paradigm and toward a model of monopoly. Veblen's argument that big business is primarily interested in maximizing profits rather than maximizing production is illustrated in skeleton form in the pure monopoly model. But Veblen went beyond this, arguing that the instinct for workmanship declines and the importance of salesmanship increases when money takes precedence over goods. Big business is also more interested in vending goods than in making them serviceable to meet people's needs. In other words, the nature of the institution of manufacturing and distribution determines production and pricing outcomes. This would explain why, as an economy moves to a higher plateau of production, the numbers of salespeople, advertisers, and accountants increase. Veblen also believed that, as the economy develops, entrepreneurs are required to take fewer risks. (As we shall see, Galbraith continues this line of reasoning in his work.)

OTHER VIEWS OF THE "ECONOMIC MAN"

The evolutionists believe that humans interact with and are shaped by outdated institutions, a more complicated view than the neoclassical's pure "economic man." Veblen had attacked the hedonism of the neoclassical school, which would have "a gang of Aleutian Islanders slushing about in the wrack and surf with rakes and magical incantations for the capture of shellfish . . . to be engaged on a feat of hedonistic equilibration in rent, wages, and interest."[4] The belief in a more complicated prototype of behavior has gained increasing currency over the years and provides a convenient approach to some of the ideas of evolutionary economists Karl Polanyi and Kenneth Boulding.

Like Veblen, Polanyi (1886–1964) was heavily influenced by anthropological descriptions of styles of economic life that differed from Western capitalism. Polanyi contends that in preindustrial societies the common economic as well as noneconomic reference point was not the individual but the community of which that person was a part. For example, in primitive societies, people did not gather or hunt food for themselves or for their families but for the entire community. The community often ate together and shared the benefits of interaction with other tribes. Furthermore, no member of the community ever risked starvation unless the whole community was facing it, too. Polanyi believes that the "maximum material gains" motive is unnatural to humans; he reasons that it is not natural for people to expect payment in the economic sense for work (1) in which they do not naturally function at a minimal level, and (2) which they perform for noneconomic reasons.[5]

Polanyi believes that modern people have become maximizers since the Industrial Revolution, but unwillingly. The fear of starvation has been the main driving force for the "new man" as families have been driven out of agriculture by technological change and into the cities where food has to be bought. Polanyi viewed both the fear of hunger and the quest for profits as motives that are socially divisive and humanly destructive. The avoidance of hunger may well have been the "original sin" that led to materialism, although it does not explain Veblen's notion of conspicuous consumption for enhancing self-esteem. Perhaps in competitive societies, people accumulate more than they need as a form of symbolic interaction with those who have higher incomes.

Polanyi is calling our attention to the collective elements in societal organization. Primitive society was not organized to maximize *individual* satisfactions. An open, mobile society is required for the full satisfaction of individual social desires, but primitive societies were often organized according to inherited social roles. Furthermore, these roles—priest, chief, head warrior, etc.—were often noneconomic. In a similar way, as Marx suggests, roles were also ascribed in feudal societies, and this is still largely the case in some nations, India, for example. In the more modern United States, too, roles are to some extent still ascribed and certainly limited by race, sex, and ethnic background. Whereas Adam Smith's harmonious economy was the result of chance interaction, Polanyi suggests that society organizes itself by choice. For example, humans might provide for certain collective economic needs through a government organization because all their needs are not being met in the marketplace.

More recently, Polanyi's view has been supplemented by modern psychology. The late psychologist Abraham Maslow has postulated a ranking of human needs in ascending order, beginning with the most basic, the physiological (for example, the need for food and water). People who have not satisfied this primary human drive will view both present and future reality in terms of their deprivation. Having satisfied the hunger drive, people will next worry about safety needs—"security; stability; dependency; protection; freedom from fear, anxiety, and chaos; need for structure, order, law, limits; strength in the protector; and so on."[6] Third, people desire to belong and to be loved, to be part of a group, and to experience acceptance. They want to be Elks, church members, part of the "management team," Republicans, union members.

This need fulfilled, people next want to be esteemed, and they need both internal satisfaction and external recognition. Finally, people want to actualize their potential, to do whatever they choose, and to do it as well as they desire. This picture of the human being, though more complex than the economic man, appears both more realistic and more logical.

Contemporary social scientist Kenneth Boulding views the person as a social being who loves and hates, who gives gifts and exacts tributes, who engages in two-way economic exchanges. Thus, he sees a "social triangle" in which total threat is at one corner, total exchange at another, and total love at a third. Both Adam Smith (as moral philosopher) and Kenneth Boulding would have people operating inside this triangle rather than exclusively at the pure exchange extreme. Thus, the U.S. GNP would be a point inside the triangle with, perhaps, 60 percent of GNP going for exchange, 30 percent for love (gifts), and 10 percent for threats (tribute).[7]

Boulding's pioneering work on the "grants economy" as a social process concentrates almost entirely upon nonmarket decision making. One of the virtues of Boulding's approach is that it focuses attention upon balancing the forces of individualism and common concern. According to various definitions, between 20 and 50 percent of the American economy currently is organized by grants rather than by exchange. In contrast to two-way exchange, the grant is a one-way transfer of an economic good or service, such as the individual contributions of goods to Goodwill Industries for the needy. Boulding categorizes these grants as either *gifts* or *tribute*. A gift is given out of altruism, whereas a tribute is a grant made out of fear and under threat. Public assistance programs to the poor are gifts; a robbery would involve the extraction of a tribute by threat. An economics encompassing only two-way exchanges may be ignoring 40 percent of the American economy!

There is support from other fields of knowledge for this view. Still another system for balancing the forces of self-interest with social requirements comes from Harvard philosopher John Rawls.[8] Rawls ponders what principles of justice would be chosen by members of society if they were placed in an "original position," one in which they did not know the particulars of the positions they would occupy in an ongoing society. The social contract they would agree upon is presumed to be final, a kind of constitution. Although the individuals are assumed "rational"—self-interested, as orthodox price theory assumes—the parties are nonetheless capable of a sense of justice because of their knowledge about the accumulated general facts of society.

The conception of justice that Rawls envisions is not egoistic (as is the pure economic man) but is based on the understanding that social cooperation makes possible a better life for all than any would experience in isolation. Furthering one's own ends requires the cooperation of other members of society. Thus, the individuals in the original position are forced to be fair because they themselves are among those treated by the accepted principles. In this hypothetical state, one of the chosen principles of justice is the difference principle, which holds that social and economic inequalities are to be arranged so that they are (1) to the greatest expected benefit of the "worst-off" members of society, and (2) attached to offices and positions open to all under conditions of equality of opportunity.

Rawls views the distribution of natural assets as "morally arbitrary" and considers the distribution of natural ability as more or less a "collective asset," much as European peasants once viewed the commons. Everyone then has some entitlement or claim on the totality of natural assets. The ideal Rawlsian society is one that encourages cooperation within a setting in which the natural endowments of individuals and resources are the society's common property. The "better-off" in society make transfers to the "worse-off" in order to gain and maintain their cooperation. Rawls presumes that the better endowed already enjoy special advantages and do not require the extra consideration given to the economically disadvantaged.[9]

The views of Adam Smith, Kenneth Boulding, and John Rawls all depict the human being as an entity with an instinct for social behavior, a feature of humanity for perhaps the last 100,000 years. Cooperation and community life must have advantages, for people seem universally to choose this lifestyle. Despite this instinct for community, conflict is an inescapable element within the contemporary community, and some kind of social contract for the resolution of such conflict appears inescapable. This brings us to John Kenneth Galbraith, who has advocated mandatory wage and price controls to resolve the struggle between workers and managers for their shares of the national income.

THE POLITICAL ECONOMY OF JOHN KENNETH GALBRAITH

John Kenneth Galbraith is probably the most widely read of all economists. In addition to the three major works on economics mentioned earlier, he has also written historical works (*The Great Crash, 1929*);

books on politics (*The Liberal Hour* and *How to Get Out of Vietnam*); memoirs (*The Scotch* and *Ambassador's Journal*); and a novel lampooning the U.S. State Department (*The Triumph*). And at six-foot-eight, Galbraith is otherwise difficult to ignore. Yet with customary public modesty, he suggests he is conspicuous only because other people are abnormally short. His combination of wit and literary style is unmatched by any living economist (with the possible exception of Robert Heilbroner) and links him to Veblen; both men are evolutionists and, as such, have little patience with the neoclassical economics paradigm.

Galbraith's Background

Galbraith has been a confidant of presidents; a speech writer for Adlai Stevenson, Lyndon Johnson, George McGovern, and the Kennedys; an ambassador to India; and an escort of first ladies. One measure of Galbraith's renown is that in 1968 he was interviewed by *Playboy* magazine, that opulent reminder of the surrogate pleasures open to those with too much money, Veblenian leisure, and limited expectations. (Not to be out-jet-setted, Milton Friedman was later interviewed by the same magazine.)

Galbraith's early life was an excellent background for his later career as a social critic. He was born in 1908 in a Scotch farming community near Iona Station, Ontario, Canada. His father began as a teacher, turned to farming, and was a leading political liberal in this rather isolated community. When he was about six, John Kenneth began to go to political meetings with his father, and perhaps this is when he began to develop his sardonic humor. In *The Scotch*, Galbraith recalls an occasion on which his father made a speech critical of his Tory opponents from atop a huge manure pile, apologizing for having to speak from the Tory platform.

Galbraith attended high school in Dutton, a village split by social discord between the rural Scotch and the English townspeople. Most of the Tories were English merchants, whereas the Liberal Party was predominantly Scotch. The economic disagreements were substantial. The village merchants prospered while the farmers suffered in the post–World War I years. The Scotch, who thought they were superior in every way to the English (Galbraith agrees with this assessment), believed that the merchants were better off because they were buying cheap and selling dear. The superior bargaining power of the merchants apparently made a lasting impression on the young man. Galbraith worked his way through Ontario Agricultural College and took his doctorate in agricultural economics at the University of California at Berkeley in 1936, where he first began to read Veblen and Marx. Most of his subsequent academic life has been spent at Harvard University as professor of economics and, now, professor emeritus.

Galbraith's Attack on the Neoclassical Paradigm

Galbraith's most effective book is probably *Economics and the Public Purpose* (1973), the object of which is nothing less than the destruction of the neoclassical paradigm. Galbraith attaches himself to no schools, no movements, no ideologies, and no earlier economists, although his indebtedness to Veblen is abundantly clear. He concedes that the neoclassical paradigm is useful when applied to the market system, but, he says, the modern economy has spawned *another* system that exists side by side with the conventional market system yet far transcends it in massive wealth and power. Galbraith calls this other system the *planning system*, by which he means the 1,000 (or so) very largest industrial firms. The 1,000 industrial giants in the United States produce a larger share of the gross national product than the remaining 12 million business firms combined. The four largest U.S. corporations have total sales in excess of those of the 3 million farmers whom Galbraith keeps down in the market system and who produce the food supply. The combined revenues of General Motors and Exxon far exceed the combined revenues of California and New York. The neoclassical paradigm, Galbraith believes, cannot begin to explain the economic reality of the giant corporation.

Galbraith calls his theory of the way giant corporations operate the *general theory of advanced development*. It differs from neoclassical theory in two important ways. First, the theory of pricing is not of special importance in planning systems. Second, whereas neoclassical harmony is maintained because no single element in the economy has enough power to control prices, the giant corporation *has* the power to impose its purposes on others. The only reason that corporate power does not corrupt absolutely is because the power is not quite absolute. At present, the corporations do not control all the sources of political power. Nonetheless, planning-system power is sufficient to impose an "irrational" mode of life upon individuals. According to Galbraith, the monster corporation grew because technology became so complex that a new organizational entity was required to deal with it.

The first Model T car was built in a small plant in a short time. But, writes Galbraith in his *New Industrial State*, the Ford Motor Company's Mustang, produced in the mid-1960s, required expert knowledge, specialization of labor, a huge outlay of capital, a precise plan for production, and sophisticated organization. From drawing board to the road

necessitated years. Years of what? Years of *planning*. Galbraith emphasizes in *Public Purpose* that the planning is at the *firm* level. However,
he goes on to show that the plan for the firm is often in the interests of
the entire industry.

In the neoclassical textbook world, consumers are kings and queens
who can maximize their happiness by freely choosing whatever shirts,
skirts, soaps, bath oils, beer, and aperitifs they prefer. In contrast, the
Galbraithian planning system perceives serious disadvantages in such
freedom of choice. It takes a lot of time and many dollars of capital to
get the Mustang to the dealer's floor. The corporation wants to do everything it can to make sure that the consumer will buy that Mustang rather
than choose a car of a different horse or perhaps even a horse itself.
Therefore, part of the corporate plan becomes the management of what
consumers want. By means of advertising, promotion, and salesmanship, the producers create many of the wants they seek to satisfy, an
economic phenomenon Galbraith calls the *dependence effect*. Rejecting
the neoclassical concept of diminishing marginal utility, Galbraith—
going a step beyond Veblen—argues that in the American economy
there is something more like *producer* sovereignty.

For example, in a discussion of cars, Galbraith observes that "since
General Motors produces some half of all the automobiles, its designs
do not reflect the current mode, but are the current mode. The proper
shape of an automobile, for most people, will be what the automobile
majors decree the current shape to be."[10] Once necessities are satisfied,
a whole new world of possible wants is just waiting to be created by
billboards of young women in bathing suits, TV commercials with giant
green men, and magazine ads of liquor in velvet cases. Galbraith elsewhere notes that "mass communication was not necessary when the
wants of the masses were anchored primarily in physical need. The
masses could not then be persuaded as to their spending—this went
for basic foods and shelter."[11] In *Economics and the Public Purpose*,
published in 1973, Galbraith qualifies his want-creation argument somewhat, conceding that, though no one may actually need a pink, fully
automatic dishwasher, any alleviation of the tiresome job of washing
dishes for a large family certainly does satisfy a want. Many giant firms
spend part of their resources on research aimed at discovering what
these wants—even subliminal ones—are.

Thus, "selling the sizzle" may increase sales and growth for an
individual firm, but it also benefits the entire industry. It is a safe form
of competition between existing rivals and makes it difficult for new
competitors to enter or become entrenched in the field. The combined
market research–advertising–promotion expenditure of the three big-

gest automobile manufacturers increases the allocation of the consumer's budget toward automobile purchases and promotes the growth of the whole industry. Although Galbraith has not extended his analysis to the international economy, the Japanese appear to have benefited from the United States' "selling" of the automobile to the world.

The Technostructure

In the planning-system world of giant corporations, groups rather than individuals make the decisions. All the officials who take part in group decision making are members of the *technostructure*, a collective term that includes not only the most senior officials of the corporation but certain white- and blue-collar workers as well. It embraces only those who bring specialized knowledge, talent, or experience to group decisions. In a very large corporation, it might include the chairman of the board, the president, vice-presidents who have important responsibilities, and people with other major staff positions, such as department or division heads. Galbraith says that the technostructure cannot be specifically defined, but it has taken over corporations in a way that supports Veblen's prediction that all firms would logically be operated by technicians rather than risk takers.

The technostructure displaces the old entrepreneur and the captain of industry with something that more closely resembles a huge committee. Committees have different goals than the steady (or unsteady) hand of the captain at the helm of the company. Whereas neoclassical economics has the individual capitalist aiming (and succeeding) at profit maximization, Galbraith's controlling technostructure has two principal purposes rather than one. First, there is its *protective* purpose: the technostructure's collectively made decisions attempt to ensure a basic and uninterrupted level of earnings that will keep the stockholders happy and the bankers away from the door, as well as provide savings and capital. Second, it has an *affirmative* purpose, which is the growth of the firm. Growth becomes an important purpose of the entire planning system and hence of the society that is dominated by giant business.

One way to assure firm growth is by acquisition. Galbraith points to the fact that between 1948 and 1965 the 200 largest U.S. manufacturing corporations acquired 2,692 other firms, and these acquisitions accounted for about one-seventh of all growth in assets by these firms during this period. In the next three years, the 200 largest corporations acquired some 1,200 more firms.

Unlike Marx and Veblen, who believed that industrial concentration was motivated by a thirst for profit, Galbraith sees the technostructure's motive as one of bureaucratic advantage, a motive that can also be spelled POWER. Each member of the technostructure sees the logic in growth. A unit of the firm, such as a department, expands its sales. With increased revenue flowing into the firm, the department can expand its employment and make new claims on promotion, pay, and perquisites that go with its increased size. The members of a nongrowing corporation cannot lay claim to any of these rewards. And bigness begets bigness, because revenue growth gives the firm more to grow on. When a firm is so large that its production alone can cause price fluctuations, it is far safer for this firm and the few others like it to set prices *first* and then adjust their production to sell their products at the predetermined price.[12]

The planning system and the technostructure are closely associated with the state because government expenditures are responsible for a large share of corporate revenue. There are still other reasons for an extremely close relationship between government bureaucracies and corporations, a bureaucratic symbiosis. Public regulatory agencies, such as the Federal Trade Commission, tend to become captives of the firms they were set up to regulate. The government often supplies capital for technical development, such as for nuclear power, computers, modern air transport, and satellite communication equipment. Sometimes the government can act as a lending agency of last resort, as in the case of the historic bail-out of the Lockheed Corporation. The goal of corporate growth thus becomes inseparable from the goal of national economic growth. What is good for the government is good for General Motors. National economic growth is also an important goal of organized labor, and this goal fits well into the ambitions of the technostructure: giant firms set prices, so they can usually pass increased wages on to the consumer in the form of higher prices. Everybody wins—except perhaps the consumer.

Galbraith's Concept of Uneven Development

What Galbraith is describing is an uneven power distribution between the planning system and our old friend, the market system. This uneven development is organized along the following lines: the planning system requires highly skilled workers, and it can afford to pay them very well, often more than they would be worth in the market system in terms of their ability to produce revenue. The market system is thus at a disadvantage in its competition for skilled personnel. Furthermore, the influential planning system can obtain services from the state, which the market system largely does without. Uneven development that favors the planning system influences significant social attitudes. For example, consumers have maintained a love affair with private transportation partly because the planning system has convinced them that automobiles are essential to their lives. Public transportation is slighted, even though it may be ultimately more beneficial for society.

Galbraith is concerned with social imbalance. The private sector is a glutton and the public sector is starved, a starvation that extends into education, the arts, and a variety of public services. General fiscal and monetary policy serves the technostructure's own policy of steady economic growth so that individual consumers can purchase the products of giant business. Inflation may be the result of this marriage, but large corporations are largely immune from restrictive monetary policies because the giants have access to their own immense financial resources. As long as demand in the economy remains high and the public cannot effectively oppose the technostructure, the upward wage-price spiral goes on and on.

Galbraith has clearly departed from the prevailing paradigm. His focus is on planning, not the market. He examines in detail the giant firm, not the small. He sees prices and outputs decided by the technostructure, not by the market mechanism. He is a believer more in producer sovereignty than in consumer sovereignty. The goal of the firm is growth rather than maximum profit rates. The relation of the state to the corporation is cooperative. He sees the quality-of-life concerns in the *composition* of output, not its magnitude. In this respect, the ethical base of Galbraithian economics probably is closer to the public's perception of reality than is neoclassical economics.

Perhaps because he is an economist concerned with what *people* may or may not choose to believe about their economy rather than what economists think people ought to believe about it, Galbraith is not universally admired by other professional economists.[13] He has been dismissed as a trivializing journalist, a superficial Mickey Mouse of scientific economics. But many distinguished economists respect him, particularly those whose reputations are large enough to accommodate his iconoclasm, such as Paul Samuelson, Kenneth Boulding, and Robert Heilbroner. Like John Stuart Mill, Galbraith has reminded economics of its vast humanistic implications. He has persuasively questioned once again the primacy of pure economic choice over the balance of what is important in life. In particular, Galbraith as a social critic has brought to light in dramatic fashion the unevenness in the development of the American economy in contrast to the presumed smoothness depicted by the neoclassicals. In a sense he, too—like Adam Smith—is the Scotch moralist urging us to move toward a more fulfilling society. As you have witnessed by now, the economists who are historically most important (such as Smith, Marx, Mill, Keynes) have tried to break the ruling paradigm. That is what Galbraith is doing, and Galbraith's terrain is a part of the time-honored country of *political* economy.

12

NEW
RADICAL
ECONOMICS:
THE LEFT

▼

*In the middle and late sixties we studied orthodox economics
(Weisskopf at MIT, Edwards and Reich at Harvard), and at the
same time participated in current struggles against racism,
poverty, and the Vietnam war.... we were studying a well-
established and sophisticated discipline, but we became
increasingly aware of its inadequacy. Not only did it deny or
ignore most of our political concerns, but even worse, it
constituted a system of belief that justified the status quo by
defending the capitalist system.*

RICHARD C. EDWARDS, MICHAEL REICH, AND THOMAS E. WEISSKOPF,
THE CAPITALIST SYSTEM, 1972

Among the largest and most articulate group of economists opposed to the conventional neoclassical paradigm is the mixture known
as *New Left radical economists.* This group includes orthodox Marxists,
those sympathetic to Marx's economic methods, democratic socialists,
a few Maoists, a few anarchists, and some people who are simply critical
of what they believe is the narrow tunnel vision of contemporary economics. The bonds that unite them are the convictions that capitalism
as practiced in the United States is responsible for many of this country's problems, that orthodox economics is a de facto defense of capitalism, and that reform can occur only along with a wholesale change
in the economic system.

Marx and Veblen attacked the unequal distribution of income and
the monopolistic control of wealth. The New Left radicals are opposed
to the poverty and alienation they believe are rampant in an affluent
economy and the adverse results of unbridled private consumption and
production that are a product of growth capitalism. Marx advocated
replacing the Newtonian world view, which was based on natural

physical laws, with a Hegelian world view that returned human beings to the center of the universe. In the United States, Veblen saw many of the same evils in capitalism that Marx had identified and urged social reform. Yet the basic neoclassical paradigm remains intact, and neither the Marxists nor the institutionalists have provided a new one. By the end of our discussion of the New Left radical economists, the reasons for this failure will become clear.

THE RISE OF THE NEW LEFT RADICALISM

When a brigade of young radical economists stormed the stage of the American Economic Association (AEA) convention in New York in 1969, most of the other economists present dismissed them as a fringe group of rebels with a cause but no theory and maintained that economics would little note what they did there, much less recall what they said. This prediction is not the only one in economics to miss its mark in recent years. The radicals of the Left did not go away. They are very much alive and have come to command the allegiance of some older, established scholars as well as many first-rate young economists. John Kenneth Galbraith, Kenneth Boulding, Robert Lekachman, Robert Heilbroner, Daniel Fusfeld, Douglas Dowd, Warren Samuels, Andreas Papandreou, Benjamin Ward, and Robert A. Solo are among those sympathetic with the radicals. Other established economists, including Martin Shubik (Yale), Lester Thurow (MIT), Vincent Tarascio (University of North Carolina), the late Oskar Morgenstern (New York University), E. J. Mishan (London School of Economics), Nobelist Kenneth Arrow (Stanford), and Wassily Leontief, advanced criticisms of the subject matter and the methods of conventional economics similar to the critique of the radicals, although without the passion and rhetoric of the New Left. More than a dozen radical adherents or sympathizers appeared on the 1971 program of the AEA convention, probably because John Kenneth Galbraith was then president of the association and the largest group of young radicals is from Harvard, where Galbraith taught.

Beyond this, even the economists who have vigorously disagreed with the radicals are now inclined to regard radical left-wing economics as a legitimate branch of academic economics. New Left radical economics has joined Marxism and evolutionist economics as an accepted critique of neoclassical theory. By 1980, the New Left radicals could claim 1,500 members in their organization, the Union for Radical Political Economics (URPE). Its journal, *The Review of Radical Political Economics,* is thriving and being sold in the private-enterprise marketplace. By 1985, a number of books had been published on radical economics, including David Mermelstein's *Economics: Mainstream Readings and*

Radical Critiques, Howard Sherman's *Radical Political Economy*, Sherman and E. K. Hunt's *Economics*, Samuel Bowles and Herbert Gintis's *Schooling in Capitalist America*, James O'Conner's *The Fiscal Crisis of the State*, Bowles and Richard Edwards's *Understanding Capitalism*, Bowles, David M. Gordon, and Thomas E. Weisskopf's *Beyond the Waste Land*, Raymond S. Franklin's *American Capitalism: Two Visions*, and the work that provided the epigraph for this chapter, *The Capitalist System*.[1]

The New Left radical economics had its formal, academic origin at Harvard University in the autumn of 1967. A group of graduate students and faculty organized a course that they hoped would help them resolve the contradictions they perceived between what they were studying and teaching and what they actually saw in the world around them—poverty, racism, the Vietnam War. They called this course Social Sciences 125, "The Capitalist Economy, Conflict and Power," and requested that the course be added to the curriculum so that students could get credit for it. As the tradition of normal science behavior would predict, the Harvard Department of Economics did not grant their request. At about the same time, a smaller group of young radicals was emerging at the University of Michigan. Others began to appear at schools throughout the country, including the New School for Social Research, American University, the State University of New York at Stony Brook, Cornell University, the University of Massachusetts, and the public universities in California.[2]

There are several causes for the rebirth of radical economics in the United States in recent years. Among them are certain economic crises (to be discussed in Chapter 13) such as environmental pollution, poverty amidst plenty, and the apparent inability of the capitalist system to reconcile full employment with price stability. Another condition that affects the state of economic science is the decline in extra satisfaction from income and wealth increases in America as the general level of affluence rises.[3]

The radical economists' concern for poverty is extended to the issue of economic development in Third World countries. For example, the radicals charge that the developed countries are draining the mineral resources and "surplus value" of Third World countries without giving them adequate compensation. The developed countries use tariffs and quotas and other means of unfair competition against developing countries' products. Like Marx, the young radicals depict a growing gap between rich and poor countries. In international economics particularly, the New Left radical economists' use of such terms as *economic imperialism* and *neocolonialism* adds to the Marxist-Leninist tone of their literature. The radicals' concerns also embrace racial problems and localized wars, which they see in part as a consequence of the widening economic gap between rich and poor countries.

Despite its debt to Marx, however, New Left radical economics cannot be viewed simply as a rebirth of Marxism. (Marxism is anathema to the evolutionist school.) The radicals are influenced more by the broad, humanistic social thought of Marx than by his revolutionary side. This statement from *The Capitalist System* may be taken as a fair summary of the radicals' general attitude toward Marx and Marxism:

> *We do not find everything that Marx or his followers have written to be useful, or even relevant or correct. On the contrary, readers familiar with the Marxist literature will notice (and may complain) that many strands of Marxist thought are not represented in this book. Nonetheless, our primary intellectual debt is to Karl Marx. His approach to social problems has influenced us deeply.*[4]

THE RADICAL CRITIQUE OF NEOCLASSICISM

New Left radical economics offers the following basic criticisms of conventional economics:

1. Orthodox economics makes analysis of the sources of income, product distribution, and product choice difficult because it concentrates on small, marginal changes and shifts within a capitalist system rather than on large, qualitative changes that may alter the system. This interest in relatively minor changes within a given system makes the system appear to be essentially harmonious and ignores large discontinuities, such as the concentration of power and wealth.

2. Neoclassical economics does not take into account the actual socioeconomic determinants of productivity, such as corporate structure and ownership, education, job training, or family background; it ignores the intimate relation between the distribution of power and the distribution of wealth.

3. Conventional economics assumes that consumer choices are somehow "given" and therefore excludes from discussion the impact of production, advertising, and the desire to have what others have that help form such preferences.

4. The radicals argue that the separation of positive and normative economics is impossible and that earlier economists did not attempt any such separation. Policy emanates from normative economics.

5. Overspecialization has eliminated important political and social variables from economic model building because these variables

are "outside" the theory. Overspecialization, in combination with the other four factors above, has caused economics to ignore the quality of life under a given economic system—the way decisions are made, the presence or absence of collective services, the natural and created problems of the environment, for example.

All in all, argue the New Left radical economists, the normal science curriculum of modern economics teaches conventional marginalist theory, an analysis that has to be based on the status quo in social relations because it cannot accommodate anything beyond the ownership and decision-making systems typical of existing capitalist societies and then only the money-making behavior of firms and individuals within that context. Even when the overall operations of these individual units are studied, modern economics focuses on the fiscal and monetary adjustments necessary to keep the system functioning. They sound a plea close to that of the evolutionists when they argue that "the marginalist approach is useful only if, accepting the basic institutions of capitalism, one is primarily concerned with its administration."[5]

According to the New Left radicals, the neoclassical paradigm is useful primarily as a justification for existing institutions, and it has adverse welfare results. (That is, resources are poorly allocated; "welfare" in this sense has nothing to do with federal or state welfare programs.) The radicals join Marx, Galbraith, and Veblen in attacking the distribution of income and wealth, particularly in the United States, and here they have hit orthodox economics in its softest spot, because both personal wealth and personal income distributions are simply "given" in the standard paradigm.

The Radical View of Preference Formation

The radicals also join hands with Veblen and Galbraith in rejecting the idea of consumer sovereignty, the idea that consumers control what producers produce. Herbert Gintis, who appears to be the radicals' chief theoretician, argues:

First, this body of theory [neoclassical theory]
Views
Individual welfare
As a direct function
Of the "objects" available to the individual.
That is, it considers
Objects as "ends in themselves"
In that
The individual's welfare depends only on the "objects"

Under his jurisdiction
Or his control.[6]

But this view is only one of many on how preferences might be formed. Gintis suggests that the neoclassical theory of preferences could be seen as a subsystem within an alternative theory of changes in an individual's development and preferences.

Along with the evolutionists, the radical economists argue that it is institutions themselves (including values) that determine preferences. Moreover, there is a feedback effect between the individual and the institution. In reality, suggests Gintis,

The individual
At a point in time . . .
May act
Either
To increase his welfare based on his existing preference structure
Through the provisionment
Of additional goods and services
Or
He may improve his preference structure
So as to be capable
Of increased satisfaction
Based on available material goods.
The trade-off
Between material welfare and individual development
Faced by the individual
Is mirrored on the level of society as a whole.
Thus we may pose
A central question
For any adequate welfare economics:
Does the structure of socioeconomic institutions
Adequately reflect
These individual trade-offs?
Moreover,
An adequate welfare theory
Must analyze
The ways in which
The set
Of "approved" institutions
Itself
Biases the individual's approach to the problem
Of personal development.[7]

Interpersonal Utility Comparisons

Gintis also attacks conventional economics for avoiding comparisons between the levels of satisfactions that different consumers receive
from the same products—interpersonal utility comparisons.

Interpersonal comparisons
Represent
A bitter pill
For neo-classical welfare economics,
Which traditionally argues
That
As value judgments,
The prima facie *must be excluded from a welfare analysis.*
This argument is surely
Confused
As the fact that certain judgments
Are normative
Can never justify their exclusion from an explicitly
Normative analysis.
In fact,
We would expect recognition
Of the normative nature of such comparisons
To lend
To an argument for their inclusion....[8]

In other words, Gintis believes that the exclusion of value judgments
from normative economics is a contradiction in terms. A welfare economics that bears no relation to what people value beyond economic
efficiency makes little sense.

Again like the evolutionists and Galbraith, the new radicals attack
specialization in economics and the unwillingness of economists to
adopt broad approaches. Galbraith reminds us in *The New Industrial
State* that "specialization is a scientific convenience, not a scientific
virtue." To Galbraith, specialization, at least in the social sciences, is
viewed as a source of error: "The world to its discredit does not divide
neatly along the lines that separate the specialists. These lines were
drawn in the first instance by deans, department chairmen or academic
committees.... Excellent though the architects were, they cannot be
credited with a uniquely valid view of the segments into which society
naturally divides itself."[9] Gintis also attacks

... the application with quite rigorous
"Separation schema,"

To the effect that the ways in which neo-classical theory
Goes about
Efficiently allocating resources
Does not itself affect
The way in which individual preferences
Develop.
. . . I hold that this separation schema
Is unjustifiable,
And that neo-classical
"Efficient economics"
Must be rejected even within its own realm of application. . . .
The types of institutional mechanisms
Indicated by neo-classical theory
And embodied in capitalistic society
Have implications
Which are not restricted to maximal material product
But directly affect
The way society handles
The problem of individual development.[10]

The frequent, if sometimes vague, references to "personal" or "individual" development have the humanistic ring of the younger Marx.

THE CRITICISM OF THE CAPITALIST SYSTEM

The major focus of the New Left radicals' criticism is the contemporary
economic system in the United States, which is a mixed capitalist system. I shall summarize five separate but overlapping aspects of their
general criticism.

First, the New Left radicals believe that the market system is unstable, unfair, and amoral, and leaves people unfulfilled. By its very
nature, they argue, the market system creates negative costs outside the
market that others must pay, such as the various pollutants that are
fouling lakes and streams and the air we breathe. As one new radical
article puts it,

> *Because the capitalist [capital owner] controls the work process*
> *and his goal is profit maximization, there will be no tendency to*
> *minimize costs which fall on others. . . . These extramarket costs*
> *take the form of fracture of the community, water and air*
> *pollution, congestion, "urban sprawl," etc., —a general destruction*
> *of the environment which cannot be viewed as a secondary issue*
> *but one of dominant importance in the society.*[11]

Thus total output per se is rejected as a reliable measure of welfare because the effects of output expansion may become detrimental to that welfare.

I want to make a slight digression at this point to clarify some terminology. In the above quotation, I put the phrase *capital owner* in brackets next to the word *capitalist* because the latter term is not always clearly defined in the New Left radical literature. Presumably, a capitalist is Marx's idealized owner of capital, but the new radicals only recently began to recognize the difference between capitalism as an idealization and American capitalism as it exists.[12] Baran and Sweezy, the "old Marxists," had always seen in most American industry a separation between ownership and control (management). Many industry managers share the radicals' concerns regarding poverty, racism, sexism, and pollution. Their differences appear to be on matters of policy. The managers, such as those on the Committee for Economic Development, petition the government to enact humane policies. The New Left radicals, who are antibureaucratic, envision some kind of organization for production that relies neither on profit incentive nor on government control. Like Marx, the radicals assume that the government is merely an extension of the power of the capitalist.

Bowles, Gintis, and Edwards envision a form of modified socialism in which individuals structure their lives through direct participatory control. The core of the society would be the development of an alternative to the wage-labor system. They see progressive democratization of the workplace as the key. An egalitarian and democratic economic life would lead to greater political democracy. Bowles and Edwards would have all banks and insurance companies under public control in order to ensure popular accountability for the investment uses of personal savings.[13]

Second, the radicals attack the way ownership of capital is distributed, a criticism advanced in the quest for a more equal distribution of wealth and income. They deplore the pockets of poverty in the United States and the general acceptability of the Phillips curve trade-off between price stability and higher unemployment. (The Phillips curve—discussed in more detail in the next chapter—is the relationship between the percentage of unemployment and the rate at which wages increase; it implies that unemployment can be reduced only at the cost of higher rates of inflation.) However, if one prefers the collective ownership of capital—as some radicals do—one still cannot be certain that power will also be equally distributed. To the extent that power is *not* in fact decentralized, the emergence of inequalities of wealth will not be far behind, a statement for which one can find ample evidence in a number of communist bloc nations. This prospect has led Bowles and

Gintis to place high priority upon economic equality in order to reduce the wealth differences that lead to political power imbalance. Corporate wealth has tipped the power scale in favor of the corporation. Not only must investment be democratized, according to Bowles and Edwards, but the United States needs an Economic Bill of Rights to counter corporate "trickle-down" economics.

Third, the New Left radicals want to rely less on wage and salary differentials as work incentives. It is true that for a number of reasons, including worker alienation, the power of these incentives is declining in the United States, but no one seems to know what will replace them. What incentives will be used to decide which occupational or leisure positions individuals will fill? Bowles, Gintis, and Edwards's answer is that democratic social relations in production will lead to highly motivated and productive workers. Increased efficiency will reduce the workweek and free persons for creative leisure and more informal production. Worker cooperation in production and participation in decision making is the carrot that replaces the stick of present work rules.

Fourth, the radical economists see competition as an evil to which cooperation (except monopolistic cooperation) is morally superior. Many—perhaps even most—people who have thought about it would probably agree that the American product-and-money rat race can have extremely bad effects on collective goals and individual personality development. Moreover, many of the most severe problems in the United States are caused by competition for profit (of some form) and are amenable to solution only through collective decision making. But intensive cooperation may have its own problems: many individuals who stress cooperation prefer to "cooperate" on their own terms. For example, would the radicals really prefer the paternalism of Japanese industrial organization or the regimentation of communal economies? Would they prefer the Yugoslavian model of management by the workers?[14] Bowles and Gintis prefer a uniquely American socialism that seems to be a cross between Yugoslavian worker democracy and Swedish cooperative socialism. Yet very little is actually known about the relative merits of competition and cooperation. The worldwide search appears to be for some middle ground where the efficiency attribute of competition could meet with the personal benefits that are supposed to derive from cooperation.

Finally, the radical economists argue, much like Galbraith, that the capitalist system takes resources away from the collective needs of education, health, the fine arts, public transportation, and social welfare. With respect to the last of these needs, certainly the quantity and quality of welfare services in the United States compare unfavorably with those in several socialist countries. This gap widened in favor of the socialist countries during the early 1980s. The mixed capitalist system in the United States may well misdirect attention away from collective needs that should be financed through taxation, but the Galbraithian and the New Left radical rhetoric is an input in the education process even though it has fallen into disfavor in the 1980s.

The foregoing recital of criticism and complaint does not mean that the New Left radical economists believe that capitalism has *no* virtues. Instead, they are saying that a society as affluent as ours should and can begin to rearrange its priorities in such a way that the technological success of capitalism can be taken for granted, and the society can concern itself with increasing the nonmaterial sources of satisfaction. For Gintis,

> *The virtue of capitalism*
> *Lies*
> *In its ability to generate*
> *Vast quantities of goods and services.*
> *It accomplishes this*
> *By devising a set of economic institutions*
> *Which*
> *Organize the development of society*
> *And the allocation of resources*
> *Over time*
> *Around the criterion*
> *Of "economic efficiency"*
> *In the sense of maximal physical output per unit of resources.*[15]

For Bowles and Edwards, however, the corporate system is at the same time wasting resources as it generates more and more supervisors and salespersons to coerce and persuade workers to do what they dislike and consumers to buy what they little need even as it has laid off *production* workers. Marx would have agreed. In this country, for example, land is a resource used primarily for making marketable commodities. The location of cities and farms and people may conform roughly to the efficiency criteria of competition and profit maximization but not necessarily to what people may actually want in terms of jobs or location.

DOOMSDAY CAPITALISM

A very pessimistic view of the long-run survival capabilities of capitalism stems from the writings of Karl Marx and of Joseph Schumpeter (1883–1950). Some of the new radicals are doomsayers in the Marx-Schumpeter tradition, and they see a worldwide economic slowdown similar to the Great Depression of the 1930s. In addition to the failure of Keynesian remedies, these pessimists see American capitalism becoming stagnant not only because of the failure of Keynesian remedies but also because of the absence of product and technological innovations. Schumpeter identified a "long wave" of forty to sixty years that overrides the shorter-term business cycle and leads to progressively deeper crises.

Among those interested in the long waves, Raymond Franklin argues that American capitalism may be at the end of an elaborate investment boom launched in the early 1940s. He sees the growth of state expenditures as instrumental in this most recent wave. These expenditures financed infrastructure such as highways for the automobile industry and research and development such as that underwriting the growth of the aircraft and electronic-communications industries.

Marxian class structure becomes important in the upward swing. The new forms of production lead to upward mobility in the population, especially in middle ranges of the class structure. When the upward swing culminates in a major crisis, the status of the newly established middle class is threatened. The ultimate crisis occurs after a long inflationary binge, and the downswing culminates in an unusually severe depression.

Since the 1930s, the middle class has been taxed in order to transfer income and services to the poor as well as to provide the funds for new infrastructure and research. This threatened class balked at being taxed at higher levels during the hyperinflation of the 1970s. In short, the crisis created a condition that foreclosed the means previously used to support the upswing. Franklin expected all this to culminate in a worldwide depression during the 1980s, accompanied by a crisis of the state. On the first fear, he was correct; on the second, the correctness depends upon what we consider to be a "crisis of the state." In Chapters 14 and 16, we will return to the long wave and to the economic crises of the 1980s.

CONFUSION BETWEEN CARICATURE CAPITALISM AND THE STATUS QUO

Next we arrive at a crucial point that has been a source of confusion among radical economists of the Left *and* the Right. The New Left radicals combine a criticism of the neoclassical paradigm with a criticism of caricature capitalism in a way that suggests that the paradigm is just another product of capitalism. Kill off capitalism, the New Left radicals seem to be saying, and the neoclassical paradigm is dead. The New Right radicals (see Chapter 14) *defend* the same caricature, but they wish to preserve it. The point of confusion is that the paradigm/capitalism duality is false. Capitalism in its stereotyped, Smithian incarnation is *already* dead; it is the neoclassical contrivance that has lingered for so long. As we established in earlier chapters, the scientific content of the neoclassical paradigm has far more to do with Isaac Newton than it does with capitalism. The "equilibria" and "optima" that are so essential to the paradigm occur in an imagined world of atomistic competition derived from Newtonian science and Cartesian method. Any claim that the details of caricature capitalism have been sighted in real-world capitalism is pure science fiction. Economics has been drugged by science far more frequently than by capitalism. It is the neoclassical model as a flawless machine of internal consistency that has claimed the admiration of most economists. Indeed, economists have shown that the neoclassical pricing and resource allocation mechanism can be used under socialism and that the ownership of private property has absolutely no theoretical importance in neoclassical theory, which means that, as a *tool*, the paradigm exists in its own right, independent of capitalism.[16]

Nevertheless, the neoclassical paradigm is flexible enough to be twisted into a defense of the status quo, of whatever form "capitalism" has taken, and economists and politicians have been busily twisting it for some two centuries. Moreover, the paradigm is, as Edwards, Reich, and Weisskopf suggest, "a system of belief." It expresses—or at least seems to express—a number of significant Western values, such as freedom and individual initiative. The Marxist paradigm, on the other hand, is uncongenial to Western ethics in some respects and has had the further disadvantage of a birth that took place outside the gates of Cambridge. This lower birth denied it a proper upbringing by academic apostles.

The New Left radical economists are better understood as a paradigm-demolition squad and as advocates of economic democracy than as anticapitalists. Just as the neoclassical paradigm has survived the demise of caricature capitalism because economists have failed to endorse a better machine, the conventional paradigm will also survive the radical assault unless the criteria for a new scientific paradigm are met. Neoclassical economics survived the brilliant critique of Marx and the inspired passion and logic of Veblen, criticisms to which the New Left radicals owe a great deal. Thus far, these criticisms and challenges have emerged in their new form because contemporary conditions prove their relevance, not because economic science has unveiled new analytical insights.

13

ECONOMIC CRISES OF THE 1970s

▼

*. . . corporate economic, product, and environmental crimes
dwarf other crimes in damage to health, safety and
property, in confiscation or theft of other people's monies,
and in control of the [government] agencies which are
supposed to stop this crime and fraud. And it all goes on
year after year by blue-chip corporate recidivists.
Why? It is easy to answer—"power."*

RALPH NADER, INTRODUCTION TO *AMERICA, INC.*, 1971

Social crises precede revisions of the social science paradigm. A
dramatic omen of the crisis in economics during the 1970s occurred
on August 15, 1971. On that date, President Richard M. Nixon, who had
based his political career upon the defense of free market laissez-faire
capitalism, stunned the nation by adopting extensive wage and price
controls. Indeed, if one did not know better, one might presume that
John Kenneth Galbraith himself had drafted the plan. The initial price-
wage freeze obviously was not desired by the president but was a desperate policy play dictated by an impending international monetary
crisis. Nixon's policy reversal was an admission of the failure of all conventional economic policy devices to slow inflation without causing a
severe depression. A major crisis of economic science surfaced: its failure to explain why price stability apparently can be bought only with
very high unemployment levels. By the end of the Nixon Administration, this crisis had reached a dangerous stage. The same type of economic crisis was experiencing reruns by late 1979, and again, two new
administrations engineered economic recessions in attempts to slow
inflation.

But the inflation-unemployment crisis was only one of several
emerging economic crises in the 1970s. The persistence of poverty,

particularly in urban ghettos, indicated that a large number of Americans were not participating in the widespread affluence. At the same time, ecology emerged as an economic crisis. Planet Earth was showing signs of stress and strain. Rapidly accelerating pollution levels and the possibility of depleting certain vital resources reminded the ordinary citizen, if not all economists, that the earth is a finite planet.

Social values regarding economic betterment were also changing. We have seen how a sizable group of radical economists of the Left rejected the "efficiency economics" of price theory. They argued that orthodox economists, claiming ethical neutrality, had advanced the notions of efficiency and production growth to the benefit of private enterprise and to the detriment of the general public. Galbraith had long contended that private enterprise was starving the public sector, where society's new needs lay. The views of the new radicals and Galbraith were applauded by many who were growing disenchanted with strict materialism within postindustrial society.[1]

There is a good reason for juxtaposing social crises with values in economics. Nothing is a social crisis unless society's ethics say it is. Poverty and racism were not considered social problems prior to Dickens's time, except by a few intellectuals. Ecology was not a widespread concern in the 1950s. Overemphasis on material values is never deplored until large numbers of people fail to find satisfaction in "meaningless" work and ostentatious consumption. The purpose of this chapter is to provide a survey of the economic crises of the 1970s. First, I shall describe the effects of industrial concentration, a concern that we can share with Adam Smith. Second, I shall focus on the problems of poverty and income and wealth distribution. Third, I shall describe the twin and separate crises of inflation and unemployment. Finally, I shall outline the ecological crisis. The next chapter will cover the response of first-term Reaganomics to these crises, the new crises of the 1980s, and President Reagan's policy reversals. In the final chapters, I shall discuss the implications of these emerging social crises for new economic theory and policies.

THE CORPORATE CONCENTRATION CRISIS

Suppose that every company west of the Mississippi River had merged into one corporation called Samson Securities, and every company east of the Mississippi had merged into another, Delilah Company. In 1966, Art Buchwald developed a scenario about what might happen when Samson and Delilah applied for clearance to a merger from the Antitrust Division of the U.S. Department of Justice. It ends up like this:

> *The Antitrust Division of the Justice Department studied the merger for months. Finally the Attorney General made this ruling. "While we find drawbacks to only one company being left in the United States, we feel the advantages to the public far outweigh the disadvantages.*
>
> *"Therefore, we're making an exception in this case and allowing Samson and Delilah to merge.*
>
> *"I would like to announce that the Samson and Delilah Company is now negotiating at the White House with the President to buy the United States. The Justice Department will naturally study this merger to see if it violates any of our strong antitrust laws."*[2]

The fear that this indeed is the future direction of corporate economic power relations is dramatized by Justice William O. Douglas's appending the satirist's entire column to his concurring opinion in the antitrust case of *U.S.* vs. *Pabst Brewing Company* (1966). This fear seems justified, for today only 200 corporations do control most of the American economy. The state of industrial competition does not resemble in fact, in evolvement, in motivation, or in consequence the contemporary economics paradigm. American society continues to face a crisis of immense proportions from concentrated corporate-political power.

The Reality of Business Concentration

Fortune magazine's annual list of the 500 largest companies in the United States tells us a great deal about American industrial competition. The largest American manufacturing corporations by size of total assets for 1947–1983 were oil, automobile, computer, steel, communications, and chemical producers. Exxon (formerly Standard Oil of New Jersey) was still at the top of this heap in 1983, followed by General Motors, IBM, Mobil Oil, Texaco, Standard Oil (Indiana), E. I. duPont de Nemours, Standard Oil (California), Ford, and General Electric. In the interest of increasing competition, antitrust action decades ago "broke up" Standard Oil, but the effort had modest consequences. Now there are three Standard Oils among the top ten corporations instead of only one.[3] A fourth Standard Oil (Ohio) ranks sixteenth. But few giant corporations have been broken up by the antitrust authorities, and relatively few mergers have been blocked.

The share of total sales held by various firms in an industry provides an index of the degree of competition in that industry. Table 13.1 lists the leading producers in major industries. From this table, we can see that many industrial and consumer markets are dominated by a few large corporations. Even among the 500 largest industrial (manufacturing and mining) corporations, the top 25 garnered 41 percent and the top 50 more than half of the total sales of the 500 companies in 1983. How did the American economy arrive at a point so far short of perfect competition?

A Short History of the Merger Movement

A tendency toward the combination of industrial units under centralized control has been apparent since the development of the factory system and machine processes made possible a larger scale of production. Such a tendency has been even more pronounced since the beginning of the Industrial Revolution in the United States. Shortly after the American Civil War, the Robber Barons' attempt to gain control of industries led to the trust movement, which reached its peak between the 1880s and the turn of the twentieth century. The Standard Oil Co., the American Tobacco Co., and the American Sugar Refining Co. were among the many trusts formed during this period. The peak of this trend was marked by the formation of the billion-dollar U.S. Steel Corporation in 1901. By 1904, 40 percent of all manufacturing capital in the United States was held by the U.S. Steel Corporation. The trust included such diverse products as gunpowder, lead, linseed oil, matches, petroleum, photographic materials, window glass, whiskey, cash registers, bicycles, and chewing gum. By the time the wave of concentration had crested, a mere twenty-six corporations controlled four-fifths or more of the production in their respective industries. At the turn of the century, large corporations dominated the American economy.

The trend toward industrial concentration continued. The 200 largest nonfinancial corporations increased their relative importance from the ownership of one-third of all nonfinancial assets in 1909 to ownership of more than one-half of all nonfinancial assets in the early 1930s. Those heights of concentration were attained largely through mergers and consolidations in the years between the two world wars. The important industries affected by consolidation were iron, steel and machinery, oil, food products, textiles, and chemicals. The wave of mergers and acquisitions was interrupted by the Great Depression, but the interruption was only temporary.

Much of the increase of industrial concentration between the two world wars was a result of vertical integration. *Vertical integration* is the operation of a company in two or more industries representing successive stages of production.[4] For example, in the movie industry, theaters were organized into chains under the control of, first, film distributors and, later, film producers. The avowed purpose of vertical integration

TABLE 13.1. Major American Corporations with Substantial Market Power, 1983 (Apart from Utilities and Financial Corporations)*

Markets and leading firms	Approximate share of these firms in relevant markets (percent)	Markets and leading firms	Approximate share of these firms in relevant markets (percent)
Telephone equipment Western Electric	90–100	Aerospace Boeing United Technologies McDonnell-Douglas General Dynamics	75–85
Motor vehicles General Motors Ford Chrysler	85–95	Flat glass P.P.G. Industries Libby-Owens-Ford Corning Glassworks	80–90
Computing equipment IBM	40–45	Aluminum Alcoa Reynolds Kaiser	70–80
Heavy electrical equipment General Electric Westinghouse	55–60	Copper Amax Phelps-Dodge Kennecott	80–90
Petroleum refining Exxon Mobil Texaco Standard Oil (Indiana)	50–55	Primary lead Fluor Amax Asarco	95–100
Iron and steel U.S. Steel Bethlehem National Intergroup Republic	65–70		

Industry Group	Market Share (%)
Drugs	45–55
Johnson and Johnson	
Am. Home Products	
Pfizer	
Merck	
Soaps, etc.	65–75
Procter & Gamble	
Colgate	
Avon Products	
Industrial chemicals	55–65
DuPont	
Dow	
Union Carbide	
Monsanto	
Refrigerators, laundry appliances	80–90
General Electric	
Westinghouse	
Whirlpool	
White Consolidated	
Beer	60–70
Anheuser-Busch	
Coors (Adolph)	
Heilman	
Pabst	
Photographic supplies	70–80
Eastman Kodak	
Tires and tubes	80–90
Goodyear	
Firestone	
Goodrich (B.F.)	
Uniroyal	
Dairy products	45–55
Borden	
Carnation	
Metal containers	60–70
Continental Group	
Owens–Illinois	
American Can	
Cereal breakfast foods	65–75
General Mills	
Kellogg	
Soup	80–85
Campbell	

*Estimates derived from data published in *Business Week,* March 21, 1984; *Fortune,* April 30, 1984; and U.S. Department of Commerce, *1984 Industrial Outlook,* January 1984. Companies are listed by order of their market share within each group.

is to reduce costs by becoming the supplier of one's own materials, parts, and components. The effect of vertical integration, however, is to limit the number of independent firms operating in the marketplace, to centralize control of an industry under a few large corporations, and thereby to limit economic competition.

Domination by the Few

As dramatic as these data on business concentration are, they underestimate the fact that mere handfuls of huge financial interests dominate the economy. Besides direct stock ownership, there are several other ways of controlling corporations: interlocking directorates, investment trusts, banking affiliations, and proxy machinery. It is mostly through these more indirect methods that the great financial interests of the country—the Rockefellers, the Mellons, the DuPonts—exercise their tremendous power and control over American industry. Financial interest groups in particular are important in the control of corporate enterprises. The National Resources Committee (1939) was able to determine eight more or less clearly defined large interest groups. Nearly one-third of the corporate assets of the 250 largest corporations in 1935 were controlled by these eight interest groups, representing the control of 106 large corporations. The largest of the eight was Morgan–First National, whose influence was through two institutions—J. P. Morgan and Company and the First National Bank of New York. Three of the interest groupings were derived from the family interests of the Rockefellers, Mellons, and DuPonts.[5] To this day, these financial groups remain intact, except that the Rockefeller interests (through Chase Manhattan Bank, etc.) now control more companies than the Morgan group, and the Mellon group has superseded another of the eight.[6]

Most of the research on the economic elite has focused on the role of major manufacturing corporations and their heads, but the role of financial intermediaries has been grossly neglected. Although internal self-financing is the most important aspect of corporate life among the giants, external sources of guaranteed lines of credit can often be reassuring and sometimes useful. Furthermore, sociologist Maurice Zeitlin sees concentration in the financial sector overlapping with the industrial sector so as to contribute to industrial concentration. He cites the study by the Subcommittee on Domestic Finance of the House Banking and Currency Committee, chaired by the late Representative Wright Patman, and popularly titled the Patman Committee Report, to show that, as of the end of 1964, the 100 largest commercial banks held nearly half of all the deposits in the 13,775 commercial banks in the United

States.[7] By 1983, the 50 largest banks held more than half of all deposits and 60 percent of the assets in the 14,550 banks in the United States.

Financial intermediaries in turn exercise power over the major industrial corporations. Although the trend toward managerial control of the major corporations is still increasing, as Galbraith contends, the Patman Committee reports that the situation also involves bank minority control. Most important, the degree of open coordination between the elites of the banking sector and those of the industries is great. The Patman Committee data suggest that the financial sector of the service economy, a largely neglected area in descriptions of competitive conditions, is becoming increasingly important in the economic system and, by inference, in the present distribution of power among industrial elites.

The trend is shifting economic power back to a small group, repeating in a somewhat different manner the patterns of the trusts of the late nineteenth and early twentieth centuries.[8]

The Conglomerate Rush

Whereas the vertically integrated corporation produces functionally related products and services, the *conglomerate* enterprise, as its name implies, is typically a combination of unrelated enterprises. General Dynamics, for example, turns out a diversified product line ranging from Atlas Missiles to gravel.[9] The growth of these large multi-industry firms proceeded at a feverish tempo during the 1960s. More than 4,500 firms disappeared through merger in 1969 alone. By that year, the top 200 manufacturing corporations controlled two-thirds of all manufacturing assets.

When a firm holds conglomerate power, its operations are so widely diversified that its survival no longer depends on success with any given product market for any particular geographical area. Its sheer bigness can discipline or destroy its more specialized competitors. Thus, in an important distinction not found in economic theory,

> *a conglomerate giant is powerful . . . not because it has a monopoly or oligopoly control over a particular product, but because its resources are bigger than those of its specialized competitors, and because these resources are diversified over many different markets. Its power . . . derives from the fact that it can outbid, outspend, and outlose a smaller firm. It occupies a position much like the millionaire poker player who, in a game of unlimited stakes, can easily bankrupt his less opulent opponents— regardless of his comparative mastery over the dizzy virtues of probability theory.[10]*

These corporate forms and resultant types of economic market organization lead either to the monopoly feared by Adam Smith, or, more
likely, to oligopoly, where a few firms dominate the industry. The only
legitimate economic-efficiency justification for these variations of "ideal"
theoretical types is economies of scale, which, since Alfred Marshall,
have constituted the main defense for industrial concentration. In a
popular text, Edwin Mansfield contends that "in some industries, low
costs cannot be achieved unless a firm is producing an output equal to
a substantial percentage of the total available market, the consequence
being that the number of firms will tend to be rather small."[11] This
economic-scale argument is especially pertinent to the standardized
production technology to be discussed in more detail in Chapter 16.
Large corporate enterprises use this explanation to justify their size,
even though such economies of scale cannot be the true reason for
growth through merger across industry lines or through conglomerate
mergers.

THE POVERTY CRISIS

We are now facing a poverty crisis in terms of both human suffering
and welfare costs. For the decade ending in 1969, the number of people
in the United States regarded as poor grew steadily smaller. Then, this
downsweeping trend went into a stall. By 1969, according to conservative official definitions of poverty, the number of people who were
poor had shrunk to 24.1 million. Yet, during the 1970s a plateau was
reached in which the poor still numbered almost 25 million. The number and share of the poor rose steeply from this plateau and had reached
35.3 million by 1983, or nearly 15.2 percent of the population.[12] Thus,
some 15 percent of the American population is nearly invisible because
the poor have not always fit neatly into the orthodox economic paradigm, and both have suffered for it.

The Nonmarket Poor

Although Keynesian economics holds that the creation of new jobs
is the most effective possible cure for urban poverty, some four-fifths of
the poor consist of children, adults in households headed by females,
adults in households headed by disabled males, and adults in households headed by the aged. This means that about four-fifths of the poor
are *nonmarket poor* in the sense that they do not even enter the labor
market. We cannot ascribe their poverty to an inability to respond to
free enterprise incentives. Most of the metropolitan poor are not em-
ployable for one reason or another.

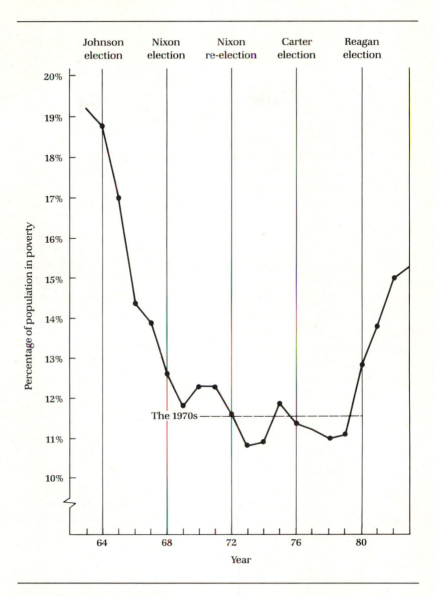

FIGURE 13.1 A twenty-year trend in U. S. poverty rates. [*Source:* U.S. Bureau of the Census, *Current Population Survey,* Series P-60, Nos. 134, 140, 1982 and 1983.]

Further, poverty takes the form of an unbroken cycle. This cycle makes our society less viable and greatly reduces the social contributions that otherwise could be made by the poor. The children of the poor grow up, are married, remain poor, and usually raise poor children. These needy children in turn form the poverty households of tomorrow. A study for Congress concludes that "poverty data would seem to indicate a low degree of economic mobility among the poverty population."[13] To the extent that such people become dependent upon welfare support, society bears an additional burden. Although there are some who break out of the cycle, they cannot be used as a rationalization for ignoring the low quality of life experienced by those who are left behind.

Income and Wealth Redistribution: A Cure for Poverty?

Whether or not one is poor, the best measure of ability to purchase goods and services is after-tax income. However, the job markets decide the level of before-tax income.

Some studies suggest that there was a significant reduction in the inequality of money income distribution in the United States during the period 1929–1947 but that there has been no change since that period. This conclusion is not unanimous. It is the judgment of most experts that the data are biased toward overestimating the decline in income inequality. This bias occurs because capital gains and income supplements in the form of expense accounts, automobiles, stock options, and so on accrue faster to higher-income families than to the lower, who do not find their way into the income-distribution statistics. Unadjusted post–World War II data indeed suggest little change in income inequalities.

Since World War II, the poorest 20 percent of all American families have received less than 6 percent of total family money income (income *un*adjusted for price changes), while the richest one-fifth have received over 40 percent. Money income is even more concentrated at the very top. The top 5 percent of all families have been receiving about 15 percent of total family money income, or roughly three times as much as the entire bottom fifth. In 1981–1982, the share held by the poorest 20 percent declined, while the share held by the top 5 percent rose to 16 percent.

It is an all-American cliché that income tax rates have been progressive—that is, the Feds tax the rich at a higher rate than the poor. It's more than a cliché; it is a myth. Loopholes such as low rates on capital gains benefit higher-income families more than the lower. So, the federal income tax has turned out to be almost proportional to one's family money income. In fact, the use of abusive tax shelters led to a multitude of tax reform proposals and the introduction of tax reform bills in the U.S. Congress during 1985 and 1986.

Of course, there are taxes other than federal income taxes. Nonetheless, when all taxes are considered together, there is little difference in the distribution of before- and after-tax money income. An important study by the Brookings Institution estimated adjusted family money income before and after all taxes under various assumptions about the degree to which businesses and landlords pass on taxes to consumers. Even under the "most progressive" assumptions, they found essentially no change between the before- and after-tax distributions of money income.[14]

The distribution of wealth comprises another part of the picture of the distribution of economic welfare. A person's or family's wealth includes all of the property or assets owned. Some of these assets, such as stocks, bonds, and real estate, produce income; other properties, such as automobiles and homes, are for personal use. Personal property is, as one would suspect, distributed more or less the same way as incomes. Income-producing wealth, however, is heavily concentrated in a few hands. Indeed, its concentration for the most part explains the great inequalities in income.

In 1969, 40 percent of all total personal and income-producing assets were held by slightly more than one-tenth of all American households. If we soar into the rare air at the peak of this mountain of wealth, we find that the wealthiest 1 percent of the asset holders held almost one-quarter of total wealth, and the top *one-half percent* of wealth holders held nearly one-fifth of total wealth.

The rich have not been very closely studied in the United States. Among the few extensive surveys of the rich, the most recent was conducted by the Federal Reserve Board.[15] In the year of their latest (second) survey (1983), the typical American household had a net worth of a little under $25,000. Nearly a fifth of families had a *negative* net worth. The top 2 percent of American households, however, held *between a quarter and a third* of the nation's household wealth. This affluent minority owned 71 percent of all tax-exempt bonds, 38 percent of all taxable bonds, 22 percent of the individual checking accounts, 13 percent of the money market accounts, 23 percent of certificates of deposit, and 12 percent of the money in savings accounts. They also owned 62 percent of all stocks in private hands and 42 percent of all the real estate purchased as investments. The basic trend of the surveys indicates a growing concentration of wealth in the coffers of a small number of families with high annual incomes.

For both political and economic reasons, poverty again became a problem in the 1980s. Voters are likely to favor redistribution of income only—if at all—when a majority are poor. But the growth of the middle class between 1929 and 1947 has shifted the balance of political power toward them. Moreover, the lower middle class became the nouveau poor during the 1970s hyperinflation in the prices of necessities. Unless the Phillips curve trade-off is illusory or can be eliminated, increased poverty through higher unemployment rates will probably be the price that society chooses to pay to maintain a slow rate of price inflation.

INFLATION AND THE PHILLIPS CURVE

Suppose that the average practicing economist, a male household head of prime working age, at the end of the 1970s had been faced with the awesome prospect of personal unemployment and higher prices for his necessities out of a zero current income. Would his policy advice or forecasts have been different? A fanciful answer to this question has been provided by Art Buchwald, and it creates a good backdrop for inflation and the Phillips curve.

> *Ebenezer Tanklips was pleased with himself. As chief economist for the Bilgewater Corporation he had just handed in his projection for the year 1979. It was a masterful job, he thought to himself. . . . His report indicated a continual high inflation rate, more attacks on the dollar, a drop in the GNP, and what he considered his masterpiece—a prediction of full-scale recession.*
>
> *When he walked into his office his secretary said, "The chairman of the board wants to see you."*
>
> *"You wanted to see me, B. J.?" Tanklips said.*
>
> *"Yes," the chairman replied. "I just read your projections for 1979. You're fired!"*
>
> *"Fired?" Tanklips said, "but why?"*
>
> *". . . As you so ably state here on Page 45, it's time to retrench, get rid of the deadwood, and dig in for the long pull until the economy turns around."*
>
> *"Did I say that?" Tanklips cried. "I must have been crazy, B. J., . . ."*
>
> *The chairman said, "I'm sorry, it's too late. You predicted that, in order to resolve the inflation dilemma, we would have to live with an 8 percent unemployment rate. This company is willing to live with it, as long as you are."*
>
> *"But," said Tanklips, "I wasn't including myself in that unemployment rate. . . ."*
>
> *"Why not?" the chairman asked.*
>
> *"Because it would be a conflict of interest. We have to stay out of the unemployment projections or our figures would be tainted by self-interest. B.J., please don't fire me."*

> *"I'm sorry, Tanklips, but your report speaks for itself. We're going to have to play hardball in 1979."*
>
> *"Let me look at that a moment," Tanklips said, grabbing the report off the desk. "My God, I put a decimal point in the wrong place! And I forgot to carry the two over when I added up 7, 4 and 9. This changes everything. We can't cut back in '79! It's going to be our greatest year."*
>
> *"You wouldn't be snowing me, Tanklips, just to keep your job?"*
>
> *"Of course not, sir. As an economist that would be unethical."*[16]

This story puts the human side of the trade-off between inflation and unemployment into perspective—for the average worker *and* the economist. For, no doubt, the greatest embarrassment for much of orthodox economics occurred during the 1970s, with double-digit inflation *and* high rates of unemployment. It was a social crisis that demanded resolution. In economic theory, however, it also was a crisis because neoclassical and Keynesian economics had concluded that unemployment and inflation could not be coincident events. Nonetheless, since the mid-1950s, prices have tended to rise even in times of slack labor markets and substantial gaps from full employment. Especially after the 1965 escalation of the Vietnam War, the momentum of inflation was such that little control was secured from the creation of socially acceptable levels of unemployment.

Before we examine the policy dilemma created by the neo-Keynesian trade-off between employment and inflation, let us consider some of the problems created by inflation (hinted at above), particularly when it is severe. Inflation is an invisible tax that redistributes income. Rising prices take real purchasing power away from those whose money incomes rise less rapidly than the prices they pay and redistribute it toward those whose money incomes rise faster than the prices they pay. As a rough generalization, those on fixed incomes, such as old-age pensioners and college professors, are heavily taxed by inflation. Highly organized union workers are impacted much less. For example, between 1967 and 1978 the average steelworker's income (after taxes and effects of inflation) increased 32 percent, whereas that of the average university professor *declined* 17.5 percent.

Of course, the budgets of the poor and middle class are substantially different from the budgets of the rich. Even after comparing the rate of inflation with the pace of money income growth, we still cannot define precisely who ends up relatively better off. In part, this depends on *which* prices are rising. For example, if the price of necessities (basic foods, clothing, and shelter) is rising the most rapidly, the lower- and middle-income classes, who spend a larger proportion of their budget on necessities, may experience a substantial decline in their purchasing power even if their wage rates are rising. For example, between 1967 and 1978 the price of hamburger increased 153 percent and that of a loaf of bread, 109 percent in Atlanta, Georgia. (We shall return to this issue in Chapter 15.)

Inflation also redistributes wealth from creditors—those who are lending money—to debtors—those who are borrowing—when debts are stated in fixed dollar terms. Whether you bemoan this redistribution depends greatly upon your value judgments. Some would argue that creditors are richer than debtors and little worry should be wasted because of a diminution of their relative wealth because their wealth is already so high. The relatively lower income debtors are paying back their borrowings with lower-valued money. Even if you do not lament the relative decrease in creditors' wealth, you would still need to consider that the poor and middle-class families would have to pay higher and higher interest rates on their borrowings as inflation continues.

Inflation also redistributes wealth from those whose assets rise more slowly in price to those whose assets rise more rapidly. A complete analysis of this issue again turns upon *which* prices are rising. For example, homeowners might experience a great increase in relative wealth because the price of housing has been rising so rapidly during the inflation of the 1970s, whereas those who are holding bonds during inflation see the value of their assets diminish. This dichotomy is the result of the inverse relation between the price of a bond and its interest rate, discussed in Chapter 7. As interest rates climb during inflation—raising the price of shelter, a necessity—the capital value of bonds declines. In any case, higher-income families have the financial flexibility to shift their resources from one kind of asset into another that would appreciate more rapidly.

Without engaging in a very complicated analysis, it is very difficult to assess with any precision the differential effects of inflation upon various income groups. Suffice it to say that significant inflation creates the greatest social problems when the prices of necessities are rising most rapidly. This is because the purchasing power of most of the population is greatly diminished by such inflation. Much of the inflation of the 1970s was of this variety.

Inflation can be classified by its *causes* into at least four types: demand-pull, cost-push, structural, and expectational. (Although useful, this delineation is difficult to identify in practice.) Pure *demand-pull inflation* is a consequence of total demand exceeding potential output. This is the type of inflation identifiable in the Keynesian cross diagram. *Cost-push inflation* can be the result of union pressures for higher wages (and management acquiescence) or of higher costs of raw materials and other commodities used in production. The latter variety of cost-push inflation was identified as "seller's inflation" by the late Abba P. Lerner, the distinguished American economist. It can orginate with highly concentrated industries, such as steel, that face little competition from products that are substitutes for their wares. The price rise for one industry becomes a cost increase for the next, and so on. Seller's inflation from market power can sometimes spread; for instance, from the price of steel to the price of automobiles.

Structural inflation is a consequence of both demand-pull and cost-push forces. If total demand is less than potential output, inflation can occur where there is a shift in the *pattern* of demand. Because of the historical downward rigidity of U.S. prices and wages, an advance in wages and prices in one section of the economy is not offset by comparable declines elsewhere. Hence, the overall average price level rises and continues to rise so long as wages do.

Expectational inflation occurs as a result of the actions of individuals and institutions in reaction to anticipated inflation. In its purest form, we have expectational inflation because we expect inflation, and we expect inflation because we've been experiencing inflation. There are many variants of expectational inflation; however, they all share the same basic labor market explanation. Workers demand higher rates of increases in wages because they anticipate (correctly or incorrectly) higher prices for the products and services they buy.

These alternative explanations of inflation are often compared by reference to the Phillips curve, named for its inventor, A. W. Phillips, an Australian economist. The curve relates to the percentage of change in the money wage rate and the associated cost-of-living inflation on the vertical axes, with unemployment, expressed as a percentage of the labor force, on the horizontal axis (see Figure 13.2). Note that wage inflation does not result in price inflation until it exceeds the long-run rate of productivity growth (about 3 percent per year). The explanation for the shape of the Phillips curve lies in competitive labor markets. During booms the enhanced demand for labor drives up the rate of increase in wages, which translates into higher production costs and accelerated increases in product prices. (Labor remuneration comprises the largest share of production costs.) At such times the unemployment rate falls. The opposite sequence happens during downturns.

The Phillips curve of the 1950s and 1960s suggested that the tradeoff for a greater share of workers employed was price inflation. Price stability had to be sacrificed in order to gain high employment levels. For presidents and prime ministers, who hoped to have both stable prices *and* lower levels of unemployment, this curve was perplexing. If the real-world relation is depicted by the righthand curve in Figure 13.2,

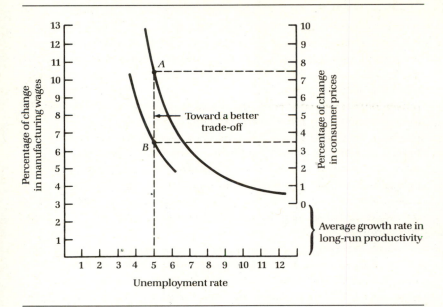

FIGURE 13.2 The Phillips curve

a policy that would reduce the inflation rate from 7.5 percent to 3 percent would raise the unemployment rate from 5 to 7 percent.

There was only a slight glimmer of hope. Some economists detected a rightward shift in the curve (toward more inflation and more unemployment) during the 1950s and 1960s. If the curve could shift right, why not left? In short, could the behavior of individuals and institutions important in determining the curve's position be altered? If economic reforms could shove the curve, would left be the proper direction to move? If the shift leftward results in a curve parallel to the old one (as illustrated in Figure 13.2), the inflation rate would fall from 7.5 percent (point A) to only 3.5 percent (point B), while the unemployment rate would remain constant at 5 percent. Of course, a society would prefer less inflation if it meant a stable unemployment rate.

A rightward shift and an upward shift toward worse trade-offs are associated with two inflation types—the structural and the expectational, respectively. We first consider the structural inflation explanation associated with the Keynesians of Chapter 8. In their view the Phillips curve correctly amends their Keynesian models in a way that accounts for inflation. During full-employment years, when labor markets are tight, wages are bid up. When national income falls during economic recessions, average wage rates continue to rise, although less rapidly, and thus add to the mounting costs of manufacturers. Now, introduce the market power of highly concentrated industries; such industries not only pass the higher costs off as higher consumer prices, their power, plus "adequate" consumer demand, is reflected in higher profit rates during periods of high employment. This shift in the power (higher profit rates) of institutions would indeed yield rightward shifts in the Phillips curve. Whether this profits-push inflation is subsumed as cost-push inflation depends upon whether profits are considered a cost of production or a residual. Irrespective of which way we look at profits, we can say that the profits-push variety of inflation shifts the Phillips curve rightward. In point of fact, any increase in nonlabor input costs—such as higher oil prices—will shift the Phillips curve rightward.

A second explanation for a worse trade-off in the short run is the upward-shifting Phillips curve caused by expectational inflation. Workers demand higher rates of wage increases because they expect higher product prices. For any unemployment rate, the higher the anticipated rate of inflation, the higher the actual inflation. If we go only this far, the result is not much different from structural inflation. If workers expect a rapid inflation, they will demand more generous wage contracts, and firms will then pass these higher wages along as the higher prices that the workers expected. (By the same token, if people expect little or no inflation, then wage inflation will be modest and firms will restrain product-price inflation.) In this view, however, the long-run Phillips curve is much steeper than the short-run Phillips curve because it would trace out all those points at which the actual and the anticipated inflation rates are equal.

Because of completely anticipated inflation, the monetarists see *no trade-off at all* between inflation and the unemployment rate in the *long run.* Their conclusion stems from their concept of the natural rate of unemployment (see Chapter 8). This vision depends upon a classical view of the perfectly adjusting labor market (in real terms). Any increase in anticipated inflation is matched percentage point by percentage point by wage inflation, leaving the real wage rate unchanged. With the real wage rate unaltered, the level of employment and therefore the unemployment rate remain constant (at the natural unemployment rate). Only *unanticipated* inflation can lead to *temporary* reductions in unemployment below the natural rate. In the long run, inflation is fully anticipated, and there is no trade-off whatsoever between inflation and unemployment; the Phillips curve is vertical, as in Figure 13.3.

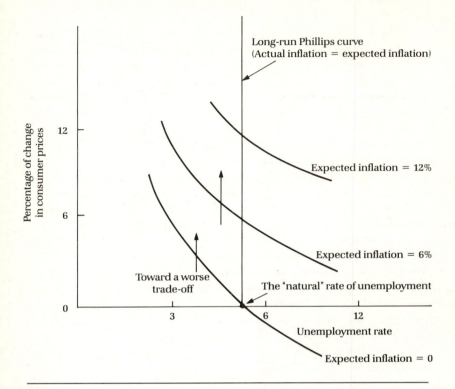

FIGURE 13.3 The Phillips curve, expectational inflation, and the natural rate of unemployment

Note: Three short-run Phillips curves are shown in the figure: there is a different curve for each rate of expected inflation. In the long run, the "natural" rate of unemployment is fixed at that level at which actual and fully anticipated inflation are equal. Monetary and fiscal policies can reduce unemployment below the "natural" rate temporarily by creating an unanticipated inflation (movement up the relevant short-run Phillips curve). However, as soon as workers realize that the actual inflation is greater than what they anticipated, they will leave their jobs and again be voluntarily unemployed. Then, employment and unemployment will return to their higher "natural" levels. Since equilibrium is always determined by the equality of actual and anticipated inflation, an increase in the anticipated inflation rate shifts the short-run Phillips curve up the "natural" unemployment rate line to the corresponding rate of inflation (vertical axis). For an expected inflation of 6 percent, the short-run Phillips curve intersects the "natural" unemployment rate at an actual 6 percent change in consumer prices. All such intersections (for all short-run Phillips curves) yield the long-run Phillips curve, the vertical line.

Still another school of thought lands on the same curve, though it is vertical even in the short run. This particular monetarist branch out-Friedmans Milton Friedman. This group is called the rational expectationists and emerged in the late 1970s. The more conservative members of this branch are Friedman inspired with a vengeance that distinguishes them from economists who use the idea of rational expectations, only to find that the expectations themselves are denied by empirical study. Robert Lucas of the University of Chicago, as well as Thomas Sargent and Neil Wallace, both of the University of Minnesota, appear to be the leaders of the Chicago offshoot.

The notion of rational expectations is really an extension through future time of the rational economic man prototype. The new super-rational economic man bases his choices upon perfect knowledge about not merely today's conditions but also the situation in the future. The usual monetary or fiscal policy manipulations will not stop the inflation because, on the basis of their knowledge of the past, superrational individuals will presume that the government will go on doing what it has always done, encouraging governmental deficits and rapid growth in the money supply. Persons who expect prices to be higher tomorrow than today buy now to beat the price rush and thus cause prices to rise even faster. Calibrations by superrational man are faster than the speeding, but misguided, bullet of the governmental decision. Only *random* changes in governmental policies would go unanticipated and lead to lower inflation rates, which sounds like a justification for irrational economic policies but instead is intended to be a reason for minimal government action.

A similar argument has been advanced to explain unemployment, bolstering Friedman's view of the unassailable natural unemployment rate. Only when the labor-force members fail to anticipate higher prices will they offer themselves in so great a number that they become unemployed. This view equates the workers' money illusion with inexcusable ignorance. The superrational workers, of course, will not be fooled into thinking that a higher money wage means greater real income, and they will withhold their labor until the employers offer the "correct" real wage. Then all people will be employed at the natural unemployment rate. Monetary and fiscal policies are powerless even in the short run.

The same economists who see central bankers as ill-informed, misguided, and foolish argue that even the least skilled blue-collar worker has perfect foresight. Behind the superrational man is the notion that information about prices and jobs is so abundant that knowledge is a free good. Everything else has a cost and, therefore, a price. There is no such thing as a free lunch, but information is born free. Moreover, the decisions made by the individual are painless (costless) as well.

No doubt the expectation of inflation can be a self-fulfilling prophecy as consumers and retailers stock up on goods in order to beat the coming price rise. However, this assumption tells us little about how inflation got started in the first place. Certainly every person on the street does not live up to the expectations of the rational expectationists. In general, rational expectations are suspect because they are at the end of the arm of an already idealized prototype, the rational economic man.

The difference between the structuralist Keynesians and the others has to do with contrasting views of the labor market. The structuralist view of the labor market is one of disequilibrium in which lower unemployment rates can be reached at higher and higher inflation rates. The monetarists and the rational expectationists have a classical view in which labor markets always clear exactly at full employment. Therefore, only unanticipated inflation can lead to temporary deviations from the long-run natural unemployment rate.

The message of the Keynesians is abundantly clear: the suppression of demand by Keynesian economic policy creates unemployment in the short run, whereas doing nothing allows the inflation to continue. The intentional creation of unemployment even for the short run may result in urban riots, voter retaliation, and social hardships and dissatisfaction. Unless policies are implemented that change the structure of the economy so that it behaves according to the postulates of classical theory, an even more ingenious solution must be invented.

THE ECOLOGICAL CRISIS

During the 1960s and 1970s, people realized that, despite circumstances within human control, tomorrow may be canceled. On the present voyage of what Kenneth Boulding has called "Spaceship Earth," we became worried about where the earthship is going to end up. There is little time to take swimming lessons; besides, the water is becoming too polluted. There is no use trying to tread water in order to keep breathing; the air is becoming dirty. There are lifeboats of a sort, but they are available to only a few first-class passengers with the money to buy them and the desire to use them. Though the poor and the middle class may suffer the most from pollution, eventually the rich will be unable to escape it either.

Ecology is the study of the relationships and interdependencies between living organisms and their environment at both a micro and a macro level, a science that attempts to describe and analyze the delicate relationships that constitute the web of life. Today most economists recognize that air, water, and land are natural resources used in common by the entire human population and that people's impact on the environment can be ignored only at the peril of the extinction of life. One individual or one firm cannot consume these resources without influencing the quality of their consumption by others. Under the capitalist system, each producer has a vested interest in concealing his or her preference for such factors of production as clean air and clean water. Each firm hopes to force its competitor to pay for the jointly created costs of pollution. The inevitable result under laissez-faire in those cases where social consciences are underdeveloped is that industry creates social costs without reimbursing the general public. The automobile industry, for example, adopted safety features and emission control devices only under governmental pressure.

The fact that important natural resources are common property has led some to argue that environmental problems can be solved by increasing the size of the public sector of the economy relative to the private sector. To the extent that pollution control adds to the cost of production but not to the market value of the product, combatting pollution is unprofitable to the private producer. Yet during the same period that pollution became an important issue in the United States, newspapers in the Soviet Union carried reports of wildlife being destroyed by the improper use of pesticides and of smog blanketing their industrial cities. (Later, the United States had its Three-Mile Island and the Soviet Union, its Chernobyl.) In the United States, among the most offensive pollutors are local municipalities. Whether the production unit be privately or publicly owned, domestic or foreign, it appears that the presently dominant cult of efficiency requires managers to trim internal costs as much as possible. Until recently, Soviet economists have also regarded natural resources as "free goods." These facts suggest that the pollution crisis is related more to economic knowledge in general than it is to any particular political or economic system.

CONCLUSIONS

During the late 1960s and the 1970s, was there any cause for optimism in what appeared to be a rather bleak contemporary landscape? There were several. Rapid technological change, the reduced requirement for direct labor as an input, and ecological problems were occurring at the same time that attitudes appeared to be changing toward both material consumption and the Puritan work ethic. The Yippies, the cultural movers and shakers of the time, no longer saw the maximization of materialistic desires as life's sole purpose and were seeking psychological satisfaction in activities that were only indirectly related to work or are work substitutes. Though these twin forces were operating at an individual level, they had yet to congeal as a collective force greatly influencing governmental policy. In the meantime, there have been institutional adjustments such as the increasing popularity of flexible working hours and a reduced workweek. Most important, the neomaterialism of the 1980's Yuppies did not jettison these concerns. Already a new breed—call them "neo-Yuppies"—is beginning to restate at a different level the values of the Yippies of the New Age movement. The New Age people condone profits accumulated from the provisions of services that improve the quality of others' lives.

As we will next see, the issue of whether the Phillips curve existed was settled by Reaganomics. Many of the problems of the 1970s were aggravated—unemployment and poverty soared. However, pollution declined because factories were producing less, much less. The problems of industrial concentration, financial concentration, income inequality, and lopsided distribution of wealth became more acute, but ideologically more acceptable. Inflation subsided with born-again Phillips curvism. The revolution in government policy quickly led to new crises, the crises of the 1980s. But, deep valleys often precede high peaks. Lessons were learned, and policy reversals were the order of the day by 1985.

14

NEW
RADICAL
ECONOMICS:
THE RIGHT

▼

*A capitalist is always also virtually an entrepreneur
and speculator.*

LUDWIG VON MISES, *HUMAN ACTION: A TREATISE
ON ECONOMICS,* 1949

*Material progress is ineluctably elitist: it makes the rich richer
and increases their numbers, exalting the few extraordinary
men who can produce wealth over the democratic masses
who consume it.... Material progress is radically
unpredictable (to foresee an innovation is in essence to make
it) ... is inimical to scientific economics: it cannot be explained
or foreseen in mechanistic or mathematical
terms.... Capitalism ... is the only appropriate system for a
world in which all certitude is a sham.... Jack Kemp and
Ronald Reagan alerted me to the emergence in America of
Republican politicians who crave and celebrate ideas.*

GEORGE GILDER, *WEALTH AND POVERTY,* 1981

*Whenever there are great strains or changes in the economic
system, it tends to generate crackpot theories, which then find
their way into the legislative channels.*

DAVID STOCKMAN, QUOTED IN *ATLANTIC MONTHLY,* DECEMBER 1981

What do orthodox economics, Austrian economist Ludwig von
Mises, pop sociologist George Gilder, President Ronald Reagan, and Reagan's onetime budget director (1981–mid-1985), David Stockman, have
in common? All were connected to the rise to power of the New Right
in the United States during the late 1970s and early 1980s; all expressed
contempt in various ways for orthodox neoclassical and Keynesian

economics. The rise of the New Right, like that of the New Left, was a reaction to the economic crises of the 1970s. Oddly, the economists from Left *and* Right criticize orthodox economists for roughly the same *methods*—overreliance upon an imaginary positive economics, hypothetical mathematical equilibria, and unreliable econometric tests. Indeed, the neo-Austrians who helped to lay the intellectual groundwork for the New Right even attacked the Chicago school's monetarism and rational expectations doctrine, despite the affinity of both schools for free market capitalism.

The New Left and the New Right part company at the point of faith in capitalism, for the radicals of the Left see capitalism as the problem, whereas those of the New Right see it as the solution, the *only* solution. The political success of the entrepreneurial New Right was not foreseen at a time when the intellectual stars were rising on the Left. It took a movie star, Ronald Reagan, and Reaganomics to stall the Left's progress. As long as we are paying respect to serendipity, however, we cannot ignore insider David Stockman's admonition about the time being ripe for "crackpot theories." Reaganomics comprised a baffling array of ideas, some of which were conflicting. In this chapter, we may give Reaganomics the appearance of a coherence that it did not possess; this is the ever-present danger in defining a school of thought.

Ideology from the distant past played a role in the dangerous economic crosscurrents of the 1980s. Values from classical and neoclassical economics were revived. The libertarian Austrian school of nineteenth-century Vienna evolved into a neo-Austrianism that proudly acknowledged its normative tenets, past and future. Still, it took popularizers of libertarian ideas such as George Gilder to link up with the political Right. Gilder may be on to something with his idea of the "unpredictable." As we will see, New Right ideas contributed to Reaganomics, a depression, a precarious recovery, and a debt cloud over the global horizon. The crises of the 1970s were pushed off center stage by new crises, legacies of Reaganomics. Since we have already discussed the free market value system of the classicals and neoclassicals, we will begin with the Austrians.

THE NEO-AUSTRIANS

Neo-Austrian economists are about as self-conscious of their adherence to the fundamentals of a "school of thought" as the Marxians and neo-Marxians. Neo-Austrian literature is replete with references to "Austrianism" and the neo-Austrians' role as "methodological outcasts" and thus "radicals." Unlike their neoclassical brethren, the neo-Austrians wear their values on their sleeves, deliberately proclaiming their "Austrianism" to spite their Keynesian, neoclassical, and Marxian detractors. The fervor of neo-Austrian economists and their lay followers often makes neo-Austrianism seem like a *doctrine* in which an almost religious commitment sometimes motivates economic theorizing. These doctrines include the analysis of human action, the theory of capital, and the idea of entrepreneurship.

Forerunners of Austrianism

Austrian-style economics has not been confined within the borders of Austria (or even within the ancient walls of the University of Vienna), irrespective of such a preference on the part of many economists. "Austrianism" refers to a philosophy or doctrine that, though originating with economic thinkers of Austrian nationality, nowadays is practiced outside Austria, notably in the United States. (Today's Vienna, which otherwise memorializes its past, views Austrian economics as quaint or irrelevant to a mostly socialized Austrian economy.)

Austrian economics began in 1871 with the publication (in Austria) of Karl Menger's *Principles of Economics*. A descendant of Austrian civil servants and army officers, Menger studied law at the Universities of Prague and Vienna, turning to economics in 1867. Two years after the publication of his *Principles of Economics*, Menger, a cofounder of marginalism (see Chapter 6), had sufficient stature to be appointed to the chair of economics at the University of Vienna and to serve as tutor to Crown Prince Rudolf. The refinement of Menger's views by students Friederich von Weiser (1851–1926) and Eugen von Böhm-Bawerk (1851–1914) ignited the "Austrian tradition."

Weiser, born into the Viennese aristocracy, studied law at the University of Vienna and traveled with his boyhood friend, Böhm-Bawerk, to various European universities to study economics. A student of Weiser's and Böhm-Bawerk's, Ludwig von Mises (1881–1973), found his way to Great Britain and, later, to the United States. Von Mises's great colleague, Friedrich von Hayek (1899–), also taught in England and the United States, where he influenced many in the Chicago school. The number of neo-Austrians working in Britain and the United States today is far from clear; nor is it clear who will inherit the positions of Mises and Hayek as major exponents of Austrianism in the Anglo-American world.

Karl Menger, the "father of Austrian economics," said that four qualities distinguished an economic good. An economic good required a human need for it, satisfaction of this need by the good, human knowledge of the good's capacity to satisfy the need, and the engineering ability to direct the good toward satisfactions of the need. As we noted in Chapter 6, Menger believed these satisfactions varied in their rank-order of importance. Life itself relies upon the fulfillment of the highest needs; a person who has a choice between a bed to sleep in and a personal computer will forgo the latter more quickly than the former.

Although Menger stressed the need for formal models of the marketplace, he rejected Newtonian mechanics and the calculus as the ultimate scientific expression of economics—hence, his objections to marginalists Jevons and Walras (see Chapter 6). Menger saw marginal or incremental utility, for example, as a series of steps, a staircase, not a smooth curve. He was concerned about the *essence* of economic reality in the individual, especially in the acting individual's determinations of such economic phenomena as value, rent, profit, and the division of labor. Menger's unit of analysis was the individual choice and not Newtonian-like equilibria among economic variables.

Menger's view of the role of individual choice in economic activity became a fundamental building block for later theories. The building block is most clearly delineated in Ludwig von Mises's *Human Action*; the economic implications of Menger's approach are explored in Böhm-Bawerk's *Pure Theory of Capital* and, more recently, in Israel Kirzner's *Competition and Entrepreneurship*. Indeed, Kirzner and Murray Rothbard, both contemporary self-conscious propagators of Austrianism and both of New York, aggressively defend the rights of individuals to pursue, however capitalistically, their own ends. We will now turn to the unique approach of Austrian economics. Here, the tradition or perhaps potential paradigm, in Thomas Kuhn's sense, becomes most visible.

Human Action and the Preeminance of the Marketplace

Neo-Austrianism's overarching concern is with human action, a technical, well-defined term. Kirzner states, "In so far as human behavior is guided by logic, then, conduct will follow a path that has been selected by *reason*. This path of conduct is what is known praxeologically as human action."[1] Economic affairs are not unique in this regard; all conduct is dictated by "human reason." Praxeology, the distinctive methodology first applied to Austrianism by von Mises, rests on the "undeniable" axiom that individuals engage in conscious actions toward chosen goals. Praxeological economic theory shows how human reason and actions work their way to specifically economic phenomena such as rent, value, and profit. Von Mises states that multidimensional human action is ". . . put into operation and transformed into an agency, is aiming at ends and goals, is the ego's meaningful response to stimuli and the conditions of its environment, is a person's conscious adjustment to the state of the universe that determines his life."[2]

The basic units for economic study, for Austrians, are individuals, who by their own will and powers of reason, come to guide their brute physical behavior toward their own ends and goals. The Keynesian-neoclassical orthodoxy is "economics betrayed," or indeed, "human action betrayed," in that Keynesian economists focus, not upon individual will and reason, but upon forces beyond the individual's control. Keynesians (really the "bastard Keynesians" of Chapter 8) begin their analyses with macro-forces, the unintended consequences of a sum of *other* individuals' behavior, or "aggregate behavior," in the social system. Keynesians thus ignore individual choice. Like the Keynesians, the neoclassicals have displaced the real agent of economic—and all—activity, the individual will. Where there is will, according to the neo-Austrians, there are ways; where will does not exist, there is only neoclassical equilibrium.

The radical nature of the Austrian conception of human action cannot be overstressed. Still, neo-Austrians do wish to account for aggregate economic phenomena such as the operation of the market and general price or wage levels. Here neo-Austrian theory moves toward a normative view of the market, or the "necessity of the market"—a sentiment that is the radical-individualist equivalent of Paul Samuelson's revealed preference theory (see Chapter 9). No doubt, each viewer considers his version to be revealed truth.

To account for wages and prices, the neo-Austrian might use the following reasoning: since each person is the best, and perhaps only, judge of her own ends, the individual always makes the best, and most reasonable choice, in the marketplace for herself. From the "macro point of view"—a conception distasteful though not poisonous to Austrians—we can observe the "prevailing wage" or "prevailing price" of labor or cheddar as, say, $10.00 an hour or $2.50 a pound. But this only says that a large number of individuals decided that, first, the market was the most reasonable means for obtaining their goals, and, second, that particular wages or prices were acceptable on the basis of their assessment of less reasonable alternatives. That $10.00 or $2.50 is "prevailing" means nothing more than that more people offered and accepted that price than did not. All wages and prices need not equilibrate at that level, though the presumption is that reasonable individuals, upon recognition of the higher-wage or better-price alternatives, will find those more suitable to their ends.

The receipt of the better wage or higher price is conditioned, however, on other individuals' offering that wage and that price on the basis of *their* ends—and this might not be true. Since individuals who cannot get what they want in the marketplace will leave it, the market will always reveal wages and prices—including rents—that are most reasonable to individuals. For the neo-Austrian macro-observer, therefore, the market will *always* present the best solution at the time to individual problems of choice of means to ends. Lesson: individuals ought, perhaps, to give the market a try since it works so well.

In order for the neo-Austrian economics to work, the psychology or praxeology must hold. For example, the psychology undergirds the theory of capital and entrepreneurship, where entrepreneurship constitutes the human actions of producers of goods. Von Mises's insight into entrepreneurship recognizes that humans are not only calculating agents but are also keenly alert to opportunities that are "just around the corner." *Dis*equilibria reflect widespread ignorance that provides profit opportunities. The entrepreneur, a persona embodying superior knowledge, foresight, alertness, and willingness to act, is alert to prevailing prices that *do not* clear the market and therefore provide profitable opportunities. The mechanistic, allocative decision making of neoclassical economics is displaced by human action: entrepreneurship transforms market equilibria into *market processes*. (The entrepreneur superalert to opportunities also defines the heroically entrepreneurial role for Austrian Joseph Schumpeter and Chicagoan-Austrian Frank H. Knight.)

Von Mises's conception of capital is based on human action taken because of uneasy feelings. Individuals reason about ends and means only because they are dissatisfied with their current situation; getting from this disvalued present state to a future valued state is, of course, a job for human reason. An immediate change is most reasonable since it is simplest, most direct, and least costly in producing a desired alteration in the present. From this, von Mises formulates his famous theory of *positive time preference*; people choose not the present, but the immediately succeeding state in time, through action. Positive time preference does not exclude, say, the building of a solar collector for reducing the chill—though it takes materials and time—rather than burning the furniture to heat the stove.

For von Mises, Böhm-Bawerk, Hayek, Kirzner, and the others, the moves of the long-distance rational planner are indicative of the successful functioning of human reason in human action. It is therefore no accident that praxeology, in its psychological underpinnings, focuses upon the action of the entrepreneur in capitalist trappings as one who has effectively used his or her expanded powers of reasoning to produce higher states of satisfaction. Praxeology *is* the point of view of capitalistic individuals, maximizing personal satisfactions in the marketplace through their increased access to alternative means to chosen ends and their capability to exploit those means to planned-out ends. In fact, the entrepreneur is the standard against which *all* human action is judged rational.

Capital, the Entrepreneur, and "Roundaboutness"

The Austrian theory of capital is well-known in economic circles; in fact, sometimes one is led to believe that capital theory is all there is to Austrianism.[3] In an important sense, this is true, for in the theory of capital all of the elements discussed above—human action, the normative marketplace, entrepreneurship as long-distance rationality—are implied. In this regard, Böhm-Bawerk's *Pure Theory of Capital* is a paradigmatic Austrian work, even though the significance attached to capital (which includes labor and raw materials) has its roots in Menger. The latter distinguishes goods by order. First-order goods satisfy persons' needs *directly*; higher-order goods (raw materials, labor, machines) can satisfy human needs only *indirectly*. No human need, for example, can be satisfied with the labor service of a baker or by flour. Only when these inputs are combined in a *complementary* way to produce bread can they satisfy a need.

Still, the value and character of first-order goods such as bread decide the value that can be imputed to higher-order goods. The radical subjectiveness of Austrianism stems from the role of the consumer as the ultimate arbiter of value and the entrepreneur's role as the sole creator of value. Menger's capitalist is the person who puts the higher-order goods—labor and flour—to productive use. Bread would never reach the table or even be invented in the absence of the capitalist baker! The baker gives rise to bread rather than vice versa. Indeed, in Menger, economic progress itself was the gingerbread to be snatched from the tree of higher-ordered goods. Böhm-Bawerk and Schumpeter elevate the entrepreneur above the capitalist, who earns only interest; the entrepreneur takes on a romantic quality. Kirzner's economic universe revolves around the entrepreneur; the romancing of capital goes on.

Austrian capital theory itself comprises two simple declarations: (1) production takes time; (2) the longer the time, the greater the productivity. Böhm-Bawerk attempts to show that the longer a stock of raw material can be labored over, the greater will be the value of the final product. This is because the roundabout way in which a good is produced will ultimately be made to command a higher market price. Contrary to classical labor theories of value, this "roundaboutness" adding to the value of the final product has little to do with increasing intrinsic or objective value in the product itself. Rather, roundaboutness depends upon the entrepreneur's increasing the value of the product by withholding the end product from the market until the entrepreneur's subjective value is realizable. Also contrary to labor theories of value, the value of goods produced through greater roundaboutness necessarily lies in the marketplace rather than in the factory. Only goods that are ready to return their value to the entrepreneur will be marketed; this is the ultimate test and truth of the rational choice-revealed nature of markets.

Böhm-Bawerk is concerned to show precisely how it is the time involved, and not, say, applications of greater quantities of technology or labor, that enhances the values of produced goods. In the Austrian waiting game, time is something to be killed. On the one hand, it is true that faster machines or more workers can yield greater quantities of a good in the same time; however, even Karl Marx noted that increased *physical* output decreases values of products, which may ultimately decrease even physical productivity should the capitalist not receive an adequate return on investment. Böhm-Bawerk turns Marx's claim into a necessary truth: unless the entrepreneur can expect to market the increased amount of goods at the price he wants for them, the entrepreneur will decrease productivity in the physical sense—or wait to market the additional items until he can get what he wants. Each stage in the production of, say, automobiles, is "capitalized" by the entrepreneur as he decides that the time past and the time remaining will ultimately yield him the greater value on his investment. Although capital and time (also capital?) create the product, the value of, say, the Oldsmobile, is still decided by its utility or marginal utility as a first-order good by its driver. Time is therefore the important element in the production of subjective values for the entrepreneur.[4]

Disputes within Austrianism have not altered the basic premise upon which the analysis of capital rests—namely, that capital is whatever entrepreneurs put to use in producing a final, marketable product. In this regard, capital is a *category of thought*—anything the entrepreneur thinks is capital *is* capital.[5] More exactly, capital is whatever the *Austrian* economists think the entrepreneur thinks is capital, which makes it still another Cartesian ("I think, therefore I am") invention. We can see, finally, how this notion at once embodies and fully explicates the neo-Austrian view.

NEO-AUSTRIANISM AND LIBERTARIAN SOCIAL IDEAS

In neo-Austrianism, capital is the only factor of production. All apparent dissimilarities between labor and machines and money dissolve into the fact that, to the entrepreneur, each must be put to use to serve his or her ends. All factors are only increments to the entrepreneur's time of production. Since *everyone* cannot be an entrepreneur, the neo-Austrians appear to have little concern for the laborer or for human non-entrepreneurial capital, presuming apparently that the blessings of worker as consumer are sufficient solace for the worker. Despite this view, the neo-Austrians are decidedly optimistic about the implications of human action—and this, as expounded in their political and social values, is to what we now turn.

Despite the abstractness of Austrian economic categories like capital, neo-Austrians are concerned with making the most out of entrepreneurship and capitalism as social practice. The inherent reasonableness of the capitalist and the unreasonableness of natural or artificial constraints upon the capitalist's weaving—human action—are threads woven into all Austrian cloth. In this way neo-Austrian thought embodies or, at the very least, is easily pressed into the service of libertarian social philosophy. Thus, we find leading neo-Austrian economists such as Murray Rothbard espousing the values of capitalism, the free market, and, in general, entrepreneurship in his work in political philosophy, *Man, Economy and State.* We also find Harvard philosopher Robert Nozick, author of the libertarian treatise, *Anarchy, State, and Utopia,* and defender of "capitalism among consenting adults," engaged in what can only be called an "in-house" criticism of some of the implications of the neo-Austrian theories of time preference. Nozick envisions unrestrained free exchange and a "minimal state" as utopia. Ultimately, George Gilder's *Wealth and Poverty* joins neo-Austrian nostalgia for entrepreneurship with public no-policy. The ease with which neo-Austrian economics and libertarian political ideas are exchanged in various research institutes and organizations is also indicative of a "kinship" of spirit, if not a direct mutually justifying relationship.

The neo-Austrians have especially strong patrons in Charles Koch, the head of Koch Industries, a family-owned oil distribution company that is often called "the U.S.'s most profitable private business," and in Lewis E. Lehrman, New York drugstore heir and unsuccessful candidate (1982) for governor of New York. In 1974, Koch established the Charles Koch Foundation to seed the views of laissez-faire economists such as von Mises. It has since become the Cato Institute, a full-scale, public policy institute that publishes and distributes (free) short paperback books dominated by neo-Austrian authors Rothbard, Hayek, and like-minded persons, as well as full-length books. Cato's main function, however, is to provide an intellectual infrastructure for the Libertarian party's political development. Thus, the institute supports libertarian-oriented research into the flaws of Social Security, the income tax, and foreign policy. It also publicizes libertarian ideas through radio shows, magazines, and conferences of neo-Austrian economists. The goal of the Libertarian party is thinly disguised: it is to greatly shrink the government.

Austrian economists have been, almost from the outset, radically antisocialistic and antigovernment in general. Early on, Böhm-Bawerk took on the task of refuting Karl Marx's economic justification of socialism. Later, Hayek, especially, repeated the pattern, though von Mises and now Rothbard and Kirzner position themselves diametrically opposite Keynesian government fiscal policies. The Austrian theory of human action and rational capitalization of means toward individual ends carries a heavy normative baggage of "oughts." Free choice in the marketplace will necessarily produce the best results, an "optimum" that leads neo-Austrians on to a further normative judgment concerning public policy—the "no-policy policy." In this regard, neo-Austrians agree with other free market advocates, such as the monetarists. But the force and direction of neo-Austrianism suggest that the "no-policy policy" is not just preferable for the Austrians—it is rationally necessary. They maintain that without collective interference, human nature and interpersonal relations will flower; with any external interference, we are doomed.

No doubt the legal training of the founders of the Austrian school has influenced the judicial tone of neo-Austrianism. They believe the only good decisions by the state are judicial ones. So long as private property rights are clearly defined, the judicial system can solve all disputes and all economic problems. They argue that the main legitimate function of government is to stop aggression and that only courts and police are required for that. Take pollution as an example. The neo-Austrian would say that Lake Erie is polluted because the government owns lakes and rivers. "True" ownerships do not exist because government officials cannot sell lakes and streams or equities in them. Therefore, there is no basis for the pride in ownership that would incite the preservation of purity. If a private firm owned Lake Erie, the first person to dump garbage into the lake would be hauled into court by the owner and forced to pay damages. But what if a private firm bought Lake Erie expressly for the purpose of turning it into a garbage dump for profit? Since such human action is entrepreneurial, it must be reasonable. The lake as a landfill is something of future value, the Austrians would answer. The Libertarian might say that what the firm does to the lake is the concern only of the firm.

In their favor, Austrian praxeologists often cite the realistic optimism embodied in their theories. They believe in the perfectability of man through the marketplace of goods and of ideas. That praxeology says little, however, for its truth or for its claim to be a "science of human action," let alone economic conduct. Despite these doubts, we will return to some of the Austrian concepts of entrepreneurship and production that have vitality outside the radicalism of Austrian normative preferences. Obviously, the political appeal of neo-Austrian (and monetarist) ideas to Ronald Reagan lay in their free market ideology. We now turn to Reaganomics.

REAGANOMICS AND THE SUPPLY-SIDERS

Just as monetarism was a reaction to the perceived failure of bastardized Keynesianism to end stagflation, the "supply-side" economics identified with Reaganomics was a set of policies aimed at ending inflation without reducing output and employment. In other words, supply-side economics was pressed into service as the way out of the stagnation afflicting the U.S. economy during the 1970s. Tight monetary policy would be used to curb inflation while supply-side incentives would be used to expand employment and production.[6] The program would eliminate the Phillips curve trade-off discussed in Chapter 13.

In January 1981, President Ronald Reagan faced an inflationary problem whose beginning could be traced to the Vietnam War. At the same time, however, the recovery from the Carter Administration's 1979 recession was not complete; the unemployment rate hovered near 8 percent. Though the Reagan Administration considered inflation to be by far the greater evil, it faced the continuation of the stagflation malaise, a condition afflicting Great Britain and Western Europe as well. The centerpiece of Reaganomics, the Economic Recovery Act of 1981, was enacted in August of that year. The act aimed to cut personal tax rates by 25 percent over three years, drastically liberalize business depreciation allowances, and provide handsome tax credits for business investment. Additionally, Reagan planned to raise defense spending, cut nondefense spending, deregulate various industries, and, finally, balance the federal budget by 1984. The federal government's role, expanded by the New Deal programs of the 1930s and by World War II, was to be reduced, except for national defense and the criminal justice system (which were to be enlarged).

As it turned out, a Phillips curve appeared to rise from the ashes of Reaganomics. The American economy plunged into a deep and prolonged economic recession before inflation began to subside. Moreover, because of the magnitude of goods and services purchased by Americans from other countries, the U.S. depression became global as it was transmitted through trade balances to most of the rest of the world. In order to understand Reaganomics and supply-side theory, we will trace their origins. We also will try to understand what went wrong.

Contemporary supply-side economics was a media event begun by Wall Street journalist Jude Wanniski, writer Bruce Bartlett, and pop sociologist George Gilder. All three writers make devoted reference to the second-generation Austrians—von Hayek, von Mises, Schumpeter, Knight—and the neo-Austrians Kirzner and Rothbard.[7] The Laffer curve, the Rosetta Stone of Reaganomics, drawn for Wanniski on a napkin in a Washington, D.C., "insiders' " hotel bar by Arthur Laffer, a former business professor at the University of Southern California, was given celebrity status in Wanniski's book, *The Way the World Works*. The Laffer curve traces the relationship between tax rates and government revenue. At two extremes (0 percent and 100 percent), there will be no revenues for the government. As tax rates rise above zero, the provision of public goods essential for markets to operate (justice, defense, law and order, and primary education) contributes to productivity, output, and, thus, tax revenue. However, as tax rates are raised further, relative price changes cause a decline in the after-tax rewards of saving, investing, and working for taxable income. People begin to shift out of these activities and into leisure, consumption, and tax shelters. The national output and income base upon which tax rates apply is eroded, and the tax revenue from higher tax rates falls.

George Gilder gave a further boost to Lafferism even while embracing neo-Austrian entrepreneurship in his *Wealth and Poverty*, required reading for the 1981 White House staff. (David Stockman distributed thirty copies to White House staffers immediately upon its publication.) Gilder, the chief nonordained evangelist for Reaganomics, argued that personal income tax cuts for the rich would stimulate output by the same class; eventually, the expansion in production and the additional tax revenue that such increases would bring would allow further tax cuts for low- and middle-income families. Gilder further contended that the welfare state motivates the poor to choose leisure over work. Since only the rich have enough savings to stimulate capital formation, their reduced tax rates would stimulate economic growth.

The neo-Austrian spirit of entrepreneurship blitzed the White House long after the planned tax cut had been drafted. That is, the initial impetus for Reaganomics came from Laffer's version of neoclassical economics; Gilder's assurance that faith in God and enterprise, tempered with contempt for women in nonsubmissive managerial roles, apparently reassured the president, even after David Stockman had become convinced otherwise, that Reaganomics would stimulate output and employment. Therefore, Reaganomics stressed those elements that presumably would affect the supply of labor and productive capacity, but the full program went beyond tax cuts to cuts in government spending on welfare programs and decreases in government regulation. The unique proclamation of conservative supply-side economics is its dual promise of stimulating economic growth without accelerating inflation. We now will turn our attention to the bricks and mortar of the Reaganomics archway.

Say's Law and the Entrepreneurial Spirit

The first canon of supply-side economics was our old friend, Say's law, or the idea that supply creates its own demand. Say's law connected Reaganomics to economic growth. Saving was the starter key for the growth engine because of the guaranteed transmission of saving into investment. The engine always starts no matter how chilly the investment climate since every dollar saved is predestined to become a dollar invested. Since Reaganomics viewed the upper-income class (over $50,000 a year in 1980 dollars) as the dominant personal savers, the sole economic purpose of the well-to-do was to save. This provided the analytical basis for lowering marginal tax rates for the well-to-to as an incentive to enlarge personal saving, which ends up as new plant and equipment. As a failsafe, special tax benefits to corporations such as larger tax credits, lower tax rates, and faster depreciation would add still more *incentives* for investment. No doubt the neo-Austrian optimism regarding the alertness of the entrepreneur in responding to changed profit opportunities belatedly provided some basis for the belief that saving would become investment. (Neoclassical optimism is based upon the belief in the drive to *optimize* profits; in this regard, no conflict exists between neo-Austrianism and neoclassicalism.)

Thus, even though the various tax cuts would increase disposable income, their presumed effectiveness did not stem from their effects on Keynesian aggregate demand, which were presumed to be nil. Rather, following the neoclassical lead, the effectiveness of tax reductions would come from their changing of relative prices. A reduction in tax rates would induce decision makers to substitute productive activity (investment, work, and exchange) for leisure and idleness, causing output to rise. Moreover, entrepreneurs would play a role here as they would be freed from the constraints of taxation. The shift away from nonproduction (and consumption) toward production would enlarge total supply, causing real income to expand rapidly. The market supply of goods and services—i.e., aggregate supply and, hence, economic growth—would be enhanced.

Did Reagan's advisers really believe that workers were so sensitive to small real-wage increments that meager marginal tax reductions would energize work effort? The answer was provided by David Stockman, then Reagan's director of the Office of Management and Budget (OMB), in his Christmastime 1981 "confessions" to the *Atlantic Monthly*. "The hard part of the supply-side tax cut is dropping the top rate from 70 to 50 percent—the rest of it is a secondary matter," Stockman explained. "The original argument was that the top bracket was too high, and that's having the most devastating effect on the economy. Then, the general argument was that, in order to make this palatable as a political matter, you had to bring down all the brackets. But, I mean, Kemp-Roth (the name of the original supply-side tax bill) was always a Trojan horse to bring down the top rate."[8] A Trojan horse? Supply-side economics was rolled into the enemy camp of labor with a horseload of entrepreneurs. Rather than a Calvinistic response by workers, the Reagan Administration apparently was counting on a more literal interpretation of Say's law and on entrepreneurship for the stimulation of output—either Puritanical investors or superalert entrepreneurs. Stockman conceded as much: the supply-side theory was really new clothes for the naked doctrine of the old "trickle-down theory"[9] in which benefits to the rich "trickle down" to the workers.

The Reaganauts' Trojan horse ploy was as successful as it had been for the Greeks in their Trojan War victory of 1200 B.C. As a result of the Reagan fiscal revolution, affluent Americans made robust real-income gains, while poorer Americans actually experienced income losses during 1980–1984. These outcomes are highlighted in Figure 14.1. When families are divided into quintiles—five groups of equal size rank-ordered by real disposable income—the top fifth gained by far the most over the four years, with its average leaping by nearly 9 percent. But the poorest fifth suffered an average decline of more than 7.5 percent, and the second least-fortunate quintile lost 1.7 percent. About half of American families endured real-income losses over Reagan's first term. The Reagan Administration was successful in reducing some welfare programs even as Social Security benefits cushioned the drop in real disposable income of the "statistically average" family to 1 percent in 1979–1984. If there were to be "trickle-down" benefits, they had not materialized by the end of 1984. This lopsidedness had no significant impact on the 1984 presidential election because the affluent have a much higher propensity to vote than the less fortunate (in the 1980 election only 44 percent or so of eligible voters with family incomes of $10,000 or less actually voted, in contrast with 74 percent of those with incomes above $25,000).

The full period from 1979–1984 looks much like the Ford-Carter years of 1973–1979. Each era got off to a fast start with hyperinflation inspired mostly by OPEC's crude-oil price increases (and food-price

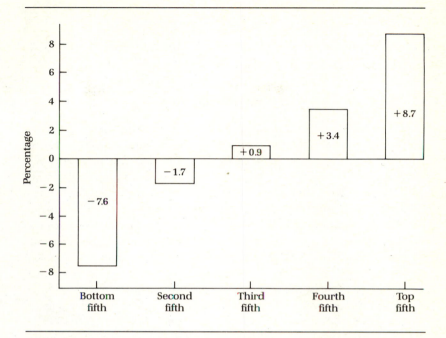

FIGURE 14.1 Percentage change, real disposable family income, 1980–1984. [*Source:* Urban Institute household income model. John L. Palmer and Isabel V. Sawhill, eds., *The Reagan Record* (Cambridge, Mass.: Ballinger, 1984), p. 321. Copyright 1984, The Urban Institute. Reprinted with permission of Ballinger Publishing Company.]

inflation in the first period); the governments in each era created a severe economic downturn in order to slow inflation, although the Reaganauts claimed no recession was necessary or would happen. Government policy made life more difficult for many people, especially the poor. President Reagan apparently believed so avowedly in "trickle-down" that he saw little further need for public welfare programs that, he and the supply-side economists presumed, were Darwinian burdens on the poor.

Though federal income taxes for the "average family" actually rose by 1 percent, the U.S. Treasury's accelerated depreciation allowances and special tax credits left most major corporations with little or no corporate income taxes to pay. A large number of major corporations such as U.S. Home, Dow Chemical, General Electric, General Dynamics, and Boeing actually received a *negative income tax* (refunds or other tax benefits) during 1981–1983 even while earning large profits. All things considered, the fiscal revolution was stunning, but the President did not get everything he asked for.[10] President Reagan pushed for these further domestic program reductions in his second term.

The Golden Enthronement of Monetarism

The second canon of Reaganomics was the quantity theory of money, as amended by the modern proponents of monetarism. Though promoted by Milton Friedman and Harvard's Martin Feldstein and embraced at the outset by President Reagan, the tight money experiment in the United States began in 1979 under President Jimmy Carter. The belief was that reducing the money supply or slowing its growth rate would halt inflation. President Reagan's own first-term conversion to monetarism was eased by its underlying free market principles. Supply-siders Wanniski and Gilder, however, took the prevailing neo-Austrian view that monetarism was wrongheaded: don't interfere with the otherwise correct decisions of the omnipotent entrepreneur.

Tight money was no Trojan horse; administrations as early as Eisenhower's (1953–1961) and as recent as Carter's (1977–1981) had demonstrated that monetary policy could reduce aggregate demand to the point that inflation would slow. Moreover, in 1979, the Federal Reserve faced no ordinary inflation: the rate was running as high as 20 percent. Strictures on money supply growth led to a recession that helped to elect Reagan in 1980. If the proposed tax cuts based upon the supply-side theory succeeded in increasing output (as the supply-siders claimed), however, a tight monetary policy to reduce inflation could be implemented without reducing output or (more important) employment.

The monetary authorities cooperated fully with the Reagan Administration in constricting money supply growth. The Reagan Administration and the Federal Reserve agreed that the money supply should be allowed to grow about 2.5 percent per year. At the same time, President Reagan promised that nominal gross national product (GNP) would grow at an annual rate of 12 percent between 1980 and 1984.

The Laffer Curve

The third and last maxim of Reaganomics was the Laffer curve, also a central feature of supply-side economics.[11] The 1980–1981 supply-side advisers to President Reagan believed that the relation between the tax rate and revenue in the United States was such that a reduction in tax rates would *increase* tax revenue. Although no empirical evidence to sustain this faith existed, from this belief came the conclusion that a massive tax cut would so swell the U.S. Treasury's revenues that the national budget would be balanced by 1984, if not sooner. Most economists believed that, in fact, tax rates were well below this range of perversity.

KEYNES REDUX

Instead of a nominal GNP growth rate at the promised annual rate of 12 percent between 1980 and 1984, the United States' economy spun into the greatest decline since the Great Depression. What went wrong? What went right (besides a wing of the Republican Party)?

Despite a variegated *General Theory*, in the folklore of the economics profession, Say's law presumably had been put to rest "forever" by the Great Depression and John Maynard Keynes. "Forever" turned out to be a relatively short historical time. And yet, the overemphasis by orthodox economists on equilibrium economics and their ideological preference for free markets left even the fiscal Keynesians helpless in any effective counterattack against the rising tide of Reaganomics. The New Deal liberals were diminished to jokes about the Reaganomics tide "raising all yachts." Attacked from the supply side, orthodox economists were submerged by the media blitz. Nonetheless, as the global economy plunged to depths unvisited since the Great Depression, many economists began to remember the mathematics of Keynes's multiplier in reverse and its implications for Say's law. The tight monetary policy of the Federal Reserve combined with rising budget deficits sharply raised interest rates. The real GNP dipped 1.5 percent in the second quarter of 1980; a depression was on its way, inspired by Keynesian interest-rate effects upon effective aggregate demand. The tight money policy overwhelmed the business tax cuts aimed at encouraging capital formation.[12] Where were the heroic entrepreneurs? Accelerated depreciation allowances do not help if slow sales eclipse capacity utilization and the *need* to expand plant facilities. Tight money continued to reign; the depression ground on. Real GNP plummeted 5.3 percent in the fourth quarter of 1981, 5.1 percent in the first quarter of 1982, and remained unchanged in the next quarter. The unemployment rate steadily climbed to 8.4, 8.8, 9.5, and, by the end of 1982, 10.8 percent, the highest rate since the Great Depression.

Keynes and the Velocity of Money

The most obvious and perhaps most critical problem with first-term Reaganomics is revealed in a direct comparison of the classical equation of exchange with Keynes's attack on it. Let us consider the equation of exchange of Chapter 8 again (now expressed in percentage changes). President Reagan's 1980–1984 targeted nominal GNP growth rate of 12.0 percent and money supply growth rate of 2.5 percent annually implied a growth rate in the income velocity of money of 9.5 percent,

$$\underset{\substack{\text{Percent Change,} \\ \text{Money Supply}}}{2.5} + \underset{\substack{\text{Percent Change,} \\ \text{Velocity}}}{9.5} = \underset{\substack{\text{Percent Change,} \\ \text{Nominal National} \\ \text{Income}}}{12.0}$$

an annual growth rate of velocity far in excess of the historical average growth rate of 3 percent for 1946–1980. Even more important, this historical 3 percent growth rate of velocity combined with a 2.5 percent growth rate for money would allow *nominal* GNP to grow only 5.5 percent a year. At a hoped-for inflation rate of 6 percent, the real growth in GNP would be −0.5 percent annually (5.5 − 6.0). Real GNP declines!

Data are the advantage history often provides. Let us consider the same data for two one-year periods:

3d quarter 1980 to 3d quarter 1981   3.4 + 5.9 = 9.3

2d quarter 1981 to 2d quarter 1982   1.6 + 0.6 = 2.2

The first period is the recovery year from the trough of the 1979–1980 recession. The second period is the first year of the Reagan depression. (All of the percentage changes apply to nominal values.) Since the rate of inflation was 9.0 percent in the post-Carter recovery year, the growth rate in *real* output was a meager 0.3 percent (9.3 − 9.0). Even in terms of the quantity theory of money, this means that tight money policy contributed to a very sluggish or nil recovery from the 1979–1980 economic recession. In the second period, Reagan nearly achieved his inflation goal, as inflation dipped to 6.6 percent. However, this also means that real output *declined* 4.4 percent (2.2 − 6.6 = −4.4).

The historical outcome begs for the Keynes-type interpretation provided in the "Money and Uncertainty" section of Chapter 7. Keynes had the public demanding money for its own sake, as the ultimate "safe" asset, a view of the demand for money that once again damages with a single blow both Say's law and the quantity theory of money. The income velocity of money declined from the 5.9 percent rate of the post-Carter recovery year to an anemic 0.6 percent rate during the first year of the Reagan economic decline. Job prospects were dim, and expected returns from investment dismal and increasingly uncertain: households and corporations held on to their money. The act of holding-on decreased the income velocity of money.

This behavior of velocity naturally raises the question of why the growth in the money supply slowed so sharply. In this regard, Keynes's original perspective also is enlightening. The money supply growth influences business activity (mostly through the interest rate), and business activity affects the money supply. The demand for bank loans by businesses and consumers was minimal during 1980, not to mention 1981 and 1982. Since the extension of loans creates demand deposits (checking accounts), the major share of the money supply, slowdowns in bank-loan demand cause a slippage in bank deposits and slow money supply growth. In this lowly state of business expectations, the Federal Reserve could stay near its 2.5 percentage target only by creating an enormous supply of money which it chose not to do in 1981 in order to stay on the tight money course.

The massive tax cut added still another dimension to the interest rate equation. The depression required an enormous increase in unemployment compensation and welfare payments because of the rapid climb in unemployment. On the other side of the fiscal ledger, the income tax cuts, especially those for giant corporations, led to a sharp fall in federal tax revenues, a decline speeded by the slowdown in the growth of incomes and profits. The gap between government expenditures and government revenues widened, a federal deficit that had to be financed by the issuance of historically massive amounts of U.S. Treasury securities. Even with the meager demand for loans by households and businesses, the historically unparalleled government demand for funds kept real interest rates at levels 100 percent above their historical averages. The massive tax cut in conjunction with the depression gave the nation a legacy quite out of step with Ronald Reagan's original intent to balance the federal budget in 1984. Quite the opposite was evolving as budget deficits began to shatter historical records, soaring to annual rates of $200 billion. Even after a modest attempt in 1984 (an election year) to reduce the deficit, the Congress and a now deficit-defending president would see less than $200 billion of red in fiscal 1985 only with the luck of the Irish. Without a dramatic change in tax and expenditure policies, the nonpartisan Congressional Budget Office (CBO) predicted a federal deficit approaching $300 billion in 1989.

By 1984, Dr. Laffer, a millionaire from his consulting firm's profits, had resigned his professorship at the University of Southern California. Meanwhile, a president who had campaigned on a plan to balance the federal budget became the biggest deficit spender in history. Despite these deficits, the same president went back to Laffer for advice during the 1984 presidential campaign and appeared determined to further weaken the president's already crippled Council of Economic Advisers.

Nonetheless, the U.S. Congress aborted born-again supply-side economics in President Reagan's second term and prolonged a massive
Keynesian deficit spending program (though in supply-sider drag) bolstered by Keynesian monetary policy in monetarist skirts.

Reagan's Ersatz Keynesianism

As we know, history is replete with irony. By 1980 Keynesian economics was at a nadir among U.S. economists. The Reaganomics depression greatly altered this perception. For one thing, unemployment
compensation and other programs from the New Deal placed a floor
under disposable income and therefore the decline in consumer spending. Even the officials of the Reagan Administration looked to gains in
consumers' disposable income stemming from the personal income tax
cuts and easy money policy to stimulate Keynesian effective demand
in 1982 and 1983. Fiscal Keynesianism became the way out of the malaise. Federal Reserve officials—in near panic as the 1930s flashed before
their eyes—began to pursue in 1982 an incredibly expansive monetary
policy. Monetarism was scrapped. The tremendous increase in federal
military expenditures (about 7 percent annually in real terms), though
a part of Reagan's original budget plan, provided a sorely needed
Keynesian demand yank for the depressed economy. The tax cut—
lopsided as it was—gave some impetus to Keynesian aggregate demand.
Moreover, the accelerated depreciation allowances plus tax credits became usable tools to swell corporate cash flow as consumer demand
in housing, automobiles, and other durables began to expand in 1983.
President Reagan and the supply-siders began to defend vigorously
Keynesian budget deficits greatly in excess of amounts acceptable to
modern Keynesians.

THE ECONOMIC CRISES OF THE 1980S

The U.S. economic recovery of 1983 and 1984 came with unusual vigor,
especially in light of the still historically high real interest rates. Even
so, by mid-1984 the U.S. economy had recovered only to its pre-Reagan
level. Moreover, the historically high real interest rates remained a cloud
over the sustainability of the recovery. After mid-year 1984, the combination of more intense business loan requirements and gigantic U.S.
Treasury borrowings began to exert upward pressure on already high
interest rates. By mid-1985 the economy was flirting with a recession.
The recovery had always been precarious—going all the way back to
the Democrats in 1979. Moreover, as we have said, the recovery was very

uneven inasmuch as its benefits were enjoyed only by the upper two-fifths of families and especially by the richest. Of the 9 million unemployed in 1983, only half as many received benefits from unemployment insurance programs as they would have in January 1981.

Other threats were posed by rising interest rates. Interest rates in the United States—far above those in Great Britain and Western Europe—were attracting a flood of foreign funds. The purchase of dollar-denominated securities by foreigners exerts an upward pressure on the international value of the dollar (the price foreigners pay for the dollar). A high-valued U.S. dollar makes American goods and services expensive and foreign goods cheap. For a century, between 1870 and 1970, the United States enjoyed a virtually uninterrupted string of trade surpluses. Although the 1970s brought trade deficits, they could be blamed almost completely on high-priced oil imports from OPEC. As recently as 1980, the trade deficit was a tolerable $36.4 billion. But by 1983 the trade deficit had reached $69.4 billion and in 1984 was roughly double that. With the reduction in foreign purchases of U.S. goods and services, the United States had from 2.5 to 3.0 million fewer jobs by the end of 1984 than it would otherwise have had. Moreover, the threat to workers and to industry profits had led to demands on the Congress and the president for trade protection. By the mid-1980s, imports had captured about one-quarter of the U.S. steel market, up from 15 percent in the 1970s. Between 1979 and mid-1984, the steel companies had laid off 45 percent of their work force. Especially ominous was the erosion of industries that produce capital and high-technology goods. (As we will see in Chapter 16, other elements besides a strong dollar contributed to the trade problem.) Still, on the plus side, the gigantic trade deficits contributed to a low inflation rate because concentrated industries at home faced stiff competition from the flood of foreign goods.

The rest of the world did not recover from the global depression as quickly as the United States. In fact, the slow global recovery contributed to the U.S. trade deficit. Western Europe's recovery was especially slow, but the situation with respect to the developing countries was even more drastic; many were still mired in depression. Because the bulk of industry still resides in the developed countries, their collective economic growth train still is required to pull along the developing economies. The linkage between the engine and the freight is international trade. The severe economic downturn in the developed nations meant forgone export earnings in the developing nations; historically high interest rates added to the debt-servicing cost of non-oil-producing developing countries; and the oil-price shocks of 1974 and 1979 added to the oil-imports costs of many developing countries. In this way, forces outside the control of most of the afflicted countries added about $400 billion to their external debt in 1973–1982, leaving only about $100 billion in self-inflicted debt. The external debt, funded by robust trade growth in the 1970s, was greatly aggravated by an unexpected export collapse and extraordinary interest rates.[13]

Nations such as Mexico and Brazil became so burdened by foreign debt and so short of ready cash that they were forced to reduce imports drastically. Latin America's trade balance with the United States had gone from a $4.7 billion surplus in 1980 to a deficit of about $20 billion by 1984. Foreign debt probably is the greatest problem that Latin America has faced in this century. By fall 1985 Cuba was finding an audience throughout the hemisphere by advocating default on the debt, a debtors' revolt. The crisis is global because the developing nations owe so much to so few private banks in the developed countries (especially in the United States) that these countries now depend upon a resumption of economic growth in the developing countries in order to avoid a collapse of their banking systems and of global liquidity. The interest-rate dilemma at home and the debt problem abroad were among the crises of the 1980s, legacies of first-term Reaganomics.

Moreover, the crises of the 1970s were being accelerated by the Reagan Administration's views on the environment, public welfare programs, deregulation, and the effects of corporate tax advantages. The hazardous-waste "cleanup" program had become a scandal during the first term; a second-term reversal on environmental problems has yet to be unveiled at this writing. The depression plus budget cuts during Reagan's first two years increased the number classified as poor by 5.5 million and elevated the official poverty rate to about its height at the beginning of the War on Poverty in 1965. The merger trend, especially the merger of unrelated enterprises and the conglomerate rush, was encouraged by both tax policy and by aggressively lax antitrust policy. Upon the heels of a historical record of mergers of companies collectively valued at $83 billion in 1981, the *first half* of 1982 featured 1,198 corporate acquisitions, somewhat higher than the 1,184 of the same period one year earlier. By 1983 the *arrangement* of mergers had become a growth industry led by the legendary Texas tycoon, Slim Pickens. (Slim "pick'ens" indeed!)

The effects of Reagan Administration policies were epitomized by the bidding war between U.S. Steel Corporation and Mobil for Marathon Oil Company. Mobil, which earlier had acquired the Montgomery Ward department store chain (apparently, according to Senator Edward Kennedy, in order to drill for oil in Montgomery Ward's aisles), tried to buy Marathon. Contrary to the claims for the effects of the Reaganomics tax incentive program, Mobil expressed an interest in buying *existing* oil reserves rather than going to all the trouble of looking for them. Earlier,

Mobil had attempted to buy Conoco for the same reason; the chemical giant Du Pont had been the successful White Knight bidder. In its boldest gamble since the company was put together by Andrew Carnegie and J. P. Morgan in 1901, U.S. Steel bid $5.15 *billion* for Marathon. Even though Mobil raised its ante to $6.5 billion and took its case to the Supreme Court, the Court ruled in favor of U.S. Steel because it had never been and was not then in the oil business. As a result of the acquisition, U.S. Steel became the nation's twelfth largest industrial company. Industrial assets become even more concentrated even though no new industrial capacity or apparent productivity improvement had been created by such mergers. Deregulation in the airline and banking industries—begun under the Carter Administration—was having similar effects, as cutthroat competition was driving even giants into bankruptcy, while more and more mergers and takeovers loomed on the horizon. By the end of 1983, the top ten U.S. commercial banks held about 35 percent of U.S. total banking assets and the top twenty, nearly 50 percent.

CONCLUSIONS

Reaganomics did not yield all the benefits that it had promised. Inflation slowed for the same reasons as in prior monetary-policy-inflicted recessions; production plunged and the unemployment rate reached depression heights. Social welfare programs were reduced, but the poor, rather than benefiting from the "trickle-down" doctrine, increased in number and desperation. And, ironically, the fiscal revolution, which promised to reward entrepreneurship and restore nineteenth-century capitalism, enhanced merger trends and nationalized a private bank, Continental Illinois (then the seventh largest U.S. bank), even as it provided federal bailouts to other giant financial institutions around the nation. The failures of Reaganomics revived Keynesianism—originally designed by Keynes to save capitalism from itself—at a time when neoclassical Keynesianism appeared comatose.

15

THE POST-KEYNESIANS

▼

To me, the expression post-Keynesian *has a definite meaning; it applies to an economic theory or method of analysis which takes account of the difference between the future and the past.*

JOAN ROBINSON, *JOURNAL OF POST KEYNESIAN ECONOMICS,* FALL 1978

Post-Keynesian economics . . . holds that industrial society is in a process of continuous and organic change, that public policy must accommodate to such change, and that by such public action performance can, in fact, be improved.

JOHN KENNETH GALBRAITH, *JOURNAL OF POST KEYNESIAN ECONOMICS,* FALL 1978

A number of economists most sympathetic to Keynes but less so to bastard Keynesianism have been dissatisfied with the prominence and proliferation of the bowdlerized version of Keynes and with zealous monetarism. Some of this disaffection began before the *General Theory* saw print, but the 1970s crisis of simultaneous inflation and unemployment has speeded the growth of a post-Keynesian economics. Post-Keynesianism has flourished on two sides of the Atlantic—on the European side in Cambridge, England.[1]

As we have seen, the response to two of the flaws in Keynes's *General Theory*—the absence of an explanation for economic growth and Keynes's presumption that the state of competition was not critical to his theory—was quick, as Keynes's associates and followers at Cambridge University tried to drive a sharper wedge between Keynesian and neoclassical economics. The concern of Keynes's followers had shifted beyond the "unjustness" of gigantic inequalities of income and wealth; the post-Keynesians saw income inequalities leading to economic instability.

A new problem in the Western industrialized nations, double-digit inflation, gave the post-Keynesians still another challenge. The new brand of inflation—cost-push and profits-push—was especially onerous because the fiscal Keynesians had no practical remedy. Fiscal demand management worked well only on demand-pull inflation. Inflation itself was a double challenge to Keynes's followers because the monetarists claimed to have the only effective weapon against the malady, money-supply contraction. If the more extreme monetarists won the intellectual battle, macroeconomics would be forced to retreat to Say's law, which guaranteed that demand would always be adequate. The post-Keynesians perceived the conservative implications of the monetarists' views—namely, the blanket indictment of the public sector as the sole source of inflation. The post-Keynesians were not content to assail the bastard Keynesians; they also aimed their analytical big guns upon the monetarists. As we witnessed in Chapter 14, the monetarists and Say's law won the first battle. But—after the heat of Reaganomics and the smoke of deindustrialization had cleared—the problems of giant federal budget deficits, high interest rates, high unemployment rates, and stagnation were still there.

It is difficult to follow the post-Keynesians without a road map. We shall start by going back to an early crossroads. Departing from Smith, Ricardo went one direction, followed at a respectable distance by Marx; the neoclassicals followed a separate route. The post-Keynesians believe that the neoclassicals took a wrong turn, and the post-Keynesians go back to the basics of Ricardian production. Then, in a roundabout way, the distribution of income becomes the focal point for an explanation of how the national income is decided.

You don't have to go down the production route very far before you encounter explanations for inflation and disinflation (the slowing of inflation). The post-Keynesians modify the classical notion of pricing based upon cost of production to explain modern inflation. The key departure from both classical and Keynes's thought is found in a notion called the *price markup*. Once production, its division between capitalists and workers, and imperfect competition are placed on the same track, it is but a short distance to an understanding of the business cycle and the long-term growth trend of the economy. The *very* long run is postponed (appropriately) until Chapter 16; then the implications of post-Keynesian economics for economic policy are assessed in Chapter 17.

POST-KEYNESIAN THEORIES OF PRODUCTION
AND THE INCOME DISTRIBUTION

Some of Keynes's pupils and followers, such as Joan Robinson, Piero Sraffa, Richard Kahn, and Nicholas Kaldor, went on to articulate systematically a theory of income distribution in Keynes's spirit. Initially, however, the income distribution was secondary in their writing to the general topic of economic growth that Harrod had reintroduced. Later, Keynes's followers faithfully built their income distribution arguments from the same aggregates or totals that Keynes had used—namely, labor's wages and capitalists' profits in national income. The post-Keynesian income distribution theory is thus primarily macroeconomic. Moreover, the income distribution is such an integral part of post-Keynesian theories that it is not really distinct from the theory of *how* the national income is determined.

Two lines of criticism were directed at the neoclassical theory of the income distribution, the first emanating from Keynes himself. The *General Theory* states that the wage rate for labor services will not necessarily be determined at an equilibrium *real* wage rate, as the neoclassicals contended. If labor is not paid its real extra value in production, the distribution of income between labor and capital cannot be based upon marginal products. A second criticism stems from Sraffa's return to a classical view of production (his criticism is expressed somewhat differently by the late Joan Robinson and myself). Sraffa shows that, once the services of capital are recognized as deriving from various unlike commodities used in production, any measure of the "quantities" of capital in terms of a common denominator (such as another good or money) will vary as the prices of the commodities vary. As luck would have it, the prices of the commodities will fluctuate with wage and profit rates.

The printing of this book, for example, is accomplished with a computer, a printing press, and a binder. The money values of capital, however, depend upon the price times quantity of all these capital goods (and others) combined. The printing press, the computer, and the binder all sell at varying prices. These prices, or the "rentals" for the services from these capital goods, in turn depend upon the distribution of income between workers and capitalists.

Therefore, the value of capital (its price times its quantity) is not decided by capital's *productivity*, as the neoclassicals argued. Furthermore, reason the post-Keynesians, the neoclassical economists must also be wrong about the income distribution because it is not decided by the market's demand and supply of the factors of production.

In order to dramatize how central the income distribution is to post-Keynesian theories, we will first consider the contributions of a modern Ricardian. (You will recall that Ricardo, like Marx, thought in terms of social and economic classes.) The reincarnation of Ricardo is not as remarkable as the manner in which the results are interpreted. *No* economic explanation of the income distribution emerges from this modern version of Ricardo, and *that* is its central message for those seeking a substitute for the neoclassical theory of distribution.

Sraffa's Neo-Ricardian View of Production and Value

Piero Sraffa, Keynes's pupil and the editor of a modern version of David Ricardo's works, published in 1960 an enigmatic book with an appropriately curious title, *Production of Commodities by Means of Commodities: Prelude to a Critique of Economic Theory.* It puts Ricardo in modern dress. At first glance, Sraffa's highly abstract work appears to bear little relation to the real world. However, his conclusion that changes in the shares of the national income held by workers and capitalists do not alter the level of national output has been applauded by some post-Keynesians (such as Robinson and Kaldor) as an accurate description of industrial reality.

What was a mere puzzle now becomes a labyrinth. It is precisely because Sraffa has no theory of how the income is distributed between workers and capitalists that some of the post-Keynesians have embraced his ideas. This vacuum—unexplained sharing of income between income classes—waits there to be filled by explanations based upon class struggle, administered wages, and relative bargaining power. In other words, if we can adopt Sraffa's theory about the process of production, we can separate issues of production and economic efficiency from income distribution concerns. As you will recall, John Stuart Mill divorced one from the other and was given low marks by later economists for trying to break up the production-distribution family. John Maynard Keynes, for the most part, ignored the distribution of income; it was a "given" in his system.

Sraffa's reincarnation of Ricardo is an abstraction of the system of production and of the way that the real value of goods is decided. *Real* in this sense means the value of one good expressed in terms of other goods. The real value of any one good is decided by the shares of other commodities required to produce it. At the economy's core are *basic commodities,* goods that cannot be produced independently of each other. Basic commodities appear in two roles—as inputs and as outputs. In agriculture, for example, crops are produced with seed stored from a prior growing season. When such goods are inputs or intermediate commodities, it is helpful to think of them as capital goods.

Therefore, capital consists of reproducible capital *goods*, which are combined with labor to reproduce themselves and other commodities.[2]

At every level of production of a particular commodity, the same ingredients are always combined according to the same recipe. As the techniques of production vary by industry, different products will be produced by different combinations of labor and intermediate commodities. However, in any particular industry, labor and intermediate commodities will be mixed in the same proportions regardless of how much of the final product is being produced. The recipe or technology is not changed, and although demand affects the level of production, it plays no further role in deciding prices. In the system, *either* wages or profits are a given. Sraffa nullifies neoclassical demand theory even as he leaves open the theory of personal income distribution.

From this framework, Sraffa defines a *standard commodity* as a special kind of basic commodity that can serve as an "invariable" measure of value or relative prices, invariable to changes in the income distribution between wages and profits. Such a measure is achieved if a wage-rate change alters the measuring rod itself in the same way that it alters the pattern of prices it is measuring. You will recall that Adam Smith and David Ricardo had difficulty with labor as a standard of value because labor's current wage did not always reflect labor's past or cumulative contribution to output. Therefore, Sraffa has something else in mind: he sees *relative* prices (or values) and wages or profits (depending upon which one is "given") decided by the technology used in the production of basic commodities. In this way, Sraffa answers a question posed by Ricardo: How can the profit rate (as a share of "capital") be determined when the income distribution between workers and producers changes? Also, with such an invariable standard, relative price movements can be correctly assigned either to income distribution changes or to changes in the characteristics of the products themselves. Again, however, we must caution, Sraffa's prices are production prices or physical costs, *not* market (exchange) prices.

Sraffa points to corn production, an example used (correctly, Sraffa believes) by Ricardo, as a basic commodity in an agricultural economy. Corn was depicted as the only output of agriculture *and* its only commodity input. As input, corn as food was advanced to the workers and corn as seed was planted. Sraffa's economy is self-replenishing in the sense that gross output must be *at least* sufficient to pay for all inputs, including labor, so that production can reproduce itself. For example, imagine that corn wages are 35 bushels and the amount of seed corn required is 80 bushels to generate an output of 130 bushels at prevailing technology. In Sraffa's world, only commodity inputs count, so *net product* is 130 bushels minus the 80 of seed corn, or 50 bushels. Some of this net output would go to wages, supplying the workers with 35 bushels of food and leaving 15 as producer profits. Corn would then be a perfect (invariable) measure of value, because what happens to wages or profits must affect corn both as an output (food and seeds) and as an input (food and seeds), leaving the relative price of corn unaltered. As full employment and fixed technology prevail, gross output is constant. Therefore, an increase in wages (corn payments) would have to come out of profits. "Capital" cannot be substituted for labor.

Suppose wages rise to 40 bushels. With a fixed production technique, the ratio of seed-corn input to gross output would remain the same (80/130), as would the ratio of the number of workers to the amount of seed corn. Moreover, to replace the 80 bushels of seed corn and 40 bushels of corn as food would require outputs of 80 and 40, respectively. A *standard commodity*, then, is a basic commodity whose outputs appear in the same proportions as the reproducible inputs with which it is produced. A unit of such a commodity can be used as a common denominator with which to express the prices of all other commodities.

In the undecomposable core of the economy consisting of production of basic commodities, there is an entire group of commodities that enter into production in the same proportion as they exit from production. In other words, we can identify a *composite* commodity, which is our historically elusive standard commodity of invariable value, one that has the same property as the corn in Ricardo's example. Sraffa shows that the ratio of net outputs to "capital" inputs in this composite standard subsystem of the economy and the share of net output going to wages in that subsystem determine the rate of profit in the economy as a whole.

This outcome can be illustrated with our version of Ricardo's corn model. [I have greatly simplified Sraffa by expressing his model (which includes all prices) in corn-model terms. You would need to understand how to solve a large system of simultaneous linear equations to duplicate Sraffa exactly. However, his results are identical to those derived with my simple illustration.] Recall that the original corn wages of 35 bushels and seed corn input of 80 bushels produces 130 bushels of corn. Profits equal the residual of gross output after the wage payments and the seed corn costs are subtracted, that is, $130 - 35 - 80 = 15$. Sraffa considers only the seed corn as capital (unlike Ricardo, who included the wage advance as capital). The physical profit rate on capital is 15/80, or 19 percent. After a wage increase of 5 bushels, the profit level drops to 10 ($130 - 40 - 80$). The profit *rate* drops to 10/80, or to 13 percent. A higher wage share necessarily results in a lower profit rate because labor is paid from the standard commodity. (If, instead, the profit rate is predetermined or given, the profit rate could be raised and then the wage share would fall.)

The result for corn as *the* standard commodity can be extended to a multitude of basic commodities. As wages are not connected with any change in production technology in Sraffa's view, an increase in wages does not change the relative prices of the commodities *within* the *composite* yardstick. The composite standard commodity also would be produced with a ratio of inputs identical to the ratio of outputs. Therefore, any jump in wage costs (paid in composite commodity) does not alter this relationship; the consequent change in the prices of inputs is reflected equiproportionately in the prices of outputs so that the input-to-output ratios remain intact.

Sraffa derives another important result that holds equally for the standard commodity and for other basic commodities. A move in the wage (and profit) rate leaves the ratio of net output to means of production unaltered. In the corn example, the initial ratio of net output to commodity input cost is 50/80, or 0.63. After wages have increased by 14 percent, the ratio of net output to the means of production (the commodity input) is still 0.63. There is no mystery in these numbers: this consequence follows directly from the fixed factor proportions, in which productivity is determined solely by the technical conditions of production rather than from the distribution of product or income between wages or profits.[3]

The invariability of the yardstick, of course, does not mean that prices do not change because the world is not all corn or composite standard commodity. So let us move on to another of Sraffa's intriguing conclusions. As labor and the other means of production are used in unequal proportions in the various basic industries (the ratio of labor to "other input" in steel will not necessarily be the same as in corn production), a general wage increase (and profit-rate drop) will cause relative prices to change—say, the standard commodity value of steel compared to corn—because labor will be a larger share of production costs in some industries than in others. Still, the new income distribution will not alter the ratio of net output to the means of production because input requirements remain unaffected. (A change in technology of production also will alter relative prices of basics. The proportion of labor and commodities used in production are altered, and their prices and quantities will vary from those of the old recipe. Therefore, production costs must change.)

Consider the *non*basic commodities, those (including services) that are not used in further production and enter only into final demand. They are strictly consumer goods or services, such as hairstyling or medical treatments. Changes in the prices of nonbasic commodities alone do not alter the relative prices of basics. The reason should be obvious by now.

By definition, a nonbasic commodity is never used in the production of basics, so a change in the price of a nonbasic does not alter the price of a basic. For example, an increase in the price of hotel rooms does not increase the cost of producing automobiles, because hotel rooms (a nonbasic) are not inputs in the automobile production plant. The impact is limited to changes in the exchange ratios between the nonbasic commodity involved (hotel rooms) and all other commodities.

We need to be judicious in our selection of inferences from Sraffa's abstract world, no matter how appealingly tidy his analysis. As formulated, his results depend crucially upon the presence in a modern economy of a unique collection of industries producing basic commodities, the commodities used to produce each other. The kernel of truth in Ricardo's purely agricultural economy must extend to a large area of a modern economy in which nonbasic consumer-goods (and service) industries constitute a fairly small share of total national output. As we shall see, Sraffa's treatment of labor as neither a basic nor a nonbasic service raises questions about the nature of demand. Nonetheless, Sraffa's notion of a standard commodity group in the economy drives a wedge in the neoclassical system sufficiently wide to allow room for new theories of demand and the income distribution.

Sraffa's approach returns economic theory to the classical description of production, especially the view of David Ricardo. The classical system of fixed input proportions was swept away by the marginalists, for reasons that will now be apparent. In an industry in which equal amounts of, say, labor are always combined with a unit of capital, the marginal product of capital is not merely difficult to find—it is not there to be found! Profits can no longer be said to be a return on capital because the profit rate varies with the wage rate. Moreover, the neo-Ricardian theory tells us that relative (real) price movements are driven by changes in the income distribution and technology rather than by demand movements. Finally, the income distribution can be altered without changes in net production levels relative to the available means of production. There is little room for the usual supply-and-demand considerations so central to neoclassical price theory because the wages-to-profits relation becomes a social-political question.

Now that we have seen what *doesn't* decide the income distribution, let us turn to a post-Keynesian story of what *does* determine it.

Kalecki's Pre-Keynes Prodistribution Vision

Given the attempt by post-Keynesians to build on the earlier work of the classical economists as well as on Keynes's aggregates, the Cambridge economists have turned to the work of the Polish economist

Michal Kalecki. In 1933, Kalecki had developed a Keynes-type theory of the level of employment—prior to and independent of Keynes's *General Theory.* Kalecki's approach to the income distribution, however, was more in tune with the Ricardian and Marxian chorus about income classes. In fact, Kalecki's version of the national income determination *and* distribution theory can be summed up in the adage: "The workers spend what they get; the capitalists get what they spend." This view can be expressed with the national income accounts, Keynes's aggregates.

The national income or product can be measured from the flow of income or from the flow of expenditures, so:

Income

Profits (Capitalists' income) + Wages
(Workers' Income) = National Income

Expenditures

Investment + Capitalists' consumption + Workers'
Consumption = National Product

This simple schema says that the national *income* is divided between profits received by capitalists and wages received by workers. The composition of the national product is somewhat less simple, being divided among the investment *and* consumption spending of the capitalists and the consumption expenditures of the workers. The definition of investment is the standard one used in national income accounting—purchases of fixed capital (tools, machinery, buildings, etc.) and changes in inventories or unsold finished goods.

In this schema, all worker earnings are spent on consumption, which means that workers' wages must equal the value of consumption goods they purchase. Whereas Sraffa's system reveals the *inputs necessary* to produce particular outputs, Kalecki's defines the amounts of *necessary consumption goods.* A worker receives, say, $8,000 per year in income and spends $2,800 on food and drink, $2,000 on housing and utilities, $1,300 on durable goods such as an automobile and a washing machine, $800 on medical care, $800 on clothing, and $300 on miscellaneous goods and services. ($8,000 income = $2,800 + $2,000 + $1,300 + $800 + $800 + $300 expenditures.) No savings are accumulated by the worker. Consumer installment purchases are assumed zero (not surprising, as Kalecki developed these ideas when consumer credit buying was rare).

A similar formula describes the spending of capitalists: their profits will equal the sum of the value of their purchases of investment and consumption goods. A diligent capitalist might receive $800,000 in annual profits, which he divides between $700,000 for new machinery to replace some outmoded equipment in his plant and $100,000 for living expenses ($800,000 profits = $700,000 investment + $100,000 consumption).

As we have seen with the monetarists' theory, simple classifications often have surprising results. The first surprise is that capitalists can add to their current share of the national income (profits) by having increased their investment spending in a prior period. Investment, Keynes-style, is multiplied in terms of total output. Out of a larger output come greater profits. The second, more shocking, outcome is that, even if the capitalists were to consume their profits in high living—buying yachts, building vacation homes, supporting lovers—they would not experience a decrease in profits income. The total income of capitalists is insensitive to *how* it is spent because increases in the purchase of goods lead to higher levels of production. Capitalist profits are like the water of the artesian well; no matter how much water is taken out, the well never empties.

If the wages of workers are spent entirely on consumption, they are expended for necessary goods: the food, shelter, and clothing required for life as well as for transportation to and from the workplace. (In reality, of course, today's workers spend income on some goods and services that are not strictly necessities, but Kalecki is using Marx's notion of cultural subsistence.) This consumption can be related either to the level of income or to the level of employment. If we further simplify by saying that *all profits* are diligently plowed back into the business to purchase new investment goods, savings as well as investment are equal to profits. The capitalist is the lone saver in this simple economy. Although the capitalists are "masters of their own fate" in this sense, Kalecki sees outside elements, such as uncertainties regarding profitable investments, causing unavoidable fluctuations in profits. As we have been concerned here primarily with the rudiments of Kalecki's thought, these complications need not detain us at this point.

The Simplified Process of Economic Activity

A Kaleckian view of production can be made to conform with Sraffa's subsistence model (in chapter 1 of *Production of Commodities*). This synthesis is not surprising if we pause to appreciate the unbroken lineage from Ricardo to Marx to Kalecki and from Ricardo to Marx to Sraffa.

Let us retain the above distinction between the worker and the capitalist income classes. Suppose further that the economy is divided Kalecki-like into two distinct industries, one producing necessary consumption goods, the other producing necessary investment goods, mostly machines and buildings. In Sraffa's admittedly simple world of fixed technology, the amount of business investment and the prevailing production technology then decide the level of employment as well as the division of labor between the production of necessities and the manufacture of investment goods. This technology and the prevailing level of capacity to produce (the size of plants equipped with vintage technology) also decide the total amount of each class of good produced.

The introduction of subsistence wages into Sraffa's model transforms it into a Kaleckian world of income distribution. Workers' incomes generate a flow of spending that decides the quantity of necessities manufactured. The quantity of investment goods produced is determined by the entrepreneurs' expected future profits. These investment goods are combined, of course, with labor effort. Suppose one worker is employed for every two machines in steel production—that is, machines and workers are utilized in a 2:1 ratio. If steel production is doubled, even though more workers and more machines are used, the increase in the units of each must be such that at the higher level of output each worker still is using two machines and the 2:1 overall ratio remains intact. That is, capital and labor are combined in fixed proportions in the short run.

Where do funds for investment come from? Now we pick up another line from the story being told by Kalecki. Realized profits depend upon the relation of the current costs of production (for the sake of simplicity, wage costs are the sole production costs) to the prices of necessary finished goods. The demand for these "survival goods" equals the workers' income from both the necessities sector and the investment goods sector. The sensitivity or price elasticity of demand of workers to price changes in necessities is zero or nearly so because price concerns vanish near death. Therefore, the producers of consumer necessities will receive revenues in excess of their costs of production, that is, in excess of labor's wages in the production of survival goods. These profits (the excess of revenue over costs) provide the funds for the purchase of investment goods by the industry that produces necessities.

Investment goods are produced in part by investment goods. It is helpful here to imagine Sraffa's commodities being produced with commodities. Machines and labor have to be combined in order to reproduce machines. Therefore, the sales receipts of the investment-goods industry from the necessities-goods industry must cover the investment-goods industry's labor costs plus the cost of the machine-babies, that is, the investment-goods industry's own machines. Those required investment outlays are equal to the profits of the investment-goods industry.

Obviously, the combined profits from both industries must equal the value of produced investment goods. With equal predictability, *real wages* (money wages adjusted for the price of necessities) equal the amount of necessities produced. Likewise, the profits from both industries combine to purchase the output of the investment-goods industry. This means that the larger the investment-goods industry of the economy, the greater will be the profits for capitalists! As leaders, the capitalists are their own followers. The accumulation of capital is both the rainbow and the pot of gold.

The distribution of income between workers and capitalists becomes the hallmark of this approach. The division of income between wages and profits is the mirror image of the distribution of national output between consumer necessities and technologically necessary investment goods. The allocation of labor between the production of necessities and investment goods has already been decided by the technology for producing the two general classes of goods.

Now we have a result identical to that in the national income account schema. If a greater share of national output is devoted to investment goods, the level of employment in the investment sector will be greater relative to the consumer necessities sector, and (given that investment = profits) a greater share of the national income will go to the capitalists. Conversely, if a greater share of output is devoted to consumer necessities, the workers will have a larger piece of the national income pie. However, there remain some major difficulties with this Sraffian-Kaleckian system.

After introducing his classical subsistence model, Sraffa moves on to a production surplus economy, one that produces commodities in excess of labor's physiological necessities plus actual depreciation of all the means of production. In Sraffa's model of the surplus economy, basic commodities or goods that appear as inputs *and* outputs are necessities *only* in a *technological* sense.

In the surplus economy, nonbasic commodities or goods and services entering only into final demand include both consumer necessities and luxuries—even for workers. Only in Sraffa's subsistence model are basic commodities necessities in consumption as well as in production. In his surplus economy, Sraffa makes no attempt to separate the allocation of extra-subsistence wages between necessary and "luxury" consumer goods. Kalecki's simplified model does not allow workers to consume luxuries. Moreover, Sraffa's treatment of labor as neither a basic nor a nonbasic service in the surplus economy raises additional serious questions about the nature of demand.

Ironically, then, a critical insight into the advanced economy lies hidden in the model so quickly dismissed by Sraffa, his subsistence model in which both necessary consumption and necessary capital goods coexist. Such a model reveals that labor is best treated as a basic "commodity" or, better, basic service, because labor is still necessary to produce subsistence commodities. Labor is an input *and* an output in the (at least) self-reproducing economy. Nevertheless, in the long run, just as the standard commodity must change with new technology, the quantity of consumer "necessities" must change as what is necessary is redefined.

The Personal Income Distribution

Beyond his subsistence model wherein labor requires a subsistence wage in order to meet basic physiological needs, Sraffa provides no guide to the distribution of surpluses. What happens then to Sraffa's *and* Kalecki's theories when—as is the case in a modern economy—we find some "workers" with sufficient incomes to indulge in nonspending, that is, saving? If such persons purchase income-producing financial assets, they can then share (albeit indirectly) in total profits. The incomes of such persons then include labor earnings plus some capitalistic profits. In this case, of course, the "working class" receives a larger share of the national income than that derived from their labor efforts alone.

Because such earners also receive some nonwage income—interest on savings accounts, rents, or profits—more than two income classes exist, and the simple distinction between "workers" and "capitalists" dissolves. Such income intervals would identify the *personal* income distribution. However, this refinement of the income distribution does not alter Kalecki's general conclusions as long as there is *one* group that receives only profits income.[4] Such a group of income receivers does exist (coexist?) in modern capitalistic societies.

In short, the reliance on a stereotyped income division between workers and capitalists is an inadequate explanation for the income distribution of an affluent society. Moreover, it tells us little about the characteristics of the labor receiving differential income payments beyond the color of their collars. We need to know more about why different households occupy varied places in the income distribution. Our concerns go beyond the extremes of Wayne Newton's $1 million per month "wage rate" for singing in Las Vegas, Mike Schmidt's $1.6 million 1983 income for playing with the Phillies (baseball), or Moses Malone's $1.7 million in 1983 for playing with the Seventy-Sixers (NBA basketball). In medicine, 1982 average compensation for the neurosurgeon (incorporated) in the United States was $140,070 compared with $77,860 for the general practitioner. In insurance, the salary for a Class A accounting clerk in Atlanta in 1980 was $9100 but $11,752 in Philadelphia. The maximum UAW-member hourly wage for a (miner) assembler was $9.55 in

1982 whereas that for a "machine repairer" was $11.81. The nonunion worker performing the same tasks received substantially less. The median income of the white male in 1980 was $19,719; the white female, $11,702. Finally, inheritance accounts for about half of the wealth of the richest 400 Americans.[5] As we will see, the members of these diverse income classes end up spending their incomes in equally distinct stores, restaurants, and nightclubs. My *vita theory* provides a more eclectic explanation.

A *vita* is a brief summary of the main attributes and events of one's life, a kind of autobiographic sketch. The *vita theory* is a way of saying that an individual's life history is important in deciding his or her income, and that income is important in deciding the person's life.[6]

The main thrust of a vita theory can be simply stated. Imagine that one labor market exists for each general class of labor, such as plumbers, medical doctors, electricians, or elementary school teachers. The individual's quality as a productive member of the economic system determines which labor market that person enters. A person "qualifies" for a particular labor market by the state of his or her vita at that time. The vita begins with birth, when race, sex, religion, national origin, inherent or initial mental and physical capacities, inheritances, and family background (endowments) are duly noted.

The autobiography is added to over the life span by education, other training, and experience. An individual does have some control over the length and depth of his autobiography. However, production "recipes" change in the long run. Because labor demand is related to technology as well as to product and services demand, only the rarest of individuals can predict with any accuracy the amount of future demand for workers with his or her own emerging or mature autobiography. Beyond this, specific labor supply conditions are a collective outcome that is beyond personal control.

Thus, given his vita and the characteristics of the applicable labor market, the individual's basic wage rate depends upon the average wage for such services. Upon closer examination, however, the individual's personal income exhibits differentials from potential labor market earnings. The differentials—occupational, geographic, interindustry, union-nonunion, discriminatory, and so on—often can be traced back to the first vita stage, the birth vita. Second and third stages are the precareer vita, and the career or mature vita. Speaking in terms of life stages highlights those events and times in which the individual often loses control over important choices. At birth, the genetic code has already determined one's *initial* or *innate* IQ, sex, race, and initial state of health. The precareer vita is the time for education, when earning qualities can be enhanced. For example, 35 percent of all white householders earned

$30,000 or more in 1981 while 15 percent of black householders earned as much. Of these above-average whites, 63 percent were college graduates compared with 14 percent who had completed elementary school education. Of the above-average blacks, 47 percent were college graduates whereas 7 percent had completed elementary school. Education adds substantially to the income of blacks, though not nearly as much as to that of whites. Education beyond that which is mandatory and free normally depends heavily upon parental contributions. Individuals thus have only moderate control over their precareer vitae because voluntary schooling and training is often directly related to inherited material endowments. By maturity, the options of the individuals are greatly narrowed. From the view of earnings prospects, the autobiography is for the most part written, although one new consideration enters at this life stage—years of experience.

The labor force, the supply side of the labor market, consists of those people who are of working age, who wish to work, and who have either precareer or mature vitae, which identify the person's occupational characteristics. In the short run, individuals can enter only that labor market they "fit"; in the long run, they potentially can change their characteristics and qualify for a different labor market, perhaps one with a higher wage rate. In general, however, the number of vitae directly applicable to the labor market decreases with increases in skills, special aptitudes, and required credentials. For example, the number of people who qualify as unskilled labor greatly exceeds the number who qualify as medical doctors. Similarly, the possibilities for substitution of different types of labor are greater among occupations within unskilled labor markets. The least labor substitution occurs within the most specialized occupations. At the higher skilled extreme, in fact, the professional occupation *is* the labor market.

There is no assurance that all vitae will be employed at any particular time, for employment levels depend upon demand. However, it is presumed that, wherever involuntary unemployment exists, it involves those of lowest ranked employment vitae, including young people with precareer vitae who lack job training or are being newly considered for on-the-job training.

During production and employment expansion, upward occupational mobility can occur. However, labor institutions—craft unions and industrial unions—are a major part of the real-world conditions for mobility. Industrial unions, for example, organize entire industries. They consist of persons with diverse autobiographies and occupations, including both the unskilled and the semiskilled. The main economic effect of the industrial union is the negotiation of a wage floor for its members. However, the industrial union attempts to gain some of the advantages of the craft union through apprenticeship regulations, seniority practices, and (in some cases) discrimination. These practices alter the mobility conditions for union workers as they attempt to change occupations within the unionized plant.

The vita theory points toward a structural view of labor demand. In the short run, employment and wages are not always determined by the same forces. In describing such a process, we lose the determinism of the neoclassical labor market but gain some realism.

In the short run, product prices, the state of technology, and industrial competition are givens. Employment is a fixed proportion of production, so the quantity of labor demanded is tied directly to the production level. With fixed capital-to-labor combinations, employment levels are unrelated to the wage rate and therefore vary with output levels.

Technological progress can alter the demand for a particular labor type in two ways. First, it can change labor-quantity requirements. Though capital and labor complement each other in the short run or even the intermediate run (two workers may be needed for each new machine), they can become substitutes for each other in the longer run. The long-run trend of wages in the concentrated sector is known to be upward, and it is not surprising that the main purpose of new equipment in industrialized economies is to reduce labor employment. Technological change also exerts a more indirect effect on labor demand. A new, more complex technology can cause a shift to labor of a different type altogether. Workers who once combined the ingredients for frozen cakes may be unqualified to monitor the automated machines that now perform this task, and unemployment of these workers results.

The labor markets dominated by industrial unions are akin to "administered" wages and prices. If the labor union is strong, industry's ability to pay the demanded wage is enhanced by its ability to impose price mark-ups upon the consumer. The industrial union's tool is the wage rate rather than the labor supply. This means that in the short run employment is not related to the wage rate, and the wage rate is related to employment only if full employment extends across all labor. (At full employment, wages can be bid up by Keynesian excess demand.) Therefore, a high wage can be associated with a high unemployment rate because employment is decided by the level of production.

Union labor sets the pace for the wage structure across the industrial economy. Moreover, the price mark-up is not limited to concentrated industries. Competitive industries producing industrial or consumer necessities can pass along rising costs because the industry or consumer supplied does not have an alternative to the product.

The long-run labor supply is related to what individuals *expect* the wage rate to be, because the supply over time represents the maturing of vitae that have been directed along a career path designed years earlier. In the long run, increases in the expected market wage rate, for whatever reasons, are likely to attract new entrants, and the labor supply for that class of worker is increased. Even in this longer run, it is probable that the labor supply will be controlled in craft union areas. It is not mere historical accident that skilled workers were the first to organize in craft unions and successfully raise wage rates.

The actual and expected wage rates may tend to converge for industrial labor, but this by no means assures a full employment equilibrium for such labor. The substitution of newer industrial processes that require less labor may have advanced to the point that long periods of idleness are traded off for higher wages. Full employment under such conditions might require extraordinarily high production levels and a glut of goods. An unused supply of unskilled labor is a characteristic of recent experience in the United States, England, and Western Europe.

The vita theory explains several kinds of wage differentials. If we impose the assumption of "rational man" or "superrational man" with respect to income, these differentials represent an opportunity for a worker to move from a low-wage market to a high-wage market. Unfortunately, the mobility of labor is a complex, difficult, and cumbersome process. Studies attribute only 53–69 percent of migration to purely economic motives, leaving considerable room for the motivations of regional preference, health, education, housing, marriage, lifestyle, and so on.

Nonetheless, according to the vita theory, a higher wage rate for individuals depends upon their mobility. Significant upward mobility requires the acquisition of a "higher quality" set of skills, whether in response to changing technological requirements or because of the individual's desire to increase income and status. Despite the training and education that require a substantial amount of time and personal investment, this search for higher earnings may end with still another barricade. The individual may not receive the wage rate of the labor market and occupation of his choice because of genetic characteristics—race, sex, nationality. Even age is a source of discrimination that can bar a worker from receiving the desired wage. Studies suggest that more than half of the earnings differential relates to racial discrimination. In short, earnings and income differentials are wider than wage differences. Under such circumstances, the best advice is that children be very selective with regard to their parentage.[7]

In light of the vita theory an economy of workers demanding only minimal necessities cannot be described as robust. If we are looking for an "invariant" measure of value from the demand side, the quantity of necessities per worker seems a better candidate than Sraffa's composite standard commodity. Nevertheless, in the long run, just as the standard commodity must change with new technology, the quantity of "necessities" will change as workers redefine what is necessary. Whether necessities are a constant or a variable market basket of goods and services, their quantities and prices will determine their dollar value and the required dollar value of the wage bill. For example, in the autumn of 1980, the Bureau of Labor Statistics (BLS) estimated the annual cost of a "lower" consumption budget for a four-person family in the urban United States at $14,044. This household's budget included expenditures on food, shelter, furnishings, transportation, clothing, personal care, and medical care. If $14,044 represented the cultural subsistence requirements for an average family in the urban United States, the wage bill paid to the household had to be at least $14,044.[8]

Surpluses, a characteristic of the capitalistic economy, are production increments in excess of what is required merely to sustain life. Although it cannot be denied that there are American households that exist at the biological subsistence level, ours is indisputably a supra-surplus economy, or Galbraith's affluent society.

The estimate for the "higher" consumption budget for a four-person family in the urban United States in 1980 was $34,409, nearly 2.5 times the lower budget. The "intermediate" budget was estimated at $23,134. Does this mean that the higher one's income goes, the greater the number of necessities the individual must meet? The answer, though not definitive, is illuminating. In an economy such as ours, we need to distinguish between absolute physical necessities and "wants." The satisfaction of a greater number of wants is usually associated with higher standards of living. Leaving aside for the moment the question of whether people continue to be better off at higher and higher income levels, we can say with certainty that the ratio of the dollar value of absolute biological necessities to the wage bill paid to the U.S. higher-income family is much less than one.[9]

THE HOUSEHOLD BUDGET AND MACROECONOMICS

As we prepare to shift our attention back to the vagaries in national income, the question arises concerning the relation of *family* or household incomes to the *national* level of personal income. The answer is surprisingly simple. Each income class in the distribution includes a given population. The population multiplied by the average income of that class is the total income generated by that part of the income distribution. The sum of the incomes in all such classes equals the nation's personal income.[10] For the most part, expenditures that give rise to the demand for goods and services come out of current personal income. The distribution of the population among these income classes affects consumption and therefore the national income and the business cycle.

If the transition from individual prices and quantities in product markets to macroeconomics is to be made, we will have to dispense with the idea of general equilibrium, which requires that we know every price and every quantity. The explanation of the failure to integrate neoclassical price theory and Keynesian macroeconomic theory is simple: it cannot be done because we do not know the quantities that will be demanded and supplied of every product at every possible price. Economists should not be criticized for failing to do what is impossible.

The alternative way of handling this difficulty is to rearrange the price theory so it can be "added up" to macro-theory. Setting aside the theory about market supply and demand for every product is a modest loss from the point of view of the individual. For any particular household, prices are presumed to be given by the markets. As Joan Robinson has intimated, in the theory product markets do not move to equilibrium; they are already there.

I will assume that prices are determined by prevailing technology and the cost of production. In addition, I will adopt the view of the institutionalists that consumption is dominated by mores and habit and that the stage of economic development, and therefore the culture, of the society decrees consumption patterns. Finally, we will see how the income distribution goes a long way toward explaining why thousands of budgetary investigations have led to the same conclusion.

There is a certain regularity in the way households allocate expenditures on food, clothing, transportation, and other items. This uniformity is related to income level. The poor, for example, spend their incomes primarily on necessities such as food, shelter, and clothing. After these needs are met, the discretionary income remaining meets "needs" or wants that are difficult to pigeonhole. The uncertainty increases as we shift focus away from specific needs, such as the need to be clothed, and toward the particular way such needs and wants are met, such as attempts to be fashionably dressed. Although households tend to eat more (and perhaps better) as their income increases, there is a limit to the amount of extra money that people spend on food as their incomes rise. That is, beyond the income level that meets basic nutritional needs, food expenditure as a share of the household budget grows slowly. This general behavior pattern was first identified by the nineteenth-century Prussian statistician Ernst Engel (not to be confused with Marx's friend, Friedrich Engels), and the relation was named *Engel's law*.

Engel's law is as successful as Sraffa in suppressing the role of product money prices, but without eliminating prices from the crucial aspects of economics. The prices are still there insofar as the *price index*, or unit costs of product-service groupings, affects real income. It is more meaningful to speak of budget shares allocated to *bundles* of consumer inputs than to individual consumer products.[11] Such a relation among product-service groups, money incomes, and average group prices means that, once we have identified the household's income level, we also have come close to identifying the share of the household budget that goes to meet particular needs or wants and therefore to necessary bundles of inputs. Thus, what is important to the household is the ability to meet needs and wants with its real income levels, given its budget shares. To keep things simple, we will confine the present discussion to the following general categories: food; clothing; housing; automobiles and transportation; and medical care, education, and recreation. (Ideally, basic medical care should be classified separately.) Of course, whatever remains in the way of non-consumption out of household income is personal savings or "forced savings," going to governments as taxes.

The relation between personal income and expenditures by category for American families in 1980 is illustrated in Figure 15.1. The budget shares equal the income level divided into the related expenditure for a selected category. For example, the higher-budget family spends about 26 percent of its income on food whereas the lower-budget family's share is almost 31 percent. (This gap is about twice as wide if we use after-tax disposable income.) The curves are "forced through" the aforementioned BLS budget values, so that the general configurations are correct, but the expenditure values for some incomes are approximations. The consumption budget level for each of the three BLS budgets (lower, intermediate, and higher) is denoted by vertical solid lines so that expenditures by categories can be read off of the left-hand vertical axis for each budget. The arrows above the graph point to the estimated number of households (in millions) that have budgets close in value to the respective BLS budgets.

In terms of shares, we note a pattern, which conforms to a complex "economic man" prototype (see Chapter 11). First, the more "necessary" the product or service, the lower the level of income at which expenditure for it begins to slow. Second, this pattern suggests a hierarchy of rankings. Expenditure shares for food begin to slow down at a very low level of income; clothing at a somewhat higher income level; housing at a substantially higher income level; automobiles and transportation at a still higher level; and medical care, education, and recreation appear not to slow much at all at higher income levels. Evidently, the income

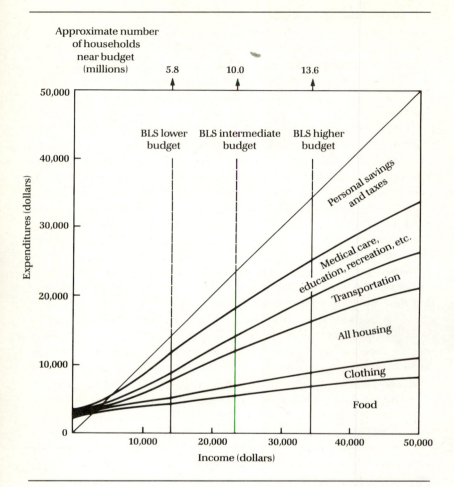

FIGURE 15.1 U.S. personal income and expenditure. [Compiled from data
of the U.S. Bureau of Labor Statistics, 1981, Autumn 1980 urban family
budgets *News* USDL 81–195; *Family Economic Review,* Agricultural Research
Service, U.S. Department of Agriculture, Fall 1981; and U.S. Bureau of the
Census, *Current Population Reports,* Series P–60, No. 142 1984.]

distribution has a lot to do with the overall *level* of demand in the
economy as well as with the composition of production. Furthermore,
expanded consumption by those households above the middle budget
requires that households either satisfy certain wants at a higher level
or discover new wants. The consumer once satisfied with a black Model

T must now be motivated to buy a streamlined, racy, colorful machine designed for maximum road comfort and perhaps fulfilling exotic fantasies.

Discretionary income is to consumption what physical surplus is to production. Budget shares are to consumption what production prices are to production in Sraffa's system. The difference between the consumer's physiological necessities budget and the higher-income budget motivates producers to create many of the wants they seek to satisfy—Galbraith's *dependence effect* (see Chapter 11). Only in the affluent society can wants be created in a Galbraithian manner. As Galbraith states, "Mass communication was not necessary when the wants of the masses were anchored primarily in physical need. The masses could not then be persuaded as to their spending—this went for basic foods and shelter."[12]

An excess of income above physiological subsistence leaves a demand wedge that provides breathing space for producers. Imperfect competition abhors wedges and sets into motion forces to fill the space. As we now will see, the price markup tool accomplishes the task. In this regard, we will also find a connection between investment spending and the price level. Kalecki, in particular, sees the oligopoly assuring its needs for investment funds through its pricing powers. In this post-Keynesian perspective, the money wage—the *actual* wage negotiated—separates itself from the real wage or labor productivity. This separation underlies the post-Keynesian theory of stagflation.

THE PRICE MARKUP AND STAGFLATION

The introduction of imperfect competition into macroeconomic theory is due mostly to Kalecki in Europe and Sidney Weintraub in America. John Kenneth Galbraith's conception of the New Industrial State is consistent with Kalecki's notions of pricing behavior. Weintraub's version is a logical extension of the post-Keynesians' eclectic interpretation of Keynes's *General Theory*. Kalecki's and Weintraub's vision of pricing in the manufacturing sector can be dramatized in one word: *markup*.[13] Hyman Minsky, a laconic but persistent American post-Keynesian, sees the retained earnings from the markup levered by debt as financing the acquisition of additional capital assets.

The Markup

The post-Keynesians agree that the firms in the manufacturing sector are oligopolistic; that is, a handful of firms produce the products of each industry. They have sufficient market power to pass on to the consumer most cost increases as well as price increases required by a substantial share of investment needs. Somewhere between 75 and 90 percent of gross (including replacement investment) fixed capital investment in the United States is financed from retained profits. The giant firm has the power to select a percentage markup over production costs (mostly wages) that is sufficient to complete its investment plans much of the time without going hat in hand to a banker for loans. Nonetheless, in the aggregate—as Minsky contends—business debt is used to finance additional plant and equipment purchases.

Capacity utilization may move up and down with the demand for products, but the firm usually will stick with the markup that will provide its target level of retained profits. This target depends upon its dividend payout ratio to stockholders, its amount of debt relative to its equity, and (most important) its perceived investment needs.[14] The target's highest limit is determined by the current number of firms in the industry and by the firm's perceived price elasticity of demand or consumers' sensitivity to price changes. Generally, the fewer the firms in the industry and the lower the sensitivity of consumers to price increases (the lower the price elasticity of demand), the higher the upper limit to the price markup. As long as the firm's capacity is sufficient to meet demand for its products, and as long as production costs do not vary greatly from expectations, the firm will cling to the price derived from its careful planning. Although the margin of prices over current costs already reflects the market power of the firm in a concentrated industry, even a fixed markup allows for a higher price when the unit cost of production goes up.

An example will clarify the role of the markup. If the wage cost per typewriter in the business machines industry is $700 and the markup is 10 percent, the profits flow per unit of production is $70. If 1 million typewriters are sold yearly, industry profits reaped are $70 million. If wage costs rise to $800 per typewriter, the unchanged markup rate of 10 percent over current costs would now generate an earnings flow of $80 million, given the same number of units sold.

Kalecki's measure of the "degree of monopoly" of the firm conforms neatly with the idea of price leadership under oligopoly and with Galbraithian power. The essence of the degree-of-monopoly formula is that a firm can raise its own price in proportion to its increase in production costs (as in the typewriter example) if other firms in the industry do likewise. When General Motors, the most efficient American producer of automobiles, signs a union contract with the United Auto Workers of America for higher wages, the corporation also raises prices more or less in proportion to the wage hike. Chrysler and Ford then follow suit.

The markup and investment plans are inexorably linked. Because of the degree-of-monopoly factor, actual prices charged by the industrial firms do not reflect current demand conditions; they more closely mirror the funds requirements for the planned investment expenditures and debt servicing (payments on principal, interest, and dividends) that the giant firm deems sufficient to increase capacity (plant size or number of machines) to meet *expected future* demand. When costs of production rise, the firm "protects'" its profits-for-investment flow by raising prices according to its established markup over costs. It is likely that the prices of investment goods will rise also as wage increases ripple through the economy. At times the capacity accumulated with these retained profits will be in excess of that needed to meet current demand, but this situation is no problem for an oligopoly.

Money Incomes and Inflation

In order to understand the implication of firm and industry pricing behavior upon the general price level, it is best to revert to the equation of exchange as a starter. If we have

(Price Level) · (Real Output)
= (Money National Income), or (Price Level)
= (Money National Income) / (Real Output),

stable prices require that money income grow no faster than real output. A 4 percent increase in money income and the identical advance in real production leaves the price level unchanged. In other words, if the money income per employee rises no faster than output per employee (productivity), the price level remains stable. There is no inflation.[15]

Contrary to Kalecki's simple worker-capitalist duality, money income arises from a whole spectrum of sources. It includes wages and salaries, profits and depreciation, business taxes, rents, and interest payments. If money wages are administered by union-management agreements, the balance of income is provided by the markup over wages, most of which will be retained profits (profits plus depreciation) and dividend payouts. If this markup remains constant throughout the economy and productivity remains unchanged, any cost increase from a boost in average wages will be reflected as an increase in the price level.

If prices are set with a constant or even a variable markup over wage costs, money wages become central to the price level. Though it is a short-run process, the "short run" can become rather long. Labor contracts are negotiated and then prevail over some future time. The money wages are inflexible downward (as Keynes argued for a different reason) because to reduce money wages violates the labor contract. If the Teamsters' Union signs a contract for a 30 percent wage increase divided equally over a three-year term, no one would expect the second-year increment to be sliced to, say, 5 percent. In the short run, therefore, product prices must adjust to money wages and the cost of production rather than vice versa. There is a revised sequence in which the price level and inflation are resolved after the money wage rates and increases are determined. Money wages, *outside* Sraffa's system, are endogenous in Galbraith's system but determined by social-political conditions, not by the technology of production.[16]

When demand shifts up or down, for whatever reason, the neo-classical response of rising and falling prices is absent. The adjustments made by the firm are in output levels. If GM is not selling its inventory of cars at the current prices (based upon markup over unit costs), GM produces fewer Chevrolets next month and may even lay off production workers. The main message is sufficiently short that it could be sent by Western Union (incidentally, a monopoly): "Rather than responding to lower demand by reducing prices, giant producers reduce production levels."

You will note that this view of pricing is more in line with classical thought (especially that of Smith, Ricardo, and Mill), in which prices are determined more by production than by demand. Although production adjustments occur in the short run, pricing is based upon long-run behavior. The role of consumer (and investor) demand is futuristic. Demand shifts resources among industries over the longer calendar period via its effect upon planned investment and therefore upon required profits. Private enterprise competes for market shares or for new markets, both of which require wise investment decisions and capital accumulation under conditions of uncertainty.[17]

NECESSARY STIMULATION

From the viewpoint of production economic efficiency, there is no purely economic reason for any firm to have more than one plant of optimal size. Firms that build more than one such plant or build plants to produce unrelated products are not doing so in the interest of economic efficiency; they are attempting to increase their flow of revenue to finance growth or gain still more power. Such firms follow the growth patterns described by Galbraith's planning system. The existence of such firms is characteristic of supra-surplus capitalism and leads to a form of competition largely unrelated to prices. Imperfect competition that resorts to nonprice devices for luring customers widens the wedge between absolute and cultural necessities even as it enlarges the price markup.

Budget shares lead to an understanding of nonprice competition that is lost when disputes are confined to market pricing. Veblen's snob appeal takes on concrete meaning in the face of the 2.5 ratio of the higher to the lower urban budget in the United States. The large gap between the lowest and highest incomes inspires management and the entrepreneur to transcend their roles of simple producers of goods and services. Although the difference between the necessities budget and the higher-income budget could in theory be devoted entirely to household savings, the producer tries to divert these household dollars toward consumer goods and services. Not surprisingly, in such an economy, a large share of the GNP goes to salespeople, marketing efforts, and advertising. Indeed, the very lifeblood of capitalism as we know it is the exchange of surpluses for desired extras, whether those luxuries are perceived as needs or not. Galbraith and others have described how products are differentiated by imaginary innovations, stylistic alterations that leave the functions of the goods intact. Beyond these widely discussed elements of imperfect competition, market researchers long ago discovered that products and services can be further differentiated by making the outlets in which they are sold disparate. That is, customers above subsistence buy ambiance as well as products. If this were not so, people would not attach a different status to Neiman-Marcus stores than to K-Mart or to New York's Four Seasons Restaurant than to a humble deli.

Differing retail outlets also provide for varying markups. With the low-budget and middle-budget stores meeting the needs of their own clientele, the high-budget outlets can satisfy the more imaginary "needs" of the rich and the great pretenders. Indeed, retail outlets are designed with particular shares of the income distribution in mind. There is an intense competition, not so much among products as for the dollars of different income classes. Supra-surplus capitalism is more a struggle for class than it is a class struggle.

Supra-surplus capitalism is a system of great complexity. David Warsh, a financial writer for the *Boston Globe*, describes the "idea of complexity" in graphic terms. "The best currently available rough indicator of the complexity of the [U.S.] economy," says Warsh, "is a standard industrial classification (SIC) code, a kind of Yellow Pages for the Nation."[18] Warsh's idea of complexity encompasses increased specialization and interdependencies; the SIC code begins with ten divisions that include agriculture, mining, and manufacturing, moves on to some 800 major classifications, such as mining and quarrying of nonmetallic minerals, and finally ends up with dimension stone, cordage and twine, and so on. In the finest division, there are nearly 10,000 U.S. industries today. The required division of labor is far finer than could ever have been imagined by Adam Smith, for the layers of value added generate a hierarchy of tasks, jobs, and industries that vary in complexity. In one of Warsh's least elegant examples,

> *The modern pig climbs on the assembly line at birth, lives its entire life indoors, is fed a computer-formulated diet loaded with vitamin and mineral supplements, and goes to the slaughterhouse five months later. Instead of having his throat cut by a man, he is stunned with a hammer and killed by a jolt of electricity, often as not generated by a nuclear power plant.*[19]

He might have added that the pig is fed antibiotics that are later ingested by humans who may require medical attention from a newly required "specialist." Moreover, meat inspectors now use sophisticated instruments designed and produced by persons as far removed from the Omaha stockyards as most people prefer to be. This more complex division of labor requires a theory of a segmented personal income distribution since some tasks are simple, others ridiculously complex, some overpaid, others underpaid.

THE INCOME SHARES OF WORKERS AND MANAGERS

Where corporate and union powers reside in supra-surplus capitalism and are symbiotic, *physiological* subsistence for labor gives way to *cultural* subsistence. The notion of cultural subsistence in the complex society brings the income distribution in line with a Veblenian-Galbraithian state of consumption. The technology of production and the prevailing level of production capacity decide the total amount produced of two types of goods: now-"necessary" consumption goods and the requisite investment goods. However, realized output depends upon effective demand and income distribution. We, of course, do not have to be content with Sraffa's abstract and "given" output level.

The distribution of income between workers and capitalists reenters the picture, but in a more complex way than Kalecki would lead us to believe. There are two tugs-of-war between the manufacturers and the consumers-workers; producers seem unaware of one of them and workers unaware of the other. Displaying the instincts attributed to corporate management by Galbraith, corporations create and stimulate new demand for their goods and services. However, in the planning (concentrated) system, the wherewithal to fulfill both the manufacturers' and the workers' dreams is decided at the labor-management bargaining table. Only in the guise of consumers are there any losers. Goodbye, Adam Smith, in which consumers wear crowns.

The planning systems' producer has succeeded all too well in convincing consumers that they should expand the number of goods and services they consider necessary. In response to these culturally determined desires, the giant labor union demands higher wages so that the workers can pay for the newly defined standard of living. The corporation capitulates, knowing that the higher cost of production from a larger wage can be passed on to consumers. The illusion that a higher wage is always a good thing—a money illusion—is enjoyed by the workers, who don't quite sense the implications of their dual role as both laborers and consumers. In the workers' budget referred to above, these increases merely cover the "cost of living." As Galbraith implies, it is not mere historical accident that the highest paid workers reside in the protected part of the economy, the planning system.

If the process stopped at this point, the working class would increase its share of the national income, at least in money terms. However, the defensive weapon of the manufacturers is the markup, which diverts saving from consumers to producers. It is little understood, but the consumption (nonsaving) of consumers is, in large part, the source of saving (for *potential* investment) for manufacturers. The concentrated industries can use the markup, augmented by ready access to capital markets, the largest banks, and the lowest rates of interest, to generate funds for investment purposes. Throughout the history of capitalism, the idea that workers have to be employed in order to purchase the producers' goods has always eluded manufacturers. Though it is in the interest of any single producer to minimize his wage bill, if all producers succeed in that calculus they will find there is no outlet for their products.

It is this failure to see the forest for the fees that seduces sales managers into replacing their secretaries with cybernetic typewriters. Of course, there is more to technological change than this. Nonetheless, the salutary effect of adopting a new mode of production is its potential for replacing labor. Beyond the reduction of the wage bill, replacement of human beings with machines has further advantages: machines do not demand fringe benefits and do not talk back. It is not surprising, therefore, that the markup is used to generate investment funds for acquiring a production process that utilizes less labor.

As my vita theory suggests, in the short run, industrial employment is not related to the wage rate, and the wage rate is related to employment only if full employment extends across all labor. Therefore, the high wage associated with a high unemployment rate is decided by technology and effective demand rather than by the marginal product of labor.[20] This process is so deeply imbedded in the economic system that it took a four-year global depression (1979–1982) to slow wage (and price) inflation in the United States.

The wage differentials between the union-certified skilled and the unskilled is the consequence of (at least) dual labor markets that reflect the duality between the planning system and the competitive system. Even though the primary or raw materials sector may contain competitive industries, the planning system of the advanced economy is in charge, wielding its power in the marketplace to control production and pass on rising costs (including money wage increases) to all of us. The usually benign countervailing power of an earlier Galbraith (1952) gives way to (as Galbraith admits) nonbenign compensatory power (1983).[21] The well-funded investments in new technology that replace workers have the effect of redistributing income away from the working class, particularly away from the least skilled. Although the working class receives a share of profits, most "nonearned" income from high technology is accumulated by the entrepreneurial, managerial, and professional classes.

Where union power resides, "cost-of-living" wage increments will cover at least the rising prices of necessities. Those whose incomes rise less rapidly, however, will experience a diminished standard of living. In order to maintain a one-to-one relationship between culturally defined necessities and the wage bill, wages must rise proportionately each time the average price of the market basket of necessities increases. If the prices of electricity and gasoline go up, the wage bill would go up in either case. This is what is meant by the popular term *wage-price spiral.*

The constancy of the production recipe (fixed input ratios) is used under specific conditions—to explain outcomes during periods too short for industrial technology to change—and provisionally as an abstraction that can explain the true nature of real or relative prices. Under alternative conditions, technological change—unpredictable and not widely understood—plays a major role. Its impact is readily seen when we accept the wage settlement as largely a political solution based upon the relative power of organized labor and organized production. It is precisely the more advanced secondary or manufacturing sector of the economy that shifts over time toward more and more complex, automated ways of delivering its product. However, there is no guarantee that productivity will grow steadily faster than the wage rate. When effective aggregate demand is expanding rapidly, inflation is the logical consequence of income share or distributions based upon political and social relations mostly unrelated to productivity.

STAGFLATION

The post-Keynesian view of the price level provides a possible explanation for the simultaneous presence of inflation and unemployment, the "stagflation" that plagued the industrialized nations with increasing intensity during the 1970s. If wage acceleration is passed on to the consumer, we have a cost-push inflation. If production costs remain rather stable relative to productivity and the markup is steadily increased, we have a profits-push inflation. The short-run response to any consumer resistance or any other cause of declining demand for goods and services will be *not* wage reductions or price cuts in the concentrated industries but slower production. Substantial production cutbacks will lead—with a lag—to worker layoffs. Production shortfalls and unemployment can therefore happen during times of rising prices. Inflation is treated as delicately as sin: every economic class denounces it and every economic class participates vigorously. By the same token, disinflation, or a slowdown in inflation, depends upon slower wage growth and declines in raw materials prices.

In the Sraffa-Leontief input-output sense, the raw materials, or primary, sector feeds inputs into the secondary sector. Thus, an increase or decrease in the price of raw materials has the same effect as an increase or decrease in the wage rate—a higher or lower cost of producing manufactured goods. Moreover, the primary sector serves a dual role in production because it supplies a biological necessity—food—to fuel the labor input of manufacturing as well as services.

This view of production sectors helps explain the recession (combined with inflation) of 1974–1975, which followed the tripling in world oil prices as well as the recession beginning in 1979. The production of many necessities requiring the use of oil and its derivatives was profoundly affected. Leaps in tractor fuel and fertilizer prices carried over into higher food prices, and the surge in crude oil prices meant a higher price for gasoline used for transportation. Slowdowns in sales of durables, the most expensive postponables, meant inventory accumulations at factories as well as production and associated employment cutbacks. The rolling advance in prices for necessities rippled through the economy, toppling workers from payrolls even as it raised prices to consumers, an anomaly in Keynesian and neoclassical economics. The tripling in oil prices is only the most dramatic example of how cost-push inflation can lead to production and employment reductions.

The foregoing suggests the difficulties of separating monetary and real effects in the economy. In fact, the consumption–production necessities nexus suggests that the separation of the monetary from the real can be done only with mirrors; such reflections are not without interest or importance. As we turn our attention toward the business cycle, however, we will see the arbitrariness of such a dichotomy. This does not detract from the insights we now have from the provisional abstraction from money such as that suggested by Sraffa.

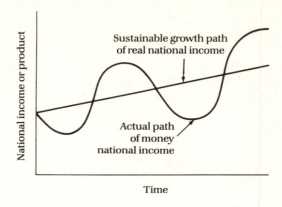

FIGURE 15.2 Growth paths: post-Keynesian national income

THE SHORT PERIOD: THE BUSINESS CYCLE

The legitimate heirs of the Harrod-Domar framework for capitalistic growth are the post-Keynesians. Economic models that could generate busts as well as booms in capitalism flourished during the 1950s. These outpourings were in the spirit of Keynes; however, as we have seen, they also had bastardized neoclassical versions. At this juncture, we want to pick up the thread of Keynes rather than those created as Keynesian spinoffs. In this regard, the contributions of Nicholas Kaldor, Joan Robinson, and Hyman Minsky are consistent with the macroeconomics of Sraffa and Kalecki.

The writings of Harrod, Domar, and Robinson are bullish on capitalism in a special sense. They see the capitalist system growing over time, but in a highly irregular pattern. Capitalism is characterized by intermittent cyclical fluctuations in output and employment. True to Keynes and Kalecki, Kaldor, Robinson, and Minsky see investment playing a key role in such cycles. The existence of short-run variations in economic activity suggests that capitalism is usually in some kind of disequilibrium. Despite these ups and downs of economic activity, however, there is a long-run upward growth path for the economy.

This view presents something of a puzzle. The capitalist economy fluctuates, and yet it grows. Figure 15.2 shows a hypothetical path for such an economy expressed in terms of national income or product. What causes the variations? What sets upper and lower limits to the fluctuations? Why doesn't production fall in the downward cycle to the point that the unemployment rate reaches 20 percent? Whatever it is, the post-Keynesians agree that there is no automatic self-correcting mechanism that can be counted on. The post-Keynesians have noted that different economies, even different capitalistic economies, tend to grow at different rates over time. Economies also grow at different rates at the same time. Why?

Kaldor, Growth, and Income Distribution

Kaldor suggests that the ratio of savings (and thus investment) to income in an economy depends upon the distribution of income. We can best see the explanation for this phenomenon in Kalecki's description of the behavior of workers and capitalists. Kaldor also begins with a Sraffa-like fixed relation between labor and capital so that the number of workers per machine in any particular industry remains constant. This assumption, of course, means (again) that the capitalists have positive savings, and—as in Sraffa—the rewards to capital and to labor are not based upon their productivities.

The income distribution is thus variable (unlike Keynesian or neoclassical economic views), and neoclassical-style wage or price adjustments do not guarantee that the economy will grow along a smooth path. In this simple version of the model, therefore, profits are the only source for financing investment. In turn, the level of profits depends upon the level of investment goods demand by producers. When demand slackens, the level of production in the affected industry falls below the capacity of its plant and equipment to produce it; in other words, the physical facilities of production are underutilized. When this happens, the national income is on the downswing. Whether existing profits will be invested depends upon the attitude of the producers about future sales prospects. Even though there is an upward trend in the economy's capacity to produce goods and services (the straight line in Figure 15.2), variations in demand can swing actual national output away from that trend line as well as toward it.

If production techniques (technology) and the money wage rate are givens, the faster the growth rate of national income, the higher will be the ratio of profit (nonwage income) to wages. Now we are fully in the world of Kalecki. The relatively high level of profits will result in a higher level of investment and a greater share of national income going to capitalists. Kalecki and Weintraub arrive at the same destination by route of the markup deciding the capitalists' share. Thus, the focus remains on the distribution of income even in the growth process. Money wages are decided outside the production process (they are among the givens) and reflect the bargaining power of unions relative to management's ability to pay.

How can a division of income described so long ago by the classical economists be at all relevant to a modern industrialized economy? Supra-surplus capitalism is dominated by large corporations so that a great share of the economy's savings do come out of the corporate sector. Therefore, the savings-out-of-profits behavior of large corporations is a key determinant of the distribution and level of income because profits are a prime source of investment expenditures. Following Keynes, then, we can see that investment expenditures are the main factor deciding the level of economic activity. Whenever such expenditures are insufficient to keep the national income and product growing at a steady rate, the economy will turn downward in a cyclical pattern beneath the trend line. Nonetheless, the strength and duration of booms shapes the trend rate of growth, suggesting that the straight line of Figure 15.2 is an oversimplification.

Minsky and Financial Fragility

Virtually all post-Keynesians agree that fluctuations in business investment open the door to the business cycle. Such a view—consistent with the *General Theory*—nonetheless has been expressed in different ways. Hyman Minsky's theory of investment focuses on how uncertainty, speculation, and an increasingly complex financial system lead to cycles rather than an "equilibrium growth" pattern for capitalism. According to Minsky, Keynes developed a financial theory of investment and an investment theory of business cycles. Any sustained "good times" stagger off into a speculative, inflationary binge and a fragility of financial institutions.

Minsky begins with Kalecki's accounting: workers' consumption equals workers' wages. Moreover, he accepts the Kalecki-Weintraub markup, except, in Minsky's elaboration, the internal funds so generated by the firm are levered by debt to finance the acquisition of additional capital assets. The acquired assets may be purchased out of the existing plant and equipment (corporate takeovers, etc.) or through the production of new investment goods. Only in the latter case will new increments and industrial capacity be added to the economy's productive potential. *In the aggregate,* investment requires *external* financing. Even so, at the level of the individual firm, Minsky is not departing sharply from the views expressed above: investment is financed from both internal *and* external funds.

The income distribution still plays a dominant role because Minsky sees household consumption depending upon household income, which includes, for the higher-income households, interest and dividend income from lending to business. The income constraint for the firm is provided by retained earnings (internal funds) and the amount financed by debt (loans from households and other businesses). If, in the aggregate, the external funding needs of business exceed the household saving made available to finance investment, the shortfall will have to be met by some combination of an increase in the money supply and a decrease in households' money holdings, that is, by an increase in the velocity of money. Since (unlike the monetarists' view) the money supply is endogenous, private banks respond by providing finance and altering the money supply. The way banks, households, and firms respond to uncertainty and financial market conditions is the essence of this Keynesian theory of investment.

Rising wage costs during an economic expansion at a constant markup elevate production costs. Since the amount of markup is not unlimited (price elasticity of demand for products is not zero), only a generalized inflation can assure full employment. In this process a rising share of investment is financed by debt. Bankers and businessmen go along with the rising ratio of debt to internal financing so long as they are reasonably convinced that inflation will continue. Any slowdown in wage rates does not alter contractual debt commitments so that the burden of debt rises during disinflation or deflation. Debt-financed investment decreases, and purchases of investment goods financed by money supply increments decline. Business firms will begin to pay off debt instead of buying new plant and equipment. If capital and labor are used in fixed proportions (Sraffa and vita theory), employment falls with the decline in use of the existing capital stock. Once again, business conditions are at the mercy of uncertainty and financial market behavior.

These models express profound truths, but we need to be cautious. Kaldor, Robinson, and Minsky focused upon the instability of business saving and investment. However, since the markup and sales revenue growth or decline sets the profits (corporate savings) pace, instability in consumer expenditures means instability in corporate savings. Since the *personal* income distribution comprises more than two income classes, the diversity of income classes adds another element to the instability of supra-surplus capitalism. The central notion can be said succinctly: the higher nominal and real family income, the greater the discretion exercised in its expenditure and the greater the potential volatility in consumption behavior. In this way, the multilayered income distribution can magnify the amplitude of the business cycle. Therefore, we turn our attention toward the relation of consumer behavior to national income.

The Instability of Consumption

Consider at this point the classical to neoclassical shift in focus with respect to the consumption choice. Most of the classicals presumed that workers receive a subsistence wage, with "subsistence" defined culturally. Irrespective of the culture, discretionary income can be spent on anything—more necessities, luxuries, or unadulterated frivolity. The neoclassical stress was upon the discretionary part of income, discretion being the better part of value. The truth recognizes both elements of income, with the degree of discretion enlarging as the household moves upward in the income distribution.

In the advanced industrialized nations, discretionary income in the upper reaches of the income distribution is sufficient to generate substantial savings. These upper-class personal savings are only *indirectly* important to the investment plans of the giant corporation and *directly* important to the saver-household itself because the giant corporation generates its own savings and borrowing leverage through price mark-ups on goods sold to the masses. Savings allow households to move funds among cash, checking accounts, stocks, bonds, and other financial assets. Families saving and "balancing portfolios" in this fashion probably constituted no more than 10 percent of American households during the 1970s and 1980s.[22]

Large amounts of discretionary income in the higher-income households constitute a source of instability. From the standpoint of the industries that are concentrated—constituted of only a few corporations—this instability is channeled initially through the tides of consumption expenditures rather than through the rises and falls in the level of investment. Anticipated job losses, pessimism about the future of the economy, higher prices for necessities, changes in the prices of assets, and shifts in taste can be reflected in sales fluctuations in particular industries that may not be offset by opposite movements in other industries.

Most of these sources of consumption volatility have been explored elsewhere. However, the least examined aspect of consumption is the interface between spending for necessities and spending for discretionary items. Whether biological necessities are produced under conditions of competition or by the concentrated sector, the effect upon the consumer's budget is the same: increases in production costs are passed on to the consumer. Any unanticipated jumps in the cost of necessities must be diverted from discretionary income (which is a given in the short term). That is, the discretionary income of the household diminishes, and so must the sale of discretionary items produced mostly by the concentrated sector. The importance of this relation is underscored by recent patterns of price changes for basic necessities (food, energy, shelter, and medical care). The annual inflation rate for these basics was 7.5 percent in 1970–1977, whereas the rate for non-necessities was 5.1 percent.[23] This differential inflation rate *greatly* widened in 1978–1979. By the same token, slowdowns in the inflation of the same necessities (especially food and energy) in 1981–1983 added to the discretionary income and spending that contributed to an economic upturn. Unfortunately, the production decline that contributed to these results also raised the unemployment rate to the highest level since the Great Depression.

The Variable Consumption Function

Instead of looking at alternative hypothetical income and related consumption levels, let us plot an aggregate consumption relation from our three BLS budgets. This would give a "consumption function" across the urban society at one point in time. Such a curve also would show how consumption spending rises with income. Multiply the number of households near the family personal income (before taxes) required for each of the three BLS budgets by the family personal income level. These calculations are detailed in Table 15.1 for each budget. The result will be total personal income for families at this budget level. This is the income generated by this part of the income distribution. The total consumption expenditure for each budget class in Table 15.1 is the product of the expenditures from Figure 15.1 and the same numbers of households. From these estimates, the total personal income of those near the lower-budget level was $82 billion in 1980, $230 billion for those near the middle-budget group, and $468 billion for those near the higher-budget group. However, total consumption as a share of these summed incomes varied greatly, from 80 percent for the lower group to 74 percent for the middle and 68 percent for the higher. The United States average consumption share was 77 percent, down from 79 percent in 1976.

For simplicity, let us draw a straight-line consumption curve (Figure 15.3). We need only two points, but *which* two shall we use? If every dollar increase in personal income resulted in a dollar advance in consumer expenditures, the consumption curve would be the 45° guiding line. As the marginal propensity to consume is less than 1, however, we can exclude this possibility. As the first data point, we plot the total consumption expenditure of the lower-budget families against their

TABLE 15.1 Calculation of U.S. Personal Income Budget Data, 1980

	Budgets below lower	BLS lower budget	Budgets between lower and middle	BLS middle budget	Budgets between middle and higher	BLS higher budget	Budgets above higher	U.S. totals
Total family consumption*	...	$11,243	...	$16,969	...	$23,266	...	...
Family personal income (before taxes)	...	14,044	...	23,134	...	34,409	...	...
Number; households near budget (millions)*	...	5.8	...	10.0	...	13.6	...	82.4
Total personal income (billions)	...	+ 81.5 +	...	+ 230.1 +	...	+ 468.0 +	...	= 2,160
Total consumption expenditure	...	+ 65.2 +	...	+ 169.7 +	...	+ 316.4 +	...	= 1,673
Consumption shares	...	80%	...	74%	...	68%	...	77%

*From Figure 15.1

Sources: U.S. Bureau of the Census, *Statistical Abstract of U.S.*, 1981;
and U.S. Bureau of the Census, *Current Population Reports*, Series P-60, No. 142, 1984.
Data for 1972–1973 are available for the "other budgets" represented by the ...'s but not for 1980.

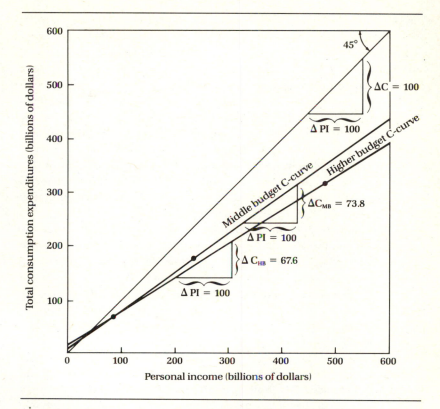

FIGURE 15.3 The budget-sensitive consumption curve

Note: The Δs signify discrete changes. For an increase of $100 billion in personal income ($\Delta PI = 100$), consumption increases by $73.8 billion along the middle-budget C-curve ($\Delta C_{MB} = 73.8$), which is read off the expenditures axis, but only $67.6 billion along the higher-budget C-curve ($\Delta C_{HB} = 67.6$). If all extra income of $100 billion ($\Delta PI = 100$) were spent, then the change in consumption would be $100 billion ($\Delta C = 100$), as along the 45° guiding line.

total personal income ($65.2, $81.5). If we use the middle-budget income and consumption levels, we have a steeper sloping consumption function than if we use the higher-budget levels for the second data point. That is, the consumption-to-income connection is sensitive to the budgets available in the society. Moreover, a society with an income distribution that allows a BLS higher budget will experience a smaller increase in consumer spending ($67.6 \div 100 = 67.6$¢) from a dollar increase in personal or national income than will a society with only the lower and middle BLS budgets ($73.8 \div 100 = 73.8$¢ in Figure 15.3). What Keynes credited to a "psychological propensity" (the tendency for consumption to rise by less than income) is explained by budget habits that are conditioned by the family's income class. If all households had the spending habits of the lower-budget households, the consumption-to-income relation would be even steeper than the middle-budget C-curve, and a dollar increase in national income would result in an even greater leap in consumer spending.

There is an Engel's law in the aggregate. It is true that households tend to consume only a given maximum of food (even lobster and caviar), and it is also true that they can reasonably utilize only a certain number of houses, automobiles, and years of education. In other words, any type of consumption has its limit, whether it is circumscribed by the size of the stomach or by sheer space and time.

The American income distribution is such that, for higher-income families, the share of personal income is greatly out of proportion to the number of households. In 1982, for example, the top 20 percent of families garnered 42.7 percent of all income, and the top 5 percent of families, 16 percent of income. Yet households with high incomes are not insatiable in their consumption. The higher incomes rise in an advanced economy, the greater the difficulty such households experience in spending the bulk of their incomes.

The use of the term *Engel's law* itself is a matter of habit. The relationships I am describing prevail with given states of technology and cultural preferences. Technology, cultural preferences, and thus budget shares can change, but they are not likely to mutate quickly. In the long run (discussed in more detail in Chapter 16), of course, individuals and households can move to different positions in the income hierarchy.

ECONOMIC REALITY AND THEORY: A SUMMARY

Economic instability is probably the best way to characterize the crisis facing supra-surplus capitalism. The threat to democratic governments from powerful concentrated special-interest groups has transformed the economic crisis into a political crisis. For the most part this is a moot issue, for the causes of the economic crisis are political: the problems raised by poverty amidst affluence, a middle class alienated by hyperinflation, high rates of unemployment, and sometimes both. As life, especially postindustrial life, is not simple, it should not be surprising that these problems are intermixed in a fairly complex way. Therefore, it is useful to summarize.

The *composition* of employment, incomes, prices, and production as well as their levels is important. That is, if we are to understand why people are poor or unemployed, we need to know the ingredients of success as measured by their economic system. In order to fill the vacuum left by Sraffa, a new theory of the income distribution that relates incomes to job markets as well as to other elements is required. We find the worker buffeted by forces such as demand changes for products, technological innovations that can replace or displace workers, powerful labor unions, discrimination, and other factors often outside worker control. In terms of policies for dealing with failed incomes, we have to consider whether to place all blame upon the individual. Within this framework, Sraffa's conclusions can be reached while explaining what determines the personal income distribution.

If labor is treated as a basic service, demand can be introduced into Sraffa's model. When demand is considered, the true nature and importance of necessities compared with luxuries in an advanced economy producing surpluses beyond worker subsistence is revealed. Income earners are then viewed as allocating expenditures among goods on the basis of a budget. In this view, personal income levels are critical to personal welfare, and we are thus able to suppress orthodox price theory in such a way that the consumers' budget can be incorporated into an aggregate consumption function.

Within the context of the business cycle—the summary measure of economic instability—the purpose of defining the income distribution and the nature of demand by income class becomes clear. Any income above that required for absolute biological necessities is truly discretionary in that it can be spent or saved. The greater the amount of such income (as in a supra-surplus capitalistic economy), the less reliable is consumer behavior. This instability can be amplified by price inflation or disinflation among necessities, which shrinks or only dampens *real* discretionary income. The presence of persons or families with a variety of incomes and thus alternative levels of discretionary spending power leads to a variable consumption function, which adds to a volatility of total demand traditionally assigned only to business investment. If this were not adequate cause for alarm, as we shall see in Chapter 17, the financial asset holdings of the small share of the population with such wealth are a source of *monetary* instability.

There is a connection among consumer budget shares, production technology, and inflation that has not been widely appreciated. One kind of inflation is instigated by nonwage elements. However, in Galbraith's planning system, giant business firms separate the affluent from their money by stimulating new wants. There is a kind of poetic justice in this, for the organized workers in the concentrated manufacturing industries demand higher wages to indulge their whetted appetites. This round-robin is usually consummated at a (round) table at which Big Business and Big Labor have consumers for lunch. The post-Keynesian price markup enables producers to pay the wages required to purchase the products the workers have been persuaded they truly need. In this process, the basic cost of remaining in the economic system keeps going up as both what is believed culturally necessary expands and the prices of these "necessities" rise. As such wage settlements are "political," we cannot expect them to be related to productivity. If not, unrestrained wage settlements cannot provide a limit to inflation unless the society is willing to endure a depression. As we next observe, technology also has implications for long-run stability that cut across production, consumption, *and* personal incomes.

16

STAGNATION
AND THE
LONG WAVE

▼

*Without this type of change which we have labelled
development the capitalistic society cannot exist, . . . the
classes which serve the capitalist apparatus—would
collapse, . . . without innovation there are no entrepreneurs,
without entrepreneurship there are no capitalist profits and
no capitalist momentum. . . . The atmosphere of industrial
revolution—of progress—is the only atmosphere in which
capitalism can survive.*

JOSEPH A. SCHUMPETER, *KONJUNKTURZYKLEN II*, 1961

The post-Keynesians now recognize that the two key assumptions of Kaldor's growth theory must be relaxed so as to provide a more sophisticated explanation for the longer-term growth of the economy. The composition of output as well as the methods of producing that output (technology) do change. Though the production techniques and the amount of labor relative to machines may remain constant for several years or even decades during stagnation in any particular industry, at any moment in time other industries may be switching to different methods of production. It is likely that any new techniques will exhibit different mixes of inputs.[1]

Consumers change as well. Consumer tastes vary. Teenagers who adored denim in the early 1970s may prefer corduroy (the cloth of kings) and the preppie look in the 1980s. Lifestyles may change so that families who once almost invariably dined at home may now dine frequently in restaurants. Even deathstyles change as people today (even the Rockefellers) apparently prefer simple and inexpensive burials.

Finally, there is a connection between the availability of technology to produce hitherto unknown products and consumer demand. Producers did not manufacture microwave ovens because consumers were

313

clamoring for this cooking device. Rather, the marketing specialists for the durable goods and electronics industries are always looking for methods of saving the time and effort of housework, an *idea* that sells well in an affluent society. A microwave oven saves both, but consumers did not demand this specific product because they cannot demand a nonexistent product. Once this new product was marketed, however, it was then "in demand."

As we look across the economy, we see some industries in decline, some booming, and some simply marking time. New products give rise to new firms and even to new industries. The use of the computer in the home was undreamed of less than a decade ago; it has become a growth industry that already is approaching maturity. In the United States, the textile industry is in decline, but the leisure-time industry is on the upswing; people are having a good time even with fewer clothes. All this is to say that the kinds of technologies will vary drastically as we look at different industries. Moreover, there will be an uneasy co-existence between high-tech firms and backward and inefficient firms. Wages and profits will vary among these types of industries.

How then is technological advance related to variations in the national income? New technologies are simply abstractions unless they are somehow embodied in new equipment and processes of production. Technology is transformed into factories through doses of investment. The absorption of technological change in this fashion will be more rapid the greater the share of national income devoted to expenditures for real capital formation (investment).

Given the changing composition of demand, the uncertain timing of new products and new technologies, and the uncertainty of when investment will take place, we would clearly have to conclude that economic growth necessarily proceeds at an uneven pace. We would not expect the private economy to perform an impossible balancing act. The rate of growth in total sales revenue is unlikely to match the rate of growth in the capacity to produce. It is more probable that the Chicago Cubs will win a World Series again.

Our post-Keynesian vision of capitalism is incomplete. I have attempted to piece together different strands of thought derived from independent scholars. As a group, these scholars can be said to represent a post-Keynesian trend, the development of an approach that takes account of the differences between the future and the present, the present and the past. In this chapter we will extend post-Keynesianism to the *very* long run. As it turns out, capitalism's stage of historical development critically alters the amplitude of the business cycle and the effectiveness of traditional, short-run fiscal and monetary policies. In

Chapter 17, we will reexamine economic policies in the light of post-Keynesian ideas and this excursion into the long run.

THE PRODUCT CYCLE AND THE EVOLUTION OF INDUSTRY

Schumpeter: Innovations and the Business Cycle

The ideas of an Austrian will provide a surprise ending to what was, in the beginning, a post-Keynesian story. Joseph Alois Schumpeter (1883–1950), a second-generation Austrian, elevated the role of capitalism's entrepreneur to the highest plane—to be the central force in capitalistic development. Schumpeter came to the same conclusion as Karl Marx—namely, capitalism was doomed. Unlike Marx, Schumpeter decried the self-destructive tendencies inherent in capitalism. No doubt Schumpeter's grief was more for the euthanasia of the entrepreneur than for capitalism itself. Although various research efforts continue to flow from Schumpeter's theory of capitalism, the neo-Austrians have kept Schumpeter at a respectful distance, perhaps because of the volatile mixture of his respect for Marx and his pessimism regarding the future of capitalism.

Born in Triesch, Moravia, now part of Czechoslovakia, Schumpeter was the only child of a cloth manufacturer and a physician's daughter. A typical Austrian mixture of the many nationalities that lived in the Austro-Hungarian Empire, Schumpeter grew up in the aristocratic milieu of prewar Vienna. From 1893 to 1901, he attended the Theresianum, an exclusive school for the sons of the aristocracy; and from 1901 to 1906, Schumpeter studied law and economics at the University of Vienna. While there, he studied under Wieser and Böhm-Bawerk, even while being exposed to the most brilliant young Marxists of the day. Vienna has been described as one of the pleasantest places on earth during the closing years of the Hapsburg Empire, at least for those as properly born and properly endowed as Schumpeter. To the end, Schumpeter remained the cultivated, egocentric Austrian gentleman of the old school who found from 1914 onward little evidence of progress in civilization.

After several appointments in continental Europe, Schumpeter moved permanently to Harvard University in 1932. Although he enjoyed international fame, he was overshadowed by John Maynard Keynes, whose ideas were gaining ascendancy at Harvard during the Great Depression. Belatedly, in 1948, two years before his death, Schumpeter became president of the American Economic Association. His contemporary role in economics would have been enhanced had he accepted those Keynesian ideas that could have been integrated into his business cycle theory. He stubbornly resisted this, however, in deference to himself as the grander economist.

In Schumpeter's theory of capitalism, the entrepreneur *is* the innovator, the agent of economic change. Although to Schumpeter, there are cycles within the cycles of capitalism, we will focus upon the long wave or Kondratieff cycle, credited to the Russian economist Nikolai Kondratieff. In Schumpeter's vista, the Kondratieff or long wave is spread over roughly a half century. Schumpeter related the first long wave— starting in the late 1780s and ending in the 1840s—to the development, in England, of steam power and textile manufacturing. We recognize this era as the period of the Industrial Revolution (see Chapter 4). Schumpeter connected the second wave—continuing to the end of the nineteenth century—to railroads and iron and steel. The third long wave—ending around the mid-1960s—was charged by electricity and supercharged by the automobile.[2] When the lows of all cycles—inventory, investment, and long wave—coincided, the economic system was in for a particularly bad forecast; Schumpeter laid the 1929–1933 great contraction in the United States to this unhappy coalescence.

Schumpeter begins his system in a stationary condition of Walrasian equilibrium, about the only ground Schumpeter is willing to give to Walras. As Schumpeter notes, there is no extraordinary opportunity for profits in this stationary state; only a circular flow of economic activity takes place, and the system merely reproduces itself. The extraordinary person, the entrepreneur, daringly raids the circular flow and diverts labor and land to investment. Since savings are inadequate for such ventures, the entrepreneur must be provided credit created by the capitalists. Since only the more enterprising and venturesome persons act, innovations appear in "swarms." The innovations include setting up new production functions, techniques, organizational forms, and products. Even though they stand above the reluctant crowd, the heroic entrepreneurs create favorable conditions for other, less venturesome businesspersons to follow. These glowing economic conditions (business prosperity) are enhanced by the creation and expenditure of new incomes.

The boom, however, limits itself. Paradoxically, innovations contribute to the downswing. The competition of new products with old ones causes business losses even as rising prices deter investment. Entrepreneurs use the proceeds of the sale of their new products to repay indebtedness and, in this way, bring deflation. The depression results from the slow process of adaptation to innovation and from this secondary deflation. When adaptation to the innovations is complete, deflation ends and Walrasian equilibrium is restored. In equilibrium, a time when all vital signs are stable, there is little cause for capitalism to suffer cardiac arrest. Left to itself, capitalism even has "trickle-down" benefits—Schumpeter told his students at Harvard how "The capitalist achievement does not typically consist in providing more silk stockings for queens but in bringing them within the reach of factory girls for steadily decreasing amounts of effort." The presence of innovations helps to explain why new industries with these new products for the masses emerge and old ones—with great reluctance and stubborn resistance—die.

It is industrial concentration—the rise of big and stubborn business—that weakens capitalism. The early monopoly of the individual, venturesome entrepreneur who makes the breakthrough and corners the market is always acceptable to society. However, the maturing of an industry into a gigantic monopoly generates the political and social attitudes that ultimately destroy it. Andrew Carnegie was a majestic figure, but the United States Steel Corporation cast a foreboding shadow of death across the face of capitalism. The growth of giant business deprives capitalism of its individual entrepreneurs even as it makes itself vulnerable to political and social assault. Though New Deal nostrums could sustain "capitalism in the oxygen tent" by artificial means—paralyzed in those functions that had guaranteed past glories—inevitably the beneficiary of capitalism's fatal disease was socialism. Whereas most of neo-Austrianism wears blinders to giant business, Schumpeter's singular prophecy for capitalism is Marx's denouement; like the Biblical whale that saved Jonah, capitalism is swallowed by the state in order to save it.

The Product Cycle: A Post-Keynesian Amendment

Post-Keynesians consider stagnation to be related to the *composition* of aggregate demand and aggregate output. Although Schumpeter treated demand with nonbenign neglect, he nonetheless saw some branches of industry flourishing while other branches floundered. Schumpeter's "process of creative destruction" is evolutionary, with firms and industries coming into existence, growing, declining, and disappearing. This process is characterized by structural change, not only in the composition of output but throughout economic life. When change is the constant, we see the necessity of viewing Sraffa's (and Leontief's) fixed production coefficients as provisional (as indeed they themselves did). The very long run is one of industrial evolution or even revolution, even though a Sraffian slice out of historical time reveals much about the way value is determined in the economic system.

We can amend Schumpeter in a manner perfectly consistent with the way that we amended Sraffa. In Chapter 15, we said that for the supra-surplus society, satiation in product markets (contrary to neo-classical theory) takes place. Specialists in marketing research have known for a long time that products have a sales life cycle. Initially, a product innovation coming from one of Schumpeter's entrepreneurs will be sold (perhaps experimentally) to a handful of consumer pi-oneers, who are often the richest families in the society. Since a new product is usually very expensive to develop, its introductory price will be very high. However, if a middle-income class exists, Veblen's class emulation emerges, and the product (perhaps drinks, dinner, and dance combined in one establishment like Studebakers, a 1980s chain) is grad-ually diffused among a larger and larger number of families. When the product hits Main Street, the sales growth is exponential; the product "takes off." Any market is limited only by its human population and the distribution of income. When virtually every family of the society has at least one of the "new products," the market is satiated. This product cycle looks like a flattened S and is often called, appropriately enough, the product S-curve. It is illustrated in Figure 16.1.

Mass production of a product eventually turns the emulator's gold into fool's gold. When products are sufficiently diffused throughout the society, they can be standardized in gigantic factories (perhaps Gil-ley's, the "world's largest nightclub") and produced with a large-scale technology that yields low prices. Not only does everyone have at least one of the once-prized possessions, the products all begin to look alike. Surely, clever manufacturers and advertising agencies can post-pone mass realization of sameness (in the manner described by Gal-braith), although eventually the cause becomes hopeless, especially when all opportunities for *real* as opposed to imaginary product "im-provements" have been made. The picture reception of the first TV, a black-and-white, was roughly as good as that provided by the win-dow of a front-loading washing machine. Then, the quality of the pic-ture and its size were enhanced. Color was added even as the TV set became a carefully crafted, elegant piece of furniture. Eventually, the size of the picture could be further increased only with a severe loss in its clarity. TV sets all began to look alike. More important, the U.S. family having fewer than three sets was viewed as impoverished (eco-nomically, though certainly not intellectually). The market was sated, the price elasticity of demand was low, and the top of the TV product curve was in sight.

Economic development brings standardized technology even as it increases the complexity of the *overall* production system. In the agrar-ian society, generic goods from the land, such as raw potatoes mashed or sliced at home, are the only goods required in consumption. Value

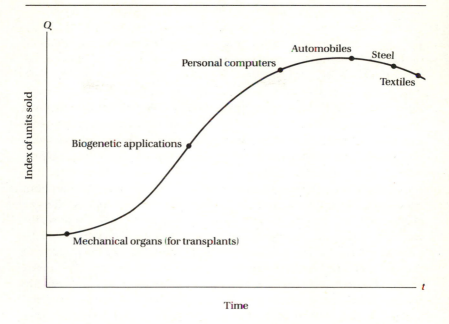

FIGURE 16.1 The product S-curve in supra-surplus countries

Note: Each product, of course, would have its own curve, each being uniquely shaped except for the generally flat-S configuration. In this illustration, however, I assume that each product follows the same life cycle in order to show where (approximately) each product is in its life cycle in the supra-surplus economies.

added or the difference between the value of sales and the costs of production (and therefore economic surplus) does not exist because goods are not marketed. In contrast, the supra-surplus society relies upon a highly interdependent production system in which a longer and longer chain of suppliers supply each other—adding layer upon layer of value added—until the final product emerges. Sraffa and Leontief would call the production system a matrix of inputs and the technological coefficients of these inputs; the Austrians would call it "roundaboutness" in the production process. Be it a post-Keynesian or a neo-Austrian description, Warsh would call the supra-surplus economy complex. In any case, the complex and fine division of labor leads to a theory of segmented personal income distribution such as the vita theory.[3]

BUDGET SHARES AND THE SIZE OF THE FIRM

The personal income distribution is important in a surprising way: a reduction in income inequalities is a precondition for a middle class (see Chapters 4 and 15), and a middle class is essential in providing a product market size sufficient to warrant the standardized technology. Thus, income levels and the number of households with those incomes are related to the size of the firms and industries producing goods and services. The linkage derives from the value of total expenditures given by budget shares (see Chapter 15), which defines the overall size of the market for a particular product.

You will recall that we began with a specific mode of production. However, the particular technology is not entirely independent of the size of the market afforded by income levels and populations. Suppose, for example, upon first commercial introduction (at the initial state of technology), household personal computers appeared only in the budgets of the very rich. Indeed, household computers would not have been produced at all in an economy without a certain threshold population of the rich. Suppose the introductory average production cost for the personal computer was $10,000, and that 1,000 households included the computer in their budgets that year. At a 10 percent markup over production costs, a sales revenue of $11 million is forecast for a monopoly corporate producer.

After production costs, the producer is left with $1 million profit, which can be used for further investment. After selling the 10,000 household computers during the first year of production, the producer uses a portion of the revenue to conduct market research on the potential for expanding her market. She finds that if she could lower the price of the computer by 50 percent, she could entice a slightly lower income class of 4,000 into the market. If the producer could devise a way to cut production costs in half, she now could sell 5,000 computers (4,000 + 1,000) at a unit price of $5000, for a total revenue of $27.5 million ($2.5 million in markups). With diligent research, the company's engineers emerge with a new patent on an improved memory chip for a computer that can be produced with less labor and fewer expensive parts. The corporation sells additional common stock, issues more bonds, or borrows funds from its bank to equip its plants for the production of the Model II household computer. With successful Model II sales, the firm can now rely upon its profits flow for any new investment.

This example illustrates the general case rather than the exceptional one. Plant size is usually decided by the lowest-cost technology. Given technology, even the smallest plant may be too large for the market. If so, the plant will not be built until incomes, budget shares, and population warrant it. In some cases, the smallest plant is gigantic, and its level of production may absorb all the revenue available for the particular product. The telephone companies, regional monopolies, fall into this category.

INNOVATIONS AND STAGNATION

In Chapter 15 we described the post-Keynesian view of capitalism as one of frequent ups and downs but with secular ascension. The idea of a cycle over the cycles or a Schumpeterian long wave of a half century is both more pessimistic *and* more optimistic than the world of Harrod, Domar, and Robinson. The long wave of Kondratieff, Schumpeter, or Kuznets appears smooth over time. This is an illusion, for, if we look at a set of data over a sufficiently long historical epoch, they are "stretched out" so much that the *appearance* is one of continuity. Yet, the historical reality is quite different: the world economic crises of 1825, 1873, and 1929 were a bit more like falling off cliffs than gliding through gentle valleys. Moreover, the ups and downs of the 1970s and (thus far) the 1980s are enough to give continuity a bad name. As we saw in Chapter 10, Karl Marx depicted the crises of capitalism as cataclysmic. Much more recently, another German economist, Gerhard Mensch, now at Case Western Reserve University, has taken his lead from Schumpeter but favors the pattern of the discontinuous path of capitalism.[4] Mensch's model, which he calls the metamorphosis model, is based upon the product cycle or product S-curve. The configuration of Mensch's theory is displayed in Figure 16.2.

Innovations can be either of the product variety, such as laser disc recordings, or of the production-process kind, such as computer-assisted design (CAD) of an automobile or a house. In turn, Mensch has made a useful distinction between *basic* innovations and *improvement* innovations: *technological basic* innovations produce new markets and industry branches; *nontechnical basic* innovations lead to new activities in the cultural arena of public administration or social services. An *improvement* innovation might be an improvement upon an existing product or production technique.[5] The production of electricity (1800), the first use of the coke blast furnace (1796), the first commercial use of photography (1838), the production of the jet engine (1928), and the production of nylon (1927) were basic technological innovations. The institutionalization of mercantilist commercial policy (1743), the restriction of guild control over industry (1754), and the introduction of a general protective tariff (1775) were nontechnical organizational inno-

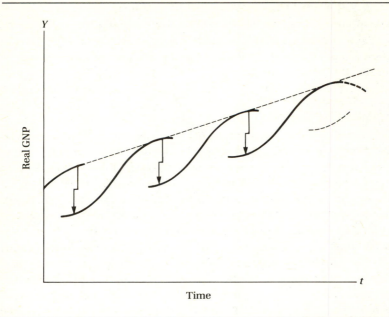

FIGURE 16.2 Mensch's (modified) metamorphosis model

Note: In the metamorphosis model, long periods of growth are interrupted by *relatively* short intervals of turbulence. Despite these breaks and upheavals over time and the variation in tempo of change, there is a regularity that conforms with the S-curves of those industrial complexes that lead the particular expansion. This is a "modification" only in the sense that general economic progress is extended over several centuries despite the sharp disruptions. See Gerhard Mensch, *Stalemate in Technology* (Cambridge, Mass.: Ballinger, 1979), p. 73, for the original.

vations. Quality control was an improvement innovation in assembly-line production. For now, we will confine our discussion to technological basic innovations.

Innovations, of course, do not emerge from thin air. An inventory of scientific discoveries and inventions exists at any time; this inventory is the outcome of an intellectual tradition of idea development, the construction of new scientific paradigms (see Chapter 2), and the transfer of knowledge. The time lag between inventions and their commercial application often is very long, but variable. The development of neoprene, a synthetic rubber, provides Mensch with an interesting example of a six-stage innovation process that begins with the development of a new theory (perception).[6] In 1906, Julius A. Nieuwland observed the acetylene reaction in alkali medium and worked for more than ten years to obtain a higher-yielding reaction (invention). In 1921, Nieuwland showed that his material, a polymer, can be manufactured through a catalytic reaction (feasibility). In 1925, Dr. E. K. Bolton of du Pont attends a lecture by Nieuwland at the American Chemical Society; du Pont takes over the further *commercial* development of the "rubber" material (development). Finally, more than a quarter century after its invention, the synthetic rubber is marketed as a new product by E. I. du Pont de Nemours and Company (basic innovation). Today, in the advanced industrialized economies, synthetic rubber is at or past the top of its product S-curve; the product and the industry are now mature. Interestingly, then, serendipity plays a major role in the path from theory to commercial application: Albert Einstein did not know that his ideas would lead to the nuclear bomb, the nuclear power industry, or laser-beam products and services (such as medical removal of cataracts).

An entire industry unfolds as a basic innovation generates various new industrial products. If we follow the Sraffa-Leontief input-output approach, we can understand the complementary nature of these various branches of an industry. In Chapter 15 we explained how iron ore, coke, energy, and labor are complementary inputs in the production of steel. Further downstream is automobile production. Interdependence means that the lesser branches of industry that supply necessary inputs to a mature industry such as automobiles rise and fall together.

The remarkable contribution of Mensch is to provide data suggesting that basic innovations do occur in swarms, as Schumpeter claimed; and, importantly for the present malaise, the frequency of the most recent swarm of basic innovations peaked in 1935 (in the middle of the Great Depression!). If the average product life cycle—from basic innovation to maturity—is a half century, a large share of the 1935-centered swarm would reach maturity, or the top of their S-curves, in 1985. If so, the overall real GNP takes on an S-curve configuration that is flat by 1985. Our Engel curves of Chapter 15, combined with observed satiation in automotive, airline, household appliances, and even housing markets, bolster the idea that stagnation best describes the condition of the advanced industrialized economies—Great Britain, Western Europe, Northern Europe, the United States and perhaps even Japan—by 1985.

STAGNATION AND POST-KEYNESIAN STAGFLATION

Stagnation from market saturation and inflation may be two sides of the same coin; at least, this is Mensch's claim. Stagnation no doubt describes the condition of the main branches of industry in the advanced industrialized countries since the late 1960s. In automobiles, the leading

U.S. industry in the post–World War II era, the Otto-cycle engine still used is more than a century old. The last major innovation introduced in the industry, the automatic transmission, was widely diffused a generation ago. Basic steelmaking technology has not changed greatly since the nineteenth century, despite enormous increases in the scale of steelmaking plants. In the basic chemical industry, the techniques for making nitric acid, sulfuric acid, ammonia, nitrate fertilizer, and other industrial chemicals were being used prior to World War I, even though the scale of plants has greatly expanded. But, having said this, the post-Keynesian explanation for stagflation (of Chapter 15) still holds.

Sustained price explosions have occurred three times in the past 700 years—the first in the sixteenth century, a second in the eighteenth, and a third beginning around 1890. The last episode has been the most dramatic by far. The magnitude of the latest inflationary wave may be a result of social innovations such as the giant corporation, the industrial union, modern marketing techniques, and highly flexible financial institutions, plus the various floors placed under incomes and prices by government programs. Perhaps if the supra-surplus economies were not suffering the affliction of many product cycles peaking more or less at the same time, the expansion in private and public credit would have fueled a sustainable expansion in real output rather than substantial inflation as well. Finally, we cannot ignore Warsh's idea of economic complexity. The supra-surplus economies have become more complex. In other terms, each additional layer adds its own overhead and other costs. As Warsh describes it, modern marketing (which, of course, did not exist in the sixteenth and eighteenth centuries) has a lot to do with rising costs (prices) from increased complexity.[7]

Industrial concentration, complexity, technological stagnation, inflation, and recession—this collection of terms describes supra-surplus industrial societies since the late 1960s. Perhaps no single explanation will suffice. A concentrated industry, often with government aid, can stall its own doomsday. In a manner so well described by John Kenneth Galbraith, the standardized products always leave room for a few more wrinkles, a differentiation of product that displaces the necessity of price competition. Even so, the economy at the end of its long expansion sees the number of industrial branches that are peaking exceeding those beginning with basic innovations. The sunset-to-sunrise ratio of industries means that bankruptcies and liquidation of assets are just over the horizon. Those groups whose income and wealth are threatened will circle the wagons at sunset. Producer coalitions demand even more subsidies and protection from foreign imports, and labor groups become even more recalcitrant in their demands for job security.

Entrepreneurship Versus the Price Markup

Historically, stagnation has had not only a beginning, but also an ending. In Chapter 15 we described the use of the price markup by manufacturers to guarantee a cash flow sufficient to meet investment needs, based upon future expected demands. Why does this cash flow fail to lead to basic innovations? Apparently, it is because concentrated industries producing standardized products are not very innovative; rather, the market power of such giants enables them to get by with mostly imaginary product innovations and with price increases for products whose sales no longer respond significantly to price changes. In this light, we can understand why the accelerated depreciation allowances and tax credits of first-term Reaganomics led to acquisitions, mergers, and fevered money market fund activity rather than to strong increases in real investment. The lone entrepreneur, a David, does not reside generally in the house of Goliath.

During the last half of a long-wave economic expansion, the Sraffa-Leontief fixed technical coefficients industrial model takes on an unexpected realism. Once the basic process innovations that define the relations between inputs and outputs are widely diffused in the economy, the industrial branch becomes remarkably rigid in its technique. True, the size of plants and of the companies grows large, but the same technique is simply replicated on a larger scale. In the final throes of decline, ironically, the production technology finally *is* modified by *improvement* innovations; in the present wave, automation in the standardized product–manufacturing industries is being used to replace high-priced labor. Crises begin to break through the rigidities.

If Mensch's analysis of the historical data on inventions and basic innovations is correct, basic innovations do cluster during the technological stalemate. According to his data on the distribution of innovations, only a small number of the basic innovations that will be implemented in Western economies by the year 2000 were implemented during the 1970s. About two-thirds of the technological basic innovations that will be produced in the second half of the twentieth century will occur in the decade around 1989. The greatest surge of innovations occurred in 1984, a year comparable (on the scale of innovations) to 1825, 1886, and 1935.[8] Since giant industry is the home mostly of, at best, improvement innovations, there is a narrow window of opportunity for entrepreneurs every half century or so. However, much like the life of the butterfly, the Age of the Entrepreneur is short and perhaps gets shorter with each wave. The lone entrepreneur often is the one who first commercializes a basic innovation, creating a temporary monopoly in the production of a new product. In effect, the entrepreneur develops *a new production function.* Eventually an entire, new industry is born. This entrepreneurial activity well describes the recent, rapid development of the personal computer industry. Entrepreneurs Steven P. Jobs and Stephen Wozniak got the industry moving with Apple Computer in 1976; as early as 1985 the maturity of the industry was epitomized by Jobs's bitter resignation from the chairmanship of Apple. The initial monopoly profits attracted (cheaper) imitators who could experience some growth on the exponential part of the computer S-curve. Now, however, there is a major shakeout in the personal computer industry that will leave perhaps no more than ten or twelve survivors. Moreover, the largest share of the market may end up in the hands of IBM, the giant that was an innovator in mainframe computers, but merely a follower in personal computers. The Age of the Entrepreneur is like Camelot; it is only here for one brief, shining moment each (roughly) half century. If the entrepreneur is the only hero, a Queen Guinevere suffering from depression is aged by the time Sir Profitsalot rides onto the scene.

The Rise and Decline of Nations

Innovations and the timing of long waves are forces making for faster or slower economic growth rates in nations. Relatively small coalitions or special-interest groups appear to be most obstructive to economic efficiency and growth when the long upswing is aging. Mancur Olson has advanced the powerful thesis that countries that have had democratic freedom of organization without upheaval or invasion the longest will suffer the most growth-repressing organizations and combinations.[9] Olson uses his theory to help explain why Great Britain—long immune from dictatorship, invasion, and revolution—has had in this century a lower rate of growth than other large, developed democracies. A powerful network of special-interest organizations characterizes, to Olson, the "British disease." In particular, Great Britain is renowned for the number and power of its trade unions, but its professional associations also are remarkably powerful. As an example of the latter, solicitors in Britain until recently had a legal monopoly in real estate services and barristers still have a monopoly as counselors in the more important court cases. Olson seems to join hands with Mensch when he concludes that "... with age British society has acquired so many strong organizations and collusions that it suffers from an institutional sclerosis that slows its adaptation to changing circumstances and technologies."[10] These coalitions could not have emerged in the idealized conditions of the free market.

The only "good" coalition, in Olson's view, is a "highly encompassing" coalition, so homogeneous in purpose and large in population that the interests of each member is visibly tied to the entire membership. Olson points to the highly encompassing special-interest organizations established after World War II in Germany and Japan, to which he attributes at least part of the growth rate success of the two nations. Nevertheless, Mensch provides convincing data to suggest that West Germany now has reached a technological stalemate because of sated markets and the petering out of the last swarm of innovations. Is the explanation in the tea leaves of obstructive coalitions or in technology? It is probably both; in this regard, the rich tapestry woven by Olson can properly be appreciated only if we take seriously his many qualifying threads of "in part's", "some of's", and so on. Moreover, cause and effect run both ways so that we cannot afford the luxury of selecting a single cause.

Olson considers the "rent-seeking" coalition as bad because his focus is upon economic efficiency and economic growth. If, however, we shift the focus back to concerns with the income distribution, coalitions can be viewed as organized efforts to avoid the income-reducing effects of stagnation or competition, be the competition in product or labor markets. As we said, Sraffa's focus upon the power of technology opens the door to explanations of the income distribution that are (even in the short run) independent of marginal products and the "economic efficiency" implied by such solutions. The vita theory shows how most of the labor force generates wage rates unrelated to productivity. When technology is sufficient to create a surplus and inputs are complementary—as in Menger, Sraffa, Leontief, or Canterbery—it is very difficult, perhaps impossible, for even a free market to assign "marginal products" to the appropriate persons, for labor and capital goods are equally necessary. And yet, the surplus must be divided by some rule. If coalitions as "rent seekers" design the rules, the income distribution is decided by their powers. Irrespective of the political or social nature of that decision-making process, as long as the growth rates of wages and labor population do not exceed that of "productivity," the rent-seekers divide the surplus without creating much inflation. This could describe the first half of the long-wave expansion. Only when the swarm of innovations have been widely diffused do the rent-seekers create instability in the economy. At that time, the stable democracy that—in Olson's judgment—gave rise to the rent-seekers might itself be threatened.

For the most part, we have written of economies in isolation. We next consider the implications of some of these ideas for the global economy.

THE GLOBAL ECONOMY

Global industry today remains concentrated in the developed countries. Together, the (predominantly) market economics of the Organization for Economic Cooperation and Development (OECD) and the (mostly) nonmarket economies of the centrally planned economies of Eastern Europe is known as the "North," and the developing countries as the "South." North-South differences extend beyond geography or even the degree of industrialization to dramatic contrasts in income, life expectancy, infant mortality rates, unemployment rates, education, health care, and working and living conditions. By the 1970s these disparities led to a North versus South configuration in discussions of global development. The Second (1975) General Conference of the United Nations Industrial Development Organization (UNIDO) in Lima adopted a specific industrialization target, the Lima Target, of at least one-quarter of global manufacturing value added in the South by the year 2000.[11]

The global share of the South's manufacturing value added did steadily advance between the adoption of the Lima Target and 1980, but the share peaked at 11 percent and has since declined slightly. In view of the 1980s global debt crisis, the hopes and plans of many countries have turned to fears and chaos. By the early 1980s, the illusion of uninterrupted progress was displaced by a self-delusion widely shared in the North: massive unemployment in the industrial democracies was considered the only way to control inflation. Despite its best efforts and its past successes, the South has not been able to escape the punitive nature of this delusion disguised as reasonable and necessary economic policy. The consequence, an increasingly fragile international financial system, is dire for North and South alike.

The global debt crisis must be resolved if global economic growth is to be resumed. The North-to-South loans were based upon the remarkable economic growth of developing countries between 1960 and 1980. The South's growth rate in manufacturing actually outpaced that of the North's. What altered the prospects of the South? Few, if any, bankers, economists, or policymakers predicted the oil shocks of 1974 and 1979 or the depression of 1981–1982 in the United States. These events, engineered by human actors, converted the seemingly prudent lending of the 1970s into the global debt crisis of the 1980s. A *sharp* break in a quarter century of progress in the developing countries happened for the first time during 1980–1985. In 1980 the gross domestic product (GDP) growth rate in the developing countries slowed to 2.7 percent and in 1981–1984 turned negative.

A NEW GLOBAL PERSPECTIVE FOR DEVELOPMENT

Beyond Failed Paradigms

Once a viable plan for the global debt has been formulated, we need to take a fresh approach to the problem of economic development. Such a view requires an understanding of the current malaise in the affluent market economies.

In instantaneous orthodox or neoclassical time, the masses can be painlessly patient, for all things are possible in due time. This conundrum confounds reality: the critical period is the "time it takes" for leading industries to shift partially, then fully, to new techniques of production. Only particular firms and industries enjoy this exhilarating experience. The locomotive was invented in 1769, produced in 1824; photography was invented in 1727 and used commercially in 1838; the gasoline motor, invented in 1860, was manufactured in 1886. If *it* happens in a strategically placed industry and with sufficient diffusion, economic development can follow this leading industry. Such innovations combined with complementary labor skills determine productivity growth (the gains in output per worker employed). Though insufficient alone, an initial advance in technology is a precondition for economic surplus and development.

The preindustrial state in which agrarian households generally produce only enough to feed themselves characterizes the low-income nations such as Bangladesh, Burma, Haiti, and Ghana (where per capita GNP ranged from $80 to $390 in 1982 in that year's dollars). Nongeneric goods, such as frozen snow peas and canned yams, are made possible only by a surplus sector. As the textile and clothing industry expanded and cotton became a cash crop under the plantation system of the American South, for example, the cash could be used for "dining out" in cafes and for "store-bought" clothes. The workers set free (labor surplus) by productivity gains in agriculture, now organized under one roof for a definite time period, rain or shine, perform only a few tasks related to a mechanized technique. Surpluses open the opportunity for Adam Smith's division of labor. Value added is multiplied for the first time because the generics such as raw agricultural products must be processed, packaged, marketed, and delivered. This initial, halting step toward industrialization in the antebellum southern United States has features in common, except for certain details, with the process in the low-income developing countries.

Satiation in the North and Vent for Surpluses

The dream of the low-income countries—dominated by agricultural and other raw materials exports as inputs for Northern manufacturing—is to increase the size of the manufacturing sector—to industrialize. Ironically, as we said before, Northern consumers are nearly satiated with manufactured products and—because of high labor costs—the unit cost of production is substantially higher in the North than in the newly industrializing countries, such as Mexico, the Republic of Korea, Turkey, and Venezuela. The affluent nations are victims of their own excesses; a condition to be lamented only in particulars, not in general. In the supra-surplus economies, there remains the need to market the hyper-surpluses, surpluses now being produced at high and rising unit costs of production. The idea of such a "vent for surpluses" is traceable to Adam Smith, who had no way of anticipating the enormous need for such a vent in supra-surplus economies.

The International Product S-Curve

The developing countries' sales normally are nowhere near the flattening-out and turning-down range of their S-curves. The global patterns of the S-curves, neatly portrayed by economist Raymond Vernon, are replicated in Figure 16.3. The dynamic product cycle is divided among three developmental stages—new product, maturing (growth) product, and standardized product. In the early stage an entrepreneural near-monopoly guarantees a small number of firms and high prices. When the production plant becomes large enough and the product price low enough to satiate the domestic market of the supra-surplus economy, production levels off. Long before that happens, however, the marketeers of that product begin to look for sales possibilities abroad (vent for surplus). In this regard, U.S. corporations established multinational empires on foreign soil; West German and Japanese firms established mostly distribution branches abroad and kept production on domestic soil. In the mature (standardized) stage, the markets in developing countries became a vent for surpluses because the supra-surplus economy encounters competition from other affluent economies as the monopoly position is eroded. (This happened as the OECD countries became more alike in their postwar recoveries and sated each other.) The newly industrializing countries (NICs) become effective competitors because their adoption of the now-standardized technology is coupled with cheap labor.

In the stagnating developed economies of the 1970s and 1980s, charts of the top, flat part of various product cycles appeared on U.S. corporate boardroom walls. The giants moved toward conglomeration, epitomized by General Motors' move into the computer, robot, and robotics vision branches of industry. Moreover, the close correlation of the business cycles of the OECD countries since the 1950s reflects the overlap of product cycles in nations experiencing similar satiated markets. As

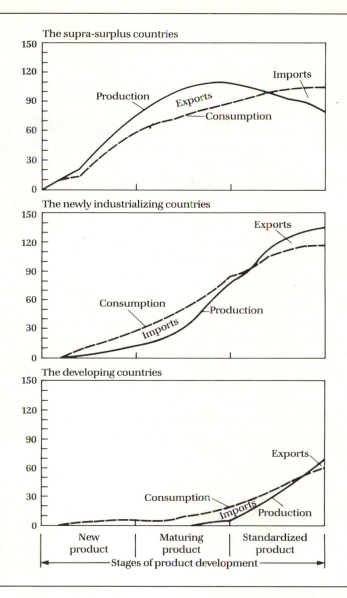

The supra-surplus countries

The newly industrializing countries

The developing countries

New product | Maturing product | Standardized product

◄────── Stages of product development ──────►

FIGURE 16.3 Vernon's international product life cycles. [*Source:* Adapted from Raymond Vernon, "International Investment and International Trade," *Quarterly Journal of Economics*, 1966, p. 199. (Reprinted by permission.)]

Note: In each region consumption generally follows the S-curve pattern. In developing nations, however, consumption is still on the exponential part of the S. In the new product stage, the supra-surplus countries are exploiting their internal markets; in the maturing stage, the supra-surplus countries' exports greatly increase (vent for surplus) and; in the standardized product stage, the technology has been widely adopted in the newly industrializing nations, whose exports rapidly grow.

a result, the rise in output of standardized products through standardized technology in the NICs has elicited outcries for trade protectionism that became louder and more effective during the 1980s as the need for a vent for surpluses intensified in the beleaguered industries of the North.

The satiation of a particular or even a collection of product markets is a concern, nonetheless, only for those who out of necessity or ignorance take a parochial view. If one takes a global perspective, for example, there is no glut of automobiles. The market for autos in Mexico is new and fresh, and the production technology is well defined and standardized. Mexico and other developing nations comprise a frontier for products commonplace in the supra-surplus countries. Around the world in 1978 only 300 million autos were available for about 4.25 billion people. We can reasonably expect a global market of about a *billion* cars by the year 2000, and at least a similar tripling (or more) can be expected for other consumer durables. From the standpoint of *global* economic development, virtually untapped markets for new product innovations also exist in the supra-surplus countries. The supra-surplus countries have an advantage in research-intensive high-technology products. Microchips, biochemistry, robots, and exotic manufacturing in outer space can propagate undreamed-of products.

We arrive at two extremes in the global economy; at one extreme, labor has yet to divide itself significantly in the low-income countries, whereas in the richest nations labor is dividing itself out of manufacturing existence. Conceivably, by the turn of the century unskilled workers will be replaced by robots and semiskilled calibrators (bookkeepers, typists, and store clerks) will be replaced by computers in the supra-surplus economies. By that time the United States and most of the other now-industrialized nations probably will be service economies with perhaps as much as 90 percent of their labor force in services. In the supra-surplus economies, the main role of people in the economic system will be once again to consume and produce simultaneously, a function that will require greater and greater imagination. Manufacturing productivity will reach perilous heights, and human employment could reach perilous depths.

Despite the setbacks of the 1980s, the drive to industrialization by the South can be resumed if certain requirements are met. Economic development derives from the changing *structure* of an economy; the inauguration of new S-curves determine potential growth rates in GNP.[12] Economic historian Walter Rostow provides a further exposition on the S-curve (at an *industry* or *product* level); at its heart, Rostow's theory is one in which a leading industrial sector complex (with many branches) evolves, rapidly grows, and then matures.[13] Rostow points to the automobile sectoral complex in mid-1970s United States, British cotton textiles in the late nineteenth century, and U.S. railroads in the 1920s as examples of mature (and giant) complexes whose decline (stability) can lead to stagnation.

Rostow's destination is one at which many scholars can congregate. Modernization, at its core, depends upon the progressive (though not necessarily continuous) generation and diffusion of basic innovations linked, in some way, to a prior accumulation of knowledge. Although the most complete histories are of the automobile and the railroad, we know enough about other innovations and industries to draw intricate inferences. However, past is not always prologue; yet, Rostow expects the future to be like the past, except everywhere. Not all inventions and innovations are born, live, and die equally.

In order to know the future, we must know the leading sector, which, in its generic form, is often a leading product. The leading sector extends itself outward in many directions at the same time, giving rise to inputs from other industries and providing inputs for others. Then, the sequence and speed of adoption of new techniques depend upon their complexity, the quality of infrastructure, and the present level of per-capita income. Since the decline of an industry is related to market satiation (the top of the product S-curve), cotton textiles in Great Britain ceased to lead during the 1860s and chemicals ceased to lead in the United States during the 1920s. Even so, industries producing consumer durables, clothing, and printing, as well as capital goods and major intermediate inputs for their production continue to grow faster than GNP up to the per-capita income levels of the supra-surplus nations. The rapid expansion of this latter group of industries characterizes Rostow's "stage of mass-consumption."[14]

All of these industries are traditional industries using well-known, standardized technology. The technologies are—at least in theory—easily transferable from one country to another. State-of-the-art steel plants are found in Brazil, Mexico, Taiwan, and the Republic of Korea. Parochial instincts telling us that every country follows the same path to economic development must be resisted. If for no other reason, this logical leap is made suspect by the speed at which these NICs have gone through their "industrial revolutions" as well as the fact that they are presently investing large sums in electronics research and development, an act ordinarily assigned to the supra-surplus nations. In terms of *production techniques*, the NICs *already* appear to be affluent.

We need to go a step beyond the supra-surplus economies in order to identify the next leading industries and to chart the next century. If the information network is sufficient, inventions and even innovations are available to every country that has the infrastructure to absorb them. The continued dominance of autos, household durables, and steel in many affluent nations is based more on social and political power than upon domestic consumer need; the illusion of innovation has masked the reality of stagnation. It is quicker and easier for oligopolists to create the illusion of a product or process improvement than to create a genuinely new and improved product from a new perception. (The neo-Confucian culture does not suffer this defect; it has a much longer time horizon.) Traditional industries are organized in Olsonian coalitions in order to protect their traditional markets, a rearguard but effective action that slows innovations. The clash of interests and the meeting of past and future is dramatized by agreements in late 1984 to limit steel imports by the United States from seven countries including *Mexico and the Republic of Korea.*

The *innovations* from the 1825, 1886, and 1935 swarms epitomize much of what Americans still consider modern today. In 1825 we find the locomotive, Portland cement, insulated wiring, and the puddling furnace; in 1886, the steam turbine, the transformer, resistance welding, the gasoline motor, Thomas steel, aluminum, chemical fertilizer, electrolysis, radar, synthetic detergents, titanium, and—to make rapid change more tolerable—the radio and cocaine; finally, in 1935 appears nylon, Perlon, polyethylene, Xerography, continuous steelcasting, and—to make recessions more endurable—cinerama. No doubt many persons have difficulty believing that these basic innovations have been a part of our lives for so long. But consider something even more astonishing: the basic *inventions* came long before the innovation (actual production). The greatest clustering of inventions, later to materialize as Great Depression innovations, happened in *1904.* The sequence that will greatly influence the early twenty-first century begins with a clustering of inventions in 1935, market experimentation in 1979, and again—according to Mensch—probably clustering of basic innovations in 1989.[15]

The lead time between inventions, practical application, and fruition, however, may be getting shorter and shorter. (Mensch disputes this.) The fastest-growing industry in the supra-surplus countries is the information industry with its microchips, satellites, and laser beams. The only possible barrier to the Chinese knowing about the technology of the supra-surplus nations is lack of Confucian concentration. Even if the time lag between invention and innovation does not shorten, surely the lag between perception and invention will. In any case, the experience of the newly industrializing countries tells us that the *diffusion* of existing technology happens much faster than in the past, mostly because information systems have improved.

The global economy may have to rely on the incentive provided to the supra-surplus societies by the long stagnation to inspire the innovative swarm. The computer and biochemical industries already contributed an apparently new, though short-lived, class of American entrepreneur. Among the other affluent nations, Japan needs no new entrepreneurial class, and the "new Japans" of Taiwan, the Republic of Korea, and Indonesia may provide some of their own surprises. All things considered, in fact, the neo-Confucian culture seems economically more success-oriented than Western culture. The American entrepreneur, small and innovative at the start, usually has been willing to "sell out," so that each successive innovation ultimately shares the same fate—namely, virtual monopolization by the giant conglomerate. This process may prevent the United States from leading the global economy out of stagnation. The U.S. corporate concentration crisis then becomes part of the global crisis.

A NEW VIEW OF ECONOMIC GROWTH

Investment and the Income Distribution

In the vita theory, we find some income recipients—particularly professionals and business managers—who are able to accumulate savings. These savings can be plowed into financial assets that yield an additional source of income. This part of labor is easily confused with capitalists; it constitutes the upper-middle and high-income classes. Meanwhile, the requisites of technology rearrange the demands for different qualities of labor.

This consequent arrangement of incomes is the stage upon which demand plays. The cultural generation of wants, though not separate from technology, plays out much of its destiny within this dimly lit area at the interface between the wants of labor and those of corporate management. Within that gray area, Veblen and Galbraith can tell us more than Kalecki can.

Even though the primary sector may contain competitive industries, the planning system of the supra-surplus economy is in charge, wielding its power in the marketplace to control production and pass on rising costs (including money wage increases) to all of us. Its symbiotic relationship with big labor and big government gives giant business an almost inexhaustible supply of funds for investment. These investments for technology that replaces workers have the effect of redistributing income away from the working class, particularly the least skilled.

We have no assurance that displaced labor will be hired elsewhere. The rehiring of such labor requires the coincidence of new products and new industries emerging quickly enough to absorb the labor reserve. Even then, it is the more skilled reserve that is needed. Meanwhile, the life plans of the more advantaged workers move inexorably

toward collectively increasing their numbers and the skilled labor supply. From the viewpoint of those who wish to have the highest possible
personal income, this collective response is unfavorable. Rather than
"rationality" being a way out of a poverty or low-income predicament,
it can be a way in.

The Unevenness of the Expansion in Capacity

It is not a great exaggeration to say that the advanced economy
fluctuates around some trend. However, to the extent that investment
in both machines and labor development (education and training) is
unstable, the capacity level or the growth trend itself exhibits ups and
downs. In addition to instability in investment, there are still other
elements that create the unlikelihood that demand and capacity will
grow at the same rate. Consumption by the affluent tends to be unstable.
The appearance of basic innovations is uncertain. Switching to new
production processes is unpredictable. The vita theory adds the extra
uncertainty that the quality of the labor force is unlikely to divide precisely in accordance with the needs of private industry. Because of these
sources of flux, industries across the economy do not all grow at the
same rate. The demand for necessities versus luxuries, the availability
of qualified workers, the emergence of new production recipes, and the
course of government policies are unlikely to follow a mutually agree-
able course—even if we ignore foreign trade sources of instability.

A wage settlement that is political cannot be decomposed into a
corporate economic decision in which the managers are engaged in a
delicate balancing act between labor and capital and whose outcome
is decided on the razor's edge of their relative prices. Rather, there is a
revised sequence, in which the amount and type of capital are predestined by the requisites of technology and the personal preference of
managers for capital accumulation. If management can generate investment growth with investment growth, the labor force most assuredly will do the rest, that is, train itself for the new pigeonhole. To
the extent that unskilled workers are slow to respond, the corporation
will replace them even faster. The government is left with the responsibility for those left behind. In such a case, being a good corporate
manager is never having to say you're sorry.

Those who would tell a different story of growth need to explain
the complex development of two recent American growth industries—
photocopying and computers. The Xerox Corporation, dominating the
former industry, owes its incredible growth to the improvement of its
original Model 914 copier. Xerox went from cumbersome, expensive
models to ones that could serve the needs of both the one-person office

and the largest corporation. Xerox's sibling, IBM, has utterly transformed business and government through the use of computers. IBM's
technology has now gone through four generations in the past three
decades; each successive technology increased the capacity, reliability,
and speed of information processing. In turn, the cost per calculation
was reduced, expanding the market for computers to small businesses
and even to households.

These two industries no longer rely solely upon photocopying and
computers for their sales growth. New growth potential must be sought
on new frontiers of technology. It is highly unlikely that decisions regarding basic innovations or their production will turn on the market
rate of interest.

The tremendous increase in global economic integration enables
us to extend the theory of economic growth in the supra-surplus economics to developing countries. All nations have backward industries:
in parts of the South it is textiles; in parts of the North it is steel. International trade links the interdependence (of inputs and outputs) of the
supra-surplus countries to the rest of the world. Once the interdependence is extended to the global economy, the monetary, fiscal, industrial, and trade policies of all nations are tied together. Still, as is the
case in domestic economics, the weakest nations economically are the
most dependent upon the strong. In this regard nonetheless, dependencies between North and South tend to run more in both directions
than once was true.

17

POST-KEYNESIAN ECONOMIC POLICIES

▼

A Hamlet-like student, poised in neutral equilibrium between eclectic post-Keynesianism, monetarism, and rational expectationism, would have to be pushed in the direction of post-Keynesianism by the brute factual experiences of America in the 1980s. That is my message.

PAUL A. SAMUELSON, *CHALLENGE*, NOVEMBER–DECEMBER 1984

After testing different macroparadigms, Paul Samuelson came to this epigrammatic verdict; post-Keynesianism had received some vindication from experience.

What kind of policy recommendations can we expect from a framework that stresses the level and distribution of income rather than reactions to price changes within the economy? With investment growth related to technological imperatives and interacting with the division of income, incomes earned can be explained without reference to individual or economic class productivity. As profits—flowing from a price markup—are not explained as the result of a "productive" factor called capital, the income distribution is more the result of social and political customs, including those institutions that generate special market-power privileges. This view leaves few strictly economic obstacles to a more equal income distribution. It also opens the door to policies regarding income payments as a means for controlling inflation.

Restrictive fiscal and monetary policies directed against stagflation are counterproductive because production and employment must slump long before inflation begins to slow. Moreover, tight money policy inflicts its damage on those who can least afford it. What savings the giant corporations generate internally can be levered by debt, whereas small business firms and consumers must rely more upon loans from private banks. Therefore, the post-Keynesians would recommend a steady growth in credit and the money supply as facilitators of business expansion but would place no reliance upon tight money policy during stagflation. The excessive costs of lost production and employment have not prevented the Nixon, Ford, Carter, and Reagan Administrations from fighting inflation with these traditional demand management tools.

A GUIDE TO POST-KEYNESIAN MONEY

One of the underlying premises of post-Keynesian monetary theory is that a sharp distinction separates logical and historical time. Only historical time is real, and the post-Keynesian view of money stresses real-world events. There is an effort in economics to restore Keynes's stress on the uncertainty implicit in the knowledge that, although the past is clear, the future remains clouded. We always move forward not backward in time. Reality is structured that way, and a real economy must follow time's arrow, which points in only one direction.

Production takes time, historical time, so that the value of a good produced today may be different several months from now. Money and enforceable contracts denominated in money units provide the link that enables persons and firms to operate reasonably well under conditions of economic uncertainty. As long as production utilizes labor at expected stable wage rates, the public is willing to hold money as a temporary store of value or reserve of purchasing power. If money wage rates and the price level were expected to rise sharply, the public would become unwilling to hold a money stock that is depreciating in value. Within this setting, money, mostly checking deposits, can affect the situation in both the short run and the long run.

"Inside" Money

Rather than money entering the economic system from the sky via Friedman's helicopter, however, the supply of money comes into existence as Keynes describes it, with private debts ("inside" money). Therefore, the money supply is related to debts created by contracts to purchase or produce goods. Because production takes time, the agreements or contracts for the goods are denoted in money units to be paid upon delivery. However, the production costs have to be paid during the time of production, so that producer debt may be incurred prior to any sales revenue whatsoever.

Add to the idea of "inside" money the notion of markup. Wage increases raise production costs. Even if sales continue at their past pace, the price markup is designed to generate enough profits to meet investment requirements. As production costs eat into this profit margin, the firm must raise prices, sell liquid financial assets such as Treasury bills, or borrow from its banks in order to finance its now higher valued inventories of goods in its warehouses. If the business sells financial assets, it must consider the price at which the assets are liquidated compared with the expectation that future sales receipts will cover the higher costs of production, including the interest payments, which are viewed as a cost.

Borrowing from banks adds to the money supply unless the increase in loan activity is offset by actions from the monetary authorities—in the United States, the Federal Reserve System. A new loan creates a new checking deposit amount, which in turn can be reloaned. This process repeats itself with the same mathematical regularity as the Keynesian multiplier. Loans beget deposits, which beget loans, which beget deposits, and so on. In this way, changes in the nation's money supply are in great part decided by business activity itself. That is, in contrast to the monetarists, we have $M \Rightarrow GNP$.[1] For the most part, the money supply is a facilitator: money greases the cogs and wheels of the giant industrial machine. In Chapter 15 we noted how savings in the discretionary-income households allow families to move funds among cash, checking accounts, bonds, and so on. In terms of economic instability, the perturbations in the demand for financial assets by these households are far more important for consumption than for savings.

The largest and most strategic savings reside in the corporation. Inspired by incorrect expectations of the producer or of the consumer, corporate financial asset shifts accentuate an economic downturn. This happens because the price of bonds held by corporations tends to be very low immediately preceding the downswing (interest rates being very high). A time of high interest rates also coincides with a sluggish stock market, so that, although the price markup can be held constant or even perhaps increased, a slump in consumer demand may culminate in a smaller profits flow and therefore less savings for investment. Even the giant corporation is then reluctant to cash in its bonds at a capital loss or borrow at interest rate peaks in order to expand its facilities or replace aging equipment. This liquidity reluctance seems to be a monetary source of instability in investment expenditures.

Although instability in the supra-surplus economy begins in the real sector, the crisis can be extended into the monetary regions of the economy. Although the monetarists are wrong to ignore union-management institutions as partners in inflation, they are correct in suggesting that an ongoing inflation can feed itself with expectations. An about-face in expectations, however, depends upon a reversal of such real phenomena as OPEC's monopoly power and stalling the corporate-union engine of inflation.

The Money Supply and Monetary Policy

In view of the dominance of the real elements among the causes of recession and inflation, the main action of money supply growth is passive; ideally, it facilitates classical-like corporate advances to workers and finances other sources of corporate debt. However, causality initially runs from businesses to the money supply and not vice versa. The expansion of the demand deposits created by the business firm and of those created by loans to the firm starts the money-supply train. A contraction in the money supply engineered by the central bank has little direct impact upon this private source of monetary expansion. It has an indirect effect insofar as the business corporation is reluctant to liquidate bond holdings that are dipping in price. Nonetheless, as long as its sales revenue is experiencing healthy growth, the firm will not be reluctant to issue additional stock or borrow from the largest banks.

For competitive firms such as small businesses and the fragmented construction industry, quite a different tale unfolds. Even with Master-Charge, the small firm does not have the markup clout of the giant. The small business leans upon trade credit financed by private banks. Moreover, when the central bank cuts back on the money supply, small businesses (considered the highest-risk firms for loans by private banks) are the first to experience difficulty obtaining loans. Interest rates for small business loans are high to begin with, and they soar into the stratosphere during tight money periods. Thus, in contrast to the giants, the small competitive firms find that the interest rate is a primary cost of production. Indeed, for the small business, loan money may not be available at all. Tight money is a midget killer.

Higher interest rates for housing and construction in general have similar effects. As every homebuyer knows, the value of interest payments usually is greater than the face value of the mortgage itself. Even a single percentage point increase in the interest rate represents a large increment in the monthly payments. It would be absurd to view such an interest rate as reflecting the productivity of capital. Rather, the interest rate is a major cost of buying the product.

The construction of both houses and commercial buildings is contingent upon the availability of loans in advance of sales. Some of these funds are paid out in wages to construction workers, and some are used to purchase building materials. When loans are unavailable, the rate of construction of all types declines rapidly. A tight money policy only

exacerbates the economic instability described above because it reduces production and creates rising prices simultaneously![2]

Keynes saw the indirect effect of money-supply changes through
investment changes via variations in the rate of interest. The monetarists
contend that the transmission effect is by way of the ultimate wealth
holders, households that spend unwanted money balances on either
goods or financial assets. However, as we have witnessed, the complete
effects of these variables can be ascertained only by a closer look at the
income distribution and a microanalytic inspection of cost.

The monetary guide of post-Keynesianism warns: (1) the wealth
holders may have an unreliable demand for money. However, as indicated in Chapter 15, this source of instability is transmitted through
consumption rather than savings (or investment). (2) The *availability* of
loans (credit) has a discrete, catastrophic impact on certain industries
that goes beyond the costs associated with the interest rate. (3) As we
shall next observe, the unrestrained expansion of credit creates monetary instability. General monetary policy is best viewed as a long-run
lubricant for sustained economic growth rather than as a tool for fine-
tuning the economy. Only specific credit controls can be used to control
credit expansion and allocation.

The differential effects of tight money account in part for the seem-
ing paradox of a decline in construction activity while the price of housing soars. This anomaly ushered in the Great Recession of 1974–1975
and (to a lesser degree) was a prelude to an economic recession beginning in 1979. Finally, the decline of 1981–1982 was led by sharp contrac-
tions in two interest-sensitive industries—construction and automotive.
The housing industry then drew household durables into the downward spiral.

Why does money have to be so "tight" so long in order to bring
down production and employment? We next consider a theory that
helps to answer this query.

THE CASINO ECONOMY

Since the late 1960s credit or finance has become increasingly important
in the United States and in the global economy. Even though real elements in the form of production and consumption rigidities underlie
the business cycle, accelerating financial fragility well describes recent
events in the American and the global economy. Financial disturbances
since 1966—those of 1972–1973, 1974–1975, 1979, and 1981–1982—left
the peak rate of inflation and the lowest rate of unemployment ever
higher. This high-flying era was characterized by a volatile but generally

upward movement in interest rates, wild gyrations in exchange rates, and a general decline in the growth of consumption. Moreover, during this era net interest income was growing nearly 18 percent yearly even as employee compensation was expanding at the rapid rate of 10.5 percent yearly. The irresistible combination of a fast-rising U.S. private and public debt and soaring U.S. interest rates is responsible for sky-rocketing net monetary interest.[3] Indeed, at the 1970s growth rates for national income and net interest income, the entire U.S. national income would equal net interest before the end of the century. The entrepreneur's share of national income has declined drastically even as the rentier's (unearned) income share has soared.

Of course, an economy can never reach a state in which 100 percent of its national income is net interest because the sum of employee compensation, proprietor's income, and corporate profits would be zero! Nevertheless, we can picture an economy whose main industries would be printing (for credit instruments and money), financial firms, and retail outlets and in which all manufactured goods and services would be imported. The central function of businesspeople in such an environment would be speculation. The society would be a giant money market fund in which households and businesses would spend each day shifting financial assets about in their gigantic portfolios. The United States would implode into Las Vegas—hence, the term "casino economy."

An economy built on the wild side of growing debt (credit expansion) and financial speculation is geared more to making money than to making goods. The necessary outcome of such a financial system—especially within concentrated state capitalism—is increasing financial fragility. Ironically, the growing importance of borrowing and lending that contributes to financial crises makes each successive crisis more severe. The theorist most important in calling attention to this increasing financial fragility is the post-Keynesian Hyman P. Minsky. In fact, Minsky had been writing since the early 1960s about the built-in instability of the credit system. He has called post-World War II global economic growth an exercise in "Ponzi finance" (a reference to the notorious swindler and innovator in the use of pyramid schemes).

Minsky's Theory of Financial Fragility

Minsky retains the insight into capitalistic profits provided by Kalecki. The price markup reflects demands that are financed by means other than wage incomes earned in the consumer goods sector. Profits in consumer goods production (the sum of the values from the markups) pay the wage bill in the investment goods sector so that total profits equal investment (see Chapter 15). However, as Minsky suggests, the increase in direct and indirect government employment since the Great Depression along with the explosion in transfer payments has reduced the dependence of profits on investment. Since government transfer payments and tax revenue are tied to national income, declines in national income during recessions greatly expand the government's deficit and its debt. The countercyclical effects of government deficits help to stabilize profits; if these fiscal measures fail, the central bank stands ready to be lender of last resort in order to prevent a depression that otherwise would deflate the debt. With the growth of financial institutions and their increased concentration, the Federal Reserve and the Federal Deposit Insurance Corporation (FDIC) have moved with greater speed in attempts to prevent bankruptcies of financial institutions. Since the survival of banking in particular depends upon confidence that deposits can be paid upon demand, giant banks simply cannot be allowed to fail unless the government is willing to let the entire system collapse.

We have noted how sales revenues of businesses bolstered by private credit provide funds for investment in a capitalistic system. Since business debt has to be serviced (scheduled payments on principle and interest made), Minsky suggests that such cash flows (and debt-servicing commitments) determine the course of investment and thus of output and employment. In this manner, Minsky has extended post-Keynesian monetary theory to include not only credit, but the special problems connected with financial speculation in a capitalistic system.

The monetary system still is at the core of the debt creation and repayment process. Money is created as banks make loans, mostly to business: money is created in response to businesses' and bankers' profits expectations. Minsky emphasizes, however, that money is destroyed as profits are realized and loans are repaid to the banks. Monetary changes are the *result*, not the cause, of behavior in the economy. The monetary system's stability depends upon profit flows to borrowers sufficient to service loans. Thus, the central problems of capitalism are connected to the ownership, creation, and financing of capital assets that, in turn, contribute to business cycles. As John Maynard Keynes would have put it, only a monetary economy can have a business cycle.[4]

Minsky's financial instability hypothesis is the lineal descendant of ideas from classical economist John Stuart Mill; neoclassicals Alfred Marshall, Knut Wicksell, and Irving Fisher; and John Maynard Keynes. In Minsky's view, the prelude to a financial crisis is some "outside" shock to the system, such as war (Vietnam), crop failure, OPEC, a Schumpeterian basic innovation such as the automobile, or some massive debt disturbance. Whatever the origin of the shock, it significantly changes profit opportunities in at least one important branch of industry. Before we throw an entrepreneur into the breach, however, we must remember the degree of industry concentration under supra-surplus capitalism; giant corporations sense the opportunities for profit in some new or existing lines and can shut down others. If new profit opportunities dominate, increased investment and production generate a boom, a boom fueled by the expansion of bank and other forms of credit.

Credit is notoriously unstable. If the need for credit in a monetary economy arises, banks as well as others who have discretionary income (and savings) are quick to meet the need (for a price, interest). Since profit opportunities create lending opportunities, booms ordinarily are financed, a process that explains why financial institutions are among the first to be regulated. The boom is fueled by an expansion of credit that enlarges the money supply. Financial innovations emerge in the forms of new financial institutions and new credit instruments, and even person-to-person and firm-to-firm credit. Policy issues emerge when knowledgeable people begin to talk about controlling the expansion of credit.

Speculation in financial assets eventually spills over into enhanced Keynesian effective demand for goods. Pressures on the capacity for goods production elevates prices. Rising prices of both goods and financial assets provide still more profit opportunities: a round robin of new investment increases discretionary income, motivating still more investment, still more income. The prices of goods now include a *speculative* "markup." Many market participants will become pure speculators who buy goods for resale rather than for use. In the United States pure speculation characterized much of the housing market during the 1970s. Eventually, the number of firms and households buying strictly for resale rather than for further production may begin to dominate the economic environment. What normally characterizes the bond and stock markets, where only about 1 percent of all transactions directly lead to real investment, becomes more and more characteristic of goods markets. A large share of the economic actors are now placing bets in the casino economy.

A continuation of the boom means higher prices, interest rates, and velocity of money. The leveling-off of prices brings financial distress for certain participants and industries. Firms, including farms, have counted upon a particular inflation rate for their products in order to service their mounting debts. Yet, those most in the know in the financial markets, the insiders, take their profits and run. This is the start of a race toward liquidity as financial assets are cashed in. As Keynes had it, the holding of money "lulls their disquietude." Outright financial panic can be avoided only if (1) prices fall so low that people move back into assets;

(2) the government sets limits to price declines (e.g., agricultural price supports), closes banks (e.g., the "bank holiday" of 1933), and shuts the exchanges; or (3) a lender of last resort steps in—as the Federal Reserve did in the financial turbulence following the Penn-Central collapse (1969–1970), the Franklin National Bank bankruptcy (1974–1975), the Hunt-Bache silver speculation (1980), and as the FDIC did in nationalizing Illinois Continental Bank (1984). Such interventions prevent the complete collapse of the values of assets.

The Federal Reserve did not function as lender of last resort during the Great Depression: we all know the consequences of that nonintervention. As Minsky tells the story, however, what the government and the Federal Reserve (as its agent) do to shore up values to avoid depressions sets the stage for still higher inflation. Since debt deflation also means profits deflation in what I call "the casino economy," the otherwise stabilizing effect of government deficits and last-resort lending has its dark side. Liabilities such as new loan instruments and other financial innovations of the boom are validated as the central bank refinances the holdings of financial institutions. This propping-up of the system creates the base for still further expansion of credit during the economic recovery, a process that helps to explain the inflation following the financial crises of 1969–1970, 1974–1975, and 1980.

The Real Economy and Economic Policy

We need not lose sight of the real elements of technology and income shares in order to be persuaded by Minsky's theory of financial fragility. Events in financial markets—happening long after he published the theory—are convincing. For example, the theory goes a long way toward explaining the plight of American farmers in the mid-1980s. Irrespective of and in part despite their high productivities, farmers are going bankrupt because their massive borrowings during the euphoria of an expansion at high interest rates could not be serviced when agricultural sales and prices slumped.[5]

Minsky emphasizes the importance of fully integrating money and credit into macroeconomics. Certainly, bankruptcy is a financial event, and financial crises are financial in nature, if not always in origin. Looked at another way, financial innovations do not seem to link up to technological innovations. Or, if they do, thus far the technological innovations alone have not been sufficient to end the stagnation and inflation of the 1970s and 1980s. Also, industrial concentration and the lopsided accumulation of 28 percent of all personal wealth within 2 percent of U.S. households must play roles in the casino economy: at the least, they provide the chips for pure speculation. Moreover, the income tax system in the United States (as late as June 1986) has been designed to offer maximum tax avoidance to those households that have sufficiently high incomes to use tax shelters as a place to play in the casino. Under first-term Reaganomics the giant industrial corporations were dealt such a hot hand that they ended up *bidding on each other*.

Surely, the markup is not always sufficient to finance all that investment required by expected demand. But the greatest need for business credit (at the highest interest rates) resides in the weakest parts of the economy, occupied by small businesses and farm families. Although the main purpose of financial markets is to provide liquidity on those relatively rare occasions when giant business issues a bond or equity and the frequent occasions when the federal government has a new bond issue, the "players" in these markets otherwise have no connection to production activity. As even the failing giants add to their markups to service rising interest costs, they are merely providing overhead for the casino. In this regard, the casino economy operates very much like the labor market in supra-surplus capitalism; the casino and the factory are not connected by productivity, just as wage rates are not tied to marginal products.

Charles P. Kindleberger, professor of economics emeritus at MIT, has extended Minsky's theory to the global economy.[6] Kindleberger sees pure speculation spilling over national borders. International links are provided by exports, imports, and foreign securities. Indeed, interest rates in the United States in 1983 and 1984 would have been much higher in the absence of massive purchases of U.S. Treasury securities by foreigners. However, at the same time these foreign purchases add to the credit pyramid that will begin to tumble should such speculators begin to lose confidence. Kindleberger points a finger at the enormous external debt of the developing countries, accelerated by rising oil prices (up to at least 1979, we must add), "as multinational banks swollen with dollars tumbled over one another in trying to uncover new foreign borrowers and practically forced money on the less-developed countries (LDCs)."[7] At the international level, however, there is no lender of last resort.

Several policy proposals emerge from Minsky's ideas. First, his theory seems to support continued or extended financial regulation. The recent policies of financial deregulation begun during the Carter Administration and elevated to a celebration during the Reagan Administration open the door for heretofore unheralded abuse. The initial euphoria of intense competition among suppliers of credit is now floundering upon the shoals of massive bankruptcies, mergers, and even greater financial concentration. Some of the worst abuses could be foreclosed by tax reform, including that proposed by the U.S. Treasury in late 1984 and later modified by the White House. Second, the Federal Reserve and the FDIC must act as lenders of last resort in order to avoid depression (which is otherwise inevitable). Third, as Minsky suggests, the priorities of the federal government should be shifted, altered in such a way that the actions of the lender of last resort do not guarantee subsequent inflation. Presently, the largest government expenditures support either private consumption (via transfer payments) or "collective consumption" (via defense expenditures). A big government that creates resources and infrastructure (capital formation) could create the real investment counterpart to its public credit creation. (I would add *human* capital formation to these tasks.) As we next observe, tax reform can reduce the size of the casino economy even as it shifts the focus of government toward various forms of capital formation.[8]

There remains the problem of overreliance upon tight monetary policy as the sole deterrent to inflation, an instrument that has been effective only as it succeeds in creating recession or depression. The Federal Reserve is unlikely to shift policy gears in the absence of an effective incomes policy. Rather, with even the scent of a vigorous economic upturn in the air, the Fed historically has put the brakes on the rate of growth in the credit and money supply. A sustained economic expansion appears impossible in the absence of an effective incomes policy.

INCOMES POLICY

One post-Keynesian, Abba P. Lerner, suggested as early as 1951 that the price level cannot be stabilized without an incomes policy. This recommendation contrasts sharply with the views of the fiscal Keynesians.[9] In terms of economic policy, the persistent advocacy of an incomes policy distinguishes the post-Keynesians to the same degree that the equally tenacious advocacy of deficit spending characterizes the bastard Keynesians. Not surprisingly, the advocated policy blatantly requires that wages be "controlled" in some sense. The profit margin will be whatever it will be because of the relative constancy of the price markup. However, every time wages go up, the price level will go up, too.

Some post-Keynesians recognize that problems of equity and political acceptability arise if wages alone are controlled; others realize that a variable markup (profits-push) can be a source of inflation. It has been recommended that the part of profits not retained by corporations for financing investment also be regulated. This might require the taxing of dividends and corporate salaries at a rate in line with the growth of wage income. Irrespective of *which* income source policies are applied, all incomes policy variations have the same theme: money income changes are to be geared to the pace of productivity.

Recommended incomes policies have ranged all the way from voluntary wage and price guidelines to mandatory wage and price controls. Such controls have been utilized in different forms and with varying vigor by the Kennedy, Johnson, Nixon, Ford, and Carter Administrations. Mandatory controls have been recommended repeatedly by John Kenneth Galbraith.

One alternative to wage and price guidelines or controls is tax incentives, the purpose of which is to cause modification in the behavior of labor unions and concentrated industry. Such policies use the incentives and deterrents of the price mechanism. This mixture of governmental controls and the market system in the post-Keynesian world seems a bit of a paradox. In this case, however, the "invisible hand" is at the end of the arm of the Internal Revenue Service.

One tax-based incomes policy (TIP) was developed by the late Sidney Weintraub and by Henry Wallich, a governor of the Federal Reserve Board. TIP's authors saw the use of the tax mechanism as compatible with a market economy and democratic government. The plan is described as anti-inflation rather than antilabor. It is aimed at stiffening the backbone of industrial managers so that they will resist unreasonable wage demands by powerful unions.

Whenever a corporation grants a pay increase in excess of an established norm—say, 6 percent—the firm granting the pay raise would be penalized by an increase in its income tax. If a firm increased the average pay of its workers by, say, 10 percent rather than by 6 percent, the firm might be required to pay 10 percent more in taxes on its profits. The wage-salary norms would be the *average* increase of wages and salaries of the firm so that above-average wage stipends could be awarded to meritorious workers. The goal would be to confine average money wage increases to the gains in average labor productivity in the economy.[10] The premise underlying TIP is that individual businesses will be encouraged to resist unreasonable wage demands only when they are convinced that resistance also will come from other firms and industries. TIP tilts the individual firm in the direction of yielding only non-inflationary average wage increments. The laborers would benefit from real wage gains as inflation subsided.

A TIP is a very flexible policy: it can provide a penalty for a wage increase above the norm, a reward for a wage below the norm, or both. Others have suggested that labor or business be pelted with carrots rather than sticks. The late Arthur Okun, once economic adviser to President Johnson and later associated with the Brookings Institution, preferred carrots. If a firm holds its average yearly rate of wage increase below 6 percent and its average rate of price increase below 4 percent, Okun's plan would give the employees of the firm a tax rebate (carrot I) and the firm would receive a rebate (carrot II) on its income tax liabilities. One facet of this proposal was adopted by President Jimmy Carter in October 1978. However, this incentive is very indirect, a kind of diced carrot. President Carter promised to introduce into Congress a bill that, if passed, would have provided tax relief for those workers who stay below the wage norm if the annual inflation rate ends up above 7 percent.

Lerner's last proposed incomes policy is acronymed MAP, a market mechanism anti-inflation accounting plan. This plan would limit the growth of net sales (combined profits and wages) to the rate of growth in productivity. Credits for increasing the wage bill in excess of average productivity growth could be purchased by a firm (at the going market price) from a Federal Reserve market for such credits. In effect, the firm would be required to *buy* "anti-inflation accounting credit" in an amount equal to the "inflationary impact." The greater the "demand for infla-tion," the greater the cost of the credits to generate net sales above the productivity growth rate. Expanding firms are motivated to limit cost and price increases in order to minimize purchases of such credits.[11] MAP thus turns the inflationary pressure against itself, jujitsu fashion. As the disincentive applies to both wages and profits, MAP's authors contend that it is fairer than TIP.

TAX REFORM AND INCOMES POLICY

Since the original TIP proposal, certain conditions have changed. For one thing the effective average corporate income tax rate, the original tax penalty base for TIP, was approaching zero under the Economic Recovery Tax Act of 1981. For another, net interest income as a share of national income has increased tenfold between the end of World War II and 1982. Therefore, it is essential to obtain a new federal revenue source to exert downward pressure on interest rates as well as a TIP that acknowledges monetary interest as a new, increasingly important source of rising production costs.

In order to deal with these problems, in 1983 I proposed: (1) an equitable value-added tax (VAT) as a new revenue source and as the ideal tax base for the immediate implementation of TIP; and (2) a sim-plified personal income tax program that would satisfy those critics of VAT who view it as inequitable.[12] A streamlined tax system appears to be an idea whose time has come, for Democrats and Republicans alike in the United States have been busily designing various "flat tax" schemes.

Equitable Value-Added and Personal Income Taxes

The closing of all tax loopholes, so that all income (including un-earned income) would be taxed alike, would be the first step in raising revenue. This action would be ideologically neutral because no special privileges would be granted. Indeed this reform would greatly diminish the power of special-interest groups that have given Americans Will Rogers's "best Congress money can buy."

The next step would require a second tax reform based upon the understanding that every family, rich *or* poor, buys necessities. A value-added tax can be introduced in slow stages (perhaps 2 percent the first year) as "revenue enhancement." Such a tax raises the price level by at least the percentage of the tax and thus must be implemented in stages. In theory, the tax base for VAT is the value added to the product at each level of production. In practice, the tax base is measured by the increase in sales price at each stage of production. Each stage in the chain col-lects the VAT on its sales, takes a credit for VAT paid on purchases to other firms, and remits the net amount of VAT to the IRS. At the end of the chain, the consumer pays the full amount of the tax in the sales price of the good or service and *with no other reform measure* would bear the full burden. Thus, VAT is in its effects a national sales tax. Administrative efficiency demands that all consumption should be taxed at a single, flat rate. This means that VAT would be unfair without a reduction in the income taxes paid on the personal income allocated to necessities.

Exemptions for dependents under the income tax code were orig-inally meant to cover the above contingency—namely, to provide a tax credit equal to the amount spent simply to maintain life. As a *required* counterpart of VAT, the family income tax exemption should be raised for all taxpayers to a value close to the cost of a market basket of ne-cessities, say at least 75 percent of the official poverty-level income. Three positive flat tax rates would apply to *all* income in excess of the minimum in each income interval, a rate progressively higher at higher-income intervals. The value of the necessities budget would be the main exemption from taxation.[13] (In late 1984 the U.S. Treasury recognized the critical importance of this idea by proposing a doubling of the value of personal exemptions in its major income tax reform effort.) The mar-ginal tax rates on discretionary or *taxable* income (joint filing status) would be 10 percent up to $35,000, 25 percent up to $100,000, and 30 percent in excess of $100,000.[14] The VAT and any positive rate of in-flation would increase the size of the consumption budget each year so that "bracket creep" for all taxpayers, rich and poor alike, would be avoided. Ideological neutrality is maintained since the expenditure patterns of rich and poor alike show that both place highest value on essentials.

In the absence of other reforms, we would still have a problem with the unemployed and present unemployables who have incomes below the minimal consumption budget. The Reagan Administration dismantled many welfare services but failed to follow its most renowned conservative adviser Milton Friedman's suggestion of a negative income tax for poor households. The negative income tax for households is an ingenious system for transferring income to the poor whereby a minimum income would be guaranteed by providing income supplements. The supplements should be sufficient to maintain the social minimum for necessities and would be reduced by some fraction (less than 1) as the family earned additional income. Since an increase in earnings would always add to disposable income available to the family, the supplements would not be a disincentive to seeking employment. No "needs test" except income level would be required, so that social freedoms would be preserved. "Disincentives" are bemoaned by conservatives and "needs tests" by liberals. Moreover, the negative income tax would eliminate the need for unemployment compensation, housing assistance, food and nutrition services, supplemental security income, AFDC, and low-income energy assistance, all of which cost about $64 billion in 1985. The negative income tax would be in the form of a refundable credit administered by the IRS and paid on a monthly basis. Since the cost of the negative income tax would be no more than the social welfare program eliminated, the total federal revenue from the new, simplified system would about equal that under 1984 law. The value-added tax then could be used to reduce the size of the federal deficit.

New Incomes Policy: TIP for VAT or VATIP

The combination of VAT, tax credit exemptions, and the negative income tax has two unexpected bonuses. The redistribution of income and wealth by the Economic Recovery Tax Act of 1981 toward the *ultra*discretionary households (those with incomes of $80,000 or more) reduced the size of mass markets for new products or services and therefore penalized new industry. The guarantee of tax-free income for life's necessities and truly graduated income tax rates would assure that the middle class would once again enjoy discretionary income and the wherewithal to buy newly marketed products.

For the sake of keeping the inflation rate within manageable limits and of encouraging an expansionary monetary policy, we turn to a second advantage of VAT. It is the ideal instrument for immediately implementing a tax-based incomes policy (TIP). The Weintraub-Wallich

TIP would penalize with an extra corporate tax bite any one of the 2,000 or so largest corporations granting an *average* pay hike in excess of the historical economywide pace of productivity improvement. We know that if value added (or net sales) grows at the same pace as *real* output, inflation would be minimized. The Federal Reserve would be free to follow an easy money policy without the fear of domestically induced inflation. VAT can fill the incomes policy void. A firm with a 1 percentage point increase in value added (its payments to the factors of production, which include profits, net interest, and rent payments as well as all employee compensation) in excess of an *adjusted* real output growth norm could be penalized by adding 1 percentage point to its VAT. Why *adjusted* real output growth norm? Some 2 or 3 percentage points should be added to the historical average real output pace because some price increases simply reflect preferences for a higher-priced market basket of goods. Suppose we add a 4 percent historical real output growth rate (labor productivity growth rate plus labor force growth rate) to a 2 percent "conflation" rate. (The "conflation" rate is the part of inflation caused by the diffusion of the costs of Warsh's "added complexity."[15]) With an adjusted output growth norm of 6 percent, a giant firm allowing its value added from wages and salaries, net interest, rents, or profits to rise 7 percent would have to pay 1 percentage point extra in value-added taxes. A firm with a value-added increase of 8 percent would pay a 2 percent penalty. In actual practice, those firms raising net prices (after purchases from other firms) by 7 or 8 percent would be penalized accordingly.

A special device is required to prevent price expectations from spoiling any incomes policy. In order to prevent the giants from passing along any penalty tax in the way of higher prices, the penalty is deliberately set equal to 100 percent of any price increase above the norm. Since TIP for VAT treats all income sources alike, it has a dual advantage. First, the employer gains no special advantage in holding down wage payments alone because all his income payments are taxed. Second, it is possible to tax away *all* value-added increases in excess of the norm so that the corporation can never race ahead of the tax collector with "catch-up" price increases.

Taxation and Armament

Minsky has called attention to the adverse economic effects of massive defense expenditures. As an incentive toward a reduction in such spending, the income tax eventually could be viewed only as a defense-use tax. The United States could shift roughly four-fifths of federal revenue sources to VAT and one-fifth to the personal income tax. Ultimately the personal income tax could be used solely for financing national defense. The main contribution of the working class to defense and war efforts has been to supply manpower. More equity could be achieved by financing defense with the progressive tax on incomes. If the rich object to their taxes going to national defense, they have the resources to lobby for disarmament or slower growth in the defense establishment. On the other hand VAT is less visible, less felt. Those presently in tax shelters apparently "feel" that too much of their taxes go to social programs. With the allocation of VAT revenues to the income grants for the poor, education, and other socially necessary programs, the currently sheltered could be painlessly altruistic. Moreover, they can see each VAT increase swell their income tax credits.

Toward Industrial Peace in the United States

Political scientist Charles Lindblom has recently called attention to the "privileged position" of business.[16] Unlike the individual, the corporation has earthly immortality and is invulnerable to imprisonment. The sheer size of corporate assets is a source of possible coercion in the absence of effective corporate punishment. In this respect, the continued trend toward industrial and financial concentration is not favorable to liberty's cause. The corporation looks into a mirror, and the Leviathan looks back.

In an increasingly complex society, information may be the greatest source of power in the future. The fifty largest U.S. broadcast chains already hold three-quarters of the audience. The fifty largest newspaper chains sell more than two-thirds of all daily newspapers. Could GM, the corporation that denied Ralph Nader his civil liberties, be trusted to manage the Knight-Ridder news chain or the CBS television network? The potential for misuse of the media is compounded by a corporation's right to spend funds for political and social propaganda, a right exercised by G. W. Grace and Company in TV commercials regarding the "evils" of the federal debt. The present distribution of economic power threatens majority rule and democracy itself. Moreover, this extension of corporate power is now multinational. The conglomerate usually is a large corporation of no nationality, which does not come under the rule of law, operating in a world in which "international law" is merely a useful euphemism.

John Rawls, a representative of twentieth-century liberalism, struggles with this power dilemma. In his thought, freedom as equal liberty is the same for all, but the worth of liberty is not the same for everyone. Those who have greater authority and wealth have greater means to achieve their aims. Rawls's concern for economic justice leads him to construct the *difference principle*, a principle of "fairness" whereby income and wealth would be redistributed to some degree to the "worst-off." However, Rawls leaves us in doubt about the ability of a modern industrial state to disperse its wealth, and therefore its power, evenly. In this respect, the main hope rests in Rawls's "vision," which might motivate a society to gain order and power balance through mutual interests.[17] However, the political reform that breaks the tie between concentrated wealth and legislative bodies would be a prerequisite for a Rawlsian redistribution program. In the United States, this requires, at a minimum, public funding of congressional political campaigns, a reform already applied to presidential campaigns.

There are several further ways in which the excessive power of corporations might be limited. First, new laws and governmental regulations could establish new boundaries to corporate license. For example, in the United States the Clean Air Act and Safe Drinking Water Act required that automobile companies improve car engines to reduce air pollutants and that industrial firms reduce hazardous wastes going into groundwater. Second, the driving ethic of the business firm could be altered in such a way that its responsibility for maintaining representative democracy as well as for minimizing adverse third-party effects would be in the interests of the society of which it is a part. However, the strong cultural ethic favoring individual action is an impediment to this solution. Third, public ownership could be substituted for private ownership or control of the industrial giants.

There is yet another alternative—a new social contract that forms an "encompassing coalition" of the type favored by Mancur Olson. It is widely agreed that the combination of corporate, union, and government power is unfair to the balance of society. The corporation and the union alone cannot be expected to make fair decisions regarding the consumer if the consumer is not a party to the decision-making process. Because the corporation and the union have taken away the clout of the individual, this strength can be restored only through the political mechanism. A new social contract would require that the major price, investment, and wage decisions of the 2,000 largest corporations be made with viable public representation in the decision-making process. Federal charters could require these corporations to include equal representation from labor, business, and consumers on their boards. Similarly, some of these public representatives also would comprise the membership (along with corporate and union members) of quasi-public investment-planning panels for each concentrated industry. Each panel would deal with a limited number of firms.[18] The arrangement would make formal the kind of informal cooperation characterizing Sweden's economic system.

Furthermore, selected *new* growth industries could be supported by research and development foundations similar to the National Science Foundation but jointly supported by government and industry. Any revenue from the U.S. VATIP penalties could be used to start such funds. Such an arrangement bears more directly to the productivity point, as such foundations could speed the shift of industry structure in its postindustrial direction. Once the new social contract is working, the VATIP can be dropped. Indeed the VATIP itself would be an incentive to move from a tax penalty system to the complete decision-making flexibility afforded by voluntary arrangements.

The first-term Reagan Administration tilt toward the supra-discretionary households was precisely the wrong direction, an outcome that Reagan's Treasury attempted to turn on its head in the Treasury's income tax reform proposal of 1984. To restore an adequate U.S. real economic growth pace, the poor and a resurrected middle class must spend, and for that they need adequate real income. To restore health and equity to the American economy, only a policy reversal will do. And of course, this restoration is critical to the health of the entire global economy.

These measures may seem extreme. The alternative, however, would be complete economic planning at the governmental level or outright socialism. Be that as it may, a strong case can be made for socializing those industries, such as construction and medicine, that are among those producing absolute necessities and in which union power is one-sided.[19] The problem is immense, and the survival of an entire economic system as well as of democracy itself hangs in the balance.

THE NEW MEANING OF FISCAL POLICY

According to the view of today's New Right, the problems of inflation and relatively low levels of productivity would disappear if the government were greatly shrunken in size. But the reduction of the one-fifth to one-fourth of gross national product presently generated by government would be disastrous for production and employment. However, this fact does not absolve the government of economic guilt. Its misguided attempt to control inflation through reduced production and employment spawned the Great Recession of 1974–1975 and the depression of 1981–1982. If private industry were universally required to meet the "best management practices" or be shut down, it would have disappeared decades ago. We must not confuse our ability to design good government policy with those instances in which such policies would otherwise be defeated by poor design and misguided management. These are separate issues.

In the new synthesis of economic reality and theory, general fiscal policy can only help to stabilize the level of production and employment. It is too blunt an instrument to be employed against inflation, where a scalpel is required. Therefore, the taxing and grant-making powers of the government must be directed at specific industrial and human situations.[20] Only the shortest of steps would be required by either the government or the industry.

There already is a tight connection between government spending and the savings and investment levels of giant business. This relation is most visible in the defense industry, a joint government-business enterprise in which contractual arrangements determine the rate of growth in profits. Although some of the demands are created by the private defense industry, in a rough-and-tumble way the parties have agreed on the social purpose and amounts of investment.

However, the coziness of the defense industry and government is not unique. If, for example, the automotive giants (Ford, Chrysler, and General Motors) begin to experience losses, the government immediately steps to their sides and makes a social contract similar to that made with the defense industry (Lockheed, for example). When such industries are experiencing difficulties, they welcome the socialization of their investments (unless higher tariffs will shield their profits growth). Moreover, giant business also welcomes the role of the government in financing investment projects such as space shuttles that require great outlays exceeding even that available to the conglomerate.

Whether or not the government is involved, the regularity of new inventions and product innovations is not guaranteed. The society cannot rely upon the decisions of the concentrated sector to provide new products and still more industries at exactly the rate of growth required to fully employ the labor force. In those firms in which government revenue does not represent a great share of sales revenue, the investment decision is a self-fulfilling prophecy, in which the price markup generates the wherewithal to fund the selected investment programs. If economic growth is to proceed smoothly with a limited inflation rate under supra-surplus capitalism, a quasi-public institution in which government and private industry decisions are made jointly is consistent with democratic principles.

The present deterrent to such overt joint action is based in the contemporary myth that giant business must rely on the stock market and personal savings from individuals for its investment funds. As I have suggested, this is not the case. Some 90 percent of the investment funds of the manufacturing sector are generated internally, and the bulk of savings going into corporate common stock and bonds is concentrated within a small number of families. The connection between private wealth and corporate management decisions is indirect. It comes from the social power of fortune holders and not necessarily from the efficient deployment of their savings.[21]

The new synthesis of reality and theory has quite different implications for consumers. In this regard, the distinction between necessities and nonnecessities is crucial; governmental economic policy already makes this distinction. The concern that rising prices for necessities have a greater adverse impact on human welfare than an increase in the price of luxuries has led to such policies as price ceilings on gasoline and oil. Granted, these price ceilings make no sense within the neoclassical price paradigm. Nonetheless, this fact does not preclude a merger of two kinds of concerns.

For example, a higher federal tax could be placed on oil and gasoline while the price of both is allowed to rise. In turn, since the state of technologies in transportation and heating are givens, such a price rise to consumers represents a decline in real incomes even as consumers allocate a larger share of their budgets to transportation and utilities. (The same would happen to the food budget because it is tied to the energy supply.) The government can offset the decline in real income by indexing the personal income tax exemption and the income tax credit to a necessities price index. The neoclassicals would be given the higher price that they feel is required to stimulate increased oil exploration and to incite the development of alternative energy sources, and the basic social needs of the poor and lower middle class would be met.

Finally, if we combine Minsky's guide (shift government spending toward capital formation) with Canterbery's vita theory, the government (perhaps in cooperation with private industry) has an important role to play in education and training. In this regard, it is far more efficient to subsidize individual human capital development irrespective of the industry affected rather than subsidize indefinitely a specific sunset industry. Industries can live and die with product cycles without hurting people if the industrial transition is eased through proper care and nurture of individuals. Whereas a negative income tax would provide a safety net, well-designed education and training programs directing persons into skills that are in short supply gradually could reduce otherwise necessary income credits.

GLOBAL ECONOMIC POLICIES

As we shift our concerns to the very long run, we necessarily return to economic development and the problems of the Third World. Although the long-run view presently is blocked by the global debt crisis, global financial fragility is more consequence than cause. Even so, the debt crisis must be met first. The misguided attempts to slow the evolution of the industrial structures in the North have led to disastrous policies and a rising protectionist fever that can only make matters worse. Only a global realignment of industry and new policy instruments can circumvent punitive policies in a global economy that is moving rapidly toward economic integration. In an integrated global economy, such structural change happens because patterns change with movements in per-capita income and because technological innovations alter production recipes around the world in many ways.

Development Strategy: Getting to the Twenty-First Century

Economic modernization is a process of developing infrastructure that can cope first with standardized technologies and eventually with basic innovations. There are two distinct advantages to a development strategy of selecting those technologies that raise the share of value added in gross product the most. First, the greater the number of layers of value added among industries linked domestically, the larger their contribution to national income. Second, to the extent that domestic surpluses and foreign demand exists for the processed products, it is possible to increase the amount of value added exported. The trade connection can work two ways: (1) the replacement of imports by local production increases domestic value added and reduces foreign exchange costs; and (2) the increase in manufactured exports can raise foreign exchange earnings. As a general rule, the greater the processing stages performed locally, the further downstream in terms of advanced processing stages, the greater the value added to exports if the product is sold abroad. The Japanese first and, later, the South Koreans adhered to this rule.

In view of the advantages to lengthening the chain of values added, the developing country often will try to develop an industry having both forward and backward linkages, *a propulsive industry*. The industry selected to lead usually is a basic one such as steel or automobiles. Looking upstream over his shoulder, the steel producer (as leader) sees a backward link to blast furnaces, pig-iron manufacturing, iron ore mining, extractive equipment, and even machine tools to build the extractive equipment, the blast furnaces, and the steel mills themselves. Looking downstream, the steel producer sees forward linkages to spindles, looms, and sewing machines that in turn can be used to produce cotton, yarn, cloth, and dresses still further downstream. The most strategic industrialization instrument of all is the machine tool industry, which appears as *both* a forward and backward linkage, surfacing downstream *and* upstream. The machine tool is as unique to industrialization as seed corn is to agriculture; it is the mechanism whereby machines can reproduce themselves.

Even though these opportunities for industrial linkages have been omnipresent for a century, nonetheless, the gap between the South and the North has not closed. What appears to be a natural evolutionary process apparently is blocked by human-built barriers. Even the newly industrialized countries in the South continue to rely on imports from the North for a significant share of their capital goods and machinery requirements. Moreover, their manufactured exports consist, for the most part, of the traditionally labor-intensive items of textiles, clothing, and other goods produced under low-wage conditions. Many of the industrializing developing countries also have become increasingly re- liant on imports of essential items, particularly food, in part because their desire for industrialization has taken priority over the immediate requirements of the agricultural sector. This neglect of the agricultural sector has reduced the domestic market for manufactures even while it has constrained the supply of agricultural raw materials for industry. The consequent deficits in the balances of payments have sometimes meant periodic curtailment of imports of capital and intermediate goods for industry, thereby interrupting long-term industrial development. In- ternational institutions often have reinforced this pernicious pattern. The IMF, in particular, has been shortsighted in requiring reductions in domestic aggregate demand and imports as a form of discipline for countries needing balance-of-payments settlement assistance. Since foreign exchange earnings are necessary in order to service external debts, the IMF treatment may be worse than the disease.

This process in the developing countries contrasts sharply with that of the supra-surplus economies, where high wage payments de- pend very much on skills developed in response to high productivity derived from new production techniques. Such economies are beyond industrial maturity and on their way to supra-industrialization in which direct labor is incidental to the manufacturing process. The global economy must depend upon these supra-surplus economies of the North to exploit most of the new swarm of innovations. Because of lower wages, in one way or another the South can best do what the postindustrial nations no longer do as well—produce traditional man- ufactures. Even so, the most successful newly industrializing coun- tries have reached beyond their apparent capabilities and adapted technologies a stage or so higher than would seem prudent. This "long reach" by the developing countries should be instrumental in their development strategy.

The Evolution of Policy Institutions

The North has an important stake in the quick resolution of the global debt crisis because the United States' and thus the West's banking network is in jeopardy. Although borrowing by the South stems from international payments deficits, trade deficits in the South varied only between 2 and 3 percent of total world exports between 1950 and 1973. Since then, the deficits have only occasionally flirted with 4 percent. The financing of this narrow ribbon between the value of exports and imports is a small price to pay in order to maintain a healthy international trade system. More important, policies that restore the recent historical growth rates in North and South alike would reduce the global trade deficit. International financial institutions should be established to provide automatically sufficient liquidity to fund this tiny red ribbon of trade.

Since interest rates in the United States account for a large part of the rising cost of financing trade deficits, new U.S. policy institutions such as the aforementioned tax reform, incomes policy, and VAT that could cope with stagflation without overreliance upon "tight" monetary policies would be doubly efficient, contributing to economic growth all the way round and reducing debt-servicing costs of the Third World even while reducing its trade deficits. Other outward-looking policy innovations fall under the often misused rubric of "industrial policy." The United States *already has* an industrial policy in the guise of protectionism. By Labor Day, 1985, more than 400 bills in Congress sought to protect U.S. industry and "jobs" from foreign competition. Similar protectionist pressures were growing in many industrial nations. Peter Gray has built a strong case for a *positive* industrial policy even in the case of embattled industries, industries that have lost their traditional shares of their domestic markets because of some *transitory* phenomenon.[22] Such industries can regain their health after a period of "conditional protection" in which protection against foreign competition is provided for some specified (and finite) period on the prearranged condition that both management and labor undertake specific steps to reduce production costs.

Although special-interest coalitions—playing the role once played by Ricardo's landowners—presently stand in the way of the continued evolution of industry and new divisions of labor in the North, the "rental needs" of these coalitions can be met through generalized government income transfers combined with a human capital program. Such policies, natural complements to an industrial program, may still the protectionist cry and undercut the drift of labor unions toward job security.

If heavy industry in the United States gains the same subsidies and insulation from foreign competition as agriculture has enjoyed for the bulk of this century, the supra-surplus economy's shift toward its high-technology frontiers will be slowed. So, too, will global economic progress be endangered.

In an interdependent global economic system, what the North does in rationalizing its policies helps itself even as it assists the South, a mutually beneficial game that can be extended to an international financial system dominated by the U.S. dollar. Most of the South has "soft" currencies that are not accumulated or used by the North. Except for barter, which is notoriously inefficient, the South has to carry out its trade in "hard" currencies. Usually the major currency held as assets (reserves) by central banks is the U.S. dollar. An expansion in the United States' money supply also expands its ability to purchase imports. Since the developing nations do not possess this power and the North will not accept Third World currency, the South must borrow dollars (at high interest rates), hold them in inventory, and, then, spend the dollars in the same countries that held the dollars in the first place. The Southern country pays for its imports of goods and services from the reserve center *with currency issued by that center*. Thus, the reserve center ends up exporting goods *and* accumulating financial reserves, financing its own exports without having to import goods of comparable value. Such a system fails to maintain effective global demand anywhere near full employment levels.

The ultimate solution to the financing problem has been known for a long time. The world needs an international currency bereft of nationality. The special drawing right (SDR) of the IMF is the logical choice as a world currency.[23] I doubt whether this evolution to a truly international currency will be complete before the year 2000. In the meantime the South will have to muddle through. Its massive private debt to the North may provide the necessary leverage to keep the global trading system afloat. The South could offer to service its present debt at an undiminished pace, with payments to be made in its local "soft" currency. Instead of dollars, Mexican pesos and Brazilian cruzeiros would pile up in New York and other Western banks. Since such currency presently is acceptable only in the home countries, these banks would have to be innovative in matching prospective Northern importers with Southern exporters; otherwise, the banks would be left holding the "soft" foreign currencies. (Of course, the Northern treasuries could purchase the currencies, but then the Northern governments would have to purchase goods from the South or simply hold the currency inventories, much as the South now holds inventories of dollars.) The use of the once "soft" currencies to purchase the products of the South would transfer real goods and services at minimal transaction costs, which is what a reliable international financial system is supposed to do in the first place.

If I am correct about the importance of technology and the accelerating ease of its transfer, information-gathering institutions in the North and the South are critical in the resumption of global economic expansion. Although there is a multitude of possible recommendations for institutional change, space limits my exposition to one overarching idea. Customs unions have had limited success even in the North. Though seeds for such unions have been planted in such areas as Latin America, probably their fruition will be a consequence of further industrialization rather than a cause. The most successful cooperative arrangements, be they South-North or South-South are likely to be bilateral or, at best, trilateral. Because of the important role of basic innovations, I see joint ventures between relatively sophisticated countries and raw materials–rich countries as the catalyst for development.[24] In joint ventures, two or more firms agree to provide diverse elements of production that are both necessary and complementary. In contrast to the usual multinational firm that simply markets its surpluses in a variety of nations, the joint venture implants new technology in the chosen country.

Joint ventures are extraordinarily flexible; they generally evolve to meet the specific needs of a country. Joint ventures in Africa where infrastructure is modest, for example, tend to be concentrated in transport; joint ventures in Asia tend to be more manufacturing oriented. The most common ventures are bilateral, use modern management practices, and usually are very innovative. Although the most immediate advantage of the joint venture for the developing country is increased production (often as a substitute for some imported product), the central long-term advantage derives from the transfer of an improved technology, even though that technology may be a standardized one, such as steelmaking. In a joint venture involving two Southern nations in the same region, a license arrangement could limit standardized production capacity to one nation while a second or third nation opens its market to the good in order to provide a sufficiently wide market to warrant the preferred scale of technology. Such an arrangement provides the characteristics of a customs union without the intricate and probably impossible political negotiations required to establish a sustainable customs union. A vertically integrated automotive industry, for example, might be established across several Latin American countries that could serve the Latin American market.

Governments can play a matchmaking role in any effort to encourage joint ventures. (Some firms will be government owned.) They can provide information on local resources, special skills, and financial capital sources. In the reach for the highest possible technology, even a capital-goods industry could be developed in improbable regions through the joint venture device since capital-goods factories require considerable scale and relatively long production runs to be self-financing. Finance, managerial abilities, and skilled labor unavailable in any one country are available across two or more nations.

▼   ▼   ▼

Global policies spelled out in great detail are not as important as an altered perception. There are some persons in the North with a "bunker-state" mentality. The same individuals who see bomb shelters as the preferred solution to the moral dilemma of nuclear war presumably would wish to take the global economy with them when *their* jobs and *their* industry are assaulted by the winds of change. However, spaceship earth is the only vehicle humans now share; global interdependence means that all of us will be in the same bunker if today's strongest insist upon surviving at the cost of bringing the system crashing down. Economically, tomorrow is already here: the steel industry is not American, it is global; the automobile is not GM, it is the world car; oil resources cannot be monopolized by the North, they belong to everyone on the planet; a computer in China can utilize the same softwear as one in Manhattan. To envision the once-privileged Northern economies as separate as well as unequal is to engage in a dangerous illusion.

18

A
SUMMING-UP

▼

*The needs of the poor must take priority over the desires of
the rich, and the rights of workers over the
maximization of profits.*

JOHN PAUL II, SPEECH IN CANADA, OCTOBER 1984

*We feel the Catholic Church ... is crying out for a theory of
how you overcome poverty... capitalism was designed to
answer that question. What Adam Smith wrote about was:
What is the cause of the wealth of nations?*

MICHAEL NOVAK,[1] QUOTED IN *BUSINESS WEEK*, NOVEMBER 12, 1984

*[The best state of human nature is one] in which while no one
is poor, no one desires to be richer nor has any reason to fear
being thrust back by the efforts of others to push themselves
forward.... There would be ... much room for improving the
Art of Living, and much more likelihood of its being improved,
when minds ceased to be engrossed by the art of getting on.*

JOHN STUART MILL, *PRINCIPLES OF POLITICAL ECONOMY*, 1848

Religion and economic recovery seemed to dominate the news
during the election year of 1984. More important, people voting out of
religious conviction had a significant influence on the 1984 presidential
and congressional elections, even more than in 1976 when "born-again"
Baptist Jimmy Carter was elected president. The Republicans had developed a base among evangelicals, and the Democrats had lost their
base among Catholics. In two campaigns, but especially in 1984, candidate Ronald W. Reagan courted the white fundamentalists or "evangelicals," people who describe themselves as "born-again Christians."
For the first time in U.S. history, the end of the world, or "Armageddon,"

became a campaign issue, when, during the second presidential debate, Ronald Reagan acknowledged "philosophical discussions" about the coincidence between current events and Biblical signs portending the last days. Gallup polls indicated that 79 percent of white evangelicals voted for Reagan, a "moral majority" whose influence greatly exceeded their representation as a small minority of the American population.

We have no way of knowing how much of the fundamentalists' apocalyptic vision Ronald Reagan believed. He may have simply used Moral Majority language as metaphor. One thing is clear: these Biblical interpretations dovetail with the defense of free-market capitalism and the "trickle-down" economic doctrine of the conservative Lay Commission on Catholic Social Teaching and the U.S. Economy. In sharp contrast to these Old Testament views are the New Testament perspectives of the Catholic bishops' pastoral letter released after the 1984 presidential election. Though the letter does not attack private property or capitalism as such, it argues that the right to private property is not absolute, but limited by concern for the common good. In this Biblical view, property is communal before it is private. "Economic justice" then is to be measured not by what it does for the rich or the middle classes, but by what it does for the poor in their midst. Beyond proposed reforms such as full-employment legislation, the document rejects the "trickle-down" doctrine of first-term Reaganomics.

ECONOMICS: PRESENT AND PAST IMPERFECT

With this contemporary conflict between two biblical interpretations— with emphases on different parts of the Bible—we have come full circle to our discussion of the relation of values and ethics to economics of Chapter 1. We said there that the very manner of organizing an economy often has religious origins. An ethical system legitimates the customary, command, competitive, and cooperative economies. The Bible has most influenced the West's world view, its widely shared set of beliefs about the individual's relationship to the natural world, to other individuals, and to the Divine. And yet, as we noted (perhaps prematurely), the place once occupied by religion has been taken over by science.

Even the Moral Majority seeks scientific paradigms consistent with its economic ethics. As we saw in Chapter 5, there existed no conflict between science and religion among most American economists during the nineteenth century. Their unifying theme was that God had established the right to private property and its accumulation as a natural law. The Social Darwinism that peaked around the turn of the century was the same kind of complex combination of science and religion that characterizes the views of the Moral Majority and the Lay Commission

of 1984. Creationism as a competing scientific paradigm does not conflict with contemporary Social Darwinism any more than it did at the
turn of the century. The Western religion that took on the coloration of
competitive capitalism during the Protestant Reformation and monopolistic capitalism under Social Darwinism returned during the early
1980s. The competitive version might be seen as an "ideal," whereas the
Darwinian defense of monopoly capitalism is a defense of something
closer to reality.

There is still another thought from Chapter 5 that retains contemporary relevance. We said that when science fails, it falters as faith, and
there is a deeper retreat into religion and Spencer's Unknowable. We
noted in Chapter 13 how economic science had failed to explain a
solution to the Phillips curve trade-off of the 1950s and 1960s as well as
the simultaneous inflation and high unemployment of the 1970s. Although the orthodox neoclassical paradigm provided the analytics for
Lafferism and first-term Reaganomics, George Gilder served the White
House God and economics on the same platter. "To overcome it is
necessary to have faith, to recover the belief in chance and providence,
in the ingenuity of free and God-fearing men. This belief will allow us
to see the best way of helping the poor, the way to understand the
truths of equality before God . . ."[2] Gilder even updates the stories of
American clergyman Horatio Alger and the benign universe that we
discussed in Chapter 5. As we said, in Alger's stories wealth was the
outcome of chance, appropriate acquaintances, and deservedness. The
Gilded Age (c. 1870–1910) thrived on these extensions of the Old Testament stories of Noah, Abraham, Joseph, and David. To Gilder, economic innovation requires an ascendancy above narrow rationality and
the embrace of religious values, no matter how unconscious the worship of God. Virtue and chance meld as ". . . the lucky man is seen as
somehow blessed. His good chance—and society's redemption—is
providence." If the "miraculous prodigality of chance" is replaced by a
"closed system of human planning," all is lost because "success is always unpredictable."[3] Essentially the "moral spark" of the Gilded Age
was being offered to the Gildered Age.

Of course, economic science evolved and so did economies. In
Chapter 3 we traced the slow evolution of the market economy out of
the failures of feudalism and mercantilism. The international exchange
of goods was made possible by the emergence of physical surpluses
from the specialization of labor. The value theory of Adam Smith, the
attempt to explain the true worth of things, came out of a need to place
a "price" upon the surplus or net value added. The Industrial Revolution
involved changes in technology so dramatic that theretofore undreamed-of levels of value added were generated. It was the spread of

innovations and technology to the United States in the mid-nineteenth century that ushered in the Gilded Age. The discretionary income that was households' counterpart to surplus production generated a middle class that extended the possibility of economic choice beyond the doorsteps of the rich. Neoclassical economics was directed at the behavior of the upper middle class in England, behavior described by upper-middle-class economists such as Alfred Marshall. The paradigmatic refinements still were in line with Newtonian mechanics and used the Newtonian calculus. The harmony of markets afforded by the smoothness of the mathematical functions was a major step toward making economics a metaphor of Newtonian natural science, a hardening of the metaphor that was completed during the era of positive science.

It always has been the role of "radical economists" to call attention to the gap between reality and the prevailing scientific paradigm. Karl Marx saw instability, monopoly capital, and worker alienation while the classicals idealized the natural self-adjusting characteristic of markets. Thorstein Veblen observed the reality of the Robber Barons maximizing profits rather than production and bemoaned the rising importance of salesmanship. More recently, John Kenneth Galbraith has continued Veblen's attack on the neoclassical paradigm and suggests that production in the supra-surplus economies requires a diversion of enormous resources and a devotion to marketing and advertising so that the supra-discretionary income earners will spend rather than save. Finally, the New Radical economics of the Left extended the Marxian method and tone to the economic and social problems of the 1960s.

KEYNES AND THE POST-KEYNESIANS

Thus far, the most serious challenge to an orthodoxy ruled by dated social values and increasing professionalization is the economics (in one form or another) of John Maynard Keynes. As we have told the story in Chapters 7 and 8, Keynesianism fell on its own cutting edge. The *General Theory* was bastardized by well-meaning apostles until the theory bore more resemblance to neoclassical economics than the neoclassical heretic Keynes could have ever intended. The failure of bastardized Keynesianism led to the monetarist counterrevolution that became a canon of first-term Reaganomics. Only after neoclassical Lafferism and monetarism were merged into Reaganomics did George Gilder's embrace of the neo-Austrian critique of neoclassical economics exert influence. From the vantage point of the neo-Austrian version of the cosmic machine of the market, Gilder went beyond the last of the celestial spheres. As luck would have it, only entrepreneurs go to Heaven.

The post-Keynesians, or the more literal interpreters of Keynes, would not fault the neo-Austrian critique of neoclassical method, for they are in agreement on the unrealism of Newtonian equilibria. The post-Keynesians would not even fault Gilder for being even more unabashed than the Austrians in seeing value judgments necessarily embedded in economic reality and therefore in economics. Once we recall that Keynes was responding to the reality of the Great Depression and placed policy before theory, we can appreciate why the post-Keynesians want to have their theory and reality, too. The post-Keynesians' severe disagreement with the Austrians stems from the Austrian view of *economic* reality. This is so even though Keynes is forever writing of the entrepreneur as the key decision maker in the private economy. In Keynes the *mistakes* of the entrepreneur cause depressions; in Austrian economics the unfettered entrepreneur guarantees prosperity.

As we are in an age in which science is no longer worshipped for its own sake, economists need not be apologetic if they succumb to a new sense of realism. We do not have to accept the new Social Darwinism in order to allow ethical judgments to enter social science. Rather, if Joan Robinson were alive, she would say that the economists can best combat the new Social Darwinism by elevating the social consciousness of the society. Lives are at stake, and the modern world demands an economics tailored to human needs, one that recognizes that our behavior—especially our social behavior—is both more sophisticated and more unruly than that of particles or insects. And, no doubt, human welfare is closely allied to per-capita real income and the distribution of such income. Thus, the post-Keynesian stress upon the income distribution brings us closer to a human science.

Presently, post-Keynesian economics perhaps is best known as a research program that recommends various forms of incomes policies for stabilizing capitalism. As I have established in the closing chapters, the school is much richer and more diverse than such a narrow view. Indeed, I have shown how the ideas of Joseph Schumpeter, an economist in competition with his contemporary Keynes but for the most part banished from his own neo-Austrian school, can be utilized to generalize the post-Keynesian long run. Within historical time, the time that concerns post-Keynesians, Keynes's entrepreneurs do come on to the scene roughly each half century, however briefly. Their butterfly-like presence helps to explain why small monopolies dominate the early growth of an industry and giant monopoly power characterizes the industry's sunset years. A truly scientific economics paradigm can no more disavow history than it can ethical judgments.

Will post-Keynesian theory become the new paradigm? I cannot answer that question: by definition it must be answered collectively by the scientific community. We can state the reasons why it perhaps has the best chance. (Again, economists collectively will decide, and even the euthanasia of economists cannot be ruled out.) First, post-Keynesianism is rooted in the history of prior dominant economics schools—the classical and the Keynesian. It skips only neoclassical economics. Second, its methodological critique conforms with that of the new radicals of *both* the Left and the Right. Third, as with Keynes, the policy prescriptions of the school are running ahead of the development and refinement of its economic theory. Even so, the theoretical advances are gaining on policy. Fourth, the main contemporary competing minority school, the monetarist, has had the opportunity to experiment with its prescribed policies, and these policies have failed to live up to their promises.

Third, capitalism—now state capitalism, in which the dominant (industrial) sector enjoys government protection—faces its third crisis since World War II. The use of monetarist policy revived the Phillips curve trade-off between inflation and unemployment that undid bastardized Keynesianism, an anomaly left unresolved by the monetarist experiments. Reaganomics aggravated the problems of poverty, unsustainable budget deficits, high real rates of interest, and a global debt crisis. Unless economists have answers to these problems, economics as a discipline will die. More important, there is the possibility that state capitalism will not survive either. Keynes faced the prospect of a similar outcome, death for old-fashioned capitalism. Then, as now, the defenders of capitalism were among its worst enemies.

POLITICAL ECONOMY, AGAIN

Much of the foregoing discussion indicates that a clean line between the political, social, and economic is difficult to draw. A number of leaders in economics, such as Leontief, suggested that artificially compartmentalizing knowledge is misleading at best. Adolph Lowe and Robert Heilbroner have outlined an ambitious arch-building program across the artificial boundaries of economics, political science, and sociology in order "to produce a unified conception of society as a seamless web." [4] Heilbroner believes that such an interdisciplinary approach would enable us to understand the process of social change more thoroughly than is now possible. Already several economists have suggested that economics must be viewed as a process rather than a series of improbable equilibrium points. Heilbroner's cross-linked matrix of activity is useful in forcing the specialist to recognize the multiple ways in which one simple variable runs through society.

In the Heilbroner schema, the individual plays several roles: a factor of production, a consumer, a citizen, and a social role player. As a consumer, the person votes with dollars; as a citizen, the person votes in the political process. The two actions are interrelated. Citizens can vote for the redistribution of income and thus affect the net returns to themselves as factors of production.

Only the state has sufficient resources to change the national income distribution. Thus, the citizen gives the state the authority to alter the distribution, and the state becomes a regulator of economic processes. The business firm has substantial "dollar votes" that it can use to influence public policy by lobbying and political influence. The corporation may have political power that is disproportionate to the number of people it represents. Sufficiently outraged, the citizen as voter can change the rules that the corporation plays by or else compel the government to exercise its authority in enforcing the laws designed to lessen corporate power.

This mapping of social processes suggests that economic inequities and ecological problems created by uneven economic growth require redress through the political process, changes in motivation and lifestyles, or some combination of the two. We could, of course, go on to analyze all types of further interactions and feedbacks.

Although this topography would seem familiar to Adam Smith, the Lockean-Smithian view of liberty tied freedom of the individual to private property. Property, in turn, was an inalienable right. No social obligations accompanied rights to ownership. This conception fit well an economy of large numbers of small entrepreneurs. Freedom implied the autonomous person.

As we have seen, industrialized economies have subsequently become far more complex. There is a smaller number of dominant industrial and financial corporations, competition has been largely replaced by administered prices and wages, the government is part of big business, advance planning characterizes industrial manufacturing, and corporate ownership of the giants increasingly is divorced from management. The owner of capital can only be described as a swashbuckling individual innovator in the sunrise industries now falling prey to the giants. The corporation itself, however, inherited the autonomy without obligation that was once the sole privilege of the individual. By contrast, labor was weak, so it was impelled to organize. Consumer complaints led to governmental regulation—government became responsible for corporations that otherwise had no specific civic duties. Business became less private, more public. It was not so much freedom that was redefined as the conditions under which liberty was otherwise handicapped.

THE VOICE OF THE MASTERS

We have not wandered very far from the masters. Adam Smith did not ignore the possibility that economic power could corrupt; he simply bred an unfounded optimism. Smith did not deny the love that would lead to gifts. But, in his time, the concern was with getting the engine of industry started, not with the inability of the engine to provide *all* of people's needs.

Alfred Marshall did not lack an ethical system, nor did he lack compassion. The problem is that his apostles removed all the social variables from his engine of analysis. The engine itself is now only a caricature of Newtonian capitalism. Marx and Veblen certainly anticipated the problems of income distribution, excessive corporate power, and worker alienation. The new radicals of the Left were not the first to recognize these maladies.

Normal science has stripped John Maynard Keynes of his social progressiveness and his moral intent. But Keynes's design still is there, in the *General Theory*, for all to read. In fact, a perusal of the masters would be a good start toward formulating a new economics.

A new vision is critical. The control of inflation without sacrificing human welfare has failed, and so have the welfare system, law enforcement, and environmental protection. There is the danger that too many failures will be fatal to society. Even if all of these problems are solved, there will be no Golden Age. The real-life complexities of the past, present, and future give us only one certainty: that knowledge will continue to be a series of endless horizons.

NOTES

CHAPTER 1
VALUES AND ECONOMIC SYSTEMS

1. Georges Duby, *The Early Growth of the European Economy*, trans. H. B. Clarke (Ithaca, N.Y.: Cornell University Press, 1974), pp. 32–33.

2. Henry William Spiegel, *The Growth of Economic Thought* (Englewood Cliffs, N.J.: Prentice-Hall, 1971), p. 49.

3. John T. Gilchrist, *The Church and Economic Activity in the Middle Ages* (New York: St. Martin's Press, 1969), pp. 50–58.

4. The medieval mind never tired of dwelling on sin, death, and hell. This gloomy creed produced some devotees of original sin, such as Margery Kempe, whose faithfulness is recorded in Louise Collis, *Memoirs of a Medieval Woman* (New York: Harper & Row, 1983).

5. Douglas C. North and Robert Paul Thomas, *The Rise of the Western World: A New Economic History* (Cambridge, Eng.: Cambridge University Press, 1973), p. 12.

6. Milton Friedman, *Capitalism and Freedom* (Chicago: Phoenix Books, 1963), p. 9.

7. Adam Smith, *An Inquiry into the Nature and Causes of the Wealth of Nations*, ed. Edwin Cannan (New York: Random House, 1937), p. 726.

8. Friedman, *Capitalism and Freedom*, p. 133.

9. Adam Smith, *The Theory of Moral Sentiments*, ed. Ernest Rhys (London: Everyman's Library, 1910), p. 162.

CHAPTER 2
THE NATURE OF SCIENCE AND THE ECONOMICS PARADIGM

1. Thomas S. Kuhn, *The Structure of Scientific Revolutions*, 2d ed., enl. (Chicago: University of Chicago Press, 1970), p. 176.

2. Blaise Pascal, *Pensées*, fragment 72, trans. W. F. Trotter (London: J. M. Dent & Sons, 1908), pp. 17–18. Published by Everyman's Library and reprinted by permission of E. P. Dutton.

CHAPTER 3
ADAM SMITH AND THE MARKET ECONOMY

1. The excerpt from Rand's novel is a straightforward description of caricature capitalism. It is made by a character in the book, Hank Rearden, who is on trial for the illegal sale of a metal alloy that he has created and that has been placed under government control.

2. For a fully detailed account of the material discussed here, see Robert S. Lopez, *The Commercial Revolution of the Middle Ages, 950–1350* (Englewood Cliffs, N.J.: Prentice-Hall, 1971).

3. For original data and sources, see Douglas C. North and Robert Paul Thomas, *The Rise of the Western World: A New Economic History* (Cambridge, Eng.: Cambridge University Press, 1973), pp. 71–74.

4. Economist John H. Hotson (University of Waterloo, Canada) has suggested to me this scenario for the breakup of the "monopoly power" of the Catholic Church. I also am grateful for suggestions by Thomas W. Bonsor of the Center for Economic Education, Eastern Washington State College, which clarified much of my thinking on this period. Clearly, Margery Kempe was one of the faithful who deplored the accelerating sale of indulgences, especially after 1378, when there were rival popes, one at Avignon and one in Rome. See Louise Collis, *Memoirs of a Medieval Woman* (New York: Harper & Row, 1983), p. 23.

CHAPTER 4
THE INDUSTRIAL REVOLUTION AND THE OTHER CLASSICALS

1. William Rees, *Industry Before the Industrial Revolution* (Cardiff: University of Wales Press, 1968), vol. 1, p. 72.

2. These data are derived from the discussion in R. M. Hartwell, *The Industrial Revolution and Economic Growth* (London: Methuen & Co., 1971), pp. 120–126.

3. For additional names and details, see A. E. Musson and Eric Robinson, *Science and Technology in the Industrial Revolution* (Manchester, Eng.: Manchester University Press, 1969).

4. Rodes Boyson, "Industrialization and the Life of the Lancashire Factory Worker," in *The Long Debate on Poverty* (Surrey, Eng.: Unwin Brothers, for the Institute of Economic Affairs, 1972), pp. 69–70.

5. Richard L. Tames, ed., *Documents of the Industrial Revolution, 1750–1850* (London: Hutchinson Educational, 1971), p. 96.

6. Thomas R. Malthus, *On Population*, ed. Gertrude Himmelfarb (New York: Random House, Modern Library, 1960), p. 13.

7. Peter H. Lindert, "The Malthusian Case," unpublished note, 1984.

8. Percy Bysshe Shelley, "Queen Mab," in *The Complete Poetical Works of Shelley*, ed. George Edward Woodberry (Boston: Houghton Mifflin & Co., Cambridge edition, 1901).

9. Charles Dickens, *Hard Times*, introd. by G. K. Chesterton (New York: E. P. Dutton, 1966), p. 61.

10. Ibid., p. 3.

11. Ibid., p. 68.

12. Ibid., pp. 68–69.

13. John Stuart Mill, *Principles of Political Economy*, ed. J. M. Robson (Toronto: University of Toronto Press, 1965), vol. 2, p. 105.

CHAPTER 5
THE "AMERICAN DREAM"

1. Newton's formula for this force (F) is $F = G \cdot (M\text{sun} \cdot M\text{planet})/(\text{Distance}^2)$, where G is a number, the mysterious "gravitational constant," and the Ms are the masses, respectively, of the sun and the planet in question. Most constants such as G in the natural sciences are no longer "mysterious" when equated with a collection of natural constants such as π, e, numbers, etc.

Again, the paradigm left many loose ends to be tied up by normal science academics. In deriving his laws of planetary motion, Newton neglected all "gravitational attraction" except that between the planets and the sun. This, of course, ignores the "gravitational influence" of planets upon each other. Telescopic observation therefore yielded only an approximate agreement between Newton's theory and its application.

2. A simplification from Newton's second law provides an illustration of both equilibrium and the importance of time change and consequently the calculus in mechanics. The force required to keep a heavy ball on a string moving in a full circle is:

$$\text{Force}^* = \frac{(\text{Mass}) \times (\text{Velocity})^2 \times (\text{Change in Time})}{\text{Radius of Circle}}$$

The asterisk (*) here denotes the value of the variable as an equilibrium value. For very small time intervals, we can assume that the change in time is zero and can write in a more simple way,

$$\text{Force}^* = \frac{(\text{Mass}) \times (\text{Velocity})^2}{\text{Radius}}$$

3. For a more useful application of the entropy law to economics, see Nicholas Georgescu-Roegen, *The Entropy Law and the Economic Process* (Cambridge, Mass.: Harvard University Press, 1971).

4. Charles Schuchert and Clara Mae LeVene, *O. C. Marsh, Pioneer in Paleontology* (New Haven: Yale University Press, 1940), p. 247.

5. Richard Hofstadter, *Social Darwinism in American Thought*, rev. ed. (Boston: Beacon Press, 1955), p. 51.

6. Ibid., p. 57.

7. William J. Ghent, *Our Benevolent Feudalism* (New York: Macmillan Co., 1902), p. 29.

8. This material is summarized from Joseph Dorfman, *The Economic Mind in American Civilization, 1606–1865* (New York: Augustus M. Kelley, 1966), vol. 2, pp. 695–767.

9. Andrew Carnegie, *Autobiography of Andrew Carnegie* (Boston: Houghton Mifflin Co., 1920), p. 327.

CHAPTER 6
ALFRED MARSHALL AND THE U.S.A. PURITANS

1. See Axel Leijonhufvud, *On Keynesian Economics and the Economics of Keynes* (New York: Oxford University Press, 1968), p. 394.

2. For an excellent and entertaining treatment of the lingering influence of Descartes upon economic "fiction," see Piero V. Mini, *Philosophy and Economics: The Origins and Development of Economic Theory* (Gainesville: University Presses of Florida, 1974).

3. In the calculus, ds represent infinitesimally small incremental changes so that the rate of change in pleasure can be written as dP/dt, where dP is the small increment of pleasure and dt is the time unit. Although the ds are infinitesimally small, the resultant ratio, such as dP/dt, is not necessarily small. One-zillionth divided by three-zillionths still is 1:3.

The early marginalist economist William Stanley Jevons provides an example of both the calculus and the marginal concept. Jevons denotes a as the quantity of corn held by one person and b as a quantity of beef held by another. If the two persons exchange x of corn for y of beef and the market is purely competitive, there is one ratio of exchange, $dy/dx = y/x$, which is in differential notation. After exchange, one person has $(a - x)$ of corn and y of beef, while the second has x of corn and $(b - y)$ of beef. If $\phi_1(a - x)$ and $\psi_1(y)$, $\phi_2(x)$ and $\psi_2(b - y)$ are the *marginal utilities* of corn and beef to persons 1 and 2 respectively, then Jevons's conditions of maximum satisfaction for each of the two parties in a barter exchange is given by $\phi_1(a - x)/\psi_1(y) = y/x = \phi_2(x)/\psi_2(b - y)$. That is, the two persons are satisfied when the ratio of the marginal utilities is inversely proportional to the ratio of exchange.

4. For a similar description of the economic man concept, see Frank Knight, *Risk, Uncertainty and Profit* (New York: Harper & Row, 1921), pp. 77–78.

5. Latter-day users of perfectly competitive assumptions do take risk into account but find that their basic conclusions are not changed except for the explanation of profits. Frank Knight defended the neoclassical paradigm on the basis of the validity of consumer sovereignty. Producers, in a world of uncertainty, are rewarded with profits if they correctly anticipate what products in which quantities consumers will choose to purchase. Profits come then to producers as a residual, after all other costs of production have been met, and only if consumers actually purchase what the producers have manufactured.

6. Alfred Marshall, *Money, Credit and Commerce* (London: Macmillan & Co., 1923), p. ii.

7. Joan Robinson, *Economic Philosophy* (Chicago: Aldine Publishing Co., 1962), p. 74.

8. A reaction to this interpretation of Marshall gave rise to the only uniquely American economics school, the "institutionalists." (See Chapter 11.) Some economists contend that during the 1920s the institutionalists were as influential as the neoclassicists, both in and out of the universities.

9. Joseph A. Schumpeter, *Ten Great Economists* (New York: Oxford University Press, 1965), p. 95.

10. Alfred Marshall, *Principles of Economics*, 8th ed. (London: Macmillan & Co., 1920), p. 102.

11. John Maynard Keynes, *Essays in Biography* (London: Macmillan & Co., 1933), p. 212.

12. H. S. Foxwell, "The Economic Movement in England," *Quarterly Journal of Economics* 2 (1887): 92.

13. Dudley Dillard, *Economic Development of the North Atlantic Community* (Englewood Cliffs, N.J.: Prentice-Hall, 1967), p. 364.

14. Robert Heilbroner, *The Wordly Philosophers*, 3d ed., rev. (New York: Simon & Schuster, 1967), p. 195.

15. Frederick Lewis Allen, *The Lords of Creation* (New York and London: Harper & Brothers, 1935), p. 87.

16. Ibid., p. 91.

17. *Tribune*, November 9, 1877. Also quoted in Lewis Cory, *The House of Morgan* (New York: Harper & Brothers, 1930), p. 80.

18. John McVickar, *Outlines of Political Economy* (New York: Wilder & Campbell, 1825), p. 69.

19. Quoted by Fritz Redlich, *Steeped in Two Cultures* (New York and Evanston, Ill.: Harper & Row, 1971), p. 44.

20. See D. McCloskey, "Did Victorian Britain Fail?" *Economic History Review* 23 (December 1970): 446–459.

21. Thomas S. Kuhn, *The Structure of Scientific Revolutions*, 2d ed., enl. (Chicago: University of Chicago Press, 1970), p. 64.

CHAPTER 7
J. M. KEYNES: THE END OF FRUGALITY

1. Arthur Pigou, *Theory of Unemployment* (London: Macmillan & Co., 1933), p. 252.

2. Ibid.

3. Lionel Robbins, *The Great Depression* (London: Macmillan & Co., 1934), p. 186.

4. Among the various wages and conditions reported in 1932 are: in Pennsylvania, wages in saw mills were 5¢ an hour, in brick and tile manufacturing 6¢, and in general contracting 7.5¢; in Tennessee, some workers were paid as little as $2.40 for a fifty-hour week; in Kentucky, miners were eating the weeds that cows ate; in West Virginia, people were robbing stores for food; in California, a child that had been living on refuse starved to death (reported in Arthur Schlesinger, Jr., *The Crisis of the Old Order* [Boston: Houghton Mifflin Co., 1957], pp. 249–250). President Franklin Roosevelt came into office on March 4, 1933, and closed all private banks that week by declaring a "bank holiday." This action was necessary to prevent the complete collapse of the American banking system.

5. John Maynard Keynes, *The Economic Consequences of the Peace* (London: Macmillan & Co., 1919), p. 22.

6. See Robert G. Fabian, "Cultural Influences on Economic Theory," *Journal of Economic Issues* 5 (September 1971): 56.

7. Keynes himself drew no distinction between the classical and neoclassical schools. His term *classical economists* included Smith, Ricardo, their direct de-

scendants, plus their more distant descendants—J. S. Mill, Marshall, and Pigou. The common bond of the two schools is their faith in and reliance upon free market adjustments, but of course there were other differences. Hereafter, my references to the combination of classical and neoclassical theories will be called *neoclassical economics* (to properly suggest its more analytically refined state) wherever the discussion relates to free market adjustments.

8. The late Joan Robinson gave suggestions that greatly improved my discussion of the evolution of Keynes's pre–*General Theory* thinking as well as directed me away from some errors in interpretation of the subtler aspects of Keynes's thought. The late Abba P. Lerner provided similar guidance.

9. A number of American economists, for example, wrote popular ("nonscientific") articles advocating expansionary monetary and fiscal policies during the Great Depression. See J. Ronnie Davis, *The New Economics and the Old Economists* (Ames: Iowa State University Press, 1971).

10. Joseph Schumpeter, "Keynes the Economist," in *The New Economics*, ed. Seymour E. Harris (New York: Alfred A. Knopf, 1952), p. 76.

11. Joan Robinson, *Economic Philosophy* (Chicago: Aldine Publishing Co., 1962), p. 79.

12. To R. F. Harrod, August 27, 1935. In *The Collected Writings of John Maynard Keynes*, edited by Donald Moggridge (New York: St. Martin's Press, 1973), vol. 8, p. 548.

13. L. R. Klein, *The Keynesian Revolution*, 2d ed. (New York: Macmillan Co., 1966), p. 56.

14. Robert L. Heilbroner, *The Worldly Philosophers*, 3d ed. (New York: Simon & Schuster, 1967), p. 246.

15. The details of policy as applied theory during these years are provided in E. Ray Canterbery, *Economics on a New Frontier* (Belmont, Calif.: Wadsworth Publishing Co., 1968).

CHAPTER 8
THE BASTARD KEYNESIANS AND THE MONETARISTS

1. J. K. Galbraith, *Money: Whence It Came, Where It Went* (Boston: Houghton Mifflin Co., 1975), pp. 217–218.

2. The description of these Keynesians as illegitimate heirs of Keynes can be traced to the pen of Joan Robinson in *Economic Heresies: Some Old Fashioned Questions in Economic Theory* (New York: Basic Books, 1971), pp. 88, 95. Earlier, Sidney Weintraub had pleaded for the abandonment of the neoclassical version of Keynes in *Classical Keynesianism, Monetary Theory, and the Price Level* (Philadelphia: Chilton, 1961).

3. The entertaining story of how Keynes came to America is related by John Kenneth Galbraith in *The Age of Uncertainty* (Boston: Houghton Mifflin Co., 1977), pp. 211–226.

4. Paul A. Samuelson, "Interactions Between the Multiplier Analysis and the

Principle of Acceleration," *Review of Economics and Statistics* 21, No. 2 (May 1939): 75–78.

5. Hicks's dispatch was delivered in "Mr. Keynes and the Classics, A Suggested Reinterpretation," *Econometrica* 5 (1937): 147–159.

6. See Alvin H. Hansen, *A Guide to Keynes* (New York: McGraw-Hill, 1953), pp. 140–153.

7. See Don Patinkin, *Money, Interest and Prices*, 2d ed. (New York: Harper & Row, 1965).

8. Hicks's altered view appears in *The Crisis in Keynesian Economics* (New York: Basic Books, 1974). It is good reading.

9. John M. Keynes, "The General Theory of Employment," *Quarterly Journal of Economics* 51 (February 1937): 209–223.

10. Robert M. Solow's seminal article is "A Contribution to the Theory of Economic Growth," *Quarterly Journal of Economics* 70 (1956): 65–94.

11. Marshall Jevons, *Murder at the Margin* (Glen Ridge, N.J.: Thomas H. Horton & Daughters, 1977).

12. Many of the biographical facts about Friedman in these pages were gleaned from the fascinating little book by Leonard Silk, *The Economists* (New York: Basic Books, 1976), pp. 43–85.

13. Ayn Rand, *For the New Intellectual: The Philosophy of Ayn Rand* (New York: Random House, 1961), pp. 62–63.

14. For elaborations, see Milton Friedman, "A Theoretical Framework of Monetary Analysis," *Journal of Political Economy* 78 (1970): 193–238; and "Symposium on Friedman's Theoretical Framework" *Journal of Political Economy* 80 (September/October 1972): 837–950.

CHAPTER 9
THE ERA OF POSITIVE ECONOMIC SCIENCE

1. Quoted by Warner Wick in "Frank Knight, Philosopher at Large," *Journal of Political Economy* 81 (May/June 1973): 514.

2. John Maynard Keynes, *The General Theory of Employment, Interest and Money* (New York: Harcourt, Brace & World, 1936), p. 378.

3. See, for example, Richard Olson, ed., *Science as Metaphor* (Belmont, Calif.: Wadsworth Publishing Co., 1971), p. 232.

4. Vincent Tarascio, "Value Judgments and Economic Science," *Journal of Economic Issues* 5 (March 1971): 101. The way in which professional values are sustained and diffused is explained in E. Ray Canterbery and Robert J. Burkhardt, "What Do We Mean by Asking Whether Economics Is a Science?" in Alfred S. Eichner, ed., *Why Economics Is Not Yet a Science* (Armonk, N.Y.: M. E. Sharpe, 1983), pp. 15–40.

5. Dodgson, Charles Lutmidge [Lewis Carroll], *Alice's Adventures in Wonderland and Through the Looking-Glass and What Alice Found There*, ed. Roger Lancelyn Green (London: Macmillan & Co., 1930), pp. 167–168.

6. The fact that economists have identified "positive economics" with Friedman does not mean that Friedman is a logical positivist in the tradition of the Vienna school. Indeed, as Canterbery and Burkhardt, "What Do We Mean . . . ," maintain, economists in general have not followed the "scientific" rules of logical positivism.

7. See ibid., for the sources of these "findings."

8. Both quotations from Friedman are from his *Essays in Positive Economics* (Chicago: University of Chicago Press, 1953), p. 4.

9. Milton Friedman, *The Optimum Quantity of Money* (Chicago: Aldine Publishing Co., 1969), p. 67.

10. Friedman's methodology is discussed in far more detail in William J. Frazer, Jr., and Lawrence A. Boland, "An Essay on the Foundations of Friedman's Methodology," *American Economic Review* 73 (March 1983): 129–144. If one examines all of Friedman's works, contend Frazer and Boland, Friedman is not a positivist at all. Nevertheless, economists did take seriously Friedman's *Essays in Positive Economics*, and if he did not mean it, the selection of "positive" in the title was an injudicious choice.

11. A. W. Coats has presented some economists' alternative formulations of positive economics. See his "The Role of Value Judgments in Economics," Research Monograph 7, mimeographed (Charlottesville: University of Virginia, Thomas Jefferson Center for Studies in Political Economy, May 1964), pp. 15–16.

12. Readers wanting more detail on this issue are directed to E. Ray Canterbery and Philip Sorensen, "Positive Science and Economics" (Paper presented at the History of Economics Society Conference, Chapel Hill, N.C., May 30, 1974).

13. If the ether did exist, the motion of the earth through this medium should be detectable because the difference in the velocity of light (186,000 miles per second) moving toward the earth and away from it would be the velocity of the earth in space. In a measurement taken at such an angle that the velocity of earth itself could be added in Newtonian fashion to the velocity of light, calculations by A. Michelson and E. Morley gave the unexpected and inexplicable outcome that the speed of light *plus* the speed of the earth was still just equal to the velocity of light alone.

14. This follows from Einstein's defining a *time interval* as the distance traveled between the source of a light emission and its viewer divided by the speed of light. In word-algebra, Einstein's time definition = distance to light source ÷ speed of light. A time interval, the duration of a second, is not therefore absolute and invariable. The "time" at which an event is observed depends upon the distance of the viewer from the event. Two viewers at different places will calculate different times. The greater the distance, the "longer" the time it takes for light to reach the observer. The duration of a second is relative.

15. This does not mean that there are ultimately no differences in scientific validity between the observations made from different reference points because "all things are relative'" and hence simply a matter of an observer's point of view. Such an idea is a vulgarization of Einstein. He is adding to conventional physics the notion that phenomena are interdependent in space and time in such a way that an observation about phenomenon A can be made only in terms of its relative position to phenomenon B.

16. In the words of historian John Lukacs, "Physicists have now found that while they can reasonably predict the average reactions of great numbers of electrons

in an experiment, they cannot predict what a single electron will do, and not even when it will do it." Olson, *Science as Metaphor*, p. 294.

17. Barbara R. Bergmann, "Have Economists Failed?" (Presidential Address to the Eastern Economic Association, Albany, N.Y., October 27, 1974).

18. E. H. Phelps Brown, "The Underdevelopment of Economics," *Economic Journal* 82 (March 1972): 3–4.

19. Wassily Leontief, "Theoretical Assumptions and Nonobserved Facts," *American Economic Review* 61 (March 1971): 2.

20. The National Science Foundation supports, with federal government funds, research done in colleges and universities.

21. James H. Blackman, "The Outlook for Economics," *Southern Economic Journal* 37 (April 1971): 386.

22. Joan Robinson, *Freedom and Necessity* (New York: Random House, Vintage, 1970), p. 122.

23. Ibid., p. 120.

24. Robert Brown, *Explanation in Social Science* (Chicago: Aldine Publishing Co., 1963), pp. 178–188.

25. Marc J. Roberts, "An Unsimple Matter of Choice," *Saturday Review*, January 22, 1972, p. 46.

26. Friedman, *Essays in Positive Economics*, pp. 41–42.

27. See Joan Robinson, *Economic Philosophy* (Chicago: Aldine Publishing Co., 1962), p. 23.

28. Einstein also was able to give Newton's second law an entirely new meaning through Einstein's famous solution, $E = mc^2$. Of course, the mathematics was preceded by Einstein's intuitive insight.

29. I assure you that I have no inherent bias against the use of mathematics in the social sciences. The shortcomings to which I allude in the contemporary use of mathematics come from the historical role of mathematics in the natural sciences. The blame does not rest upon the shoulders of mathematics. Differential equations—those used in thermodynamics—still are useful, but *qualitative* variables and adjustments should directly enter the equations. Again, the fault is not with the mathematics; it is with the false belief that mathematics must also be mechanical. Ultimately, social science will require a new mathematics.

30. Alfred Marshall, *Principles of Economics*, 8th ed. (London: Macmillan & Co., 1920), p. 577.

31. Joan Robinson, "What Has Become of the Keynesian Revolution?" *Challenge* 16 (January/February 1974): 9.

CHAPTER 10
PARADIGM LOST: KARL MARX

1. See Thomas Kuhn, *The Structure of Scientific Revolutions*, 2d ed., enl. (Chicago: University of Chicago Press, 1970), p. 91.

2. If Galbraith and Boulding are on the outskirts of the profession, so to speak, then how is it that they were elected presidents of the American Economic

Association, economics' leading professional society? I can only guess at the answer. Boulding had already established himself as a highly regarded technician before he "left the fold." Veblen's, and now Galbraith's, public following is so large they could not be politely ignored. Moreover, nominations for the presidency are made by an executive committee of the AEA noticeably scarce of apostle membership. Only one nominee plus write-ins appears upon the AEA membership ballot.

3. Robert C. Tucker, ed., *The Marx-Engels Reader* (New York: W. W. Norton & Co., 1972), p. xix.

4. See ibid., pp. xix–xx.

5. Karl Marx and Friedrich Engels, "The Communist Manifesto," in *Capital, The Communist Manifesto, and Other Writings*, ed. Max Eastman (New York: Random House, 1932), p. 315.

6. Moreover, contrary to common opinion, Marx was well acquainted with a modern tool of positive economics—namely, mathematics. In fact, he produced about 1,000 handwritten pages of mathematical manuscripts from about 1858 to his death in 1883. About half of these materials deal with differential calculus. Although he may originally have written many of the concepts in *Capital* in terms of differential equations, he apparently believed that the calculus was inappropriate for his type of historical analysis, and it does not appear in the published work. Toward the end of his life, Marx became interested in finite mathematics, which would have been more applicable. See Leon Smolinski, "Karl Marx and Mathematical Economics," *Journal of Political Economy* 81 (September/October 1973): 1189–1204.

7. Karl Marx, *Capital* (Moscow: Foreign Language Publishing House, 1961), vol. 1, pp. 713–714.

8. Karl Marx, *Economic and Philosophic Manuscripts of 1844* (Moscow: Progress Publishers, 1959), p. 69.

9. See Paul Baran and Paul M. Sweezy, *Monopoly Capital* (New York: Monthly Review Press, 1966).

CHAPTER 11
THE ICONOCLASTS: VEBLEN AND GALBRAITH

1. Thorstein Veblen, *The Theory of the Leisure Class* (New York: Viking Press, 1931), p. 40.

2. Ibid.

3. Harry G. Johnson, "The Keynesian Revolution and the Monetarist Counter-Revolution," *American Economic Review* 61 (May 1971): 3.

4. Thorstein Veblen, *The Place of Science in Modern Civilization and Other Essays* (New York: B. W. Huelisch, 1919), p. 193.

5. Karl Polanyi, *Primitive, Archaic, and Modern Economies*, ed. George Dalton (Garden City, N.Y.: Doubleday, Anchor Books, 1968), pp. 20ff.

6. Abraham H. Maslow, *Motivation and Personality*, 2d ed. (New York: Harper & Row, 1970), p. 39.

7. See Kenneth E. Boulding, *The Economy of Love and Fear* (Belmont, Calif.: Wadsworth Publishing Co., 1973), p. 107.

8. See John Rawls, *A Theory of Justice* (Cambridge, Mass.: Harvard University Press, 1971).

9. For an extended discussion of Rawlsian principles compared with the ethics of completely free markets, see the articles in E. Ray Canterbery and Harry G. Johnson, eds., "Symposium on Justice, Nozick and Rawls," *Eastern Economic Journal*, January 1978.

10. John Kenneth Galbraith, *The New Industrial State* (Boston: Houghton Mifflin Co., 1967), p. 30.

11. Ibid., p. 207. This argument can be illustrated with Menger's hierarchy of wants in Table 6.1. Whenever wants I, II, and III are met, Galbraith is saying, media persuasion becomes effective with IV (to be transported) and V (to enjoy luxury).

12. Those desiring more detail on Galbraith's theory of the corporation would benefit from reading an evaluation by his son: see James K. Galbraith, "Galbraith and the Theory of the Corporation," *Journal of Post Keynesian Economics* 6 (Fall 1984): 43–60. James sees his father's most important contribution to economic *theory* to be his theory of the corporation.

13. For a thoughtful and readable critique of Galbraith's economics by a critic turned admirer, see Myron E. Sharpe, *John Kenneth Galbraith and the Lower Economics*, rev. ed. (New York: International Arts and Sciences Press, 1974).

CHAPTER 12
THE NEW RADICAL ECONOMICS: THE LEFT

1. A curious feature of much of the work of the younger radicals is the sparseness of reference to the works of their economist sympathizers, such as Veblen on institutional lag, Boulding on ecology, and Galbraith on power.

2. Besides Edwards, Reich, and Weisskopf, the other staff members of Social Sciences 125 during 1968–1970 were Samuel Bowles, Keith Aufhauser, Peter Bohmer, Roger Bohmer, Herbert Gintis, Carl Gotsch, Arthur MacEwan, Stephan Michelson, Ralph Pochoda, and Paddy Quick. We can now add to the Harvard names, Stephen Marglin.

Among those at the other schools are Michael Hudson, Howard Wachtel, Stephen Hymer, Edward Nell, Thomas Vietorisz, James Weaver, Michael Zweig, James O'Conner, Robert Ritch, Mary Oppenheumer, and a convert from the orthodoxy, Leonard Rapping. Bowles moved to the University of Massachusetts after failing to obtain tenure in the Harvard economics department. Gintis has since joined Bowles (and Leonard Rapping).

3. See Martin Bronfenbrenner, "Radical Economics in America, 1970," *Journal of Economic Literature* 3 (September 1970): 747–766.

4. R. C. Edwards, M. Reich, and T. E. Weisskopf, *The Capitalist System* (Englewood Cliffs, N.J.: Prentice-Hall, 1972), p. x.

5. R. C. Edwards, A. MacEwan, and the Staff of Social Sciences 125, "A Radical Approach to Economics: Basis for a New Curriculum," *American Economic Review, Papers and Proceedings* 60 (May 1970): 352. In this same tone, Bowles and

Gintis see the public school system as a factory that replicates workers for capitalistic production in their *Schooling in Capitalist America: Educational Reform and the Contradictions of Economic Life* (New York: Basic Books, 1976). Still later, Bowles and Edwards described in a more general way how the *postwar corporate system* has been based on relations of domination and subordination, forged into an inflexible and hierarchical structure of private privilege; see *Beyond the Waste Land* (Garden City, N.Y.: Doubleday, Anchor Press, 1983).

6. Herbert Gintis, "Neo-classical Welfare Economics and Individual Development," *Occasional Papers of the Union for Radical Political Economics*, No. 3 (July 1970): 7–8. Excerpts reprinted by permission. The article is printed in free verse, and I have presented excerpts in their original form.

7. Ibid., p. 12.

8. Ibid., p. 14.

9. John Kenneth Galbraith, *The New Industrial State* (Boston: Houghton Mifflin Co., 1967), pp. 402–403.

10. Gintis, "Neo-classical Welfare Economics and Individual Development," p. 17.

11. Edwards et al., "A Radical Approach to Economics," p. 356.

12. This recognition perhaps reaches its finest expression in Bowles and Edwards, *Beyond the Waste Land.*

13. See ibid. and Bowles and Gintis, *Schooling in Capitalist America.*

14. For a radical's view of the Yugoslavian experiment, see Howard Wachtel, *Workers' Management and Workers' Wages in Yugoslavia* (Ithaca, N.Y.: Cornell University Press, 1973).

15. Gintis, "Neo-classical Welfare Economics and Individual Development," p. 10.

16. Oscar Lange and Fred M. Taylor, *On the Economic Theory of Socialism* (Minneapolis: University of Minnesota Press, 1938).

CHAPTER 13
ECONOMIC CRISES OF THE 1970S

1. An interesting discussion of these issues by Daniel R. Fusfeld, Robert Lekachman, Marc J. Roberts, Charles L. Schultze, and Robert A. Solo appear in a Committee for Economic Development and *Saturday Review* Symposium, *Saturday Review*, January 22, 1972.

2. Art Buchwald, *Washington Post*, June 2, 1966. Reprinted by permission.

3. The Rockefeller Standard Oil trust was "dissolved" by the U.S. Supreme Court in 1911. The "old" Standard Oil was divided into separate companies whose operations were allocated to different areas of the United States. Generally, each of these same Standard companies remains the dominant factor in each of the original marketing areas. Among the dominant stockholders of each company are the Rockefeller family, Rockefeller "interests," and the Rockefeller Foundation.

4. See John Blair, *Economic Concentration: Structure Behavior and Public Policy* (New York: Harcourt, Brace & World, 1972), p. 25.

5. The complete data on these interest groups appear in Temporary National Economic Committee, "The Distribution of Ownership in the 200 Largest Non-

Financial Corporations" in *The Structure of the American Economy*, Monograph #29 (Washington, D.C.: U.S. Government Printing Office, June 1939).

6. In general, super-wealth is passed from generation to generation within the same family. See E. Ray Canterbery and E. Joseph Nosari, "The Forbes Four Hundred: The Determinants of Super-wealth," *Southern Economic Journal* 52 (April 1985): 1073–1083.

7. See Maurice Zeitlin, *American Society, Inc.* (Chicago: Markham Publishing Co., 1970), p. 48.

8. Ibid., p. 64. The committee supports this argument with data. Among the 500 largest industrials, there were 176 separate situations where the surveyed banks held 5 percent or more of the common stock of a corporation. There were 20 situations among the 50 largest merchandising companies and 23 situations among the 50 largest transportation companies in which the surveyed banks held 5 percent or more of the common stock of a corporation (see ibid., p. 75).

9. See comments by Walter Adams, Hearings before the Subcommittee on Antitrust and Monopoly of the Committee of the Judiciary, U.S. Senate, 88th Cong., 2d Sess., Part 1 (Overall and Conglomerate Aspects), *Economic Concentration*, 1965, p. 249.

10. Ibid.

11. Edwin Mansfield, *Microeconomics: Theory and Applications* (New York: W. W. Norton & Co., 1970), p. 305.

12. The "official" level of poverty income for a family of four was $10,178 in 1983.

13. Lester C. Thurow and Robert E. B. Lucas, *The American Distribution of Income: A Structural Problem* (Washington, D.C.: U.S. Congress, Joint Economic Committee, 1972), p. 13.

14. See Joseph Pechman and Benjamin Okner, *Who Bears the Tax Burden?* (Washington, D.C.: Brookings Institution, 1974).

15. The first survey is Dorothy S. Projector and Gertrude Weiss, *Survey of Financial Characteristics of Consumers* (Washington, D.C.: Federal Reserve Board, 1966); the second has not been released as of this writing, and the reported results are based upon a telephone interview with the Federal Reserve.

16. Art Buchwald, *Washington Post*, January 3, 1979. Reprinted by permission.

CHAPTER 14
NEW RADICAL ECONOMICS: THE RIGHT

1. Israel Kirzner, *Competition and Entrepreneurship* (Chicago: University of Chicago Press, 1973), p. 10.

2. Ludwig von Mises, *Human Action: A Treatise on Economics* (New Haven: Yale University Press, 1949), p. 11.

3. Historians of economic thought like Joseph Schumpeter (a second-generation Austrian himself) and Mark Blaug give this impression. This, too, is the impression I received from Abba Lerner, an early and important disciple of Keynes's, regarding his view of Austrianism. As far as I know, Lerner's last completed technical paper was on the role of time in Austrian capital theory, a paper he submitted to me (for comments) shortly before his disabling stroke.

4. See John Hicks, *Capital and Time: A Neo-Austrian Theory* (Oxford: Clarendon Press, 1973); and especially, Eugen Böhm-Bawerk, *Karl Marx and the Close of His System* (New York: A. M. Kelley, 1949).

5. On this point, see especially Israel Kirzner, "The Theory of Capital," in Edwin G. Dolan, ed., *The Foundations of Modern Austrian Economics* (Kansas City: Sheed & Ward, 1976).

6. The supply-siders were by no means unified in their views. Gilder and writer Bruce Bartlett, former legislative assistant to Republican Congressman Jack Kemp of New York, for instance, did not endorse the tight monetary policy of the monetarists as necessary to curb inflation; supply-side tax incentives were sufficient to reduce inflation by increasing productivity, they claimed. Paul Craig Roberts, a supply-sider who has served at the U.S. Treasury, moved away from his endorsement of monetarism as the economy slid into depression in 1981–1982. These views notwithstanding, Reaganomics clearly embraced both monetarist and supply-side views.

7. Less well known is an influential article in *Public Interest* in summer 1981 by Harvard economist Martin Feldstein in which he presents the "supply-side" ideas as those that will replace the "conventional Keynesian view." Ironically, upon being named chairman of President Reagan's Council of Economic Advisers, Feldstein was transformed into a standard fiscal Keynesian and made proclamations that made the White House uneasy.

8. Quoted by William Greider, "The Education of David Stockman," *Atlantic Monthly*, December 1981, p. 46. Stockman's confessions had been made to journalist-friend Greider.

9. Ibid., p. 47.

10. The United States Congress rejected Reagan proposals that would have reduced Social Security benefits by 31 percent for workers taking early retirement; reduced disability benefits for 320,000 veterans by an average $423 a year; cut federal aid to low-income families for home-heating expenses by yearly amounts ranging from 24 to 34 percent; trimmed spending on the Food Stamp program by double the amount actually approved by Congress; eliminated school-lunch programs for middle- and upper-income children; increased payments by Medicare patients for most hospital stays; reduced spending on primary and secondary education programs for the disadvantaged and handicapped by 25 percent in 1981 (Congress approved cuts totaling 10 percent); reduced the student-loan program from $2.6 billion in 1981 to $1.8 billion in 1982 instead of the increase to $3.1 imposed by Congress; cut spending for highway and bridge construction from $9.4 billion in 1981 to $6.8 billion in 1982; raised interest rates on farm disaster and Small Business Administration loans; reduced general welfare payments from $8.5 billion in 1981 to less than $6 billion by 1983, a 30 percent reduction instead of Congress's increase to $8.9 by 1984; eliminated the Legal Services Corporation and Juvenile Justice programs; cut the 1983 budget for maternal and child health care, including programs for low-income women who are pregnant, by 23 percent; and cut deeper than Congress would allow numerous other domestic programs, including energy conservation, Environmental Protection Agency, federal mortgage insurance commitments, economic development grants, American Indian assistance, job training, Medicaid, and community-services grants.

11. Again, individual supply-siders are not in agreement. Paul Craig Roberts, one of the architects of Reaganomics and once Reagan's assistant secretary of the Treasury for economic policy, began as a moderate Lafferite who, by November 1984, was belittling the "successful public relations campaign" that elevated the Laffer Curve to unwarranted heights. Roberts now defined supply-side economics as tax-incentive economics, pure and simple (*Business Week*, November 12 , 1984, p. 23).

12. In reaction to the massive tax revenue losses, in 1982 Congress repealed a scheduled further increase in accelerated depreciation allowances and eliminated safe-harbor leasing, a 1981 provision that allowed unprofitable companies to sell their tax credits and depreciation write-offs to profitable ones. These 1982 tax changes left the expected return from plant and equipment investment about 17 percentage points (rather than 28) above the pre-Reagan tax treatment return.

13. For detailed estimates compiled by the Institute for International Economics, see William R. Cline, "The Issue Is Illiquidity, Not Insolvency," *Challenge* 27 (July–August 1984): 12–20.

CHAPTER 15
THE POST-KEYNESIANS

1. Two new periodicals devoted to post-Keynesian economics, the *Cambridge Journal of Economics* in England and the *Journal of Post Keynesian Economics* in the United States, bear witness to these developments. The founding co-editors of the latter were Paul Davidson at Rutgers University and the late Sidney Weintraub at the University of Pennsylvania. John Kenneth Galbraith, one of the founding patrons of the *JPKE*, is chairman of the honorary board of directors. The late Joan Robinson and Lord Kaldor were among the founding patrons of the *Cambridge Journal*.

2. Sraffa relies upon a method invented by Wassily Leontief, input-output economics, for which Leontief received the Nobel Prize in Economics. For this reason, we will later refer to the Sraffa-Leontief system.

3. The connections among net output, the profit rate, and the wage share can be shown with Sraffa's solution to his system, which is

$$\text{Profit Rate} = \left(\frac{\text{Net Output}}{\text{Means of Production}} \right) \cdot \left(1 - \frac{\text{Wages}}{\text{Net Output}} \right).$$

In the first case, where wages are 35, we have

$$\text{Profit Rate} = 0.63 \, (1 - 0.70) = 19 \text{ percent}$$

After the wage increase,

$$\text{Profit Rate} = 0.63 \, (1 - 0.80) = 13 \text{ percent}$$

4. See Luigi L. Pasinetti, *Growth and Income Distribution* (Cambridge, Eng.: Cambridge University Press, 1974).

5. See E. Ray Canterbery and E. Joseph Nosari, "The Forbes Four Hundred: The Determinants of Super-Wealth," *Southern Economic Journal* 52 (April 1985).

6. A detailed development of the vita theory of the personal income distribution appears in E. Ray Canterbery, "A Vita Theory of Personal Income Distribution," *Southern Economic Journal* 46 (July 1979): 12–48.

7. See John Brittain, *The Inheritance of Inequality* (Washington, D.C.: The Brookings Institution, 1977).

8. The content of the BLS budgets is based upon the manner of living and actual consumer choices in the 1960s. The nutritional and health standards, as determined by scientists and nutritionalists, were used for the food-at-home and housing components. Details of the content and development of the budgets appear in BLS Bulletin 1570-5, *Three Standards of Living for an Urban Family of Four Persons* (Washington, D.C.: U.S. Department of Commerce, Spring 1967). The reported budget estimates appear in *Family Economic Review* (Washington, D.C.: U.S. Department of Agriculture, Fall 1981), p. 18.

9. An enlightening exploration of the vast gray area between needs and wants appears in David Braybrooke, "Let Needs Diminish That Preferences May Prosper," *American Philosophy Quarterly*, Monograph No. 1, 1968, pp. 86–107. Also see the interesting distinction made between necessities and comforts by Tibor Scitovsky in *The Joyless Economy* (New York: Oxford University Press, 1976), pp. 106–131.

10. In the national income accounts of the U.S. Department of Commerce, personal income also includes government transfer payments, income payments that do not require the exchange of a service or good-in-kind, such as Social Security checks or wheat subsidies. In this discussion, I am ignoring this income source. Strictly measured, the *national income* includes undistributed corporate profits, but this is another account that is useful when we consider business investment (and thus corporate saving) in our analysis.

11. See E. Ray Canterbery, "Inflation, Necessities, and Distributive Efficiency," in J. H. Gapinski and C. E. Rockwood, eds., *Essays in Post-Keynesian Inflation* (Cambridge, Mass.: Ballinger, 1979), pp. 79–103.

12. John Kenneth Galbraith, *The New Industrial State* (Boston: Houghton Mifflin Co., 1967), p. 207. For a more detailed discussion of the connections among Galbraith, Sraffa, and Kalecki, see E. Ray Canterbery, "Galbraith, Sraffa, Kalecki and Supra-Surplus Capitalism," *Journal of Post Keynesian Economics* 7 (Fall 1984): 77–90.

13. Whereas Kalecki's markup applies only to manufacturing, Weintraub's is more general and applies to all industries, including those that are nearly competitive. A markup pricing rule now is widely used in orthodox econometric modeling. See Otto Eckstein, ed., *The Econometrics of Price Determination* (Washington, D.C.: Board of Governors of Federal Reserve System, 1972); Arthur Okun, *Prices and Quantities: A Macroeconomics Analysis* (Washington, D.C.: Brookings Institution, 1981); and William D. Nordhaus, "The Falling Rate of Profits," *Brookings Papers of Economic Activity* 74, No. 1 (1974): 169–208.

14. The motivation for investment "needs" has been variously attributed to market share, growth, and power goals. These explanations, which lead nonetheless to similar outcomes, have been put forward, respectively, by Alfred S. Eichner, *The Megacorp and Oligopoly: Micro Foundations of Macro Dynamics* (Cambridge, Eng.: Cambridge University Press, 1976); Robin Marris, *The Economic Theory of "Managerial" Capitalism* (New York: Basic Books, 1964); and John Kenneth Galbraith. To the extent that borrowed funds are used to finance increments to the capital stock, new financial assets are created in the process of business investment. Hyman Minsky takes this position in his *John Maynard Keynes* (New York: Columbia University Press, 1975).

15. This discussion follows closely Weintraub's description of the inflationary process. See Sidney Weintraub, *Capitalism's Inflation and Unemployment Crisis* (Reading, Mass.: Addison-Wesley, 1978), pp. 44–50.

16. Money wages also are endogenous in Canterbery's vita theory of the personal income distribution: see E. Ray Canterbery, "A Vita Theory of Personal Income Distribution," *Southern Economic Journal* 46 (July 1979): 12–48.

17. For an elaboration of the importance of maintaining market shares, see Eichner, *The Megacorp and Oligopoly.*

18. David Warsh, *The Idea of Economic Complexity* (New York: Viking Press, 1984), p. 36.

19. Ibid., p. 41.

20. In the next several paragraphs Canterbery's vita theory is used to amend Galbraith. The dual labor market perspective is also relevant: see Michael J. Piore, ed., *Unemployment and Inflation: Institutionalist and Structuralist Views* (Armonk, N.Y.: M. E. Sharpe, 1979).

21. See John Kenneth Galbraith, *American Capitalism: The Concept of Countervailing Power* (Boston: Houghton Mifflin Co., 1952), and by the same author, *The Anatomy of Power* (Boston: Houghton Mifflin Co., 1983).

22. According to Federal Reserve Board estimates of the U.S. wealth distribution for 1983, the top 10 percent of American families—those earning more than $50,000 yearly—had average financial holdings of $125,131 compared with an average of only $18,539 for families earning $25,000 to $30,000 yearly. The top 2 percent of families—those earning $100,000 or more a year—owned 50 percent of all stocks, 71 percent of all tax-free bonds, and 20 percent of all real estate. (The complete study had not been published at this writing.)

23. This basic necessities concept was pioneered by the National Center for Economic Alternatives, Washington, D.C., and used as the basis for a "necessities price index." See Part III of Gar Alperovitz and Jeff Faux, *Rebuilding America* (New York: Pantheon Books, 1984). I have provided the more abstract theoretical justification for the basic necessities distinction in E. Ray Canterbery, "Inflation, Necessities, and Distributive Efficiency," in James Gapinski and Charles Rockwood, eds., *Post-Keynesian Inflation: Essays in Honor of Abba P. Lerner* (Cambridge, Mass.: Ballinger, 1980), pp. 79–103.

CHAPTER 16
STAGNATION AND THE LONG WAVE

1. See, for example, Joan Robinson, "Keynes and Ricardo," *Journal of Post Keynesian Economics* 1 (Fall 1978): 16–18.

2. Harvard's Simon Kuznets's Nobel Prize in economics is partly related to his collaboration with Schumpeter in identifying in historical detail the three long waves. See Simon Kuznets, *Economic Change* (New York: W. W. Norton & Co., 1953).

3. See Chapter 15 and E. Ray Canterbery, "A Vita Theory of Personal Income Distribution," *Southern Economic Journal* 46 (July 1979): 12–48.

4. Gerhard O. Mensch, *Stalemate in Technology* (Cambridge, Mass.: Ballinger, 1979).

5. Ibid., pp. 47–50.

6. Ibid., p. 192.

7. Warsh, *The Idea of Economic Complexity* (New York: Viking Press, 1984), pp. 63–65.

8. Mensch, *Stalemate in Technology,* p. 197.

9. Mancur Olson, *The Rise and Decline of Nations* (New Haven: Yale University Press, 1982). See especially pp. 77–98. In chapter 6, however, Olson extends his theory of coalitions to the often dictatorial regimes of less developed nations.

10. Ibid., p. 78.

11. UNIDO's inaugural *Industry and Development Global Report,* prepared by its Global and Conceptual Studies Branch, was published by the UN in 1985. Some of my discussion on the global economy in this chapter and in Chapter 17 is gleaned from background papers that I prepared at the Branch in Vienna for this first report. Endorsement of my ideas by UNIDO is not to be inferred; the *Report* speaks for itself. A detailed discussion of the Lima target appears on pp. 19–22 of the *Report.*

12. In 1965–1980 structural change *and* economic growth rates were greater in Brazil, Mexico, Kenya, and the Republic of Korea than in the United States, France, and the Federal Republic of Germany. See the dramatic illustrations in ibid., pp. 33–35.

13. W. W. Rostow, *The World Economy* (Austin: University of Texas Press, 1980), pp. 561–568.

14. The economist or historian need not embrace Rostow's "stages of growth" thesis in order to find his terminology adequately descriptive.

15. Mensch, *Stalemate in Technology,* p. 198. The central reason for a lag between basic invention and basic innovation is not difficult to find. Entrepreneurs seldom perceive with any immediacy a direct connection between a new invention and an application. The only initial use for the diesel locomotive was in freight yard switching. Only the military had any initial application for the transistor. Xerography initially was used in a specialized part of the lithography market, not for mass copying. Only the Census Bureau would have any use for computers, or so it once was thought. Virtually no basic invention is used as first intended.

CHAPTER 17
POST-KEYNESIAN ECONOMIC POLICIES

1. You will recognize this as Keynes's original view of the money–national income interaction. It is also the interpretation of Keynes used by Sidney Weintraub, *Capitalism's Inflation and Unemployment Crisis* (Reading, Mass.: Addison-Wesley, 1978), pp. 66–77; and by Paul Davidson in "Why Money Matters: Lessons from a Half-Century of Monetary Theory." *Journal of Post-Keynesian Economics,* Fall 1978, pp. 57–65, and in *Money and the Real World* (New York: Wiley, A Halstead Press Book, 1972).

2. More details on this phenomenon are provided in John Hotson, *Stagflation and the Bastard Keynesians* (Waterloo, Canada: University of Waterloo, 1976); and

E. Ray Canterbery, *Economics on a New Frontier* (Belmont, Calif.: Wadsworth Publishing Co., 1968).

3. See John H. Hotson and William F. Hixson, "Reaganomics and the Tax-Bond: An Escape Route for Capitalism?" (Paper presented to the Eastern Economic Association Meeting, Washington, D.C., April 30, 1982).

4. This summary of Minsky's perspective is derived from Hyman P. Minsky, *Can "It" Happen Again? Essays on Instability and Finance* (Armonk, N.Y.: M. E. Sharpe, 1982).

5. The sharp decline in agricultural exports during 1983–1984 was closely tied to an appreciating dollar (raising the cost of foreign purchases of U.S. products) that in turn was related to high interest rates in the United States *that* in still another turn were connected to gigantic U.S. federal government deficits.

6. Charles P. Kindleberger, *Manias, Panics, and Crashes: A History of Financial Crises* (New York: Basic Books, 1978).

7. Ibid., pp. 23–24.

8. Under the present tax code, the income transfers to the poor are required both for humane purposes and for economic stimulation during recessions and depressions (see Chapter 15). However, government human resource development programs that successfully educate and train persons to fit the open employment niches in the economy would go to the root causes of poverty and greatly reduce the necessity for income support programs (see references to the vita theory in Chapter 15).

9. Abba P. Lerner, *The Economics of Employment* (New York: McGraw-Hill, 1951), p. 127.

10. For much more detail on the administrative features of this plan, see Weintraub, *Capitalism's Inflation and Unemployment Crisis*, pp. 121–144. Weintraub recommends the calibration of a firm's annual average labor productivity by dividing the year's value added (net sales) by the number of employees.

11. For more detail, see Abba P. Lerner and David Colander, *MAP, a Market Anti-inflation Plan* (New York: Harcourt Brace Jovanovich, 1980).

12. E. Ray Canterbery, "Tax Reform and Incomes Policy: A VATIP Proposal," *Journal of Post Keynesian Economics* 5 (Spring 1983): 430–439. Portions of the Tax Reform and Incomes Policy section in Chapter 17 are adapted from this article.

13. A later, more detailed version of the proposal allows deductions for business expenses and alimony paid. See E. Ray Canterbery, Eric W. Cook, and Bernard A. Schmitt, "The Flat Tax, Negative Tax, and VAT: Gaining Progressivity and Revenue," *Cato Journal* (Fall 1985): 521–536 (based upon a paper given at the Conference on the Flat Tax Proposals, Florida State University, March 14, 1985).

14. The comparable marginal tax rates in the 1984 U.S. Treasury proposal are 15 percent up to $31,000, 35 percent up to $63,000, and 35 percent in excess of $63,000.

15. David Warsh, *The Idea of Economic Complexity* (New York: Viking Press, 1984), pp. 92–93. When the prices of highways, American tanks in El Salvador, and pollution control equipment are diffused into the prices of automobiles, what we are undergoing, Warsh suggests, is not inflation but "conflation," which describes what happens to old costs when new ones are added. Yet we appear to want what the new costs deliver.

16. Charles Lindblom, *Politics and Markets: The World's Political-Economic Systems* (New York: Basic Books, 1977).

17. For further explication of Rawlsian principles, see the articles in E. Ray Canterbery and Harry G. Johnson, eds., "Symposium on Justice, Nozick and Rawls," *Eastern Economic Journal*, January 1978.

18. I first outlined this proposal as a contributor to David Mermelstein's "The Threatening Economy," *New York Times Magazine*, December 30, 1979. Alfred S. Eichner in *The Megacorp and Oligopoly: Micro Foundations of Macro Dynamics* (Cambridge, Eng.: Cambridge University Press, 1976), p. 278, has suggested the formation of a social and economic council comprising representatives of various groups in society. The council would have a secretariat to provide council members with an objective economic analysis. It seems to me that such a council would be a logical second step in order to coordinate investment policy across all the industry panels.

19. Galbraith presents such a case because these industries are outside the planning system. See *Economics and the Public Purpose* (Boston: Houghton Mifflin Co., 1973), pp. 274–285.

20. See Gar Alperovitz and Jeff Faux, *Rebuilding America* (New York: Pantheon Books, 1984), who provide a plethora of proposals for dealing with specific sectoral problems such as medicine and energy. They also put "teeth" into Eichner's proposal by recommending that the President's Council of Economic Advisers and the Office of Management and Budget be integrated for economic planning purposes within the Executive Branch subject to review by an agency of Congress (pp. 260–261).

21. Much of this power is transferred genetically. See E. Ray Canterbery and E. Joseph Nosari, "The Forbes Four Hundred: The Determinants of Super-Wealth," *Southern Economic Journal* 52 (April 1985): 1073–1083.

22. See H. Peter Gray, *Free Trade or Protectionism?* (London: The Macmillan Press LTD, 1985), pp. 46–69.

23. For a transitional reform leading to this solution, see E. Ray Canterbery, "The International Monetary Crisis and the Delayed Peg," *Challenge* 21 (November–December 1978): 4–12, reprinted as a part of invited testimony before the Subcommittee on International Monetary Affairs, U.S. Senate Banking Committee, May 3, 1979.

24. More specific recommendations on various joint venture arrangements are presented in United Nations Industrial Development Organization (Vienna), *Industry and Development Global Report 1985.* (New York: United Nations, 1985), pp. 126–127.

CHAPTER 18
A SUMMING-UP

1. Novak, a fellow at the American Enterprise Institute, was an influential member of the self-appointed Lay Commission on Catholic Social Teaching and the U.S. Economy, which launched a preemptive strike on the bishops' pastoral letter drafted at the U.S. Catholic Conference in Washington and released just after the presidential election. The letter was presumed to be an attack on first-term

Reaganomics: the lay Roman Catholics headed by former Secretary of the Treasury William E. Simon wrote a spirited defense of capitalism as the last, best (trickle-down) hope of the poor.

2. George Gilder, *Wealth and Poverty* (New York: Basic Books, 1981), p. 268.

3. Ibid., p. 267.

4. R. L. Heilbroner, "On the Possibility of a Political Economics," *Journal of Economic Issues* 4 (December 1970): 16.

SUGGESTED READINGS

▼

CHAPTER 1
VALUES AND ECONOMIC SYSTEMS

Collis, Louise. *Memoirs of a Medieval Woman*. New York: Harper & Row, 1983.

Hicks, John. *A Theory of Economic History*. Oxford: Clarendon Press, 1969.

Hilton, Rodney. *Bond Men Made Free*. London: Temple Smith, 1973.

Keen, Maurice. *Chivalry*. New Haven: Yale University Press, 1985.

North, Douglas C., and Robert Paul Thomas. *The Rise of the Western World: A New Economic History*. Cambridge, Eng.: Cambridge University Press, 1973.

Postan, M. M. *The Medieval Economy and Society*. Berkeley and Los Angeles: University of California Press, 1972.

Smith, Adam. *An Inquiry into the Nature and Causes of the Wealth of Nations*, edited by Edwin Cannan, introductions by Edwin Cannan and Max Lerner. New York: Random House, 1937.

Smith, Adam. *The Theory of Moral Sentiments*, edited by Ernest Rhys. London: Everyman's Library, 1910.

Tuchman, Barbara W. *A Distant Mirror: The Calamitous 14th Century*. New York: Alfred A. Knopf, 1978.

CHAPTER 2
THE NATURE OF SCIENCE AND THE ECONOMICS PARADIGM

Boorstin, Daniel J. *The Discoverers*. New York: Random House, 1983.

Kuhn, Thomas. *The Structure of Scientific Revolutions*, 2d ed., enl. Chicago: University of Chicago Press, 1970.

Nicolson, Marjorie. "The New Astronomy and English Imagination." In *Science as Metaphor*, edited by Richard Olson. Belmont, Calif.: Wadsworth Publishing Co., 1971.

Smith, Adam. "The Principles Which Lead and Direct Philosophical Inquiries: Illustrated by the History of Astronomy." In *The Early Writings of Adam Smith*, edited by J. Ralph Lindgren. New York: Augustus M. Kelley, 1967, pp. 30–109.

CHAPTER 3
ADAM SMITH AND THE MARKET ECONOMY

Braudel, Fernand. *Civilization and Capitalism, 15th–18th Century,* translated from the French by Siân Reynolds. 3 vols. New York: Harper & Row, 1984.

Cipolla, Carlo M. *Before the Industrial Revolution: European Society and Economy, 1000–1700.* New York: W. W. Norton & Co., 1976.

Davis, Ralph. *The Rise of the Atlantic Economies.* London: World University, 1973.

Eagly, Robert V. *The Structure of Classical Economic Theory.* New York, London, Toronto: Oxford University Press, 1974.

Gilchrist, John T. *The Church and Economic Activity in the Middle Ages.* New York: St. Martin's Press, 1969.

Heilbroner, Robert. *The Limits of American Capitalism.* New York: Harper & Row, 1966.

Heilbroner, Robert. *The Worldly Philosophers,* 3d ed. New York: Simon & Schuster, 1967.

Smith, Adam. *An Inquiry into the Nature and Causes of the Wealth of Nations,* edited by Edwin Cannan, introductions by Edwin Cannan and Max Lerner. New York: Random House, 1937.

Tuchman, Barbara W. *A Distant Mirror: The Calamitous 14th Century.* New York: Alfred A. Knopf, 1978.

CHAPTER 4
THE INDUSTRIAL REVOLUTION AND THE OTHER CLASSICALS

Burtt, Everett, Jr. *Social Perspectives in the History of Economic Theory.* New York: St. Martin's Press, 1972.

Hartwell, R. M. *The Causes of the Industrial Revolution.* London: Methuen & Co., 1967.

Hicks, John. *A Theory of Economic History.* Oxford: Clarendon Press, 1969.

Hill, Christopher. *Reformation to Industrial Revolution: The Making of Modern English Society,* Vol. 1, *1530–1780.* New York: Pantheon Books, 1967.

Himmelfarb, Gertrude. *The Idea of Poverty: England in the Early Industrial Age.* New York: Alfred A. Knopf, 1984.

Malthus, Thomas. "An Essay on the Principle of Population, as It Affects the Future Improvement of Society: With Remarks on the Speculations of Mr. Godwin, M. Condorcet, and Other Writers." In *On Population,* by Thomas Malthus, edited by Gertrude Himmelfarb. New York: Random House, Modern Library, 1960.

Mill, John Stuart. *Principles of Political Economy,* edited by J. M. Robson. 2 vols. Toronto: University of Toronto Press, 1965.

Ricardo, David. *Principles of Political Economy and Taxation.* London: J. M. Dent & Sons, 1937.

Rima, I. H. *Development of Economic Analysis,* rev. ed. Homewood, Ill.: Richard D. Irwin, 1972.

CHAPTER 5
THE "AMERICAN DREAM"

Dorfman, Joseph. *The Economic Mind in American Civilization, 1606–1865*. 5 vols. New York: Augustus M. Kelley, 1966.

Hofstadter, Richard. *Social Darwinism in American Thought*, rev. ed. Boston: Beacon Press, 1955.

Spencer, Herbert. *First Principles*, 6th ed. New York: D. Appleton & Co., 1900.

CHAPTER 6
ALFRED MARSHALL AND THE U.S.A. PURITANS

Allen, Frederick Lewis. *The Lords of Creation*. New York and London: Harper & Brothers, 1935.

Bentham, Jeremy. *An Introduction to the Principles of Morals and Legislation*, introduction by Laurence J. Lafleur. Darien, Conn.: Hafner Publishing Co., 1948.

Heilbroner, Robert L. *The Worldly Philosophers*, 3d ed. New York: Simon & Schuster, 1967.

Keynes, John M. *Essays in Biography*. London: Macmillan & Co., 1933.

Marshall, Alfred. *Principles of Economics*, 8th ed. London: Macmillan & Co., 1920.

Oser, Jacob. *The Evolution of Economic Thought*, 2d ed. New York: Harcourt, Brace & World, 1970.

Robinson, Joan. *The Economics of Imperfect Competition*, 2d ed. London: Macmillan & Co., 1969.

Schumpeter, Joseph A. *Ten Great Economists*. New York: Oxford University Press, 1965.

Spiegel, Henry W. *The Growth of Economic Thought*. Englewood Cliffs, N.J.: Prentice-Hall, 1971.

Sraffa, Piero. "The Laws of Returns Under Competitive Conditions," *Economic Journal* 36 (December 1926): 535–550.

Williamson, Jeffrey G. *Did British Capitalism Breed Inequality?* London: Allen & Unwin, 1985.

CHAPTER 7
J. M. KEYNES: THE END OF FRUGALITY

Chick, Victoria. *Macroeconomics After Keynes: A Reconsideration of the "General Theory."* Cambridge, Mass.: MIT Press, 1983.

Dillard, Dudley. *The Economics of John Maynard Keynes*. Englewood Cliffs, N.J.: Prentice-Hall, 1948.

Keynes, John M. *The Collected Writings of John Maynard Keynes*, vols. 8, 10, 13–16, 19. London: Macmillan & Co.; New York: St. Martin's Press, 1971.

Keynes, John M. *The General Theory of Employment, Interest and Money*. New York: Harcourt, Brace & World, 1936.

Lekachman, Robert. *The Age of Keynes.* New York: Random House, 1966.

Robinson, Joan. "The Theory of Money and the Analyses of Output," *Review of Economic Studies* 1 (1933): 22–26. Reprinted in Joan Robinson, *Collected Papers* (Oxford: Blackwell's, 1967).

CHAPTER 8
THE BASTARD KEYNESIANS AND THE MONETARISTS

Friedman, Milton. "The Quantity Theory of Money—A Restatement." In *Studies in the Quantity Theory of Money,* edited by Milton Friedman. Chicago: University of Chicago Press, 1956.

Hicks, John R. *The Crisis in Keynesian Economics.* New York: Basic Books, 1974.

Hotson, John. *Stagflation and the Bastard Keynesians.* Waterloo, Canada: University of Waterloo, 1976.

CHAPTER 9
THE ERA OF POSITIVE ECONOMIC SCIENCE

Boland, Lawrence A. *The Foundation of Economic Method.* London: George Allen & Unwin, 1982.

Boulding, Kenneth. *Economics as a Science.* New York: McGraw-Hill, 1970.

Caldwell, Bruce J. *Beyond Positivism: Economic Methodology in the Twentieth Century.* London: George Allen & Unwin, 1982.

Eichner, Alfred S., ed. *Why Economics Is Not Yet a Science.* Armonk, N.Y.: M. E. Sharpe, 1983.

Einstein, Albert. *Relativity: The Special and General Theory,* translated by Robert W. Lawson. New York: Hartsdale House, 1947.

Friedman, Milton. *Essays in Positive Economics.* Chicago: University of Chicago Press, 1953.

Galbraith, John Kenneth. "Economics as a System of Belief," *American Economic Review* 60 (May 1970): 469–484.

Roberts, Marc J. "An Unsimple Matter of Choice," *Saturday Review,* January 22, 1972, pp. 46, 60.

Robinson, Joan. *Economic Philosophy.* Chicago: Aldine Publishing Co., 1962.

Robinson, Joan. "What Has Become of the Keynesian Revolution?" *Challenge* 16 (January/February 1974): 6–11.

Samuelson, Paul A. *Foundations of Economic Analysis.* Cambridge, Mass.: Harvard University Press, 1947.

Ward, Benjamin. *What's Wrong with Economics?* New York: Basic Books, 1972.

Wiener, Norbert. *God and Golen, Inc.; A Comment on Certain Points Where Cybernetics Impinges on Religion.* Cambridge, Mass.: MIT Press, 1964.

CHAPTER 10
PARADIGM LOST: KARL MARX

Marx, Karl. *Capital; A Critique of Political Economy,* edited by Friedrich Engels. Vol. 1, 4th ed., rev. New York: Random House, Modern Library, 1906.

Marx, Karl. *Economic and Philosophic Manuscripts of 1844.* Moscow: Progress Publishers, 1959.

Tucker, Robert C., ed. *The Marx-Engels Reader.* New York: W. W. Norton & Co., 1972.

CHAPTER 11
THE ICONOCLASTS: VEBLEN AND GALBRAITH

Ayres, Clarence. *The Theory of Economic Progress.* Chapel Hill: University of North Carolina Press, 1944.

Canterbery, E. Ray, ed. "Galbraith Symposium," *Journal of Post Keynesian Economics* 7 (Fall 1984): 5–102.

Canterbery, E. Ray, and Howard P. Tuckman. "Toward a Theory of the Distribution of Power." Paper delivered to a Joint Session of the American Economic Association and the Society for the Study of Grants Economics, San Francisco, December 27, 1974.

Galbraith, John Kenneth. *The Affluent Society,* 2d ed., rev. Boston: Houghton Mifflin Co., 1969.

Galbraith, John Kenneth. *Economics and the Public Purpose.* Boston: Houghton Mifflin Co., 1973.

Galbraith, John Kenneth. *A Life in Our Times.* Boston: Houghton Mifflin Co., 1981.

Galbraith, John Kenneth. *The New Industrial State.* Boston: Houghton Mifflin Co., 1967.

Gruchy, Allan G. *Contemporary Economic Thought: The Contribution of the Neoinstitutionalist Economics.* New York: Augustus M. Kelley, 1972.

Veblen, Thorstein. *The Theory of the Leisure Class.* New York: Viking Press, 1931.

CHAPTER 12
NEW RADICAL ECONOMICS: THE LEFT

Bowles, Samuel, and Herbert Gintis. *Schooling in Capitalist America: Educational Reform and Contradictions of Economic Life.* New York: Basic Books, 1976.

Bowles, Samuel, David M. Gordon, and Thomas E. Weisskopf. *Beyond the Waste Land: A Democratic Alternative to Economic Decline.* Garden City, N.Y.: Doubleday, Anchor Press, 1983.

Bronfenbrenner, Martin. "Radical Economics in America, 1970," *Journal of Economic Literature* 3 (September 1970): 747–766.

Dowd, Douglas F. *The Twisted Dream: Capitalist Development in the United States Since 1776.* Cambridge, Mass.: Winthrop, 1974.

Edwards, R. C., M. Reich, and T. E. Weisskopf. *The Capitalist System*, 2d ed. Englewood Cliffs, N.J.: Prentice-Hall, 1978.

Gordon, David M., Richard Edwards, and Michael Reich. *Segmented Work, Divided Workers: The Historical Transformation of Labor in the United States*. New York: Cambridge University Press, 1982.

Lindbeck, Assar. *The Political Economy of the New Left*, foreword by Paul Samuelson. New York: Harper & Row, 1971.

Wachtel, Howard. *Workers' Management and Workers' Wages in Yugoslavia*. Ithaca, N.Y.: Cornell University Press, 1973.

Weisskopf, Thomas. *Alienation and Economics*. New York: E. P. Dutton, 1971.

CHAPTER 13
ECONOMIC CRISES OF THE 1970s

Blair, John. *Economic Concentration: Structure Behavior and Public Policy*. New York: Harcourt, Brace & World, 1972.

Fusfeld, Daniel R., Robert Lekachman, Marc J. Roberts, and Robert A. Solo. "Does Economics Ignore You?" *Saturday Review*, January 22, 1972, pp. 33–50.

Lucas, Robert E., Jr., and Leonard A. Rapping. "Price Expectations and the Phillips Curve," *American Economic Review* 59 (June 1970): 342–350.

Mintz, Morton and Jerry S. Cohen. *America, Inc.* New York: Dial Press, 1971.

Shepherd, William G. *Market Power and Economic Welfare*. New York: Random House, 1970.

Solow, Robert. "The Intelligent Citizen's Guide to Inflation," *Public Interest* 38 (Winter 1975): 30–66.

CHAPTER 14
NEW RADICAL ECONOMICS: THE RIGHT

Bartlett, Bruce. *"Reaganomics": Supply Side Economics in Action*, foreword by Rep. Jack Kemp. Westport, Conn.: Arlington House Publishers, 1981.

Dolan, Edwin G., ed. *The Foundations of Modern Austrian Economics*. Kansas City, Kans.: Sheed & Ward, 1976.

Feldstein, Martin. "The Retreat from Keynesian Economics," *Public Interest* 64 (Summer 1981): 92–105.

Hailstones, Thomas J. *Viewpoints on Supply-Side Economics*. Richmond, Va.: Robert F. Dame, 1982.

Kirzner, Israel. *Perception, Opportunity, and Profit*. Chicago: University of Chicago Press, 1979.

Tobin, James. "Reaganomics and Economics," *New York Review of Books*, December 3, 1981.

Warsh, David. "A Trend Called 'Supply Side,'" *Boston Globe*, April 22, 1980, p. 14.

CHAPTER 15
THE POST-KEYNESIANS

Canterbery, E. Ray. "Galbraith, Sraffa, Kalecki and Supra-Surplus Capitalism," *Journal of Post Keynesian Economics* 7 (Fall 1984): 71–89.

Cornwall, John. *Modern Capitalism*. New York: St. Martin's Press, 1978.

Davidson, Paul. *Money and the Real World*. New York: Wiley, Halstead Press, 1972.

Eichner, Alfred S., ed. *A Guide to Post-Keynesian Economics*. Armonk, N.Y.: M. E. Sharpe, 1979.

Eichner, Alfred S., ed. *Why Economics Is Not Yet a Science*. Armonk, N. Y.: M. E. Sharpe, 1983.

Feiwel, George. *The Intellectual Capital of Michal Kalecki*. Nashville: University of Tennessee Press, 1975.

Kaldor, Nicholas. *Essays on Value and Distribution*. Glencoe, Ill.: Free Press, 1960.

Minsky, Hyman P. *John Maynard Keynes*. New York: Columbia University Press, 1976.

Robinson, Joan. *The Accumulation of Capital*. London: Macmillan & Co., 1956.

Sraffa, Piero. *Production of Commodities by Means of Commodities*. Cambridge, Eng.: Cambridge University Press, 1960.

Warsh, David. *The Idea of Economic Complexity*. New York: Viking Press, 1984.

Weintraub, Sidney. *A General Theory of the Price Level, Output, Income Distribution and Economic Growth*. Philadelphia: Chilton, 1959.

CHAPTER 16
STAGNATION AND THE LONG WAVE

Harris, E. Seymour, ed. *Schumpeter: Social Scientist*. Freeport, N.Y.: Books for Libraries Press, 1969 [1951].

Mensch, Gerhard O. *Stalemate in Technology*. Cambridge, Mass.: Ballinger, 1979.

Olson, Mancur. *The Rise and Decline of Nations*. New Haven: Yale University Press, 1982.

Rostow, W. W. *The World Economy*. Austin: University of Texas Press, 1980.

Schumpeter, Joseph A. *Capitalism, Socialism, and Democracy*, 3d ed. New York: Harper & Brothers Publishers, 1950.

Warsh, David. *The Idea of Economic Complexity*. New York: Viking Press, 1984.

CHAPTER 17
POST-KEYNESIAN ECONOMIC POLICIES

Eichner, Alfred S. *The Megacorp and Oligopoly: Micro Foundations of Macro Dynamics*. Cambridge, Eng.: Cambridge University Press, 1976.

Galbraith, John Kenneth. *Economics and the Public Purpose*. Boston: Houghton Mifflin Co., 1973.

Lindblom, Charles E. *Politics and Markets: The World's Political-Economic Systems.* New York: Basic Books, 1977.

Marris, Robin. *The Economic Theory of "Managerial" Capitalism.* New York: Basic Books, 1964.

Mermelstein, David, ed. "The Threatening Economy," *New York Times Magazine,* December 30, 1979.

Minsky, Hyman P. *Can "It" Happen Again? Essays on Instability and Finance.* Armonk, N.Y.: M. E. Sharpe, 1982.

Rawls, John. *A Theory of Justice.* Cambridge, Mass.: Belknap Press of Harvard University Press, 1971.

Robinson, Joan. *Freedom and Necessity.* New York: Random House, Vintage, 1970.

Robinson, Joan. "The Second Crisis of Economic Theory," *American Economic Review* 62 (1972): 1–15.

INDEX

▼